Also by David D. Hall

THE FAITHFUL SHEPHERD:
A History of the New England Ministry in the
Seventeenth Century
(1972)

THE ANTINOMIAN CONTROVERSY, 1636–1638:
A Documentary History
(1968)

Co-editor
NEEDS AND OPPORTUNITIES
IN THE HISTORY OF THE BOOK:
America, 1639–1876
(1987)

SAINTS AND REVOLUTIONARIES:
Essays on Early American History
(1984)

SEVENTEENTH-CENTURY NEW ENGLAND
(1984)

PRINTING AND SOCIETY IN EARLY AMERICA
(1983)

WORLDS OF WONDER,

DAYS OF JUDGMENT

WORLDS OF WONDER, DAYS OF JUDGMENT

POPULAR RELIGIOUS BELIEF
IN EARLY NEW ENGLAND

David D. Hall

ALFRED A. KNOPF · NEW YORK

1989

Copyright © 1989 by David D. Hall

All rights reserved under International and Pan-American Copyright Conventions. Published in the United States by Alfred A. Knopf, Inc., New York, and simultaneously in Canada by Random House of Canada Limited, Toronto. Distributed by Random House, Inc., New York.

Chapter 2 is a revised and expanded version of "A World of Wonders," which was originally published in *Seventeenth Century New England*, Vol. 63 (1982), edited by David D. Hall and David Grayson Allen. Reprinted by permission of the Colonial Society of Massachusetts. Chapter 5 is a revised and expanded version of "The Mental World of Samual Sewall" by David D. Hall, which was originally published in the *Proceedings* of the Massachusetts Historical Society, Vol. 92 (1981). Reprinted by permission of the Massachusetts Historical Society.

Library of Congress Cataloging-in-Publication Data

Hall, David D. Iskog, 1936-
Worlds of wonder, days of judgment.

Bibliography: p.
Includes index.
1. New England—Religious life and customs. 2. New England—Church history—17th century. I. Title.
BR530.H35 1989   277.4'07   88-45373
ISBN 0-394-50108-X

Manufactured in the United States of America
First Edition

781978

For
JOHN, JEFFREY, and HUGH

Now so bad we are that the world is stripped of love and of terror. Here came the other night an Aurora [Borealis] so wonderful, a curtain of red and blue and silver glory, that in any other age or nation it would have moved the awe and wonder of men and mingled with the profoundest sentiments of religion and love, and we all saw it with cold, arithmetical eyes, we knew how many colors shone, how many degrees it extended, how many hours it lasted, and of this heavenly flower we beheld nothing more: a primrose by the brim of the river of time.

Shall we not wish back again the Seven Whistlers, the Flying Dutchman, the lucky and unlucky days, and the terrors of the Day of Doom?

—EMERSON in his journal, September 14, 1839

CONTENTS

WORLDS OF WONDER,
DAYS OF JUDGMENT

INTRODUCTION

THE PEOPLE of seventeenth-century New England lived in a world that had not one but several different meanings. This book describes the cluster of those meanings that we designate as "religion"—the mentality of the supernatural, the symbolism of the church and sacraments, the ritual enclosing of sickness, death, and moral disobedience, the self-perception of "sinners" in the presence of a judging God. More exactly, this book is about religion as lay men and women knew and practiced it. Mine is a history of the religion of the people, or popular religion, in early New England.

Religion in seventeenth-century New England encompassed set procedures and precise locations. The pace of feeling quickened and emotions became more intense on Sundays in the meetinghouse. But religion was embedded in the fabric of everyday life. It colored how you thought about your children and your parents. It entered into perceptions of community, and of the world that lay beyond New England. Religion achieved system in the tight order of the catechism. Yet in the flow of experience it was partial, ambiguous, and even contradictory. Empowering with its gift of spiritual renewal, it could also result in dark feelings of unworthiness. It added to the fearfulness of life, even as it reassured the faithful of God's providence. And though its claims were total—what was more important than preparing for the Day of Judgment?—people overlaid these claims with others that arose from family obligations and the structures of community.

In describing the religion of the people, I hope to indicate some of the ways that culture works. We may think of culture as both ordered and disordered, or, as I prefer to say, ambivalent. It has multiple dimensions; it presents us with choice even as it also limits or restrains the possibilities for meaning. What I attempt in this book is to sketch some of the possibilities that were present to the people of New England, and to suggest how they may have acted on them. In the main I have ignored the rich history of the "Puritan" movement.[1] I also pass by most of the vocabulary of religion as we find it in creeds and catechisms of the times. These are important, indeed crucial, matters. But I have preferred to describe matters that are less familiar to us, or that have been misinterpreted. Above all, I have tried to deal with the vexing question of the relationship between the people and the clergy. At the center of this description of popular religion stands a political, social, and theological circumstance, the authority of the men who held office as religious teachers. In what ways was this authority effective? In what ways was it rejected or its consequences blunted?

To raise these questions is to invite definition of the term "popular religion." In borrowing this term from historians who have studied religion and society in early modern Europe,[2] I have come to realize that its meaning for my story must emerge from the circumstances of New England in the seventeenth century. These were not the circumstances to which Europeans were accustomed. The differences are great enough to force us to revise the very sense of "popular religion."

From the vantage of his personal situation, the Anglo-American novelist Henry James was unusually aware of the differences between Europe and America, and how they had affected the American writer. Describing the career of Nathaniel Hawthorne, James paused to enumerate the "items of high civilization" that were absent in America and whose absence gave our culture its "simplicity":

> No sovereign, no court, no personal loyalty, no aristocracy, no church, no clergy, no army, no diplomatic service, no country gentlemen, no palaces, no castles, nor manors, nor old country houses, nor parsonages, nor thatched cottages, nor ivied ruins; no cathedrals, nor abbeys, nor little Norman churches . . .[3]

In the spirit of this passage, it is tempting to enumerate the religious institutions and activities that were absent in seventeenth-century New England:

No cathedrals, nor abbeys, nor little Norman churches; no liturgy, as in the Book of Common Prayer; no tithes to pay the clergy, no ranks of bishop and archbishop, no church courts, nor processions of the clergy; no altars or candles, no prayers for the dead.

And let us move beyond the narrowly religious:

No saints days or Christmas, no weddings or church ales, no pilgrimages, nor sacred places, nor relics or ex-votos; no "churching" after childbirth, no godparents or maypoles, no fairy tales, no dancing on the Sabbath, no carnival!

Events that were commonplace in much of Europe were not re-created in New England. Nor was this accidental. The differences ran deep into the structure of society and the structure of religion. Six main circumstances deserve close attention: the role of the "folk," the geography of religion, the relationship between church and state, the appeal of "radical" religion, the appeal of "magic," and the sway of literacy.

FOR MUCH of Christian Europe, it seems plausible to distinguish between two Christianities, the one that clerics taught, the other of the peasants or the lower social orders. The distinction rests on certain indisputable differences: the language of the clergy was Latin, they subscribed to points of doctrine less well understood by laymen, and they practiced a demanding way of life. The distinction also flows from the perception that European peasants clung to a "folk" culture that resisted the encroachments of official Christianity. Referring to the Middle Ages, a French historian has insisted that the religion of the clerics "had incompletely penetrated among the common people." As he sees the situation of these people, "their religious life was also nourished on a multitude of beliefs and practices which, whether the legacy of age-old magic or the more recent products of a civilization still extremely fertile in myths, exerted a constant influence upon official doctrine."[4] Others have suggested that this mixture lingered well into the early modern period. Summing up this point of view, a historian has declared more recently, "In religion, therefore, popular culture within the framework of the pre-Reformation church reflected limited mental horizons which rarely extended beyond the customary pattern of religious or semireligious rituals and observances or beyond local cults and traditions. Moreover, that religion had much in common with folk beliefs relating to the magical techniques of wizards and cunning folk."[5] According to this interpretation, most of these folk beliefs were eventually suppressed or simply faded away. But it is their persistence, their intermixture with orthodox belief, that defines popular religion in early modern Europe. We shall find that folk beliefs persisted in New England. Yet otherwise the situation was quite different, for the people who came to this region in the seventeenth century were not peasants but of "middling" status—yeomen, artisans, merchants, and housewives who knew how to articulate the principles of religion, and who shunned the "superstitions" of Catholicism. Emigration simplified the cultural system by making it more uniform.

We must start, therefore, by rejecting the conception of two separate religions, one rooted in folk ways of thinking, the other maintained by the clerics and their bourgeois allies.

In New England, too, space was much less consequential than in Europe. The significance of space was that religion varied with the distance between center and periphery. In outlying regions Christianity took on the character of "local" religion as distance turned into differences of style and understanding.[6] This was true in part because so many of the clergy were but poorly educated, and because so many others chose to live outside their parish. Either circumstance enabled ordinary people to ignore the duties of religion and perhaps to remain ignorant. But space did not have the same meaning in New England. Here, *no minister held office unless he was in residence,* a rule (and practice) obligated by the "congregational" structure of the church. Here, there was no court or urban center to which the more ambitious clergy moved; the social and the spatial order of New England was radically decentralized. Dispersed throughout a hundred towns, the clergy helped maintain a common system. They had all been trained alike; they all thought alike.[7]

A third point of difference concerns church and state. In most parts of Europe, church and state were closely allied. Every citizen was obliged to profess the religion of the king; everyone became a member of the church. The church itself had social functions to perform, and perhaps courts that imposed civil penalties; it owned vast properties, though also looking to the state for revenue. Such situations tended to arouse strong currents of anticlericalism, as in protests against tithes or in folk humor that mocked fat and overbearing clergy.[8] In contrast to the normal European system, the colonists eliminated all church courts, abolished tithes, and made church membership voluntary. Here too, although the civil magistrates were quick to act against dissent, the system of control did not include an Inquisition or a central group of clergy who enforced conformity. Nor could "censure" by a church "degrade or depose any man from any Civil dignity, office or Authority." Cooperation was offset by independence, and the power of the clergy was defined as merely "spiritual."[9] No longer agents of the civil state, and practicing, perforce, a life-style of asceticism, the New England clergy were less likely to arouse anticlericalism.

These clergy had their enemies. But we cannot define colonial popular religion as the worldview of those disaffected from official creeds. Somewhere in most European countries dissenters argued that Christianity promised universal redemption, that sin did not exist, that men possessed free will, that priests were superseded by new prophets, that the coming kingdom was at hand. Some of these beliefs were circulating in

England in the fifteenth and sixteenth centuries, though they gained their widest hearing in the period of the English Civil War, when the weakness of the church made it safe to express "radical" ideas. The sects that came and went throughout this period all gained spokesmen in New England. Yet never in the colonies did such groups attract many converts; and never did they speak for those resentful of their poverty. A few Baptists emerged in the 1640s and again two decades later, enough to organize a congregation of their own in 1665. Quaker missionaries worked hard after 1656 to gain converts, but without much success. Even the most prominent of the New England radicals, Samuel Gorton, was unable to recruit more than a handful of "Gortonists," and his group, which settled finally in Warwick, was dying out by 1670. To equate any of these groups with popular religion is to eliminate the majority of people; and it is the religion of that majority that I want to describe.[10]

Indifferent for the most part to the Quakers and the Baptists, ordinary people had more sympathy for ideas originating in the occult sciences. Many of the almanacs that every household used contained bits and pieces of astrology. Some people practiced magic to defend themselves from witchcraft, and some consulted fortune-tellers. It has been argued that such "magical" ideas and practices provided an alternative to Christianity.[11] But when New England ministers lashed out at "superstitions," their anger fell on an eclectic range of practices, from celebrating Christmas to nailing up horseshoes.[12] No war broke out between magic and religion, in part because the clergy also were attracted to occult ideas; it was they who wrote most of the almanacs, and in their response to the "wonder" they relied on older lore as much as any layman. As I argue in detail in a succeeding chapter, we do better if we perceive an accommodation between magic and religion than if we regard magic as somehow the substance of a different tradition.

One other way of putting boundaries around popular religion has been to propose that religion varies in accordance with the line that divides those who read from those who share an "oral culture." Did literacy have revolutionary consequences for one's worldview, or sustain other differentiating factors?[13] Whatever may have been the case for early modern Europe, the evidence is lacking from New England to uphold this argument. It seems likely that most people in New England learned to read as children. Of no less importance is the fact that everyone had access to the Bible in his native language, and to cheap books marketed especially for lay readers. Always there were some who did not own a Bible or lacked fluency in reading. But we can safely assume that most of the emigrants to New England had broken through into the world of print—though what this meant exactly will concern us in a moment.

All of these differences point to the influence of the Protestant Reformation in transforming the relationship between Christianity and the people. This one reason, this one cause, is why New England was so different from Catholic France and Italy. Consider that the Reformation forced a shift from Latin to the vernacular in the language of church services, that it opened up the Bible to lay men and women, that it drew laymen into church government, and that it affirmed a vernacular religion, as in a Book of Common Prayer.

Then too, consider that the Reformation was a people's movement; originating with the clergy, its motifs passed quickly into images and slogans that everyone could understand, and that many took up on their own.[14] Simple people—yeomen, housewives, even laborers—became Protestants in response to the liberating message of free grace. A church trial that took place in England in the 1530s reveals a boy of fifteen years who owned a primer and New Testament in English, and who described how

> divers poor men in the town of Chelmsford . . . bought the new testament of Jesus Christ and on sundays did sit reading [aloud] in lower end of church, and many would flock about them to hear their reading. . . .

In 1541 a church court in London was hearing evidence that certain Londoners, variously employed as bricklayers, shoemakers, plumbers, grocers, haberdashers, and servants, had rejected the mass and related ceremonies. Debate occurred in such settings as a Colchester inn to which "repair[ed]" a group of men and women who discussed in this setting the divinity of Christ, while others performed "Christian exercises."[15]

In these same years, Protestant ideas were also gaining ground among the clergy. William Tyndale, who encountered Martin Luther's writings in the 1520s, completed his translation of the Bible into English while in exile. The fortunes of reformers such as Tyndale rose and fell in rhythm with political events, but by the early 1550s those more ardent for reform, some of them by now the leaders of the church, rewrote the liturgy to make it truly "common" to both priests and people and to rid it of most ceremonies. The reign of Mary Tudor (1553–58) reversed this situation. Protestantism returned as the state religion with the reign of Elizabeth, and reformers resumed their campaign to purify the church. What happened in the years thereafter would have many consequences for New England. Reformers—it is too limiting to refer to them as "Puritans"—wished to raise the level of belief and practice among people and the clergy. As described by critics, too many of the clergy could scarcely teach the Christian message. A half century later, a better-disciplined and better-educated clergy were beginning to predominate, men who shared the vision of transforming Englishmen into sincere Christians.[16] To market towns, to London, to the "dark corners of the land," they brought their ideal of a disciplined, ascetic Christianity. The way to Christ was strenuous, for God demanded action against sin. In issuing this challenge, the preachers attacked a prevailing wisdom summed up in the proverb "The God that made me, save me."[17] They lamented the sheer ignorance of many: "For what a pitifull thing is it, to come into a congregation of one or two thousand soules, and not to finde above foure or five that are able to give an account of their faith in any tollerable maner. . . ." Arthur Dent, a minister who wrote a best-selling description of the way to heaven, denounced the throngs of people who "sit idle in the streets even upon the Sabbath. . . . Many will heare a Sermon in the fore-noon: and they take that to be as much as God can require at their hand. . . . but as for the after-noon they will heare none."[18] And there were demands for a change in life-style, as in the new requirement of Sabbatarianism.[19]

Some lay men and women took up this message with enthusiasm. The social costs of doing so were high in towns where others were in control. In such towns the people who thought of themselves as "the godly" sometimes withdrew from the "mixt multitude" in order to celebrate the sacraments and hear sermons on their own. Where they had power, the godly often sought to impose "discipline" on others.[20] Thus in the town of Dedham (Essex) the ministers and magistrates collaborated in 1585 in affirming fifteen rules or principles designed to bring about "the observation and mayntenance of all christian order" and "the banishing of the contrary disorder."[21] A handful of lay Puritans renounced the church completely; a few such "separatists" fled England between 1607 and 1609 for the safety of the Netherlands, whence they removed some years later to Plymouth in New England. But most of those who sought to cleanse themselves by separating from the "mixt multitude" were less openly rebellious or less radical.

When emigration to New England began, the new colony of Massachusetts attracted thousands of the godly who had previously accepted the message and the life-style we think of as Puritanism. What these people brought with them was also a deep revulsion against older customs and beliefs. Long before the great migration to New England, reformers in the sixteenth century had gone into churches to destroy statues and stained glass. The same people had renounced the ritual calendar of saints' days and holy days. They rejected certain forms of play, as when men dressed up as animals or people danced around a maypole. This conscious attack on "pagan" ways and "superstitions" was occurring at the same time as the pace of social change was weakening folkways and ritual practices. The village feast, the pageants that once filled the streets of Coventry, the lore of fairies and of cunning folk—all these were being displaced in the sixteenth century by a sharper sense of how the pagan differed from the Christian, the holy from the secular.[22]

This "disenchantment" of the world, or what Peter Burke has called the "reform" of traditional popular culture,[23] was well advanced before the colonists set out to found New England. Occurring when it did, the process of emigration conveyed to America the substance of a transformed culture. Psalm-singing replaced ballads. Ritual was reorganized around the celebration of the Sabbath and of fast days. No town in New England had a maypole; no group celebrated Christmas or St. Valentine's Day, or staged a pre-Lenten carnival! New England almanacs used numbers for each month instead of names deemed "pagan." And in naming their children, parents largely restricted themselves to names that appeared in the Bible, preferring John, Joseph, Samuel, James, and Timothy for male children and Mary, Elizabeth, Sarah, Hannah, Abigail, Rebecca, and Ruth for females. In doing so they acted to distinguish "profane" names from those considered holy, holy being names that were "commended unto us in the . . . Scriptures."[24] This shift in naming practice signified a change of consciousness that also explains the plain walls of the New England meetinghouse. Both were signs of how the colonists had broken with the web of custom and established a new Protestant vernacular.

This is the significance of my continuation of Henry James's catalogue: no carnival, no maypoles and church ales—and in the structure of the church itself, no bishops, courts, or Latin services. The sum of all these differences was a transformation in the situation of religion and society. It was not the act of emigration or the "free aire of the new world" that caused this transformation. The impetus for change lay in two European movements, the Reformation and the steady dissolution of traditional society. What made New England special was that its founders were more Protestant than most, more ready to eliminate old customs and to liberalize the structure of the church. Some who stayed in England favored these reforms. But only in this region did a democratic and decentralized congregationalism prevail so completely.

It is likely that the emigrants preferred a "liberal" society, by which I mean a differentiated, semi-independent government and marketplace. Far from being tightly centralized or linked to one another, the market and the legal system operated freely. If not fully secular, the courts functioned more or less according to the norms of English common law. Men and women moved about New England with an independence that distressed a William Bradford. Somehow the colonists arrived at the principle that every household should own land, and own it free and clear. The General Court of Massachusetts, like those in other colonies, granted land to groups of settlers in quantities that made it possible for families to gain substantial economic independence. Empowered in this manner, townspeople were also broadly able to participate in local and colonial politics.[25]

But despite these modernizing steps, in certain ways the colonists remained Elizabethans. Their identity as Protestants did not bar them from retaining currents of opinion that derived from pagan Greece and Rome, or from the Middle Ages. I once remarked that "the culture of the European peasant may be likened to a river full of debris."[26] I used this simile in trying to evoke a muddied, multilayered process by which culture was transmitted, one that functioned to preserve and pass along many bits and pieces of past systems of belief. What seems true of European rural culture was emphatically the case for people in New England. Protestants, their faith was leavened with accustomed ways of thinking that amounted to a folklore. Many years ago, Edward Eggleston and George Lyman Kittredge described this mixture in books that still retain their relevance. I follow in their footsteps, though also taking note of ideas Perry Miller called to our attention in *The New England Mind: The Seventeenth Century*.[27]

Let me return to the crucial question of the clergy and their role in shaping popular religion. They cannot be excluded from the story; they had too much in common with the people, and too prominent a part to play in teaching certain structures of belief. It is this commonness that complicates the meaning of popular religion. In what follows I modify two arguments that many others use in speaking of the people and their mental world. On the one hand I refuse to represent the clergy as so dominating in the churches that their way of thinking always prevailed. I acknowledge that the clergy were successful in persuading many of the colonists to adopt their understanding of religion. But the power of the clergy was too mediated to make them really dominant, and "domination" is a word that simply doesn't fit the pluralistic structure of New England towns and churches. On the other hand, I reject the argument that "popular religion" refers only to the ways in which lay men and women broke with what the clergy said. This happened in New England, as I demonstrate repeatedly. But it happened in conjunction with much sharing, and with a subtle process of *selection* between choices that the clergy helped articulate. It is an interesting and important irony that three great movements of lay protest were nurtured by some of the clergy; John Cotton and John Wheelwright took the side of "Antinomians" in the early stages of that controversy, John Davenport and others spoke out against the halfway covenant of 1662, and the revivals of the 1740s involved Harvard and Yale graduates whose preaching played a major role in stirring up the New Light movement. The process of selection was abetted by print culture; the books that people read, and especially the Bible, offered them conflicting messages. Yet here too the clergy figured as the writers of these books. Thus I find myself describing *mediations:* printers mediating what the clergy said, and vice versa, and the people bringing their needs to the meetinghouse. Where we find that people agreed with the clergy, this may simply mean that lay men and women exercised their freedom to accept the same ideas.

Hence my narrative unfolds as a tale of consensus and resistance, of common ground, but also differences. It did not take much time for a dialectic of resistance and cooperation to emerge. A crucial moment was the uprising of "Antinomians" in 1636 and 1637. Taking control of the Boston congregation, and threatening to dismiss a minister they did not like, lay men and women challenged the authority of the ministers as teachers of sound doctrine. Other groups would follow in defying the position of the ministers—Baptists, Gortonists, Quakers, Rogerenes. But we miss the real dynamics of the situation if we focus only on these radicals. Conflict was intrinsic to the congregational system despite agreement on its basic principles. Too much was vague, too much was open to interpretation. It happened that the ministers initiated change; in 1646 and 1648 they met collectively in Cambridge to debate and ratify the Cambridge Platform, by which they gained the right to veto actions by lay members. I have chosen not to describe the reaction of lay men and women to the Cambridge Platform, or any of the stages in the evolution of church government. Tension never vanished from this system, and long-nurtured anger exploded in the Great Awakening. Here it is enough to know that ministers and people worked uneasily together within a framework that empowered both.

These tensions temper the significance of statements such as Samuel Stone's, for Stone, a minister in Hartford, defined church government as "a speaking aristocracy in face of a silent democracy."[28] Indeed the ministers maintained that they were "called" by God to serve as his "ambassadors" on earth. This statement of vocation clearly served to set them apart from lay Christians, and justified their independence of lay congregations. A parallel assertion was that, as preachers of the Word, they were the "means of grace" by which the message of the gospel was transmitted to the chosen.[29] Accordingly, they argued that opponents of the ministry were practicing a dangerous game; to deny the means of grace, to resist or rebel against their preaching, amounted to denying God himself. In declaring that their "office" entitled them to deference, the ministers took advantage of assumptions about "order" that almost everyone acknowledged. A further basis of authority was the learning that they alone possessed. When Boston Second Church proposed in 1653 to elect and ordain as its minister an unlearned man (i.e., not a college graduate), the ministers reacted swiftly to prevent the church from acting.[30] Though they worked within a decentralized church structure, they continued to articulate a guildlike understanding of themselves.

Much of the time lay colonists accepted these arguments and deferred to those who were their ministers—giving them large grants of land, paying them generous stipends, and listening with respect to sermons. The grief was genuine when John Cotton died, or someone like Joseph Green, whose ministry had restored peace to troubled Salem Village.[31] Yet never did church members consent to major changes in the system of church government. Nor did the people like it when a minister intruded on affairs of civil government. In the midst of a dispute about land, an irate resident of Sudbury declared to his minister in 1654, "Setting aside your office, I regard you as no more than a man." Recalling a quarrel that broke out between him and a minister, the wealthy merchant Robert Keayne warned in his will that "the reverend elders of this country [must] not . . . be too stiff and resolute in accomplishing their own wills and ways" lest they arouse in others, as they did in him, the wrong consequences. Even someone as committed to the clergy as John Winthrop complained of their meddling. In the 1640s the deputies of the Massachusetts General Court were voting against policies the ministers approved. Toleration arrived after 1660 despite protests from the clergy, and "declension" went unchecked in spite of their demands for legislation.[32] Granting the charisma of John Cotton and his generation, the men who became their successors received less attention and were drawn into more frequent quarrels. As a candidate for jobs, Peter Thacher found that he would have to please a certain man in Barnstable before he could be hired. In Boston Second Church, Cotton Mather could not implement a change of policy until he won the consent of a leading layman.[33] These stories underscore the often overlooked reality that power in New England followed closely on the social structure, though at times it also coincided with the weight of numbers. Outside the church, as in, the power of the ministry was more bounded than we usually suppose.

All this while I have been explaining why I am generously inclusive in my definition of "popular religion." I am also generous in defining what I mean by "the people" or the "colonists." Most certainly, the meaning of religion flows in part from social experience: social rank conditions how we understand the world. But it is another matter to discern specific ways in which this process worked. Did printers see things differently because of their work situation? Did shoemakers, or sailors, or chattel slaves on a plantation?[34] Or, to speak more generally, did people of the "middling orders" in seventeenth-century England support social and religious "discipline" because of their class needs?[35] As it happens, I do not find this argument compelling. Sailors in New England do seem a rowdy lot, and merchants in such coastal towns as Boston and Salem were breaking free of Puritan asceticism.[36] A more telling case is women. One clear pattern that emerges from the data on church membership is that wives and daughters were more likely to be members than husbands and sons. I have spoken of empowerment without observing that lay-women were denied the privilege of participating in church government. In the work of some historians there are promising suggestions of how women shaped religion to their needs, or found themselves the victims of its symbols.[37] Where I can, I remark on the role of gender and of occupation. But in general, the mass of people in New England seem to have been relatively homogeneous in their social rank and practices; even those who worked as sailors were gradually absorbed within the system, and merchants intermarried with the ministers. Thus, to differentiate these people into groups each with a separate point of view seems less promising than to recognize the significance of family structure in the shaping of religious practice. My term "the people" does, however, always refer to lay men and women, as contrasted with the clergy, whom I mainly cite by name.

It is crucial that we not romanticize the people and their fascination with religion. Recalling the Connecticut farmers of his youth as they sat "stoically" in midwinter in an unheated meetinghouse, the nineteenth-century minister Horace Bushnell imagined them as

> men who have digestion for strong meat, and have no conception that trifles more delicate can be of any account to feed the system. . . . Under their hard . . . and stolid faces, great thoughts are brewing, and these keep them warm. Free-will, fixed fate, foreknowledge absolute, Trinity, redemption, special grace, eternity— give them anything high enough, and the tough muscle of their inward man will be climbing sturdily into it; and if they go away having something to think of, they have had a good day.[38]

Bushnell's farmers relish the abstract logic of theology, the harsh truths of Calvinism. So, it sometimes seems, did many people in seventeenth-century England and New England—Cromwell's troopers in the English Civil War, those Roundheads who marched strictly to the rhythm of a well-regulated conscience; or else the men and women who courageously embarked in the *Mayflower*.

But we must keep this courage and commitment in perspective. Another man who knew firsthand the mental world of nineteenth-century farmers remembered things quite differently. G. Stanley Hall describes one branch of his family as believing in religion, "but always with moderation." What moderation meant was this:

> Most of them attended church more or less but few joined, or if they did they fell off later in life. In their maturer years my uncles almost never frequented public worship. They were not unfriendly to or critical of religion but, as many expressions showed, considered it more manly . . . to stand before the All-Father on their merits as livers of good lives than to be saved by a vicarious atonement.

No Calvinists these farmers! Nor were they rigorously conscientious in the duties of religion:

> In one church there was a long and bitter war of the more ardent element against the so-called "horse-shed class," composed of people who would spend the long intermission between the two services in the horse-shed talking of secular matters instead of attending Sunday School. To this class most of my male relatives here belonged, despite the criticisms of my father.[39]

The truth this portrait captures outweighs, in my opinion, the ideal picture Bushnell paints. We have no way of knowing how many of the colonists were devout Calvinists, for no one took a census of beliefs.[40] Yet common sense instructs us that religion (or the church) attracts not only a committed core, but also others who, like "horse-shed" Christians, limit their commitment. I reason that the church attracts most people intermittently—more in some seasons of the year than others, and more at certain points in the life cycle. This reasoning I share with a far better witness of New England people in the past. From her childhood experiences as the daughter of a New England minister, Harriet Beecher Stowe remembered that in winters when the farm people were satisfied with their minister, they honored their contract to supply him with his firewood by bringing logs that were "of the best: none of your old makeshifts,—loads made out with crooked sticks and snapping chestnut logs, most noisy, and destructive to good wives' aprons."[41] I wish to insist, therefore, on acknowledging variety and change, and accepting "horse-shed" Christians as part of my story.

We find such Christians in the seventeenth century. Every parish had its group of staunchly faithful members but also many "horse-shed" members like those a minister described as preferring

> between the Exercises . . . [to] Discourse of their Corn and Hay, and the prices of Commodities, of almost any thing that they discourse of on Working dayes.

Every parish had young men and women who rebelled against their elders by making mischief where they sat together in the meetinghouse or "frolicking" on Sunday evenings. In every town some men (and women) gathered at the local tavern to down beer and rum. Winter evenings, they told stories of thieving lawyers and cuckolded husbands, sang "wicked" ballads, and swapped copies of dirty books. Certainly, they laughed; if guilt and fear were proper to the meetinghouse, release through humor was the province of the tavern.[42]

Some moved an even greater distance from the culture of the meetinghouse. A handful of persons may have questioned the very premises of Christianity as it was ordinarily understood. Amid the witch trials at Salem a man named William Barker declared that "the devil promeised that all his people should live bravely that all persones should be equall; that their should be no day of resurection or of judgement, and neither punishment nor shame for sin. . . ."[43] In most European countries there were regions where few clergy lived and where the church was weak. New England, too, had its "dark corners of the land," the places or the groups of people that were less affected by religion and less likely to want clergy. The fishermen of Gloucester, Massachusetts, made life difficult for Richard Blinman, who arrived as town minister in 1642. And, as told by Cotton Mather, a minister in some unnamed coastal village urged on his audience a more active practice of religion, lest otherwise they "contradict the main end of planting this wilderness!" Thereupon, a local resident cried out: "Sir, you think you are preaching to the people at the Bay; our main end was to catch fish."[44]

It is fair to suggest that this way of thinking was limited to settlements on the periphery. New towns where people went in search of land were often lacking in trained ministers. Referring to those who moved out beyond the reach of settlements, the minister John Eliot remarked in 1678 that he had "heard of some children of twelve years old, that never were present at a publick Sabbath worship of God; they know not what it is; such as live in dark places, in the outskirts of the land, know little or nothing of Religion, of the service and worship of God." The Reverend Increase Mather used the same equivocal expression in 1686, reporting in a sermon that "some say, that there are many hundreds, nay, some thousands in this place, that seldome hear a Sermon Preached, from one end of the year to the other. . . ." The metropolis of Boston was another place where some of the inhabitants escaped the obligations of religion; the two churches that existed by the 1650s could house no more than a third of the population.[45]

What all this means is that in certain places and at certain times of life, some of the colonists abstained from or practiced intermittently the organized activities that help make up religion. Others may have manifested their indifference by flouting moral rules, as some people do in every social system. But we must look more closely at these actions before we view them as signifying fundamental disaffection from religion. Young people settled down as they formed families of their own and brought their newborn children to be baptized.[46] New towns acquired ministers, and some of those on the periphery at the beginning, like Marblehead, became more like the norm in later years. A handful of persons may have misbehaved persistently, but for others a premature pregnancy or attendance at a tavern was accidental and not a clue to a subversive politics. At another moment in the court proceedings at Salem, William Barker expressed a conventional repentance.[47] No covert or consistent atheists can be detected in New England.[48]

My point is that we risk asking more of people in the past than they themselves expected. I think back upon my grandmother, who was devoted to the minister of her church and yet never hesitated to affirm *her* judgment of the divine will and purpose. Hence I lay aside the term "Puritan," and with it the assumption that the people of New England exemplified a total or a perfect faith. I want to affirm the legitimacy of "horse-shed" Christianity as well as the legitimacy of stricter patterns of behavior. In speaking of their quest for grace, lay men and women often referred to times of moral laxity or indifference. I take these people to mean exactly what they say, that crises or life stages affect the temper of belief and action. In sum, I have no quantitative way of measuring commitment, no means of telling who brought seasoned wood or green. Church membership is one criterion, but in seventeenth-century New England it was not the only token of commitment or mentality.

These statements lead toward a definition of religion that takes in more than simply what went on in the spare meetinghouses of New England— more than sermons and the sacraments, more than the church covenant and the obligations of community that it imposed. I describe these aspects of popular religion in one of the chapters that follow. But the meaning of religion in seventeenth-century New England must also encompass the moment when parents named a newborn child or when they took their children to an old man to receive his blessing. It takes in the preamble of a will, the last words that someone spoke as he or she lay dying, the "note" put up in church to ask for prayers for a sick person, the execution of a criminal, the whipping of dissenters who took on the guise of martyrs, the reading people did, the fearful response to an earthquake, the sense of having visions, the specter of the Devil. Religion comprehends a range of actions and beliefs far greater than those described in a catechism or occurring within sacred space: it was a loosely bounded set of symbols and motifs that gave significance to rites of passage and life crises, that infused everyday events with the presence of the supernatural.

In describing popular religion, I am thus attempting to present some of the possibilities for meaning—the possibilities for making sense of experience—that circulated in New England. I cannot always specify who acted on these possibilities. Nor am I able to describe the kinds of people, whether artisans or farmers, men or women, seacoast or inland, the better-off or marginal, who may have preferred a particular position. What I hope I have accomplished is to describe several major beliefs that figured in the repertory of the colonists, to indicate that certain of these beliefs were ambivalently coded, and to suggest how and why lay people acted to select one meaning or another.

In the culture I describe, learning how to read and becoming "religious" were perceived as one and the same thing. The many testimonies to this close connection include Nathaniel Eaton's remark "My education was in a religious manner from a cradle that I was trained up to read Scripture."[49] Taking my cue from such statements, I show that religion in New England embodied a distinctive mode of literacy, a mode originating, like much else, in the Reformation, and transported to New England with the colonists. This mode of literacy was keyed to a pervasive cultural myth. Imagining themselves as the "Lord's free people,"[50] the godly in England and New England valued direct access to the Word of God as the most precious of their privileges. Thus did literacy figure at the heart of cultural politics; thus did it represent the freedom that these people proclaimed for themselves. In the books they read, moreover, they encountered narratives or story frameworks that filled out the meaning of this freedom: the movement from captivity to "deliverance," from sin to redemption, from weakness and defeat to triumph. These story frameworks may not make much sense to us; moreover, we may label them as literary formulas, which is to imply that such stories should not be confused with what people "really" thought. I argue just the reverse, in part because so many of the colonists employed in their speech or writing bits and pieces of these story frameworks: they *do* convey the substance of perception and belief. The messages in books were the very stuff of popular religion, though people may have actually learned these messages as much from sermons and oral tradition as from print itself.[51]

Yet books were something more. Not only did they represent the myth of freedom; they were also artifacts in a commercial marketplace and counters in a complex politics that sometimes set the people at odds with the clergy. Early in the history of the printed book, entrepreneurs began to "multiply the number of works of popular piety generally available." This process, already evident in the late fifteenth century and a distinct feature of the English book trade some two hundred years later, surely signifies "the depth of religious feeling among" the consumers of this literature.[52] For this reason, books may yet again be recognized as the stuff of popular religion. I also recognize that books—and how the act of reading them was represented—were means by which the ministers imposed themselves on ordinary people; a catechism, a printed sermon, an elegy extolling someone's faith—all these created and maintained an orthodoxy. But as I hope to demonstrate, the authority of the ministers was held in check by a premise they themselves affirmed, that any version of the "truth," whether learned or unlearned, must conform to the Word of God. In practice this idea proved useful to those laymen who disagreed with what the ministers were saying. Unsettled from within by their very own tradition, the domination of the clergy was resisted by the printers and booksellers who ran the marketplace for books. To trace out the history of the book trade, to follow genres like the almanac and execution sermon as they slowly became more commercial, is to perceive, once again, the fluidity of power in seventeenth-century New England.

Let me briefly sum up other arguments and themes. To the question "Did any people in New England believe in something else than Christianity?" my answer is a guarded no. It seems doubtful that any of the colonists preferred a systematic alternative such as "atheism" or, as Carlo Ginzburg has proposed for witches and some peasants in sixteenth-century Tuscany, a folk "naturalism."[53]

Yet it may surprise some readers (as I myself was surprised) to discover how much "magic" circulated in New England—the magic of "murder will out," prophetic dreams and visions, pins hammered into buildings, shape-shifting dogs, and much more besides. The religion of the colonists was infused with ancient attitudes and practices, some indeed so old as to antedate the rise of Christianity. Much of this magic was in disfavor by the close of the seventeenth century. But the persistence of such old beliefs is one reason why it is wise to look upon the colonists as Elizabethans and not think of them as protomodern.

Similarly, it is wise to temper the assumption that radical Protestants banished ritual from religion. True, Protestant reformers dismantled most of the ritual of the Catholic church and attacked many of the ceremonies that enriched daily life. Yet ritual reemerged to surround certain rites of passage, express a conception of community, and provide patterned roles that lay people knew exactly how to play. A theme of ritual practice—it also turns up in other chapters, as when I describe the wonder and the sacraments of baptism and communion—is the loving, unselfish community from which anger and greed have been displaced. This yearning for community is another major theme, as is the anger (paradoxical though it may seem) that people felt when their sense of goodwill was violated. Other historians have shown how this anger figured in witch-hunting and attacks on dissenters.[54] Building on this work, I have sketched the ritual forms of cleansing and confession that underlie a wide range of practices, like becoming a church member. So too I indicate the anger that infiltrated every effort at affirming moral boundaries.

Ritual and magic—these are not the words we customarily use in describing the religion of the Puritans. Nor have historians said much about the practice of reading, or asked how lay people (as distinguished from the ministers) thought about the sacraments of baptism and communion. The mental world of the colonists was far richer than we have supposed. That world may seem confusing as I paint it in its many colors; for sure, no simple definition of Puritanism will emerge at the end. What has mattered to me is to listen to lay men and women as they spoke and wrote (and were spoken to), and to build upon their speech an interpretation of religion that does justice to the many levels of their thinking. What emerges is a picture that, for the first time, recognizes the importance of the popular tradition.

Above all, my story is of people who had power to select among a range of meanings. Once more the key word is "ambivalence." I have suggested that lay people and the clergy shared some ways of thinking, and I make this point more strongly in describing the tradition of the "wonder." Yet when we come to matters such as baptism, the Lord's Supper, and the "practice of piety," the purpose of my narrative is to unfold different possibilities for meaning, and to argue that lay people sometimes distanced themselves from the message of the clergy. In general I describe a set of practices and situations that offered choice, that remained open-ended.[55]

There is much that I omit, and my topical approach has meant I give more emphasis to continuity than to change. Change became significant just as this story ends, for the years on either side of 1700 reveal a growing separation between clerical and popular religion. I have briefly sketched the situation in an afterword in which I also look ahead to events like the Great Awakening.

CHAPTER 1

THE USES OF
LITERACY

A TWELVE-YEAR-OLD boy, precociously alert to the literary marketplace, writes a ballad in "Grubstreet" style on the "drowning of Captain Worthilake with his two daughters." Printed as a broadside, the poem sells "wonderfully" in the streets of Boston. Young men in Dedham sit "up many a time a great part of the night" in the secrecy of the town sawmill "to hear a book read" that teaches them the art of gaining power over women. A widow wills an "old great bible" and a "littel new bible" to her relatives. A servant girl has fits that suggest she is possessed by demons. In the midst of one such fit, as witnessed by her master, she "reherse[s] a great many verses, which are in some primers, & allso the dialoge between Christ the yoong man & the divull, the Lords prayer, all the commandments & catechism, the creede & severall such good things."[1]

These scenes draw us into the world of print as it was experienced by the people of seventeenth-century New England. These were people who eagerly read street ballads on sensational events, but who also treasured Bibles; who slipped off at night to sample dirty books, but who also memorized the contents of a schoolbook with its pious verse and catechism.

That servant girls like Katherine Branch could read is one reason why this world of print deserves attention. Compared to other regions, New England may have been distinctive in the rate of literacy. But regardless of percentages, how people learned to read and how they used their literacy were deeply consequential for popular religion.

I

THE COLONISTS enjoyed privileged access to the Bible. Theirs was the privilege all Protestants insisted on, of having Scripture in the language of the people. Free access to the Word in English! So the martyrs under Mary Tudor had demanded in debating their interrogators: Christ "never spake . . . any Latin, but always in such a tongue as the people might be edified thereby." When Protestants returned to power, they viewed it as a fundamental right that (to quote a famous martyr) "the people . . . have the Scriptures."[2] Explaining why this must be so and why Catholic clergy erred in supposing that no one can "understand the Scriptures unless he were a graduate of the university," an English minister declared that "there be divers which never came in the universities, yea, and some such as have no more but their mother's tongue do understand the Scriptures, and are able to teach good and sound doctrine." Defending the same principle, Thomas Cartwright, a leader of the Puritan movement in the 1570s, put the matter thus:

> If (as hath been showed) all ought to read the scriptures then all ages, all sexes, all degrees and callings, all high and low, rich and poor, wise and foolish have a necessary duty therein; of which particularities neither do the scriptures nor ancient writers keep silent. For the scriptures declareth that women and children and that from their infancy that noble and ignoble, rich and poor, wise and foolish exercise themselves in the holy scriptures. And Theodoret liketh well that the points of religion which the Church taught were not only known of doctors and masters but of tailors, smiths, weavers, and other artificers. . . . not of citizens alone but of country-folk, ditchers, delvers, neat-herds, and gardeners disputing even of the Holy Trinity.[3]

These very kinds of people appear in *The Book of Martyrs* as literate in Scripture—people such as Rawlins White, a fisherman, who mastered the Bible by having his young son "read a piece" of it "every night after supper, summer and winter."[4] Identifying with the likes of Rawlins White, the colonists took for granted democratic access to the Bible. Never would a New England government deny Bibles to the people, as happened in the reigns of Henry VIII and Mary Tudor. Rather was it assumed that people must be readers and own Bibles in their language.

Why say that people must know Scripture? The answer lies in part in the Reformation doctrine of *sola scriptura:* truth lives in the Word of God and not in men's "inventions" or what Catholics proclaimed as the "reason of forefathers." The articles of faith drawn up in England in 1549 and reaffirmed in 1560 made this doctrine plain:

> Holy Scripture containeth all things necessary to salvation: so that whatsoever is not read therein, nor may be proved thereby, is not to be required of any man, that it should be believed as an article of the Faith, or be thought requisite or necessary to salvation.

Nor was it "lawful" (as another article declared) "for the Church to ordain anything that is contrary to God's Word written."[5]

The politics of this assertion were made vividly pictorial in broadsides that portrayed the Pope as Devil stamping on the Bible, or else a pair of scales, one holding up the Word, the other crowded with berobed and mitered churchmen.[6] Such images suggested that the shift from Pope to Word was parallel to transformations in the concept of the priesthood: knowledge was no longer the peculiar privilege of a learned, sacerdotal caste, but common to the faithful; it empowered all, not just the few. The same images aligned the freeing of the Word from clerical authority with the freeing of God's people from tyranny of many kinds. A common language, a shared empowerment, enabled English Protestants to affirm an identity as the Lord's free people.

In Luther's Germany, where the technology of printing was already well established, the dynamics of this myth transformed an emerging craft as demand soared for books. Four times as many books were published in the 1520s than in the previous decade, as printers labored to produce sufficient copies of the New Testament in German, the catechism composed by Luther, and tracts defending the new faith. In these circumstances lay the makings of a cultural revolution, a recasting of the role of books and reading and thus of the relationship between elite and popular religion.

II

THE BIBLE was a printed book, an object just as physical as any chair or skillet. People bought their Bibles in a store. After 1611, buyers seeking English-language versions had a choice between translations, though gradually the King James Version displaced the Geneva Bible. In all, some six hundred thousand Bibles passed from printers to the public before 1640, and another million of New Testaments and psalters.[7] No printer in New England was legally entitled to print Bibles; the only local version was John Eliot's translation into the language of the native Indians. But in 1640 the newly founded printing shop in Cambridge issued a new translation of the Psalms, *The Whole Booke of Psalms,* also called the "Bay Psalm Book." The work of a committee of ministers, this was the first book to be published in New England. Its sales were steady enough to warrant a reprinting in 1647 and six more by 1700. The makers of the Bay Psalm Book had shrewdly recognized a business opportunity; some copies were shipped back to England, where demand was constant for editions of the Psalms.

These facts remind us that the Bible was like other books in being a commodity. But to its readers in the seventeenth century, the Bible was unlike other books in escaping its materiality. It was priceless, though you found it in the marketplace; it was timeless, though a printer may have dated an edition; it was living, though its matter was mere ink and paper. How the Bible appeared as the living Word of God would affect how other books were represented, and how they were read.

The uniqueness of the Bible was its status as the Word. All other texts were copies of this one original; all other forms of truth were incomplete or partial next to Scripture. It was the living speech of God, the "voice" of Christ, a text that people "heard." Or else it was a "light" conveying to the eye or soul the truth that was the gospel. This light was spiritual, and somehow independent of the medium of print. So St. Paul had declared to the Corinthians in telling them that his letters "were written not with ink, but with the Spirit of the living God," and "not in tables of stone, but in fleshly tables of the heart" (2 Corinthians 3:2–3). A few lines later (verse 6), he contrasted "spirit" and "letter," equating one with life and declaring that the other was the instrument of death: "who hath also made us able ministers of the new testament, but of the spirit: for the letter killeth, but the spirit giveth life." Appropriating this distinction, Elizabethans perceived Scripture as untouched and uncorrupted by the medium of print. To read or hear the Bible was to come directly into contact with the Holy Spirit. Scripture had no history, its pages knew no taint of time. Its message was as new, its power as immediate, as when Christ had preached in Galilee.[8]

Conceiving of the Word as living Spirit, the colonists used a version of this principle to establish the authority of Scripture. The answer to the question "How do the Scriptures prove themselves to be true?" as posed by a New England catechism was that Scripture acts directly on its readers to ensure the truth of what they learned. A martyr under Mary Tudor, the minister John Bradford, made this clear in responding to the Catholic doctrine that the church confirms the meaning of the Word: "so after we come to the hearing and reading of the Scriptures showed unto us . . . we do believe them, and know them as Christ's sheep—not because the church saith, they are the Scriptures, but because they be so; being thereof assured by the same Spirit which wrote and spake them."

The meaning of the Word was evident to those who felt its truthfulness within, as in their "hearts." To understand the Word required "faithful" hearing, a faithfulness that grace made possible.[9]

It followed that the meaning of the Bible was apparent to unlearned men and women whose hearts had been renewed in faith. Jesus was the archetype, a carpenter whose wisdom arose from the Holy Spirit. "It [must be] some strange learning," a martyr retorted to a bishop who disputed his interpretation of a text, "that Christ and his apostles could never attain to the knowledge of it."[10] In Christ's own speech, moreover, he used the "humble style," the vernacular of the people. The leaders of the English church argued that the Word of God was "easy and plain for the understanding." The Word was plain in that its meaning was immediately available. Plainness undercut the distance between text and audience. Thus Archbishop Cranmer spoke of wanting to discourse "so plainly that all men may understand every thing what I say." Preachers in New England preferred the same style as Increase Mather indicated in declaring of his father, "His way of Preaching was plain, aiming to shoot his Arrows not over his peoples heads, but into their Hearts and Consciences."[11]

A book yet not a book, the Bible had a unique aura. It was unique in its priceless value—veritably "the book above all books," the very reading Christ urged on his disciples after rising from the dead. An English minister compared it to "immortall seed," to God's "last Will and Testament," and to the "Magna Charta." Another likened its "Truths" to "pillars of silver" and its promises to "gold." The martyr Lady Jane Grey declared in a parting letter to her sister that the New Testament was "worth more than precious stones." What made it precious was the ways it changed men's lives. A minister described it as a "myrrour" in which Christians saw reflected their real nature—their corrupt hearts, their willfulness, their desperate need for mercy. He went on to say that Scripture was like medicine in cleansing men of sin; it was "physicke" to the soul, "yea, by it [Christ] doth cast out Devils, and raise men from the death of sinne. . . ."[12]

Indeed, the protective powers of the Bible were extraordinary. A New England minister may have had the local Indians in mind in urging people to know Scripture and to use it as they would the arrows in a quiver to drive off enemies like Satan. Stories circulated of the Bible being used to rescue someone from the Devil:

I have read [an English collector of such tales declared] of one Cramerus, a School-Master, who had a Scholar, who had in a Writing, in his own Blood, promised to give his Soul on certain Conditions

to the Devil: . . . and the Devil in the Night knock'd at his Cham-
ber-door, and demanded the Paper of him; but he answered, I have
laid the Paper in my Bible, and in that Page where it is written, The
Seed of the Woman shall bruise the Head of the Serpent; and
take it thence Satan if thou canst. And thereupon the Devil departed. . . .

People turned to Scripture for names to give their children. At moments
of great stress, as when a young man quarreled with his parents over
whether he should join in the emigration to New England, the Bible,
opened randomly, told what he should do:

I hastily toke up the bybell, and tould my fatther if whare I opend
the bybell thare i met with anie thing eyther to incuredg or discou-
redg that should settell me. I oping of it, not knowing no more then
the child in the womb, the first I cast my eys on was: Cum out from
among them, touch no unclene thing. . . .

A woman taken captive by the Indians, Mary Rowlandson, remembered
how, unexpectedly encountering her son, she offered him her Bible "and
he lighted upon that comfortable scripture, Psalm 118:17–18. . . . Look
here, mother (says he), did you read this?"[13]

For Mary Rowlandson, the mere presence of the Bible was like having
God beside her. The Bible signified his presence; it was an icon of the
divine, it made visible the hidden. For her it also signified the truth, a
truth she understood by way of meditation, not by rational analysis. As
icon the Bible implied that the language it contained was really divine
speech or poetry, as in the psalms of David. Such speech was symbolic
in the sense that all the people and events it described were metaphors
or figures for Christ, whose coming and redemption were foretold in
the history of the Jews. Language thus revolved around an archetypal
pattern of God's intervention in the world to manifest himself and, in
doing so, to glorify a chosen people.[14] When she was rescued from captivity, Mary Rowlandson experienced this pattern for herself. Thereafter
she turned naturally to Scripture for metaphors that linked her suffering with that of the Jews, and her rescue with the gospel. She was no
more gifted as a writer than a thousand others, for her way of using
words was the common practice of most English Protestants. As it did
for her, so for the Protestant community the Bible symbolized their bonds
with one another and with God. A free people were a people of the
Word, with the Bible as their token of identity.

Always the meaning of the Bible was self-evident. It was a book that
made its message felt without there being any mediation—no interme-

diaries, no gloss, no message that called for interpretation. In the root sense of the word, the Bible was *immediately* available. Hence the only manner of translating it was to leave well enough alone. Translation was an act of reaffirming the original, not "cloaking" it in paraphrase. Thus the men who prepared the Bay Psalm Book declared in their preface they had done their best to attend "the originall," explaining that "Gods Altar needs not our polishings." If their poetry were "plaine," it was because the plainness of the Bible was synonymous with its direct reception.[15]

Yet this very understanding of the Bible was a partisan creation, the doing of a group of Protestants who imposed their own interpretation on the text. Mediation was an everyday affair, whether through the very choice of words in a translation or in how the text itself was arranged. The makers of the Geneva Bible deemed it necessary to equip their translation with a critical apparatus that included running commentary in the margins. They divided the text into numbered verses, placed "some notable worde or sentence which may greatly further" an understanding of the text at the top of every page, inserted summaries in front of every book and chapter, and commissioned twenty-six woodcuts that visually elucidated passages "so darke" that no other means would do to make their meaning "easie to the simple reader." To make the text more readable and the book less costly, its printers used roman type instead of the more difficult black letter, and reduced the size from folio to quarto. The translators of the Bay Psalm Book, though denying any role as mediators, made that role explicit in confessing they had tinkered with the Hebrew in order to insert a "meeter" that made the Psalms more readable. And more elegant: in the end an ear for "Elegance" and "sweetness" affected the translation.[16]

The paradox was of mediators who represented Scripture as unmediated, yet who made their presence felt on every page. This was a paradox that extended to the works these writers wrote themselves—the sermons, the manuals of devotion, the biographies that appeared in abundance in England in the early seventeenth century. In imitation of the Bible, these writers represented everything they wrote as truth. They said so directly in affirming they were different from the "many scribling Professors in the world" who "write . . . imperfect copies,"[17] and they also used what we may think of as truth-heightening conventions. Within the literary tradition of the Protestant vernacular, the foremost of these techniques was to include references to Scripture. Every published sermon in New England began with a text, and many others followed in the body of the discourse. This formal device was complemented by a repertory of figures and motifs that derived from the Bible, and by patchwork quoting without giving any reference. Lay writers wrote such prose and poetry as skillfully as learned ministers, and always with the same objective, to reduce the distance between what they said and what was contained in the great original, the Word. Another consequence of this ambition was a bias against preaching from a written text, or even notes, in order that a sermon would seem "in the demonstration of the Spirit." It was a telling moment when, in Hartford meetinghouse, a minister stopped in the middle of a sermon and was silent for some minutes. For those in Thomas Hooker's congregation, his silence signified dependence on the Holy Spirit: when the spirit returned he would resume preaching.[18]

The metaphors that writers used for books betoken the same goal of fusing written word (or spoken) with the Spirit. When John Norton used the title *Abel being dead yet Speaketh* for his biography of John Cotton, he played upon the interchangeability of speech, life, and the printed page. A young writer in New England was moved by Cotton's death in 1651 to liken Cotton's very self to a book that had no errors, like the Bible:

> A living, breathing Bible; tables where
> Both covenants, at large, engraven were;
> Gospel and law, in's heart, had each its column;
> His head an index to the sacred volume;
> His very name a title-page; and next,
> His life a commentary on the text.
> O, what a monument of glorious worth,
> When, in a new edition, he comes forth,
> Without *erratas,* may we think he'll be
> In leaves and covers of eternity!

Another of these metaphors was "mirrour," as in the title of an English broadside of 1643, *A Looking Glasse for the Soule: worthy to be hung up in every house in this Kingdome, and to be looked in daily.* The aura of these metaphors—their fusion of the book with life—was evoked by Anne Bradstreet in her dedication of a book of private meditations:

> To my Dear Children. This Book by Any yet unread,
> I leave for you when I am dead.
> That, being gone, here you may find
> What was your liveing mother's mind.
> Make use of what I leave in Love
> And God shall blesse you from above.

An English writer relied on the same convention in evoking a book that was and yet was not a material artifact:

There is a Book of three leaves, said one, and I have been reading it all my Life, and I have not read it over: one was a red Leaf, the other a white, the third a black Leaf; the Black Leaf was of Death, Hell, and Judgment, the white Leaf was of Heaven, the red Leaf was of the Blood of Christ.[19]

Evoking, for the books they wrote themselves, the aura of the Word, these writers asked that readers respond to their books as though they were as sacred as the Bible. In telling people how to read, writers began by reiterating the advice St. Anselm gave in the eleventh century. To read was to ruminate, as though you ate the Word of God: "Taste the goodness of your redeemer . . . chew the honeycomb of his words, suck their flavor."[20] Henry Scudder, an early-seventeenth-century English minister much favored by the colonists, used the metaphor of "chewing the cudde"—"Meditation is instead of chewing the cudde"—in arguing that readers must actively ingest the word "with an hunger & thirst after knowledge and growth of grace by it." His point was also that reading was an act of returning to the same text time and time again. Another English minister affirmed bluntly "that once or twice reading over a booke for practice is not enough." A third, a best-selling evangelical, urged those who had his book to "diligently read it over and over again, and when you have done, enter upon a serious consideration" of the substance. The import of this advice was always to transform reading into action. In offering "a few lines of Christian counsell & advise" to his congregation in the form of a printed *Farewel Exhortation,* Richard Mather urged them to "read and practise the same." He went on to distinguish between two modes of reading, one in which "you . . . give these things the reading only, and so dismiss them with a bare approvall or disapprovall," and the other in which "you . . . seriously endeavour the practise thereof."[21]

So every preface addressed to "the Christian reader" argued, in statements that imply no difference between the words of godly writers and the Word of God. Yet somewhere, somehow, these same prefaces evoke the everyday world of printers, marketplace, and competition, a world in which all books were mere commodities. Nowhere was this paradoxical doubleness more evident than in William Greenhill's introduction to the second London printing of Thomas Shepard's *The Sincere Convert.* Early in the preface that he addressed "To the Christian Reader," Greenhill insisted that "our Divines and Writers" are "The voyce of God, and not of man: Such abundance of the Spirit hath God powred into some men, that it is not they, but the Spirit of the Father that speakes in them." As in the making of the Bible, so here the text flowed from the

Holy Spirit: "The Author is one of singular piety, [and] inward acquaintance with God." Yet Greenhill must concede that Shepard's text was different from the Bible. No sooner has he affirmed that "good books . . . spring" from the Bible than he admits that "Some" say "it's enough to praise God for his Word, other books are not *tanti*." An offstage voice declares, "But they have errors in them," and though Greenhill responds by likening *The Sincere Convert* to a "Garden without Weeds," his next sentence—"Here are truths sutable, solid, and wholsome"—implies that *other* books mislead. Indeed the subtext of his affirmation is the prevalence of error in such "perilous" times. Another subtext is the marketplace, as implied in his plea that readers buy this book "though it cost us all," and in the franker plea, "Is it not a good purchase? Can you bestow your pains, or lay out your money better?" Even in the act of giving Shepard's text a sacramental significance, Greenhill reaffirmed the duality of man and God, the "good purchase" and the price*less*.[22]

The same contradictions emerge in the preface a New England minister contributed to Henry Scudder's *The Christians Daily Walke*. In the course of citing 1 Corinthians 3:2–3, John Davenport presented Scudder and his book as manifesting the work of the Holy Spirit. The hand that held the pen, the ink that filled the pages, were but conduits through which the spirit flowed. But as in Greenhill's introduction a subtext intrudes, a voice objecting that "many have already written on these subjects, and therefore this is superfluous"! Davenport himself would cite competitors. Yet he argues that the marketplace has room for more, especially since

> The Christian, & intelligent Reader shall find in this some things new, other things expressed in a new manner, all digested in such a Method, with such brevitie, and perspecuity, as was necessary to make the booke a vade mecum, easily portable, and profitable to the poore, and illiterate.

Here the tone is that of a bookseller's advertisement, a tone that directs us to admire the skill of the printer who has fabricated so pleasing a commodity. Scudder's *Daily Walke* owes its "new manner" to marketplace considerations, not to the intrinsic power of the Word.[23]

As in these two cases, so in other books that aimed to emulate the Bible human mediators ended up acknowledging their presence in the making of a text. This was so especially for the "learned" men who believed in the plain style, yet who also felt that humane learning made the meaning of the Bible more apparent. And even in the sixteenth century, though more surely by the 1640s, writers were responding to marketplace conditions of size, price, and competing products. The translators of the Bay Psalm Book expected it to sell in England, which is why the Cambridge press ran off so many copies of the first edition. Scudder's *Daily Walke,* Shepard's *Sincere Convert,* the narrative of Mary Rowlandson—all owed their appearance to market forces. Such salesmanship intruded in the delight of young Michael Wigglesworth that his poem *The Day of Doom* earned him a Bermuda vacation, in revisions of the Bay Psalm Book to make it sell still better,[24] and in the format of Geneva Bibles. "Godly" books were products of a highly mediated world, the world of merchandise where print artifacts emerged from the interaction among printers, booksellers, writers, and readers.

No matter how such books were made to look like truth, they ended up containing what printers referred to as errors. In a deeper sense they ended up as fictive, for the very effort to present them in the same dress as the Bible underscored the presence of their makers' own inventiveness. The aura of the Word, and a very human, disenchanting marketplace—two very different and mutually contradictory contexts converged in the books that circulated in New England, and the contradiction made it possible to question the authority of "godly" books. Not that many laymen did, at least overtly; printed sermons in the plain style continued to impress their readers as being nearly like the Bible. As will be clear from patterns of production and consumption in New England, lay men and women respected what the clergy wrote, preferring "godly" books to any other kinds of reading matter. An ideology of print, a way of representing certain books as truth, thus strengthened the role of the clergy as "ambassadors" of Christ. Yet the domination implied in this role was kept incomplete or partial by forces that the clergy never mastered. The marketplace transformed books into competing products. Nor were readers in New England simply passive. Docile in accepting the truth of printed sermons, they nonetheless remembered that the Word was different from "humaine inventions."[25] The interplay of clergy, printers, and readers worked in complex ways both to heighten clerical authority and to make it vulnerable to challenge from beneath.

III

I N *The Canterbury Tales* Chaucer's prioress describes a schoolchild who is learning how to read:

> This little child, while he was studying
> His little primer, as he undertook
> Sitting at school, heard other children sing

O Alma Redemptoris from their book.
Close as he dared he drew himself to look,
And listened carefully to word to part
Until he knew the opening verse by heart.[26]

Two centuries later in New England, children learned to read in the same manner. Literacy emerged from a process of instruction that began with hearing others read aloud, and with memorizing certain texts. The manner in which people in New England learned to read throws light on the vexing question of how many of the colonists were literate, and therefore on how many of them could use books. But it is the uses of literacy that especially concern us here, the meanings that the ordinary reader drew from books and the place of reading in a broader set of cultural practices.

When Chaucer and his contemporaries used the word "illiterate," it signified an ignorance of Latin. The ministers who founded Harvard College in 1636 were prompted to do so by fears that, unless New England had a school where Latin and the literary culture of the classics were the substance of instruction, they would "leave an illiterate Ministry to the Churches."[27] By this standard, all but a mere handful of the colonists were illiterate. Yet, though ordinary people were excluded from the world of Latin, they were comfortably acquainted with the language of their Bibles. To be sure, many wrote with difficulty, or not at all. But when defined as the skill of reading English, literacy was almost universal.

This was so, largely because reading had such high importance in the religious system. Wealth and occupation were significant in sorting out mere readers from those who learned to write as well: every minister in New England possessed both skills, as did merchants and magistrates. But in trades where writing did not play a major role, people often stopped with learning how to read. Women were especially lacking in the skill of writing, though it is likely they were readers as much as the men they lived and worked with. A careful count of signatures as against simple marks on wills suggests that 40 percent of adult men in 1660 were unable to write, and 70 percent of adult women. Not until a century later did the skill of writing as well as of reading become nearly universal.[28]

The evidence for widespread literacy begins with what was said in courts and churches. Literacy, it should be stressed, involved different combinations, with some people able to read printed books but not handwriting, and still others able to read everything, as well as write themselves. When people testified in court, they often indicated, directly or obliquely, the degree of their ability or inability to read and write. An Essex County man asked someone else to write his absent wife in England; the same person read him her answers. Sarah Rowe of Ipswich, unhappily betrothed to a man she did not love, "got a young maide that lived in the house with mee to write a letter" to a would-be (and more pleasing) suitor asking him "to come noe more to mee." To get "evidence" from his daughter on what was destroyed in a fire, a man requested another person to "go to his house to write" down the details. Phineas Fiske refused the post of deacon in the Chelmsford church "considering he neither could write nor read written hand" (though, by implication, he could read print). Two men in 1671 could not decipher verse that may have been handwritten. A debtor must have a bond read to him. A woman must request another to read her a "writing." George Jacobs, a victim of witch-hunting in the Salem craze of 1692, told the court he could not read.[29]

Yet rarely do these records indicate that people cannot read at least printed matter. And, while indicating that some persons could not write or read handwriting, the same records also suggest just the opposite, that many of the colonists were at ease with writing and, perforce, with reading. Dozens of court cases involve creditor–debtor settlements that refer to a merchant or storekeeper's "book." Disputes over land sometimes turned on oral memory or the ancient method of "turf and twig," but more often, and especially after 1652, on records kept in written form. Men voted in colony elections by writing names on bits of paper. Churches sent each other letters to accompany transfers of membership and to answer questions about someone's moral reputation. Printed copies of the laws enacted at each legislative session were sent to every town, where people met to read them (or to hear them read aloud). Many different sorts of personal and public records make reference to reading and writing. The depositions at the Salem witchcraft trial in 1692 indicate that George Burroughs's wife could write; Goody Trask, an accused witch, was "much given to reading & searching the prophecys of Scripture" and wrote to her church. The bewitched house of William Morse of Newbury contained an inkwell. A young woman servant in Maine, convicted of infanticide and awaiting execution, referred in her confession to learning how to read in the household where she worked.[30]

Never do these records suggest that substantial groups of people were hampered by illiteracy. The reverse is true: these records reveal a population of readers and, surprisingly, of more writers than at first we might suspect. When the Massachusetts General Court requested towns in 1668 to provide their county courts with "an account of the youth from the age of nine years and upward, who cannot read," the selectmen of the town of Beverly replied that they "doe not find any youth of the age of nine years or exceeding it that cannot read: or that are not In-deavouring to learn as those under whose tuition those are being very few doe say who have likewise promised to use their father [further] Indeavour to perfect them to read." Topsfield made no reference to illiterates at all.[31]

Literacy was achieved within the household, with mothers as the key instructors. Here took place instruction in the catechism; here, young children first learned how to read. Not every family practiced the rou-tine of family devotions that included daily readings from the Bible. But every household in New England was affected by the premise, originat-ing with the Reformation, that all godly people should be literate. In late-sixteenth-century England, towns that came beneath the sway of "Puritans" enacted statutes requiring every household to become a little school. So too in New England, the religious system merged with house-holds in ways that ensured a near-universal literacy.[32]

Yet there were other agencies involved: the system of apprenticeship, the school, the civil state. Early on, in 1642, the civil government in Mas-sachusetts urged town officials to make sure that "parents and masters" were fulfilling their obligation to instruct children and servants "to read and understand the principles of religion and the capital lawes of the country." In 1647 the same government ordered every town of fifty families to "appoint one within their own towne to teach all such chil-dren as shall resort to him to write and reade," and in 1648, that each family observe weekly catechizing. When families slackened in this prac-tice, the ministers took over. Another instrument of enforced education was contracts between masters and apprentices; as prescribed by the courts, these contracts usually obliged masters to make sure that servants be-came literate.[33] A handful of towns found the resources to establish a more advanced curriculum at a "grammar" school, where students could learn Latin.

What made this mix of institutions work was surely not the school. Enforcement of the school laws was imperfect, and towns were fre-quently irregular in providing teachers. No law required children to at-tend for a specific period of time—or attend at all! Schools were not mentioned in the law of 1642 because of the assumption that families introduced young children to the skill of reading. Schools were where you went to learn to write and cipher, and for certain boys, to begin learning Latin. A substitute for households was "dame" schools that sprang up in many towns. Inexpensive and unregulated, such schools were run by women who taught others' children as they must have taught their own. After 1660, as towns moved to organize such schools themselves, their number became large. In response to an inquiry from the Middlesex county court, the town of Concord reported in 1680 that "as for schools, we have in every quarter of our Town both men and women that teach to read and write English, when parents can spare their children or others to go unto them." The report from Billerica cited "several women that are school-dames," and two other towns referred to "English schools kept by several women." There seems every reason to assume that dame schools filled in satisfactorily for what was lacking elsewhere. A patchwork system worked, where bureaucracies have failed.[34]

Always, the first step in education, at home or at a dame school, was learning how to read. Only later, and often in more formal settings, did children learn to write and cipher. This sequencing of skills was thoroughly traditional. The norm in English schooling as long ago as Chaucer's century, it prevailed in New England well into the nineteenth century.[35] In ordering or reviewing the practice of instruction, magistrates and selectmen took for granted the priority of learning how to read. Thus in 1650 the town fathers of New Haven debated "whether parents should not be compelled to put their children to Learning, at least to learne to read English & to wright." A year later, the town explained to a newly hired schoolmaster that "his worke should be to perfect male children in English, after they can reade in their Testament or Bible, & to learne them to wright. . . ." Informal records complement these statements. A minister who took in students noted of a new pupil, "I was to perfect him in reading, and to teach him how to write." The man in charge of Christianizing the New England Indians, a process that included their becoming literate, wrote of the "praying Indians" that "many can read, some write."[36]

The same sequencing occurs in a handful of accounts in which people describe how they learned how to read and write. These stories emphasize the household setting and the role of mothers. When his mother died in 1704, John Paine of Plymouth wrote movingly in his journal that

> carefull mother eke She was
> unto her children all
> teaching them gods word to read
> when as they were but Small.

Increase Mather declared in his autobiography that "I learned to read of my mother. I learned to write of Father, who also instructed me in grammar learning. . . ." Richard Brown, a minister, wrote in a journal that his mother "caused me to read well at home" before he went off to a school to study Latin. Another man who became a minister recalled that he had "quickly learnt to read, without going to any school that I remember." In still another of these reminiscences, it was a man's grand-father who played the key role: "This Samuel [Johnson] was early taught to read by the care of his grandfather. . . ." No matter who the mentor, New England children did not need to leave the household to learn how to read. Some gained this skill in dame schools. But for many others, schooling served to confirm and/or enlarge a literacy they achieved at home.[37]

A further motif of these stories is the brevity of formal schooling, and the early age at which a child went off to school or first learned how to read. Cotton Mather may have been presumptuous in suggesting to a friend that his son "begin to Read, before he is Two years old." But there is evidence of children going off to school when they were not much older. Henry Sewall set out for dame school, hand in hand with an older sister, at the grand age of three. John Barnard went to "dame school" when he was three or four years old; when he reached six, he was made "a sort of usher . . . to teach some children that were older than myself, as well as smaller ones." Barnard also remembered that "I had read My Bible through thrice" by the age of six. The stories of pious children that Thomas White, an English nonconformist, retold in *A Little Book for Little Children*, though perhaps exaggerating the real situation, assume that children no more than three or four years old were readers. At whatever age it came, literacy arrived without much formal schooling. Some never went at all, and others enrolled for no more than a few months.[38]

This evidence suggests that reading emerged from a broader set of practices and not from segregated training. This is the significance of Nathaniel Eaton's remark "My education was in a religious manner from a cradle that I was trained up to read Scripture."[39] We sense this conti-nuity in the rest of Samuel Johnson's tale of learning how to read:

> [his grandfather] taught him many things by heart, beginning with the Lord's Prayer and Creed, and as he delighted to read the Scrip-tures, he got many passages of them by heart, which his grandfa-ther, carrying him about with him to visit the ancient people, his contemporaries, made him recite *memoriter*, in which he much de-lighted.

The same was true of Jane Colman, who "could say the greater Part of the Assembly's Catechism, many of the Psalms, some hundred Lines of the best Poetry, read distinctly, and make pertinent Remarks on many things she read"—and all this by the age of four.[40]

Many decades later, near the end of the eighteenth century, young Joseph Buckingham was placed as a servant in a Connecticut farm household. There he "read [aloud] every day, at least one chapter, and often two or three. I have no doubt that I read the Bible through *in course* at least a dozen times before I was sixteen years old." Consequently, its "incidents and the language became almost as familiar as the grace . . . said before and after meals—neither of which ever varied a word during . . . nine years." In that same household, Buckingham spent every Saturday evening reciting the Westminster Catechism and "such Psalms or Hymns as I might have committed to memory in the course of the week. There was a time when I could recite Watts's version of the Psalms from beginning to end, together with many of his Hymns and Lyric Poems." Not surprisingly, Buckingham was able to read confidently from the Bible his first day in school:

> In December, 1784, the month in which I was five years old, I went to a master's school, and, on being asked if I could read, I said I could read in the Bible. The master placed me on his chair and presented a Bible opened at the fifth chapter of Acts. I read the story of Ananias and Sapphira falling down dead for telling a lie. He patted me on the head and commended my reading.[41]

As here, so in the experience of young children in the seventeenth century, literacy had less to do with formal schooling and more with learning Scripture and a catechism. Literacy in New England was bound up with certain texts that doubled as an introduction to religion and an introduction to the skill of reading.

Apart from the Bible (and especially the Book of Psalms), the crucial texts were the primer and the catechism.[42] In functioning as the entryways to literacy, these were texts that children listened to while others read aloud, as Chaucer's little boy had heard his schoolmates chant the "Alma Redemptoris." Like him, the beginning reader in New England "listened carefully to word to part / Until he knew the opening verse by heart." This technique of instruction meant that children were reciting from memory before they understood—or in any real sense "read"—the texts in front of them. But at every level of this system students learned by memorizing. None doubted the validity of so ancient a technique. An English minister urged godly parents, "Cause your younger children to learn the words, though they be not yet capable of understanding the matter. . . . A child of five or six years old can learn the words of a Catechism or Scripture, before they are capable of understanding them."[43] Similarly, a New England minister paused in the midst of a long poem to advise children "of tender Age, / This unto you I write, and thus in Verse, / That ye might best conceive, learn, and rehearse." Proceeding from the same assumption that verses were easier to learn, writers pro-

duced rhymed versions of the Bible. Rhymed verse was a feature of the
New England Primer, as in the famous alphabet that juxtaposed pictures
with a corresponding couplet: "In Adams Fall / We sinned All" for the
letter A, "Thy Life to Mend / This Book Attend," for B, and so down to
"Zacheus he / Did climb the Tree / His Lord to see."[44]

In all likelihood, any of the primers that circulated in seventeenth-
century New England opened with an unadorned alphabet and a sylla-
barium—that is, a list of words arranged progressively from short to
long, and divided into syllables. After children learned to speak these
words and letters, they memorized a set of sentences that contained moral
rules and advice. Then came the Lord's Prayer, the Apostles' Creed, and
the Ten Commandments, three leftovers from the time when the primer
was a service book in the Church of England. By the middle of the seventeenth century, the primers used by children in New England would
probably have included verses from the Bible and stories of the martyrs.
The primer that Katherine Branch had learned by heart contained a
dramatic poem, "A Dialogue Between Christ, Youth and the Devil"; the
New England Primer added a long prose poem, an "Exhortation" to his
children, spoken by the martyr John Rogers, who was burned at the
stake in England in 1553.[45]

In using these texts to learn how to read, children in New England
also absorbed the elements of the religious system. Literacy and religion
were inseparable. So everyone assumed, and especially those in charge
of the civil state. According to the Massachusetts school law of 1647, the
very future of the Protestant religion was bound up with knowing how
to read, "It being one chief project of that ould deluder, Sathan, to keepe
men from the knowledge of the Scriptures." Catholics made the same
assumption, as did Lutherans in Sweden, where church and state cooperated to enforce a catechizing from which emerged almost universal
literacy (in the sense of knowing how to read).[46]

Yet primers and the catechism contained other messages. The very
process of becoming literate, and starting to use books, conveyed to would-
be readers the authority of print, an authority that rested on the equiv-
alence of speech and writing. Holy books were read aloud, as in the
routine of family devotions. Holy books were also living speech, the Word
infused by Spirit. What was printed was to be received as though it had
been spoken, and therefore as the truth. Whoever put together the *New
England Primer* incorporated this message into the text itself. The literary
structure of the Ten Commandments was echoed in the rhetoric of "The
Dutiful Child's Promises," which the "Child, being entred in his Letters
and Spelling," was to "learn . . . by Heart, whereby he will be both instructed in his Duty, and encouraged in his Learning." The "Exhorta-

tion" attributed to John Rogers was explicit in conflating the living Word and inanimate print, the written and the spoken:

> Give ear my Children to my words,
>   whom God hath dearly bought,
> Lay up his Laws within your heart,
>   and print them in your thought,
> I leave you here a little Book,
>   for you to look upon
> That you may see your Fathers face,
>   when he is dead and gone. . . .
> Not many days before my Death
>   I did compose this Work.
> And for Example to your Youth . . .
> I send you here God's perfect Truth. . . .

Granting, as they do, the dual nature of the printed word, these statements suppress that duality by transposing the ephemeral into the permanent: "print [these words] in your thought." They replace the decay of books with the Word that is the "perfect Truth," a truth that endures in the heart.

Thus, the texts that children learned to read from simultaneously acknowledged and denied the role of human mediation. In keeping with the Protestant vernacular tradition, they supposed that to read was to hear, to hear was to see, and to see was to receive truth (or light) communicated to the inner self, the heart. In presuming this near-identity between printed page and (spoken) Word, these texts also imposed on their readers the manner of their use. Nothing separated books from life or action; books transformed the inner self or "heart" in ways that carried over into everyday behavior. Willing a godly book to one of his sons, a minister affirmed, "I doubt not my booke will give him A hart of all sound doctrine." Anne Bradstreet shared this expectation. The book she willed her children was, as she declared, a book for them to "make use of."[47]

When people in New England talked about their reading, as they sometimes did in speaking of their progress out of sin and into grace, their descriptions were in keeping with this ideology of print. One place where people spoke of books was in the Cambridge meetinghouse, as candidates for membership testified about the work of grace. John Trumbull, a man of modest means, may have attended school in England before he went to sea to earn a living. As a sailor, he said, he had read *The Poor Man's Pathway* (he may have meant *The Plain Mans Path-*

way) at first for the purpose of practicing his literacy. But someone advised him to "read that book over"—meaning to take it seriously—and Trumbull may have done so, since he thought of it as a "serious book." He went on to read a "book of repentance" from which he learned of "some sins yet I lived in, so saw my misery." To read was to see: the act of reading was (as godly writers had insisted) akin to looking in a mirror. No wonder that some friends warned Trumbull that he "would go mad as other ministers with study," for books taught painful lessons. Returning once again to sea, he read a book that he remembered as "To Live Well and to Die Well, which affected me." To read was to feel: the act of reading involved the affective self—the heart, the will.

The same verbs recur in the testimony of a farmer, Richard Eccles. In reporting that he knew Lewis Bayley's *The Practice of Piety,* Eccles remembered reading of the "torments of hell which affected my heart with my estate by Adam's fall." He associated other books with the process of spiritual conversion: he "got light by reading The Burning Bush," and "by Mr. Perkins's Exposition of Creed I saw my condition bad." A third member of the Cambridge church had read two classics of evangelical devotion and used them to arrive at an understanding of the difference "between a true believer and a temporary." He remembered also that reading had helped him through a spell of sickness; shipmates read him out of Psalms, "which gave me much joy."[48]

In another notebook of lay testimonies, this one kept by the minister of Wenham and Chelmsford, "Sister Geere" told the church that "she first met with a promise [God's promise of everlasting covenant] in private reading." The wife of James Fiske testified that "reading Dr. Preston" helped answer doubts about her own unworthiness. Sister Green's husband had "settled" his understanding of free will by reading in Preston's *Gods All Sufficiency,* though the published sermons of another Puritan had "tended more to his misery than his comfort; he could not see that God could be just and he receive mercy."[49] Early in the eighteenth century, a Connecticut man named Peter Pratt reported in a memoir of his quest for spiritual enlightenment of finding Thomas Shepard's *Sincere Convert* "so exceedingly searching, that he shewed me from time to time, my deceits of Heart, Mistakes, Presumptions, &c. and so broke me off from every hold, drave me from every resting place, and brought me many a time to my Wits end."[50] References to reading are surprisingly absent from the testimonies spoken in the Windsor, Connecticut, meetinghouse at the turn of the century. Yet Hannah Bancroft, a married woman, spoke of "reading at home in a book of the suffering of Christ" from which she remembered "in particular" the verse (Matthew 27:42) in which Jesus cried out he had been forsaken: "I thought then

what a wicked creature I was that I could not believe in Christ and wondered that I was out of hell and was so affected that I could read no
more."[51] In her case as in Peter Pratt's, reading brought her to the verge
of psychological distress. Something like this same experience occurred
to John Green of Cambridge when he opened Thomas Shepard's catechism; as he told the church, "The Lord began first to awaken me by
Mister Shepard's catechize concerning the dread and terror of Christ
Jesus coming to judgment." Green imagined he "was one of those there
spoke of" as sinners facing judgment. From reading the same catechism
Green also learned "of man's misery by nature how he was far from God
and God far from him."[52]

Books spoke to the heart and aroused powerful emotions. And books
were also channels for the Holy Spirit. No one in New England had
quite the sensation that came to a Welsh evangelical while reading *Pilgrim's Progress:*

> . . . I were in a field reading Mr. Bunyan's book, come and wel-
> come to Jesus. I cannot tell what [were] the words but God Almighty
> pleased to show me a great light as I thought that the heaven was
> opened, and the son of God shining but not very clear. . . .

Yet the colonists were not far removed from this mystical confounding
of inward vision and the printed word. Like Bunyan, who presented
Pilgrim's Progress as originating in a dream or vision, they sometimes wrote
as though their prose were like the direct speech of Christ. Thus Edward
Johnson has Christ speaking through his "Heralds" to the English people: " 'Oh yes! oh yes! oh yes! All you the people of Christ . . . you shall
be shipped for his service, in the Westerne World, and more especially
for planting the united Collonies of new England. . . .' "[53]

More common was to suppose that true reading involved meditation
or devotion. Certain books—we will shortly describe several of them—
were perceived as guides or rulebooks to consult at key moments in the
practice of religion—the eve of a communion service, or when seeking
signs of grace. A pious woman (her father was a minister, as was her
husband) studied two books carefully before she felt sufficiently assured
of faith to partake of the sacrament. A woman who imagined she had
"Sinned against the Holy Ghost" was advised to read Scudder's *Christians
Daily Walke,* from which she gained "comfort." The Boston merchant
Robert Keayne owned a "little written book . . . which is a treatise on
the sacrament of the Lord's Supper." In willing it to his son "as my
special gift to him," Keayne described it as "a little thin pocket book
bound in leather, all written with my own hand, which I esteem more
precious than gold, and which I have read over I think 100 and 100

times . . . I desire him and hope that he will never part with it as long as he lives." Embedded in this naïve statement were all the key assumptions of the vernacular tradition: a mode of reading that involved *rereading* certain texts—and not once or twice, but "100 and 100 times"; an aura of the book as supremely "precious" because it contained the gift of life; the high significance of literacy because it granted access to this gift; the kinship between reading, devotion, and the sacraments.[54]

Spoken sermons were as sacred as the printed page. "Faith comes by hearing," St. Paul had declared, and the persons who described in public their experience of faith referred more often to specific sermons, and in more detail, than to books. Yet hearing was like reading. The response was essentially the same—a rush of feeling, a moment of sharp self-awareness, a new sense of obligation, and all because these people thought of sermons as equivalent to the very speech of God. The wife of Mr. Sill of Cambridge remembered having heard a sermon that made her think "God would destroy her." William Manning recalled six different sermons by as many different ministers. From one he learned "of seven marks of repentance"—this numbering occurs in almost every sermon as a means of making them more "practical"—and came to realize "why I could not find such signs." Another led him to "examine my soul," and a third, by John Cotton on Acts 3:8–9, enabled him to perceive the "goodness of God which had not only healed bodies but souls, which I have had thoughts of since." Alice Stedman learned specific lessons from the sermons she remembered, like one by Peter Bulkeley on God's covenant with Abraham. Seeking, like so many others, encouragement to believe God would "help" her, she found that "in [the] midst of" a sermon by John Cotton "the Lord had begun to humble and subdue and quicken and sanctify." As in the case of the Welsh mystic, a sermon had transformed her "spirit": "And so was much confirmed, and many times since the Lord hath spoken to me to help me."[55]

Once more it deserves emphasizing that spoken sermons were like books, and books like sermons, because people in New England perceived speech and writing as continuous and interchangeable. (Some took notes on sermons, and read them over afterward.)[56] So it happened in the very process of becoming literate: the texts that children listened to and memorized were texts they then began to read. To complete the circle, these same texts denied their own materiality. Their writers (or translators) passed them off as Truth, as the work not of man but of God. Preachers tried to capture the same aura for their sermons.

When Katherine Branch recited in her fits the contents of a primer, she unwittingly revealed the ease with which young people became literate, if only in the sense of knowing certain texts by heart. And even were she not an active reader, she knew what books contained; she commanded a surprising repertory of ideas and images. And yet, though granting this capacity in her and many others, we may also want to recognize the limits to the freedom she gained as a reader. In becoming literate she and her contemporaries learned to think of certain books as "godly" and to accept them as true. More, these people learned to read these books intensively—to regard them with awe, and to return to them repeatedly. Books were never divorced from contexts or mediators that gave them their meaning. What was true of books was true of literacy as well, for its uses were determined—"channeled" is perhaps a better word—by an interpretive community.

It is tempting to emphasize the restraints on the literacy of ordinary people, as though writers (most of whom were clergy) controlled the experience of reading. But this is to ignore the marketplace and the role of a quite different group of mediators, those who did the printing and the selling of most books. For them the world of print was competitive and pluralistic, and in making different kinds available, they may have altered the significance of literacy. But what were the books that circulated in New England, and how did printers manage in what seems a tightly ordered culture?

IV

READERS IN New England needed books. They were served by printers and booksellers who made the book trade in Boston the most active in the British colonies. As in every European country, the business world of printers and booksellers was regulated by the government, which helped make certain books available and attempted to exclude others. The flow of books to readers conformed in the main to the expectations of the magistrates and ministers. But it also was responsive to printers' instincts for the marketplace, and to the varied taste of readers. Not all books were "godly," and not all readers in New England turned their backs on books deemed of the Devil. Mercy Goodwin, the daughter of a Boston tradesman, was a literate thirteen-year-old in 1688 and a member of Cotton Mather's congregation. She and her siblings, all diagnosed as being possessed by the Devil, "would roar, and howl, and shriek" when someone read the Bible in their presence. Experimenting in detail with Mercy, Cotton Mather reported in his narrative of her case that "such books as it might have been profitable and edifying for her to read, and especially her catechisms, if she did but offer to read a line in them, she would be cast into hideous convulsions, and be tost about the house like a foot ball." But when Mather brought "a Quaker's book" to Mercy, "she could quietly read whole pages of it," and when "books of jests" were "shown her, she could read them well enough, and have cunning descants upon them." In thus acting out her preference for bad books, Mercy Goodwin dramatized the choices people had as readers, choices that the book trade in New England furthered.[57]

Books reached New England readers via a commercial book trade that started up as soon as settlement itself was under way. The first books arrived with the immigrants themselves, and especially with the hundred or so graduates of English universities. One of these collections, the personal books of the Reverend John Harvard, became the basis of the Harvard College library after Harvard's death in 1638. His substantial library—he willed 320 books to the college—was equaled or surpassed by other private libraries assembled by the immigrants, though ministers owned, on average, something like one hundred books each.[58] The men who had this many books—let us name them "active" buyers—kept on adding to their collections after settling in New England. At his death in 1643, William Brewster, the lay elder of Plymouth and former owner of a printing press in the Netherlands, owned books published overseas in Europe in every year but two since 1620. Brewster acquired his new books without the benefit of any local bookseller. Undoubtedly he depended on correspondents and stray travelers for information about what to order. The men who corresponded with John Winthrop, Jr., often sent him books or told him of specific titles he should ask for; more remarkably, by 1632 Winthrop was receiving the annual Frankfurt book fair catalogue (probably the English version), which he put to use in writing back to England for new titles. Such private buyers ensured that the flow of books from Europe never ceased. Meanwhile, other immigrants continued to import collections of a special breadth or quality. The Reverend Samuel Lee, a nonconformist minister who emigrated in 1684, brought with him most of the collection that was put up for sale after he died. Out of such collections Cotton Mather built up the private library of three thousand volumes that a visiting English bookseller hailed in 1686 as "the Glory of New-England, if not of all America."[59]

But to the general reader the Latin folios that went on sale in 1694— most of Lee's books were in Latin, and a third were printed in the large format known as "folio"—were of little interest. The same limitations of language and learnedness applied to a handful of town libraries. The merchant Robert Keayne willed money to the town of Boston for a market house that, as Keayne imagined it, would contain a "library" for "divines and scholars." Keayne gave not only money but "such of my divinity books and commentaries" that others would select as being "useful for such a library." Theophilus Eaton, the sometime governor of New Haven, donated books (many of them the Latin treatises he inherited from his brother) for a similar "library." The town of Concord owned a copy of Foxe's *Book of Martyrs* that it made available for borrowing. Yet none of these collections was maintained or much frequented; the New Haven books were scattered by the 1680s, and references to Keayne's collection also cease.[60]

A more effective means of getting books into the hands of ordinary people was the practice of giving them away. Thinking death was near, Richard Mather preached *A Farewel Exhortation* to his Dorchester congregation, and gave every family in the town a copy. Some years later his congregation paid the costs of publishing *The Summe of Seventy Sermons;* the size of the edition, an estimated six hundred copies, suggests that every contributor received a copy in return, with others being sold outside the town. Private patrons added to the flow of print. Samuel Sewall gave every member of his militia company in 1685 a copy of John Cotton's *Gods Promise to His Plantations.* John Cotton, Jr., the minister in Plymouth, urged Increase Mather to send him and a neighbor twenty copies of two books defending infant baptism and the halfway covenant to give away as means of quieting dissent. Several towns, including Chemsford and Dorchester, sponsored publication of a catechism in quantities sufficient for the town's population. When Chemsford needed catechisms in the 1660s, the church purchased one hundred copies of the Westminster version, selling them at cost to families.[61] The most persistent of the agencies that handed out free books was the government in Massachusetts and Connecticut. Routinely the two general courts used tax money to support the printing of collections of law codes, and saw to it that every town (as well as every deputy and magistrate) received copies. In New Haven such law books were handed out to every family. Early on, and in keeping with an old tradition, towns staged public readings of these books, a process known as "publishing." Thus in early 1649 "the whole Towne" of Springfield gathered to hear "all the printed lawes" read aloud to them. Thereafter, ignorance was no excuse, as a Springfield man discovered to his dismay. Many other books and broadsides reached the people this same way—the Freeman's Oath, the first item to be printed in New England; the proclamations calling for a day of fasting or thanksgiving; the *Platforme of Church Discipline* (1649), of which a copy went to every town; the annual election sermon; John Norton's diatribe against the Quakers, *The Heart of New-England Rent;* and in Plymouth Colony, a history of that jurisdiction, Nathaniel Morton's *New-Englands Memoriall.* Meanwhile a semipublic agency commissioned books for distribution to the native Indians.[62]

Still other, more informal practices kept books in circulation. Often someone in a will would specify who inherited a treasured book or two. The most elaborate of these bequests were made by learned men who owned substantial libraries. Recognizing theirs were books of most use to a future "scholar," they often assigned them to sons or nephews who were planning to become ministers. Edward Holyoke of Lynn, who died in 1660, left his son a collection that, as described in the will itself, was clearly meant to serve the interest of a learned preacher: "I give him that large new testament in folio, with wast papers between every leafe, allso Mr. Ainsworth on the 5 books of Moses [a famous and much cited commentary] and the psalmes, and my dixinary and Temellius bible in Latin. . . ." Yet people who owned no more than a few books went through the same process. Christopher Young, who died in 1647, willed Bibles to each of his daughters and a godly book to his son, "to be carefully preserved for them, & there use, to enjoy as a remembrance of my affection & welwishing towards them." To a friend, Young willed "my booke entitled the Deceitfulness of mans Heart . . . as a Testimony of my love towards him." Books had their place in the gift relationship alongside of cattle, tools, and other kinds of property.[63] They also played a role in the economy of borrowing. Early in the eighteenth century, a young boy in Boston borrowed frequently from men who seemed gladly to have granted him this privilege. A court case in Essex County throws another light upon this practice, for a man in 1664 testified to having borrowed a Bible from a neighbor in order that a child of his could learn to read.[64] If this practice was common—the evidence is lacking one way or the other—it explains why households without books (according to the probate inventories) were able nonetheless to introduce their children to the skill of reading.

But the main agency for putting books in circulation was a book trade run by men responsive to the marketplace. Early on, some Boston merchants ordered books along with other goods from England. Once a printing press was set up in Cambridge around 1640, one of these merchants arranged for it to print a local almanac. Thus rapidly did profit-making figure in the output of the Cambridge press. Yet the purpose of the press in these initial years was mainly to serve church and state. As in almost every European country, the magistrates and General Court perceived it as an instrument of orthodoxy. There was never any question of allowing Stephen Daye, the first printer, or Samuel Green, the man who followed him, to print freely what they wished or what anyone requested. Nor did the magistrates and ministers imagine for a moment that books which challenged orthodox opinion could be sold or circulated. Pursuing the same policy as the government in England (whether

Royalist or Puritan), the Massachusetts General Court commanded the destruction of Quaker books and condemned by name such texts as William Pyncheon's *The Meritorious Sufferings of Jesus Christ* when word reached them of its existence. To make sure that the Cambridge printers stayed in line—Green had now been joined by a London printer, Marmaduke Johnson, who began to publish on his own in 1665 after having worked for three years under Green on publications mainly for the Indians— the Massachusetts General Court in 1662 charged four ministers with the "power to allowe or prohibit printing." This too had English precedents. And like the English government, the magistrates resisted any transfer of the press to other towns. Printing finally came to Boston in 1674 when John Foster, a Harvard graduate, opened a printing office stocked with the press and type that Johnson, now deceased, had used. Shops that specialized in books (they also carried stationery) were unique to Boston, where several persons were in business as booksellers by the 1690s. Some booksellers also ran a printing office and did what we today describe as publishing—that is, issued books at their expense.[65]

The growth of publishing was slow until the 1650s, for local writers preferred to arrange for publication back in London. But after 1660 the pace of printing quickened. The key question for the profit-minded printers and booksellers was deciding what to publish locally and what to import from abroad. In making these decisions they kept in mind the needs of different clients. A "learned" clientele of ministers, Harvard students, and "gentlemen" bought books like Matthew Poole's four-volume *Annotations on the Bible* and treatises on divinity, history, the natural sciences, and medicine. Such books were ordered, a few at a time, from London.[66] Michael Perry, a Boston bookseller who died in 1700, had a shop inventory of some five thousand books comprising twelve hundred different titles. A small number of these books—the concordances and dictionaries, the apologetics for the congregational church order—were destined to be purchased by scholars or professionals. Books in Greek or Latin were surely aimed at the same clients. Duncan Campbell, who died in 1702, had in stock some twenty Hebrew, Greek, and Latin folios, another fifty-eight Latin folios, and 249 Latin and Greek books in two smaller sizes.[67]

A small group of patrons enabled Perry and Campbell to import and sell these learned folios and quartos. But Perry sold two other kinds of books to far larger groups of patrons. Schoolboys (and perhaps some schoolgirls) came to his shop—and, no doubt, to every other Boston store— to buy Latin "accidences," the basic textbook for those beginning the study of Latin. Parents came to buy the primers, catechisms, and hornbooks that their children used in learning how to read. Perry had more catechisms in his store—1,459 copies of the Westminster text that Chelmsford had preferred in 1665—than any other item. He stocked eighteen dozen "gilt" hornbooks and another fifty "plain," almost nine hundred primers, at least three hundred psalm books, and a hundred books on writing. Altogether, schoolbooks made up half his inventory. In outlying towns where no merchant specialized in books, schoolbooks must have been of even more importance in the local trade. A 1694 shop inventory of a Charlestown merchant's widow consisted mainly of ten primers, "a parcell of hornebooks & other Small books," thirteen catechisms and some almanacs. The same kinds of books were a quarter of the total stock of Thomas Short, the first printer in New London, who died in 1712.[68]

When Perry died in 1699, his attic contained 450 copies of a book by an English nonconformist minister, Henry Stubbs's *Conscience the Best Friend of Man*. The presence of this book alerts us to another audience for books than schoolchildren or learned patrons. This was the same audience for which Perry carried at least twenty-nine Bibles, more than a hundred copies of Thomas Doolittle's *A Call to Delaying Sinners, or The danger of delaying in matters concerning our Souls*, and scores of sermons by two Boston ministers, Samuel Willard and Cotton Mather. Here as in the case of Doolittle and Stubbs, Perry was printing them himself or in partnership with others. We must think of his decision to print a specific book as based on expectations of demand—demand that fell within distinctive patterns. Consider, for example, the books that merchants ordered from (or were sent by) London agents in the 1680s and early 1690s. John Usher and his Boston colleagues asked for eighty-four copies of *The Almost Christian Discovered*, by Matthew Mead; twenty-three of *Christ's Famous Titles*, by William Dyer; forty of *The Great Assize, or Day of Jubilee*, by Samuel Smith; forty-seven of *A Call to the Unconverted*, by Richard Baxter; sixty-two of *A Treatise on the Lord's Supper*, by Thomas Doolittle; forty-two of *War with the Devil or The Young Man's Conflict with the Powers of Darkness*, by Benjamin Keach; and twenty of Joseph Alleine's *An Alarm to Unconverted Sinners*. These may seem quite modest quantities. Yet what matters is that Boston merchants ordered and *reordered* the same books repeatedly. Five different invoices specify John Fox's *Of Time and the End of Time*, four request John Flavel's *Sacraments*, three contain orders for James Janeway's *A Token for Children*, Thomas Shepard's *Sound Believer*, and Baxter's *Call to the Unconverted*. Many others were ordered twice. No less telling is the presence of these very books or others by their authors in Michael Perry's inventory—Smith's *The Great Assize*, Baxter's *Call*, three more books by Flavel, and one by Keach.[69]

All these books were printed and reprinted many times in England,

and their success in the English book trade surely caught the eye of Boston merchants such as Usher. A few were best-sellers in the English trade, books that readers purchased in large quantities within a short while after publication. It seems likely that "one Impression" of Joseph Alleine's *Alarm* (first published in 1673) consisted of thirty thousand copies, and that total sales reached seventy thousand in the space of a few years.[70] Certain other books that never sold this well in one outburst had nonetheless the same significance. Such books were steady sellers in the sense of never passing out of print for many years—and "many" could mean centuries! This was the printing history of every book that Boston merchants reordered in the 1680s, and of others Perry carried in his inventory, like Edward Pearce's *The Great Concern* and Edmund Calamy's *The Godly Mans Ark*. Almost from the outset, printers in New England were alert to steady sellers and the demand for them. The men who ran the Cambridge press thus issued native editions of William Dyer's *Christs Famous Titles* and Thomas Wilcox's *A Choice Drop of Honey*, each of which had known at least a dozen English printings. They were also quick to recognize the appeal of an evangelical description of the plague and fire that struck London in 1665 and 1666, republishing in 1667 Thomas Vincent's *Gods Terrible Voice in the City of London*, and responding to strong sales by printing it again in 1668. (Copies of the eighth English printing were in Perry's inventory.)[71] All told, New England printers and booksellers put out local editions of perhaps a dozen of these English steady sellers before 1720. Michael Perry was responsible for one of these editions; hence his stock of Stubbs's *Conscience the Best Friend of Man*.

The making of these books involved a shifting coalition of ministers, printers, and booksellers in England and New England. Most were written by the ministry. But printers and booksellers played their part in making godly books available. They squeezed these godly books into formats small enough to carry (octavo, duodecimo) and less expensive to produce since they used less paper. Sometimes they took the initiative in securing manuscripts of books that became steady sellers; Thomas Shepard was surprised to find a London printer issuing *The Sound Believer* from notes someone had taken.[72] Books like these were irritatingly inaccurate in reproducing what a preacher really said. But printers did not seem to mind. Inventive in their strategies, by 1660 several London businessmen were busily producing chapbook versions, shorter still, and ever cheaper, of existing and much longer books, and hiring writers to prepare new titles. The pseudonymous Andrew Jones (he also used the pen name William Jones) may have been a minister, but his claim to fame rests on a series of chapbooks that were published in the 1650s and 1660s, their titles increasingly sensational: *The Plain Man's Plain path-*

way to Heaven (a rip-off of the famous book by Arthur Dent), *The Black Book of Conscience, Morbus Satanicus. The Devil's Disease, Death triumphant, The Dreadful Character of a Drunkard,* and *Doomsday: or, The Great Day of the Lord drawing nigh.*[73] Benjamin Keach, a Baptist minister, joined forces with the London book trade in producing works that Michael Perry and John Usher happily imported or chose to reprint. One of Keach's London publishers was Benjamin Harris, who migrated to New England in 1686 and used snatches of his work in the *New England Primer.* The inventiveness of printers extended to the format of the broadside. In all likelihood, a printer conceived the broadside of *Old Mr. Dod's Sayings,* with its pithy aphorisms of spiritual counsel; reprinted in New England in 1673, it was widely imitated in the English book trade.

Collaborating in this fashion, printers and the ministry were able to produce a string of books and broadsides that reached many readers in both England and New England. A tantalizing clue to this success is a throwaway remark by Increase Mather. Speaking to his Boston congregation in 1677, he referred to James Janeway's *A Token for Children* (yet to be reprinted in New England) as a book "which many of you have in your houses."[74] There is also direct evidence of reader preferences in wills and probate inventories. We know from the Cambridge testimonies that some of these men and women had read Lewis Bayley's *The Practice of Piety,* Richard Rogers's *Seven Treatises,* and Arthur Dent's *The Plain Mans Pathway to Heaven,* three steady sellers in the first half of the seventeenth century. Some probate inventories refer to these same books or others of their type by title. Robert Mussey of Ipswich, who died in 1642, owned "My best Bible," which he willed to his daughter; "Mr. Downham's works, and Mr. Dod's works, and Bayley's *The Practice of Piety,*" which he willed to a son. John Warren of Watertown willed a daughter "a book called *The Plain Man's Pathway to Heaven.*" William Casley, who died aboard a ketch in 1672, owned a Bible, "Mr. Smiths booke of ye great assiz.," Baxter's "Call to ye unconverted," and another entitled "ye voice of the rod." A wealthy resident of Ipswich who died in 1666 bequeathed to his wife "the Bible she uses, the book called 'The Soul's Preparation for Christ,' and Perkins' upon the Creed." A Newbury farmer owned "Dr. Gouge's book & Mr. Perking's," as well as a Bible and a book by "Mr. Dod." A woman who died in 1655 owned "one of Doctor Sebes [Sibbes] works." Michael Metcalfe of Dedham willed "Mr. Perkins second Book" and "Luther on the Gala[tians]" to one son, together with the second volume of Foxe's *Book of Martyrs;* to another son he willed the first volume of Foxe and the first volume of Perkins's works. At his death in 1672, Abraham Toppen of Newbury, a farmer, owned a Bible and "Raigner of originall sinn." Richard Webb of Boston, who died in 1659, left his son "one old great Bible, & Mr. Elton his works, one of Mr. Boultons works, one of Mr. Wheatleys," and "one smale bible." In 1706 a deacon in the church of Norwich owned two Bibles, a catechism and a psalm book, three sermons by the local ministry, and a nice assortment of steady sellers: *The Day of Doom,* Richard Rogers's *Seven Treatises,* and Thomas Hooker's *Poor Doubting Christian.*[75]

These references include a few, surprisingly, to learned books like Calvin's *Institutes.*[76] Except for books on science, all were written by well-known Puritans. Rarely do we hear of catechisms, perhaps because they cost so little or because they were expendable. Yet people did own psalm books and, overwhelmingly, the Bible. It was not uncommon to own the Bible in two formats, the size deemed "great" and worth at least five shillings in an inventory, and one in a smaller format.[77] Another book that turns up frequently is Foxe's *Book of Martyrs.* Thomas White recommended it to little children, and Samuel Sewall's sister was reading Foxe in 1671. A man who later was a minister remembered the time when

> he read over all the vollums of Foxes *Acts and Monuments,* which I much delighted in, and know much of espetially the last two vollums, which I read over diverse times, where, in my young years, I showed a tender heart, that could not forbare melting into tears, when I read of the cruelty showed against the Ma[r]ters and Blessed servants of Jesus Christ.

The farmer who willed "my great Bible" to his son John in 1656, and "my book of Masters [Martyrs]" to his son Abraham was one of many who designated a specific heir for one or both of these books. Foxe was part of Michael Metcalfe's library and was, as we have seen, the book that Concord proudly made available for borrowing.[78]

All these were godly books, the kind that people were supposed to read, and did. So they tell us in their own words, and so the probate inventories and records of the book trade indicate. This said, a paradox emerges: some inventories list no books, and in those that did the average holding was but three or four. One conclusion to draw from this data is that, in contrast to the active buyers who frequented Boston bookshops and ordered new books from the London trade, most men and women were content to own a Bible and but little else. Notwithstanding all the statements they encountered about reading as a means of grace, people limited their purchases and, no doubt, the time they gave to reading. Yet whether active or inactive in the marketplace, men and women in New England thought of certain books as ageless and returned repeatedly to texts such as the Bible. Books loomed large in popular religion not because these people owned so many of them, but because they symbolized a myth of freedom from the tyranny of priests. Equally important is the fact that steady sellers, with their story line of struggle against sin, seemed compelling to their readers. Steady sellers (and the Bible) were key vehicles of culture, transmitting to a general readership the essence of a cultural tradition; in their format, as in how they were appropriated, they both shaped and strengthened an interpretive community.[79]

Meanwhile, there were other books in circulation than the ones deemed "godly," and other messages to ponder. Five copies of the jestbook Mercy Goodwin had enjoyed were included in a shipment to a Boston merchant; a copy reached the printer Marmaduke Johnson, a gift from his brother. A street ballad of the day, its theme the pleasures of love, was copied by a Harvard student. Hundreds of such ballads figured in the London book trade, as did prose "romances," which were often issued by the very printer-publishers who put out the chapbook "penny godlies." Their product line included histories and "merriments" that told of cuckolds or astrology or repeated Chaucer's vulgar stories.[80] Humor, sex, romance—we may add to these another vein of proven popular appeal, the violence that pervaded narratives of witchcraft, war, death, and supernatural wonders. Elizabethans flocked to public executions, where violence was made visible. They also liked to read "sensational" descriptions of these and similar events.[81]

In general, London printers and booksellers worked to satisfy three broadly based and overlapping reading publics: the respectable or "middling" reader who bought godly books, the reader who preferred to be amused and therefore liked romances, and the "country" reader who, as described by contemporaries, snatched up tales of "strange" events and perilous adventures. Except for certain specialists, most printer-publishers refused to differentiate among these publics.[82] The publishers of chapbooks are a major case in point, since they also published ballads; refusing to discriminate, they issued almanacs and "merriments" alongside godly books. Printers were eclectic even though they often published the laments of moralists against their very own productions, the "unlawful bookes of ribaldrie, merry lyes and unprofitable stories . . . which doth derogate the glorie of God. . . ."[83]

This same versatility was practiced by a group of writers who, before the term came into use, were well versed in all the tricks of Grub Street. One of these men, Nathaniel Crouch, supplemented his work as a publisher by writing (or assembling) chapbooks for the London book trade after 1650. Crouch, who used the pseudonym Robert Burton, turned out godlies as readily as tales of supernatural wonders. John Hart, the man behind the pseudonym of Andrew Jones, specialized in godlies. A third, who also acted as a printer, was John Trundle, who shamelessly repackaged books that someone else had written long before. Indeed the ethics of the London book trade were far from strict in this regard. Printers and booksellers routinely disregarded rules that regulated who could issue certain books. The publisher John Dunton, who also briefly plied his trade in Boston, issued a counterfeit version of the second part of *Pilgrim's Progress* while creating pious books (supposedly written by his father) out of extracts from the work of other authors. The men who produced almanacs often plagiarized competitors. All told, hack writers and their printer-publishers poured out tens of thousands of cheap books each year.[84]

Always, printers and booksellers chafed at censorship, no matter what its source. In printing most of what they pleased, they manifested both an instinct for the market and an ideology of freedom that ran counter to the interests of the state and church. But perhaps their deepest challenge was to "truth." The ideology of truth that guided godly writers and that led them to deny their very role as mediators was of little relevance to printers as inventive as a Crouch or Dunton. Certainly it did not stop the publishing of prose romances that, in our sense of the word, were fiction. Hence the outcry of the moralists that printers often lied: taken as a whole, the marketplace for books was like the world turned upside down, a place where fiction passed as truth, and truth was mocked as fiction!

New England's was a provincial version of this book trade. At first the Cambridge press was different in being closely tied to the church and civil state. The rough-and-tumble world of London printers seemed very distant from the small brick building in Harvard Yard where Daye and Green ran their presses. But as a wider market emerged for their products, or perhaps because, by 1665, Green and Johnson were competing with each other, they became more ambitious. Thus they rapidly reprinted titles from the London book trade that had proven sales appeal, like Thomas Vincent's sermons on the London plague and fire and an account of the "late prodigious earthquake" on Mount Etna. Johnson, the more restless of the two, took a further step in this direction in 1668 by proposing to reprint *The Isle of Pines,* a "quasi-erotic forerunner of the Crusoe type of fiction." The suppression of this book and, the year before, a similar court order barring him from issuing *The Imitation of Christ* may have figured in Johnson's request—also denied—to move his press from Cambridge to Boston.[85] Some years later, the New England book trade was enlivened by a man who brought the latest trends in London publishing to Boston. Benjamin Harris came on the scene in

1686 as a voluntary exile from the London book trade, where he made himself synonymous with anti-Catholic propaganda. There he had assembled a strongly flavored primer full of histories of the martyrs; here, he issued a revised and shorter version as the *New England Primer*. Here too he issued the first newssheet. But first was also last, for the Massachusetts magistrates suppressed *Monthly Occurrences* for reasons that they did not specify. What may have threatened them (apart from a touch of erotica) was the paper's demonstration of conflicting points of view; though it played to local prejudice against the Catholic French (as Harris did in England in the campaign against James II), *Monthly Occurrences* was astonishingly modern in suggesting reasons for a military defeat different from official versions of the truth.[86]

If most printers were more cautious, the men who imported books willingly sold titles that fell outside the boundaries of the Protestant vernacular tradition. When Michael Perry died in 1700, his shop included modest quantities of two chivalric tales (now on their way to being children's stories), the *History of Fortunatus* and *The Seven Wise Champions of Christendom*. John Usher ordered romances and works of light fiction by the score, as well as jestbooks and some twenty books of modern English poetry. Someone must have sold an occasional "how to" book on magic and fortune-telling, since several colonists refer to them. Now and then a "dirty" book shows up on inventories and invoices, as do romances, plays, and poetry.[87] Some of this material also appears in one series of New England almanacs, those written by John Tully after 1687. In Tully's almanac for 1688 a closing "prognostication" evoked the pleasures of drinking ale: "January's Observations. / The best defence against the Cold, / Which our Fore-Fathers good did hold, / Was early a full Pot of Ale, / Neither too mild nor yet too stale." Under February, young men "do present their Loves / With Scarfs . . . / And to show manners not forgot all / Give them a lick under the Snot-gall." The "prognostication" for February concludes in kind: "The Nights are still cold and long, which may cause great Conjunction betwixt the Male and Female Planets of our sublunary orb, the effects whereof may be seen about nine months after, and portend great charges of Midwife, Nurse, and Naming the Bantling." In 1688 Tully inserted Anglican saints' days and secular holidays into his calendar, while referring in a brief chronology of important events to "Oliver [Cromwell] the tyrant."[88]

One way or another, the wrong kinds of books seeped into New England. A New Haven man punished for singing "filthy corrupting songs" was probably repeating verses he learned in "old England," where, as he protested, people "could sing and be merry." Early in the eighteenth century Cotton Mather warned female readers of

Books . . . seen and sold at Noon-day, among us; which I cannot be faithful unto God, and unto you, if I do not forewarn you against the Reading of them. There are Plays, and Songs, and Novels, and Romances, and foolish and filthy Jests, and Poetry prostituted unto Execrable Ribaldry.

Defender of the Protestant tradition, he lashed out against "that sham-scribler that goes under the letters of R.B."—he meant the London writer-printer Nathaniel Crouch—for books like Crouch's *Delights for the Ingenious,* which taught fortune-telling.[89] Those books were dangerous that made people laugh or let them escape into fantasy instead of meditating on the great task of salvation. Arthur Dent personified this danger in one of the characters of *The Plain Mans Pathway to Heaven,* a man who prefers the pleasures of this world to anxious striving after grace, and who urges the "remedie" of "many pleasant and merry bookes" on another of the characters who does pursue the way to grace. He has specific titles to recommend, the very titles John Bunyan remembered liking as a boy before he went through his conversion, and that English printers were producing at midcentury in inexpensive chapbook versions: "the Court of Venus, the Palace of pleasure, Bevis of Southhampton, Ellen of Rummin: The merrie jest of the Friar and the Boy," all of them recommended as "excellent and singular bookes against heart-qualmes: and to remoove such dumpishnesse, as I see you are now fallen into." From Dent to Mather and beyond, moralists condemned this ethics and the kinds of reading—romances, plays, and ballads—that seemed to embody it. What they also were protesting was the fictiveness of genres like the romance. From their point of view the writer and the book were channels for the Word.[90]

In effect, the marketplace made room for two quite different understandings of the book, the one that moralists preferred and another that printers and hack writers made their own, a frank embracing of inventiveness and competition. Yet this separation was but partial; as William Greenhill and John Davenport acknowledged in their prefaces to godly books, the marketplace imposed itself regardless. It did so even in New England, where at first the moralists were more in charge. How this happened brings us back to godly books and why they appealed to their readers.

With but few exceptions, the men who wrote the steady sellers were ordained ministers, most of them English nonconformists (that is, excluded from the Church of England after 1662). The emergence of ministers as successful authors originated in their success in the pulpit, for in mastering the plain-spoken sermon they learned how to write effectively. For the most part, they stayed clear of abstract doctrine. The main question they addressed, the focus of their exhortation, was the evangelical inquiry, Are you saved? What they offered was a *vade mecum*, or to quote again the title of Dent's steady seller, *The Plain Mans Pathway to Heaven*.

One literary technique was to dramatize this journey by personifying sin. In *The Progress of Sin*, Benjamin Keach described "Sin" as receiving a "Commission from the Devil" and boasting of his "Skill" at leading godly people into peril. Another technique was to linger on the pleasures of the life of sin, all in order to make more astounding the inversion that occurred when pleasure turned to endless suffering in the fiery pit of hell.[91] There were stretches in most of these texts when writers were "sensational" in evoking the dismal fate awaiting sinners, a fate summed up in the title of a tract by Bunyan that New England printers issued, *Sighs from Hell: Or, the Groans of a Damned Soul. A warning both to Old & Young Sinners, how to avoid the Torments of Hell, & to put them in a way to get to Heaven*. Like the melodramas that thrilled ordinary people in the nineteenth century, such texts drew readers out into a terrifying world before reassuring them that good triumphs over evil.

It was crucial to the success of the ministers that, together with their printer allies, they mated terror and the evangelical inquiry with genres that had proven sales appeal. In another chapter I describe the "wonder" as New England writers used it, and wonders (as so many critics noted at the time) attracted readers who liked any text entitled "Strange and wonderful." In yet another chapter I describe the execution sermon. A third genre unique to New England was the captivity narrative in which people told of peril among hostile Indians; its heyday came much later, but the promise of the genre was revealed by the sales of Mary Rowlandson's *The Soveraignty & Goodness of God* and John Williams' *Redeemed Captive*. Skillful in developing these genres, writers in England and New England also turned out poetry and ballads that competed in the marketplace with secular equivalents. One great success of this kind was Michael Wigglesworth's *The Day of Doom*. A minister and Harvard College graduate, Wigglesworth was thirty years old in 1661 when he composed a long poem in ballad meter describing Christ's descent in judgment on the world:

For at midnight brake forth a Light, which turn'd the night to day,
And speedily an hideous cry did all the world dismay.
Sinners awake, their hearts to ake, trembling their loynes surprizeth;
Amaz'd with fear, by what they hear, each one of them ariseth.

Though scarcely novel in its subject matter, the first printing (perhaps English) of eighteen hundred copies sold out within a year, and more quickly followed.[92]

Doomsday as a subject was "sensational." That is, the underlying tone was one of violence, and though God (or good) prevails, evildoing is described in rich detail. Often, martyr stories had these qualities; they lingered on the agonies of martyrs as hot pincers were applied to flesh or as the flames licked at the body. Stories of the Devil were similarly shocking in their tone and substance, as were those of extreme spiritual distress. It may not be surprising that the chapbooks written by John Hart ("Andrew Jones") rate high in their "attention to Satan" and in "threats of atheism" and God's judgment.[93] Chapbooks imply inexpensive printing, and inexpensive printing aimed at a mass market implies formula—presumably those elements of formula that seem of most appeal! The penny godlies make plainly evident the formula that I have referred to as evangelical. As in Jones's texts, they also depend on sensationalism. But the difference between what he wrote and what New England ministers published was one of degree, not of kind. *The Day of Doom* had company in passages in many published and unpublished sermons, texts that played on violence and that fascinated readers with their tales of evildoing.

Yet the more important point may be that these writers dramatized the lives of ordinary men and women. Long before the novel emerged as a genre that encompassed everyday (that is, not royal or chivalric) experience, evangelical writers were turning to biography and autobiography. Many of the steady sellers contained brief life-histories in which people spoke of their struggles against doubt and sin. The stories of this kind that Foxe included in the *Book of Martyrs* were background to the tales of pious children collected in a famous steady seller, *A Token for Children,* to which Cotton Mather added tales of children in New England. A common and consistently used metaphor was of life as "warfare," as an unremitting battle against temptation, as a struggle to keep oneself on the straight and narrow path that led to heaven. Ordinary people thus learned that, whatever their worldly circumstances, they were actors in the greatest drama of them all. In this light we grasp why Bunyan wrote his masterpiece and why dozens of lay men and women in New England spoke and wrote so fluently about spiritual experience.[94] Steady sellers—and remember, these were books presented to their readers as the truth—succeeded in the book trade because of their essential plot of sinners vitalized to overcome the Devil and gain saving grace.

Thus it was that ministers succeeded in creating reading matter for a general public. Using to the full the resources of the marketplace, godly writers turned out scores of books that, by every quantitative measure, far exceeded any other type in reaching ordinary people. A program of reform that insisted on people learning to read and know the Bible evolved into a major enterprise of publishing and writing for lay readers. Yet in another instance, an attempt to transform the traditional almanac, the marketplace proved stronger than the campaign for reform.

In its standard English form the almanac involved astrology. Typically these little books contained the "man of signs," a chart demonstrating the connections between the respective parts of the body and the twelve signs of the Zodiac. Often, though not always, the almanac included prophecies loosely based on astrological events. In its standard form the almanac also contained a monthly calendar with holy days in red ink ("red-letter days"). Displaying, thus, the ritual calendar of the Church of England, it added anniversaries of kings and queens and other notable events. Altogether, almanacs affirmed the dynastic and religious history of the English state and church. Depending on the author, and especially later in the century, the genre welcomed humor edged with social criticism. As Bernard Capp has noted, burlesque almanacs, like the famous series of *Poor Robins* that survived initial disrepute to become annual productions, reiterated the "tradition of crude misogynist humour found in ballads, jestbooks and other chapbooks." In times of crisis, almanacs admitted to their pages a subversive politics. Always, they were in demand as calendars. So useful were these books, and so omnipresent, that they cut across class lines: owned by rich and poor alike, they reached perhaps a wider audience than any other book except the Bible or the psalter. We know of ministers and magistrates who saved their copies, and as Cotton Mather somewhat ruefully admitted, "Such an anniversary composure comes into almost as many hands as the best of books."[95]

The Cambridge printer knew what he was doing when, almost immediately, he began to publish yearly almanacs for local readers. But what should a New England almanac contain? The almanac of 1646, the first local product to survive, was purified of red-letter days and references to Christmas, Valentine's Day, and English kings. Instead of using names for months, the almanac referred to them by numbers: "First Month" and the like. Samuel Danforth, the man who wrote some of these early books, explained why in 1646:

But we under the New Testament acknowledge no holy-dayes, except the first day of the week only: & as for all other, whether fixed or movable . . . we reject them wholy, as superstitious and Antichristian, which being built upon rotten foundations, are Idle Idoll dayes, and in the day of their visitation shall perish.

So too the "man of signs" was missing, as were "prognostications" based on the movements of the stars and planets. For lighter reading fare, Danforth inserted academic poetry on pastoral themes.[96]

This reshaping of the almanac was deliberate. Early in the century the Elizabethan theologian William Perkins had denounced the almanac because of its astrology, which, as he complained, implied that the power of the stars and planets was greater than the power of God's will. Citing Scripture, Perkins denied that the movements of the stars were signals of impending famine, war, or plague. He extended his critique to the man of signs, and concluded by pronouncing it "unlawfull to buy or use" prognostications. Perkins would have preferred an evangelical description of the world, a recognition of God's power to work "special providences" and a parallel perception of man's sinful state. What others in the same tradition wanted was an almanac that taught a different understanding of time: time as marking off the progress of the coming kingdom, time as signaling God's providential rule.[97]

This debate—for many of the makers of the almanacs defended their astrology—was background to the making of the first New England almanacs. Accepting Perkins on the errors of astrology, Danforth taught instead the doctrine of God's providence, as in his "Chronologicall Table Of some few memorable things, which happened since the first planting of Massachusetts." One reason he could modify the text was that he had no competition; his was the sole product in the marketplace. Another was his training as a learned man. He and his successors were recent Harvard graduates, some of whom stayed on as tutors at the college for a year or so. Not until the late 1670s did men without a Harvard education (or with another sense of audience) provide competition with a different product. The makers of the local almanac, most of them awaiting pulpits, displayed their academic training in mini-essays on Copernican astronomy and in a poetry that includes classical allusions. More than once, they explained the inadequacies of "judicial astrology," as someone did in verse in 1686:

> Observe, or not observe, yet me (pray) damn not
> Judicial Astrologer I am not:
> That Art falsly so call'd I loath, I hate
> Both Name and Thing I much abominate.

And, like Danforth, they displayed their piety in using numbers for the months and excluding the man of signs.[98]

Yet even in these years of Harvard authorship, piety and learning gave way to information more in keeping with the English formula. An early token of confusion was the shifting to a hybrid naming system for the months: "the first month named March" instead of merely numbers. Bits and pieces of astrology were reappearing by the 1660s; the almanac for 1674 warned of certain planetary conjunctions as bad omens, and the man of signs turned up in 1678, together with a poem explaining its significance. By the 1680s the Harvard-produced almanacs were explicating "a notable Conjunction of Saturn and Mars," an event that in 1690 was linked with "the Sweating Sickness in England. 1445." This same almanac alluded to "Astrologers" and their interpretation of eclipses as portending "Famine, great Sickness, Pestilent Diseases, and the Like." By this time, moreover, all numbering of the months had ceased, while calendars were sometimes making reference to English kings.[99]

What happened over time was mediation as writers blurred the boundaries pious critics had inscribed. The Harvard writers soon learned, it seems, that readers wanted a mixed product. It may be symptomatic that an owner of the almanac for 1648 inserted "Michelmass" into the calendar, and that a farmer in Connecticut whose diary has survived preferred names for months instead of numbers even though he was a member of the church.[100] Competition was another factor. The almanac of 1678 in which the man of signs appears represented the first competition for the Harvard product; it was also the third almanac to bear a Boston imprint, all others being issued from the Cambridge press. A poem included in the almanac for 1686 is direct evidence of how these writers sensed themselves responding to quite different expectations. It opens with a charming instruction, "Goe Little Book, and once a week shake hands / With thy Good Reader," before assuming a tone of apology:

> Forgive me yet, Good Reader, If that I
> The Names impos'd by old Idolatry
> On Months and Planets still reteyn; Because
> I'm forc't thereto by cruel Customs Laws.[101]

But how else mediate conflicting concepts of the almanac? A strategy that few would follow was to write exclusively for the Anglicans and royalists who ruled Massachusetts briefly in the 1680s. John Tully, the man who introduced a touch of bawdy humor to the almanacs he issued after 1686, pursued this approach until 1689, when royalists were swept from power. Thereafter he reversed his course. Like the poem apologizing for the names of months (and statements in the early eighteenth century apologizing for the man of signs), his actions suggest a responsiveness to market forces. A "learned" program of reform was unable to transform a genre with its own traditions.

Yet some were left dissatisfied. The vision of a godly almanac lived on, to influence a small number of the Harvard writers. The author of the almanac for 1666, Josiah Flynt, reverted to the practice of using numbers for the months and inserted a prophetic poem on 666 (see Revelation 13:18); indeed, it may have been the year, with its significance for chiliasts, that moved him to restore the stricter style. At another time of perceived crisis, John Sherman made his almanac more pietistic by including "A brief Essay to promote a religious improvement of this preceding Calendar"; the preceding year, he turned the text into a mini-sermon on "declension," lamenting the sins of New England and appealing to a providential God. In 1683 a youthful Cotton Mather aimed to turn "a sorry Almanack" into a "Noble" piece of writing. One gesture of reform was to replace the standard essay on astronomy with "A serious Reflection on Mans moral and Momentary life"; another was to list and date the contents of the Bible. Citing, as precedent, "the Parallel project of Protestant Primers," Mather announced his as a "Protestant" almanac: "Think it not strange!" Someone of his own persuasion, Samuel Sewall, undertook to censure a draft almanac by striking out the references to Christmas, Valentine's Day, Easter, and Michaelmas.[102]

These countercurrents in the making of New England almanacs illuminate the shifting contours of popular culture and popular religion. No question but that almanacs were cheap enough, and useful, so that people wanted them. No question, too, but that the ambition to make certain genres vehicles for piety had been realized once before, when two English Protestants, Thomas Sternhold and John Hopkins, aspiring to replace "all ungodly Songes and Ballades, which tende only to the norishing of vice, and corrupting of youth," used the ballad meter for a book of psalms that passed into general use in sixteenth-century England. Their achievement was not merely to be widely used, but to reshape popular tradition: the ritual of psalm-singing, like the folklore of the martyrs, passed from clerical reformers of the church into popular religion. But why then Cotton Mather's sense of strained relations with the marketplace, as in his plea that "it not be absurd to beseech the Readers of an Almanack to become Christian men"?[103] In emerging out from under the reformers and becoming more traditional, the New England almanac suggests the limits of reform, and the power of the marketplace.

V

NEVER QUITE at ease within the marketplace, reformers who aspired
to authority also faced a challenge on home ground. The very premises
on which they based their own identity as godly writers, that printed
books were secondary to the Word of God, and that faith enabled the
unlearned to understand the Bible, became potent weapons among radicals who argued that the English Bible was superior to the "inventions"
of the clergy. Quaker missionaries appealed to ordinary people to interpret Scripture for themselves. Invoking the familiar symbolism of the
Reformation, Quakers denounced the orthodox ministers for behaving
as "the Papists and Popish Clergy" did when they "abuse[d] the primitive
Protestants, the sincere sort and part of which, who, from true inward
Conviction of Truth, and zeal to Truth, did witness against the corrupt
Doctrines . . . of the Church of Rome." According to these radicals, the
authority of "learning" was antagonistic to the pure light of the Holy
Spirit, a light that everyone was able to possess.[104] "There's one thing
more that I believe," a Nantucket Quaker wrote in 1676, "is worst than
all the rest, / They vilify the Spirit of God, / and count School Learning
best, / If that a Boy hath larn'd his Trade, / and can the Spirit disgrace,
/ Then he is lifted up on high, / and needs must have a Place."[105] In
denying the authority of learning, Quakers reaffirmed the liberty of lay
prophesying—that is, prophesying in the sense of being able to expound
the meaning of the sacred text.

Anne Hutchinson saw herself as such a prophet, and her challenge to
the ministers, which occurred twenty years before the Quakers menaced
orthodoxy, was a sign of things to come. Called before a special meeting
of the magistrates and ministers in September 1637, she asserted her
right as a faithful Christian—and a woman—to interpret Scripture publicly. The ministers were quick to quote St. Paul's notorious injunction
"Let your women keep silence in the churches: for it is not permitted
unto them to speak" (1 Corinthians 14:34). But Mrs. Hutchinson retorted with the verses (Titus 2:3–5) in which Paul allowed "elder women"
to "instruct the younger." At a later point in her "examination," she
remembered an occasion when she bested one of the ministers in a con-
test over Scripture; "Upon his saying there was no such scripture, then
I fetched the Bible and shewed him this place 2 Cor. iii.6."[106]

Down through the years, Baptists and Quakers made this gesture many
times. Baptists achieved formal organization in Massachusetts in 1665,
when a handful of men organized a church of this persuasion in Boston.

Yet quite early, a scattering of individuals preferred that their children not be baptized, and Baptist books and letters were arriving from old England by the middle of the 1640s. Quaker books were also turning up soon after Quakerism emerged in the ferment of the English Civil War; in 1653, the Massachusetts government confiscated scores of books and pamphlets that three Quaker missionaries brought from overseas. Yet even without books the men and women who converted to these faiths commanded strong resources in their knowledge of the Bible and of a repertory of symbolic acts.

These resources came into play on two occasions in the 1660s when the ministers arranged public debates with the Baptists. In 1668 a group of ministers took on several of the men who had organized the Boston-Charlestown congregation. These Baptist laymen were "illiterate" in the sense of being unlearned; one farmed and made wagons for a living, another was a mariner, a third pursued the trade of potter. In claiming they were free to withdraw from the churches they had joined before turning Baptists, they based their case on Scripture and insisted that the ministers accept the same restriction. "Many answers are given, but no scripture given," Thomas Goold complained at one point. "If convincing arguments be laid it is that which answers." A gesture dramatized this principle: "Holding up the Bible in his hand he said: We have nothing to judge but this." Moreover, Goold was equal to the insulting challenge "Show but a shadow of a scripture for what you say." His response, to cite 2 Corinthians 6:17, "Wherefore come out from among them and touch no unclean thing and I will be your God," drew him into further debate when a minister insisted that this text could not be used to justify separation "from those among whom they did dwell." In the end Goold affirmed that the privilege of worshipping as he wished was consistent with "God's mind in his Gospel"—and if the ministers thought otherwise, and claimed support from Scripture, "we desire to see it." Even after Samuel Danforth piled verse on verse in an extended attack on separation, the Baptists rejected his reasoning on the grounds that his citations of King David presumed a "parallel" between the Old Testament and the New, an exegesis none of them accepted.[107]

When Goold confronted Zechariah Symmes, the minister in Charlestown, he drew on these same principles. In 1663 Goold was summoned to a neighbor's house where Symmes was waiting to rebuke him for refusing to have his newborn child receive the sacrament of baptism. As Goold recalled the moment, "Mr. Sims took a writing out of his pocket wherein he had drawn up many arguments for infant baptism, and told the church that I must answer those arguments, which I suppose he had drawn from some author; and told me I must keep to those arguments."

But Goold would not defer to this display of learning. Instead he proposed that the written word of man must yield to Scripture: "My answer was, I thought the church had met together to answer my scruples, and to satisfy my conscience by a rule of God, and not for me to answer his writing." A defensive Symmes explained that "he had drawn it up for the help of his memory." More tellingly, he put the "writing" back into his pocket! Meanwhile Goold was opening his Bible to the texts he wished to cite.[108]

Quakers were still more insistent in denying the significance of learning. They mocked the clergy for depending on "old mouldy" books instead of Scripture, and, like Goold, sought ways of dramatizing their commitment to the Word. A jeering crowd in Newbury fell silent when Samuel Bownas, a Quaker missionary, showed them a Bible. Once he started to cite specific verses, Bownas noticed with approval that "many Bibles then appeared" among the people as they followed what he said. The scene may well be fictive, for as Bownas painted it he meant to imply that the people, once enlightened, preferred Quaker principles. Fictive or real, these actions dramatized a set of values that were powerfully available to everyone, whether orthodox or radical.[109]

In the aftermath of the Antinomian controversy, the ministers moved to suspend the practice of lay prophecy. (Thirty years later, the men who founded the Baptist church were still angry at the injustice of this action and wrote into the bylaws of their church the right of every layman to "prophesie one by one that all may learn and be comforted.")[110] They acted to give themselves more privileges in church government and a higher, more formal definition of their office.[111] Then as well as later, they insisted they were faithful preachers of the Word. Employing this defense in biographies of one another, like Increase Mather's *The Life and Death of . . . Richard Mather,* they also relied on a repertory of ritual gestures to enhance their image. A woodcut portrait in some versions of *The Life and Death of . . . Richard Mather* showed him holding out a Bible in one hand. The gesture signified his status as a preacher of the Word, a Protestant who spoke the Word in the vernacular, the Word set free from popish tyranny. Appropriating in this manner the root symbolism of the Reformation, the ministers succeeded in persuading most of the colonists that they were martyrs of a sort, and also prophets. Above all, they announced themselves as bound by what was in the Word.

Yet they went beyond the symbolism of the culture of the Word to argue the significance of learnedness. What made learnedness important was the contradictions in the Bible. Learning served to clarify the Word, to make its meaning more apparent. Not only did the prophets and apostles sometimes contradict each other, they often used rhetorical devices that required careful explication. And in certain sections, as in the cryptic prophecies of Revelation, the Bible contained hidden meanings and relationships that took training to unravel. But the crucial benefit of learnedness was that it enabled those with knowledge "to read these sacred Writings in the Languages in which Holy Men wrote them as inspired by the Holy Ghost." However good it was to have the Bible in translation, to read it in Hebrew and Greek was still better. Craving to read God's Word in the Hebrew, William Bradford struggled late in life to master what he took to be the very language in which God had spoken. What he sought to achieve, those in training to be ministers learned at Harvard. There they also received practice in the "arts" of logic and rhetoric, the first a means of reconciling contradictions in the Word, the second a technique for deciphering "tropes and figures." These arts became useful in defending the validity of doctrines "by just consequence and deduction" instead of using the more limited defense of resting them on God's "express Command." As John Cotton pointed out, this skill was needed in the case of doctrines such as infant baptism, which seemed to lack explicit sanction in the Word.[112]

Each year the "arts" of learning were publicly displayed at the Harvard commencement. It must have been impressive, though confusing to the uninitiated, to listen to the degree candidates speak in Latin for and against certain "theses" and "questiones" in a formal debate. The correct style of debate involved syllogisms, or, as it was said, to reason "syllogistically." Commencement debates dramatized the privileged situation of the clergy, for only someone trained in oral discourse could follow what was happening.[113] Privilege was a matter of techniques, but also of a special language. Debating one another in the synod of 1637, the ministers used concepts drawn from Greek philosophy and scholasticism—"the order of nature," "habit," "essence," "proximate cause"— and cited books by Reformed theologians of the sixteenth century. Attempting to legitimate themselves against the critique of the Antinomians, the clergy welcomed laymen to the final session. Yet Thomas Weld's description of this event—"a plaine Syllogisticall dispute, (*ad vulgus* as much as might be)"—suggests the persisting tension between academic discourse and the plain style of the pulpit, or lay people's discourse.[114]

Much of the time, this tension worked in favor of the ministers. Far more fluent in describing God abstractly,[115] they were able to pursue the nuances of doctrine into byways that left laymen feeling confused. John Winthrop sat in on most of the discussions of 1637, but even with the benefit of university training he found it hard to follow what the ministers were saying. When Winthrop tried his own hand at theological discourse, Thomas Shepard, a much younger man though better trained, warned him that his argument contained misleading statements. Midway through the controversy, he wrote in his journal that "except men of good understanding, and such as knew the bottom of the tenets of those of the other party, few could see where the difference was" between the so-called "legal" preachers and the Antinomians.[116]

Unique in their understanding of theology, the ministers thought of knowledge differently than did the untrained laity. For the clergy, knowledge was a system, a set of principles that cohered to form an interlocking whole. This system was complete in the sense of comprehending God and his creation from beginning to end. It was truth because of how the pieces fit together, but also, in the thinking of these men, because the "arts" themselves were constituted in the image of divine perfection. Their completeness mirrored the completeness of the Deity. True knowledge was a "universal harmony," a set of lines that converged on a center and became a single "Point." The learned men who knew their way around this system, and who showed off parts of it in public at commencements, saw themselves as endowed with greater wisdom than what unlearned people gained from reading Scripture. It was to them, the learned, therefore, that responsibility fell for keeping truth unblemished; they were the defenders of sound doctrine.[117]

In articulating this role for themselves, New England ministers followed the path of tradition in writing catechisms that imposed orthodoxy on the people. Unlike various other literary forms, catechisms were a clerical monopoly. In all, some thirteen of the ministers were moved to write these works, and always for the reason Richard Mather stated in *A Farewel Exhortation:* ordinary people needed guidance, and should master a catechism *before* trying to interpret Scripture. "Acquaint your selves with principles of Catechism," he advised his congregation, "and be well grounded therein; for commonly they that fall to errour, are defective in the knowledge of Catechistical points." In urging parents to "teach your children the word of God, firstly the principles of Catechism, and afterwards higher points," he sketched a sequencing of religious knowledge in which the inculcation of lower, basic truths preceded the acquisition of higher knowledge.[118] All of his colleagues shared the same goal of limiting freedom of interpretation. Catechisms drove home the point that "extraordinarie Revellations are now ceased," a point that needed reinforcing after 1640 as the English Civil War unleashed a wave of prophesying.[119]

That ferment disenchanted many in old England, who came to feel, with John Dryden, that "The book thus put in every vulgar hand, / Which each presumed he best could understand, / The common rule was made the common prey / And at the mercy of the rabble lay." But on the whole the clergy in New England were spared such disenchantment, and found the great majority of the populace willing to grant them precedence in learning. One sign of support was practical (and costly), the donations made by towns to support Harvard College. On their own, moreover, various laymen spoke out on behalf of learnedness. Winthrop (who attended Cambridge) denounced Samuel Gorton and his followers as "illiterate men, the ablest of them could not write true English . . . yet they would take upon them the interpretation of the most difficult places of scripture, and wrest them any way to serve their own turns." Edward Johnson, a lay writer who was not one of the learned, mocked Anne Hutchinson's efforts to "dispute" in the manner of the ministers and ridiculed a Gortonist—"as shallow a pated Scholler as my selfe, far from understanding Latine, much less any other Language the Scriptures were writ in"—for having tried to retranslate a phrase in the Bible. When, late in the century, a man declined to question a minister accused of committing witchcraft, feeling, as he told a court, "it did not belong to such as I was to discourse him he being a Learned man," he articulated a sense of inferiority that many laymen must have shared.[120] This deference to learnedness was supported by the civil courts. Any layman who dared challenge what a preacher said was apt to find himself in court accused of disrespect. This happened, notably, to women like Anne Hutchinson. But men were also censured.[121]

When the time came to preach Sunday sermons, the glories of commencement—the flourishes of Latin, the ritual of debate, the reunions with one's classmates, the discourse that turned esoteric—had little bearing on the task at hand. Face to face each week with farmers and their families, the clergy set aside the style that suited Harvard Yard and fell back on the vernacular tradition, only rarely introducing learned references.[122] In the main, most had no other audience than the men and women on whom they depended for their pay. The few ministers who published knew the same constraints. Who would buy their books if they diverged into "Scholasticall Argumentations," or if, as Increase Mather realized in writing about comets, they reached out to learned men in Europe? Hence the prefatory statements that acknowledge the presence and priority of a "Popular Auditory," and that advise it were better "to insist on Truths in which the Generality of Reformers are agreed rather than to amuse [people] with notions above the reach of most of them." At almost every turn the realities of parish life combined with the culture of the Word to limit the range of the clergy.

No one was more restless with these constraints than Increase Mather. Twice he lived for periods of time in England, and he longed (alas, in vain) for a third visit. He gained modest consolation from a Boston version of a club of learned men, and he tried to keep up in his reading with the latest European thinking. When he wrote a treatise on two recent comets, he aspired to participate in "learned" discourse over "controversial" matters in astronomy. Yet his book was published locally, and he therefore had to accept as his "chief design" to "inform and edifie the ordinary sort of Readers."[123]

His frustration teaches an important lesson. Like the student authors of the Harvard almanacs, Mather had to reckon with a marketplace—his local congregation, the local press—that diluted the significance of learnedness. Nor did learnedness eclipse the principle of *sola scriptura* that the martyrs had upheld. In the early 1660s, as debate broke out among the ministers about the scope of baptism, the aged John Davenport invoked that principle against his colleagues, appealing to his readers to "receive nothing said by me, further then they shall finde it consonant to the Word of God in the Scripture, specially of the New Testament."[124] Always held in check by the culture of the Word, and of little everyday significance in this decentralized society, learnedness was only equivocally beneficial to the clergy.

VI

ONE DAY in 1650 a copy of the newly printed *Platforme of Church Discipline* arrived in the town of Wenham. The product of a synod of the ministers, the Cambridge Platform described the details of a congregational church system—the rules for choosing ministers and new members, the "power of the keys," the relationship between church and state—as now understood after some years of experience. The Massachusetts General Court, wary of so clerical a statement, arranged for Samuel Green to print five hundred copies and ordered some dispersed to all the congregations to give them the chance to respond. Thus it happened that the men of Wenham church voted "after some agitation and debate touching some expressions" to "approve" the Platform, but not "in every particular circumstance in every chapter and section." What disturbed these men was five clauses in the Platform pertaining to the rules for calling synods. These they referred to as "dark," and as principles they did not wish to "defend" or "assent" to. Notwithstanding the proof texts appended to the Platform, these church members proposed that "it may please God to cause to break forth unto us and ours or other churches hereafter" more wisdom on these matters, "conceiving," as they put it, "the fullness of the gentile light yet scarcely come in." In effect, the issue was authority: according to the hermeneutics of these people, it was premature to "impose in a way of authority . . . such drafts or determinations from which in either opinion or practice we may not in the least jot or tittle digress or alter and better our judgments by light from the holy scripture." Wenham congregation reserved the right to interpret for themselves: "as desiring and expecting the liberty of interpreting the same in our own sense and conceiving provided we may enjoy our own interpretations, the same may so pass."[125]

Here was literacy in action, all the parts of a communications circuit that ran from writers and the printing press to publishers and readers. As in the myth that John Foxe endorsed, of printing as a means of spreading truth, so in the frontier town of Wenham the Cambridge Platform was perceived as emblem of a deeper truth, but only insofar as it coincided with the Word. What these farmers guarded for themselves was the right of judgment. More exactly, they turned their familiarity with Scripture—their own capabilities as readers—into criticism of the ministers. Even in accepting most of what the clergy described as the nature of the church, these men acted out the power that was theirs because they were literate.

This empowerment was also theirs because they knew their way around symbolic language. When they talked about their cows, they drew on a stock of precisely descriptive words. But when they talked about things spiritual, they shifted to a language made up out of words like "wilderness" and "pilgrim." People learned this other language from printed books and sermons prepared by the ministers. But they also learned it from sources that were free of clerical authority and mediation. The archetypal source was Scripture. Its figures, tropes, and stories were echoed and reechoed in almost every kind of text that people came in contact with, from almanacs and law codes to elegies and steady sellers. It penetrated every milieu; it left no social group untouched. It even overrode the gap that may have separated readers from nonreaders, because it lent itself to visual presentation.

This language shaped the worldview of lay people in New England. Most men and women thought of "popery" as wrong because it falsified the Word. A young man from Haverhill translated this view into action while a captive of the French in 1708. When a priest approached him and described the Catholic service, Joseph Bartlett demanded that he "hold to no doctrine but what he could prove by the bible: what proof (said I) have you of such a place as Purgatory, or a middle place for departing souls?" According to young Bartlett's narrative, the two went on to debate certain verses in the Bible.[126] It took no special training to perceive the Catholic church this way. Nor did people have to do much reading to absorb three other story frameworks they invoked repeatedly.

One of these, the subject of my second chapter, was the providence of God as manifested in "remarkable" events. Another was the story framework of judgment and redemption: we are born in sin and perish, so this story went, unless we engage in repentance and petition Christ for mercy. A third story line extended the motifs of judgment and redemption to the very "land" itself, as though the whole community were bound in a covenant with God that obliged them to repent as a people. It was also common for the colonists to view the world in terms of "plots," with the Devil as the grand conspirator against a holy people.[127]

People put these story lines to work in countless situations. Some lay men and women (more than we might casually suppose) drew on them in writing prose and poetry. Some, dissenting from the orthodox establishment, used them to justify rejection of the ministers. Not many went this way consistently; but that lay people spoke out on their own was one important consequence of knowing how to use a language and a set of story lines. For many, the meaning of a situation could be expressed in a word or two—a word that may be meaningless to us, like "Spira," but that resonated with significance in the context of this culture.

Once again, it must be said that people did not need to read to know their way around this language. Lay men and women learned far more from spoken than from written sermons, and got most of what they had to know from custom and face-to-face conversation. Yet the ways they viewed the world were sustained by print culture, and in turning to the books that circulated widely we encounter structures of belief, or as I prefer to say, the stories that lay people knew and used to understand the world. Always there was freedom of interpretation, though a freedom held in check by catechisms and the "learned" presence of the ministers. The marketplace was crucial in providing people with alternatives. Granting printers an important role, what is striking is how easily the ministers mediated between high and low—how, in keeping both with market forces and the plainness of the Protestant tradition, they moved in and out of formulas and genres that were clearly popular. How this happened in detail will be described as we take up the tradition of the "wonder."

CHAPTER 2

A WORLD
OF WONDERS

THE PEOPLE of seventeenth-century New England lived in an enchanted universe. Theirs was a world of wonders. Ghosts came to people in the night, and trumpets blared, though no one saw the trumpeters. Nor could people see the lines of force that made a "long staff dance up and down in the chimney" of William Morse's house in Newbury. In this enchanted world, the sky on a "clear day" could fill with "many companies of armed men in the air, clothed in light-colored garments, and the commander in sad [somber]." The townsfolk of New Haven saw a phantom ship sail regally into the harbor. An old man in Lynn espied

> a strange black cloud in which after some space he saw a man in arms complete standing with his legs straddling and having a pike in his hands which he held across his breast. . . . After a while the man vanished in whose room appeared a spacious ship seeming under sail though she kept the same station.

Voices spoke from heaven and children from their cradles.[1]

All of these events were "wonders" to the colonists, events betokening the presence of the supernatural. Some wonders were like miracles in being demonstrations of God's power to suspend or interrupt the laws of nature. The providence of God was "wonder-working" in making manifest the reach of his sovereignty; such acts of "special providence" represented God's clearer and more explicit than usual intervention into the affairs of man. But he was not alone in having supernatural power. The events that Cotton Mather described in *Wonders of the Invisible World* were the handiwork of Satan and his minions. A wonder was also any event people perceived as disrupting the normal order of things—a deformity of nature such as a "monster" birth, a storm or devastating fire. Always, wonders evidenced the will of God.[2]

Many of the colonists experienced such wonders. Many also read about or were told stories of them. There was nothing odd about this practice. Everywhere in Europe people were observing the same kinds of portents and telling the same kinds of stories. Everywhere these stories drew upon a lore of wonders rooted in the Bible and antiquity. Chaucer used this lore in *The Canterbury Tales,* as did the fourteenth-century author of *The Golden Legend,* a collection of saints' lives. Whenever the colonists spoke or wrote of wonders, they relied on an old tradition; theirs was a borrowed language.

The transmitters of this language were the London printers and booksellers, who churned out tales of wonders in abundance. Portents and prodigies were the stuff of scores of English printed broadsides. "Strange news from Brotherton," announced a broadside ballad of 1648 that told of wheat that rained down from the sky. "A wonder of wonders" of 1663 concerned an invisible drummer boy who banged his drum about the streets of Tidworth. In "Strange and true news from Westmoreland," a tale of murder ended with the Devil pointing out the guilty person. Newssheets, which began appearing with some regularity in the 1620s, carried tales of other marvels. Pamphlets contained reports of children speaking preternaturally and offered *Strange and wonderful News . . . of certain dreadfull Apparitions.* The yearly almanacs weighed in with their accounts of mystic forces emanating from the stars and planets.[3]

The same events occur repeatedly. Tales of witchcraft and the Devil, of comets, hailstorms, monster births, and apparitions—these were some of the most commonplace. "Murder will out," as supernatural forces intervened to indicate the guilty. The earth could open up and swallow persons who told lies. "Many are the wonders which have lately happened," declared the man who compiled *A Miracle, of Miracles,*

> as of sodaine and strange death upon perjured persons, strange sights in the Ayre, strange births on the Earth, Earthquakes, Commets, and fierie Impressions, with the execution of God himselfe from his holy fire in heaven, on the wretched man and his wife, at Holnhurst. . . .

A single ballad spoke of blazing stars, monstrous births, a rainstorm of blood, lightning, rainbows, and the sound of great guns. Others told of dreams and prophecies that bore upon the future of kings and countries. Almanacs and other astrological compendia reported similar events: comets, eclipses, joined fetuses, infants speaking.[4]

All of these were inexpensive forms of print. Hawked by peddlers and hung up in stalls for everyone to see and gape at, they reached people who were barely literate as well as readers of more means and schooling. The stories they contained turn up as well in books that ran to several hundred pages. Big books, perhaps in the grand format of the folio, were costly and had authors who announced themselves as of the learned. But these differences in form and audience did not extend to the contents. The lore of portents and prodigies appeared in such massive books as Thomas Beard's *The Theatre of Gods Judgements* as in the cheapest pamphlet.

Thomas Beard was a graduate of Cambridge. Schoolteacher and ordained minister, late in the reign of Queen Elizabeth he published *The Theatre of Gods Judgements* (1597). Three more editions followed, the last of these in 1648. That same year Samuel Clarke, like Beard a Cambridge graduate and a minister turned nonconformist after 1662, brought out *A Mirrour or Looking Glasse both for Saints, and Sinners, Held forth in about two thousand Examples: Wherein is presented, as Gods Wonderful Mercies to the one, so his severe Judgments against the other*. Clarke's *Examples* (to call it by the title the colonists would use) went through five editions, the final one appearing in 1671. The sequel to his book was William Turner's folio *Compleat History of the Most Remarkable Providences, both of Judgement and Mercy, which have hapned in this Present Age* (1697). To this series should be added another Elizabethan work, Stephen Batman's *The Doome warning all men to Judgmente: Wherein are contayned for the most parte all the straunge Prodigies hapned in the Worlde* (1581).

As in the ballads and the chapbooks, so in these folios nature offered up innumerable signs of supernatural intervention:

> Now according to the variety and diversity of mens offences, the Lord in his most just and admirable judgement, useth diversity of punishments: . . . sometimes correcting them . . . by stormes and tempests, both by sea and land; other times by lightning, haile, and deluge of waters . . . and not seldome by remedilesse and sudden fires, heaven and earth, and all the elements being armed with an invincible force, to take vengeance upon such as are traytors and rebels against God.

Earthquakes, multiple suns, strange lights in the sky, rainbows, sudden deaths, monstrous births—these were other frequent signs or signals.[5]

Like the ballad writers, Beard and Batman reported events that often ran to violence: rats that ate a man, a crow whose dung struck someone dead, the agonies of martyrs. In one or another of these books, we learn of dreams and prophecies, of crimes detected by some form of sympathetic magic, of thieves who rot away, of armed men in the sky.[6] Much too was made of Satan. He offered compacts to young men in need of money, though also serving as God's agent for inflicting vengeance. Many tales revolved around the curse "The Devil take you," and its surprising consequences:

> Not long since a Cavalier in Salisbury in the middest of his health-drinking and carrousing in a Tavern, drank a health to the Devil, saying, That if the devil would not come, and pledge him, he would not believe that there was either God or devil: whereupon his companions strucken with horror, hastened out of the room, and presently after hearing a hideous noise, and smelling a stinking savour, the Vintner ran up into the Chamber: and coming in, he missed his guest, and found the window broken, the Iron barre in it bowed, and all bloody, but the man was never heard of afterwards.

The Devil wore a range of guises. Black bears, a favorite of the ballad writers, turn up again in stories told by Beard and Batman, as do black dogs.[7]

In telling of these wonders, the men who organized the great collections borrowed from the broadside and the chapbook; thus, a ballad tale of someone swallowed up into the ground appeared in Clarke's *Examples* and again in Turner's *Compleat History*.[8] This flow of stories meant that "learned" men accorded credibility to wonders as readily as any of the ballad writers. The one format was employed by the learned, the other by commercial printers and their literary hacks. But each participated in a common culture, a lore that linked small books and great, the reader of the ballad and the reader of the folio.

This was a lore that other Europeans were collecting and reporting in the sixteenth and seventeenth centuries. Sixteenth-century German broadsides told of comets, multiple suns, monster births, and armies in the air. Introducing an encyclopedia of portents, a Lutheran writer "attempted to define the spectrum of such 'wonder works,' " listing "signs, miracles, visions, prophecies, dreams, oracles, predictions, prodigies, divinations, omens, wonders, portents, presages, presentiments, monsters, impressions, marvels, spells, charms and incantations." In France the *livrets bleues,* an inexpensive form of book in wide circulation by the end of the seventeenth century, included accounts of apparitions, miracles, witchcraft, and possession. French broadsides reported the same wonders as their German neighbors.[9] A Huguenot writer, Simon Goulart, issued a collection of such tales, *Histories admirables et memorables de nostre temps,* of which there was an English translation in 1607. Another Huguenot, the poet Guillaume Du Bartas, incorporated wonder lore into his story-poem *La Sepmaine* (1578). On the Continent, as in the England of Clarke and Beard, writers and readers who were "learned" shared this lore with writers and readers who were not. Protestants and Catholics were alike in their receptiveness, each side, in places like the Netherlands, discerning victory in the flow of portents.[10]

Many of these continental stories were retold in England. Certain ballads were translated or adapted from a foreign source. Thomas Beard described *The Theatre of Gods Judgements* as "translated from the French." Batman's *Doome* was a translation of Conrad Lycosthenes's *De prodigiis liber* (1552), itself a new edition of a second-century text, Julius Obsequens's *Prodigiorum liber*. Whatever the specific source, the English writers culled most of their materials from printed books that subsumed the sweep of western culture.[11] The classical and early Christian sources included Vergil, Pliny, Plutarch, Seneca, Cicero, Josephus (a favorite), Gildas, Eusebius, and Bede. The Middle Ages yielded chronicles and compilations of exempla. The sixteenth and seventeenth centuries supplied a fresh group of chronicles and encyclopedias: the *Magdeburg Centuries,* the *Chronicles* of Hollingshead, and collections (some more critical than others) by such writers as Polydore Vergil, Sleiden, Camden, and Heylin. No work was more important to the English than John Foxe's *Acts and Monuments,* itself a résumé of narratives and chronicles extending back to Eusebius. A final source was that great wonder book the Bible. Its narratives of visions, voices, witches, and strange deaths lent credence to such stories of a later date.[12]

All of this borrowing enriched the lore of wonders with the debris of much older systems of ideas. To be sure, Beard, Batman, and their successors made modest efforts to be critical. As Protestants they followed Foxe's lead in dropping from their histories the visions, cures, and other miracles found in legends of the saints. As Christians, they rejected divination and believed that God had ceased to issue revelations. But otherwise the English writers were willing to retell the stories that descended to them from the Middle Ages and antiquity. No one questioned the accuracy of Pliny's *Natural History* and its kin, to which, in fact, these men conceded an unusual authority. The parting of the ways between the "ancients" and the "moderns" was yet to occur. Ancient and modern, Christian and non-Christian, Catholic and Protestant, high and low— these great lines of cleavage had but little impact on the lore of wonders. In conceding so much to their sources, whether classical or of the early Church or even of the Middle Ages, Beard and Clarke admitted to their pages a strange mixture of ideas and themes. This was a mixture that requires closer scrutiny, for the stories in these books were charged with several meanings.

Much of this great mass of materials was compounded out of four main systems of ideas—apocalypticism, astrology, natural history, and the meteorology of the Greeks. Each of these systems was in decay or disrepute by the middle of the seventeenth century, under challenge either from an alternative, more up-to-date science or from a growing disenchantment with prophetic visionaries. But even in decay these systems continued to give meaning to the wonder tales.

The most widely used of these traditions was the meteorology of the Greeks and Romans. In Aristotle's physics, meteorology referred to everything occurring in the region between the earth and moon, a region that encompassed blazing stars, comets (deemed to circle earth below the moon), rainbows, lightning, and thunder as well as fanciful or misinterpreted phenomena like apparitions in the sky. After Aristotle, the key student of this science was Pliny, whose *Natural History* "embellished Aristotle's rational theory with many elements of wonder and even superstition." Pliny was available in English translation by the 1560s, and most other major Roman writers who spoke of meteors—Seneca, Plutarch, Vergil—had been Englished by the early seventeenth century. But English readers learned of blazing stars and comets chiefly from translations of medieval and Renaissance encyclopedias, or from a widely selling English version of Du Bartas's *La Sepmaine*.[13]

No less commonplace to most Elizabethans was astrology, the science of celestial bodies. Elizabethans learned their astrology from a medley of medieval and Renaissance handbooks. These books taught a Christian version of the science, affirming that the stars and planets had no independent power but depended on the will of God. The key vehicle (as we have seen already) was the almanacs and their "prognostications." Predictions of the weather were another means of spreading astrological ideas and images.[14]

A third intellectual tradition was apocalyptic prophecy. Several different strands converged to form this tradition. The Bible offered up a vision of the end in the Apocalypse. The Old and New Testaments told of persons who had prophesied the future on the basis of a vision, or perhaps by hearing voices: "If there be a prophet among you, I the Lord will make myself known unto him in a vision, and will speak to him in a dream" (Numbers 12:6). The legends of the saints were rich in visions, as were the lives of martyrs in Eusebius.[15] A story circulated in the late thirteenth century of a monk who saw a hand writing out the message of the gathering of a new crusade to free Jerusalem. A Lutheran printer saw enough of value in this prophecy to publish it in Germany in 1532, the same year that Martin Luther, though repudiating this specific story, affirmed the general principle that God revealed his will in episodes of this nature.[16] In general, apocalyptic prophecy gained new vigor with the coming of the Reformation, for the feeling was pervasive that contemporary history manifested the great struggle between Christ and Antichrist. In an influential explication of Revelation, a seventeenth-century English Protestant much read in New England, Joseph Mede, reaffirmed the apocalyptic significance of voices, thunder, lightning, hail, eclipses, blazing stars, and the rise and fall of kings. Mede regarded all the seals and trumpets in Revelation as figures tied to real events, and in working out the parallels he made it seem that Judgment lay not far ahead. Meanwhile certain printers were reviving legendary prophecies from the past, like those of Merlin and "Mother Shipton," or even of obscure Germans whose manuscript predictions were somehow being rediscovered.[17]

A fourth tradition was natural history. The men in mid-seventeenth-century England who pursued "natural philosophy" and who founded the Royal Society in 1662 were generously inclusive in their curiosity. They wished to collect and catalogue "all the phaenomena of nature hitherto observed, and all experiments made and recorded." By "all" they meant the "curious things of nature" as much as what was normal or routine. For them the "natural" extended to the "unnatural" in the sense of prodigies and wonders, phenomena that loomed as above or beyond the merely natural. As far back as Aristotle, the men who described nature had been intrigued by abnormalities. Why were some animals born deformed, and why some humans? The answer was that "monster births" were signs from heaven of some sinful act or perhaps apocalyptic warnings of disaster. Batman took this view, as did his sources, Lycostenes and Obsequens. The ballad writers reveled in the theme, some holding that a mother's mental state could alter the fetus. The members of the Royal Society were interested, too, in spiritual and occult phenomena, like the invisible drummer boy of Tidworth.[18]

The meaning of the wonder owed much to these four structures of ideas. But the most crucial framework was the doctrine of God's providence. That doctrine antedated Luther and Calvin. Chaucer's Knight had spoken of "Destiny, that Minister-General / Who executed on earth and over all / That Providence which God has long foreseen," and the Psalmist sang of a God who stretched out his protection to the ends of the earth. Nonetheless, the doctrine gained fresh importance in the sixteenth century. Calvin gave providence a position of prominence in the *Institutes,* contrasting it with Stoic fatalism and mere chance. In the wake of Calvin, Thomas Beard assured his readers that God was immediately and actively present in the world, the ultimate force behind everything that happened: "Is there any substance in this world that hath no cause of his subsisting? . . . Doth not every thunderclap constraine you to tremble at the blast of his voyce?" Nothing in the world occurred according to contingency or "blind chance." The "all-surpassing power of God's will" was manifested in a regularity that Beard thought of as "marvellous," though never to be counted on completely since God retained the power to interrupt the laws of nature. The providence of God was as manifest in the unexpected or surprising as in the "constant" order of the world.[19]

And Providence revealed an angry God. Portents and prodigies arose within a world besmirched with sin, a world of men and women who failed to heed his laws. The murderer, the mocking cavalier, the liar, the sabbath-breaker—all these and many others could expect that someday, somehow, their violation of the moral order would provoke awful warnings or more awful judgments. Behind the logic of this theory lay a long tradition, far older than the Reformation, of foreseeing order collapse into chaos or peace give way to violence.[20] Strife and violence abound in the wonder tales, whether caused by man, the Devil, or an avenging God.

These several themes gave meaning to the wonder in any of its many forms. Take comets, for example. Among Beard and his contemporaries, comets were remarked on more frequently than any other heavenly phenomenon described in ancient science. According to convention, comets signaled drastic change, if not disaster—"drought, the pestilence, hunger, battels, the alteration of kingdomes, and common weales, and the traditions of men. Also windes, earthquakes, dearth, landflouds, and great heate to follow." Du Bartas summed up this wisdom in *La Sepmaine:*

> There, with long bloody Hair, a Blazing Star
> Threatens the World with Famine, Plague & War:
> To Princes, death; to Kingdomes many crosses:
> To all Estates, Inevitable Losses. . . .

This motif came straight from Pliny, who, in viewing comets as "a very terrible portent," had noted their appearance "during the civil disorder in the counsulship of Octavius, and again during the war between Pompey and Caesar." Another classical source was Seneca. Readers of the Bible could add Matthew 24, where Jesus described to his disciples the signs of the last days, including what seem like eclipses of the sun and moon, and the phenomenon of stars that "fall from heaven."[21]

Thunder and lightning were other portents that drew on ancient sources. In Scripture, these events were construed as the instruments of an avenging God: "Cast forth lightning, and scatter them: Shoot out thine arrows, and destroy them" (Psalms 144:6). The prophecies of St. John in Revelation foresaw the "voice" of God in thunder, lightning, and earthquakes (8:5; 10:4). Pliny had viewed thunderbolts as "direful and accursed," associating them with other wonders such as prophecy. To writers of the Renaissance, lightning seemed especially to betoken destructive violence. Prophecy and violence were linked in plays like Marlowe's *Tamburlaine*, where the hero saw himself as the scourge of "a God full of revenging wrath, / From whom the thunder and the lightning breaks."[22]

Apparitions in the sky were yet another phenomenon that portended defeat or disaster. They were credible as signs according to both Pliny and the Bible. Among Beard, Clarke, and their contemporaries, a much-repeated apparition story concerned the fall of Jerusalem. Recounting the destruction of that city, the Jewish historian Josephus had described at length "the strange signes and tokens" that appeared before the city's fall. "One while there was a comet in form of a fiery sword, which for a year together did hang over the city." There were voices, and someone who cried out, "Wo, wo unto Jerusalem." Iron chariots flew through the air, and an army became visible in the clouds. All this seemed true not only to Elizabethans, but to Englishmen plunged into civil war, when armies in the sky were frequently perceived. Some saw ships, as when a "person of credit" watched a cloud form "into the likeness of a compleat Ship, with Masts and Sails. . . . He discerned also in the Ship, the likeness of the upper parts of Men; and at the Head of the Ship he saw many Men with Pikes on their shoulders as perfectly (according to his own Relation) as ever he saw them painted."[23]

Here as in the broadside ballads and the great collections, the wonder signified God's providence. Yet most portent stories drew on several overlapping frames of meaning. An important source of meaning and motifs was astrology, which taught men to regard the heavens as infused with order. Another source, the meteorology of Aristotle and Pliny, assumed the existence of fixed laws, as did the natural philosophy of mid-seventeenth-century scientists. However old or up-to-date, science remained allied with religion in the sense of affirming a coherence that depended on the will of God.[24] But science also taught that disruption and disorder were endemic. The conjunction of two planets could send shock waves through the universe. Stars could wander out of their ordained paths, and storms arise as nature fell into imbalance. The world as pictured by astrologers and scientists was prone to violent eruptions. This sense of things was echoed in apocalyptic prophecy, and writers who described the coming of Christ's kingdom referred to comets and eclipses as presaging the Apocalypse. Meanwhile Satan raged incessantly against God's kingdom, leading many into sin and tormenting godly seekers after truth. Sin, injustice, persecution—these disorders of the moral order were mirrored in the physical disorder of monster births. An angry God was the supreme agent of disruption. Astrologers, the Hebrew prophets, the oracles of Greece and Rome, the Englishmen at war in 1645—all spoke alike of doom portended in the turmoil of the heavens and the earth. A teleological universe yielded incessant signs of God's providential plan and his actual or impending judgments.

A further set of themes, all circulating widely in Elizabethan England, affected the significance of wonders. Portents never seemed to hint at progress or improvement but at degeneration. Dissolution or decay, the notion that the world was running down and soon would be exhausted, prevailed as a concept.[25] Another theme was *De casibus,* or the fall from wealth and power of great men. In Beard as in books like the *Mirrour of Magistrates,* Elizabethans read of kings and princes who seemed driven to destruction.[26] A third theme concerned evil as a power operating almost on its own. Evil was not distant or abstract but something always present in the flow of daily life. A book like Beard's, with its grand metaphor of "theatre," made good and evil the main actors in the drama of existence.[27] Yet another motif was fortune, its symbol a great wheel that swept some people up and others down.[28]

The wonder books incorporated all these themes without fear of contradiction. No one viewed them as in conflict, though fortune and providence were competing, if not antithetical, interpretations of the world. Yet the wonder books retained their tolerance. They made room for decayed systems of belief; in their pages the pagan coexisted with the Christian, the science of the Greeks with the apocalypticism of Scripture and the providential worldview of John Calvin. Moreover, these books reached out to folklore for stories of the Devil as black dog or bear, for legends of the saints and their "white magic," for tales of fairies, ghosts, and apparitions, of "murder will out," of curses and their consequences. In their tolerance, the great collections ended up without a unifying order. Clarke verged off into sensationalism and into citing "wonders" that were merely curiosities, like the rhinoceros that was taken to the King of Portugal. Certain of the learned may have preferred more discrimination. But in the first half of the seventeenth century, the lore of wonders remained generously eclectic in its themes and audience, with writers such as Shakespeare and Milton using the same motifs as the ballad writers. Conventional, familiar, tolerant, and open-ended, the lore of wonders was a language that almost everyone could speak and understand.[29]

I

B U T W E R E the colonists this tolerant, or did they order and discriminate in keeping with their Puritanism?

The same wonder tales that circulated in seventeenth-century England turn up in the colonies, often via books imported from the London book trade. As a student at Harvard in the 1670s, Edward Taylor had access to a copy of Samuel Clarke's *Examples,* out of which he copied "An account of ante-mortem visions of Mr. John Holland." In sermons of the 1670s, Increase Mather quoted frequently from Clarke and Beard.[30] Imported or reprinted broadsides made some of Beard's stories familiar to New England readers; John Foster, the founder of the Boston press, published in 1679 his version of a London broadside, *Divine Examples of Gods Severe Judgments against Sabbath-Breakers,* a set of illustrated warning tales drawn mostly from *The Theatre of Gods Judgements.* Booksellers were importing copies of English wonder books in the 1680s.[31] Many more such books and broadsides reached New England in the seventeenth century, though leaving no specific trace of their existence.

What passed in general from England to New England was a language or mentality. Early on, New England almanacs reiterated references and formulas derived from English counterparts. The almanac for 1649 offered its readers a lengthy "prognostication" that played on the theme of earthquakes as a portent of impending catastrophe:

> Great Earth-quakes frequently (as one relates)
> Forerun strange plagues, dearths, wars & change of states,
> Earths shaking fits by venemous vapours here,
> How is it that they hurt not, as elsewhere!

In keeping with the genre, local almanacs contained cryptic prophecies:

> The morning Kings may next ensuing year,
> With mighty Armies in the aire appear,
> By one mans means there shall be hither sent
> The Army, Citty, King and Parliament . . .
> A child but newly born, shall then foretell
> Great changes in a Winding-sheet; Farewell.

The almanac for 1648 tucked portents and prodigies into a "Chronologicall Table" that successive books updated:

Mr. Stoughton and all the souldiers returned home, none being slain. Mrs. Dier brought forth her horned-foure-talented monster. The great and general Earth-quake.[32]

Soon the colonists were issuing commentaries of their own on comets, Samuel Danforth describing the comet of 1664 in a brief pamphlet, Ichabod Wiswell the comet of 1680 in *A judicious observation of that dreadful comet. . . . Wherein is shewed the manifold judgments that are like to attend upon most parts of the world,* and Increase Mather the same comet and one of 1682 in longer books.[33] Mather also undertook a more ambitious project, a collection of New England portents somewhat on the lines of Clarke's *Examples.* Mather's *Essay for the Recording of Illustrious Providences* (1684), which received a London printing, summed up the lore accumulated after half a century of settlement.

Soon too, public groups and ordinary men and women were collecting and retelling wonder tales. Certain organizations, like the churches in Dorchester and Roxbury and the town of Newbury, incorporated references to "remarkable providences"—fires, storms, eclipses, victories, sudden deaths—into their records. Three lay members of the immigrant generation, Edward Johnson, William Bradford, and John Winthrop, wrote works of history that were richly providential in telling how the colonists had overcome adversity and conflict. This public record-keeping was paralleled in private journals and interleaved almanacs—the Reverend Joshua Moodey had "kept 30. years' Almanacks together with fayr paper between every year, setting down remarkable Providences"— that functioned as individual "memorials" of notable events. People retold such stories in their letters and passed them on by word of mouth.[34]

This trade in stories is strikingly revealed in several documents. Lawrence Hammond, a merchant in Charlestown, made notes on wonder stories in his diary. The source for one was the minister of Billerica; two others he may have learned from books. John Hull, a Boston merchant, kept an extensive diary that was largely given over to the lore of portents. His entry for 1666, a year with rich prophetic overtones, reveals a wide curiosity about events in New England:

At New Haven was distinctly and plainly heard the noise of guns, two, three, five at a time, a great part of the day, being only such noises in the air. The same day, at evening, a house at Northampton [was] fired by lightning; a part of the timber split; a man in it killed. . . . At Narriganset, in Mr. Edward Hutchinson's flock of sheep, were several monsters. In July were very many noises heard by several towns on Long Island, from the sea, distinctly, of great guns and small, and drums.

The diary of Hull's son-in-law, Samuel Sewall, was even more extensive in searching out coincidences.[35]

A college classmate of Sewall's, Edward Taylor, was on the receiving end of several stories. In a notebook kept while he was at Harvard, Taylor recorded a story of "magical performances by a juggler." He heard the story from Jonathan Mitchel, the young minister in Cambridge, who learned it as a student ("during recitation") from Henry Dunster, then the president of Harvard. Dunster had it from the Reverend John Wilson of Boston—and here the chain comes to an end. In his notebook Taylor wrote down the essence of another story passed on by word of mouth. A minister and Harvard president, Urian Oakes, had done the telling:

> A child that was born at Norich last Bartholomew-Day . . . being in the nurses arms last Easterday . . . being about 30 weeks old spake these words (This is an hard world): the nurse when she had recovered herselfe a little from her trembling, & amazement at the Extrardinariness of the thing, said Why deare Child! thou hast not known it: the Child after a pause, replied, But it will be an hard world & you shall know it.

To this same notebook Taylor added his extracts out of Clarke's *Examples,* and, from some other printed source, the prophetic scaffold speech of an Englishman executed in 1651. Here too he noted an event of his first night in Cambridge rooming in the house of Charles Chauncy, the Harvard president. As Taylor and one of Chauncy's sons were "going to bed . . . there came a white peckled Dove Pidgeon & flew against the Casement of o[u]r Chamber window." The two boys opened the window and took in the dove, which "run from us & cooed & brissled at us." Setting it free in the morning, they told the president of the event, who "said he would not (of any good) he should be hurt: ffor one should not heare of the like: it was omenous surely."[36]

Such traffic in wonder stories was crucial to the making of Increase Mather's *Essay for the Recording of Illustrious Providences.* In the early 1680s, Mather solicited his fellow ministers for contributions to his impending book. John Higginson of Salem, an older man who came to Boston as a student in the 1630s, responded to this call for stories by sending word of Moodey's annotated almanacs, "so that I doubt not but besides those [stories] he hath sent you, you may have many more from him. For instance,—he speaks of 26 men therabouts, dying or cast away in their drunkennes, which calls to mind some such cases here." The following year, having learned from Mather that he did not "confine" himself "to things done in NE.," Higginson wrote out and dispatched two wonder stories attributed to "persons credible," and of events "I believe . . . to be certain." Both concerned the Devil, the one a story of a book that acted strangely on its readers, the other of a man who covenanted with the Devil to insinuate "that there was neither God nor Devil, nor Heaven nor Hell." The informant who told Higginson of the magical book, a man no longer living, had been a ruling elder of the church in Salem. Long after having the experience (it happened back in England) he remembered that

> as he read in it, he was seized on by a strange kind [of] Horror, both of Body & minde, the hair of his head standing up, &c. Finding these effects severall times, he acquainted his master with it, who observing the same effects, they concluding it was a Conjuring Book, resolved to burn it, which they did. He that brought it, in the shape of a man, never coming to call for it, they concluded it was the Devil.

The other story Higginson had collected in his days as minister at Guilford "from a godly old man yet living."[37]

As Higginson predicted, Joshua Moodey had stories to pass on. One was of a house inhabited by evil spirits as told by William Morse, the man who lived there. All was relatively quiet at the time of Moodey's writing; "the last sight I have heard of was the carrying away of severall Axes in the night, notwithstanding they were laied up, yea, lockt up very safe." From a "sober woman" Moodey also had received a story of a "monstrous birth" that he described at length, concluding with an offer "to goe up & discourse with the midwife" if Mather wanted more details.[38]

Informants from Connecticut supplied further stories. The minister in Stamford, John Bishop, had written him some years before to answer inquiries about "the noise of a great gun in the air." In his new letter, Bishop poured out a string of tales:

> We have had of late, great stormes of rain & wind, & somtimes of thunder & lightning, whereby some execution hath been done by the Lord's holy Hand, though with sparing mercy to mankind. Mr. Jones his house at N[ew] H[aven] broken into, & strange work made in one room thereof especially, wherein one of his daughters had been a little before; & no hurt to any of the family, but the house only. . . . A little after which, at Norwalk, there were nine working oxen smitten dead in the woods, in a few rods space of ground, & after that, at Greenwich . . . there were seven swine & a dog smitten all dead, & so found the next morning, very near the dwelling

house, where a family of children were alone (their parents not then at home) & no hurt to any of them, more then amazing fear.[39]

More such stories came to Mather from other hands—a narrative of a Hartford woman's bewitchment, together with the story of a man who drank too much and died, accounts of providential rainstorms and remarkable deliverances, and of "two terrible strokes by thunder and lightning" that struck Marshfield in Plymouth Colony.[40]

From his brother, finally, came a letter reminding him of stories he had not included. Nathaniel Mather had moved to England in the early 1650s. Yet he still remembered the stories he had listened to while growing up in Dorchester and as a Harvard student:

> Mrs. Hibbons witchcrafts, & the discovery thereof, as also of H. Lake's wife, of Dorchester, whom, as I have heard, the devill drew in by appearing to her in the likenes, & acting the part of a child of hers then lately dead, on whom her heart was much set: as also another of a girl in Connecticut who was judged to dye a reall convert, tho shee dyed for the same crimes Storyes, as I heard them, as remarkable for some circumstances as most I have read. Mrs. Dyer's & Mrs. Hutchinson's monstrous births, & the remarkable death of the latter, with Mr. Wilson's prediction or threatning thereof, which, I remember, I heard of in New England.

Flowing from the memories of a man who long since had left New England, this résumé of stories is revealing both of how such stories were transmitted (Mather "heard" these tales) and of the buildup of a native stock of wonders.[41]

Most of this local lore had counterparts in stories told by Clarke, Beard, or ballad writers. Many of these older stories passed among the colonists as well, enriching and legitimizing their own testimonies of the supernatural. The man in Lynn who saw phantoms in the sky could almost have been quoting from an English tract of 1662 that described similar phenomena. So it went for others: experience coincided with the narrative tradition. We may also infer the existence of a lore of wonders that approached being common knowledge. The circulation of this lore was not limited to print, as Mather's correspondence with his friends and fellow ministers so clearly indicates. Nor was it something only the rude multitude and not the learned could appreciate. When presidents of Harvard told wonder tales in class, when ministers delighted in recalling tales of "magical" books and freakish bolts of lightning, we can be sure that we are dealing with a culture shared, with few exceptions, by all the colonists.

One other aspect of this culture deserves emphasis. It relied on the same mix of intellectual traditions, the same structures of meaning, as the lore in Beard, Clarke, and the ballad writers. Consider Danforth's and Mather's descriptions of the comets they had witnessed. Like so many others who observed a comet, Danforth and Mather relied on the meteorology of the ancients, as mediated via medieval and Renaissance encyclopedias. In proving that comets were "Portentous and Signal of great and notable Changes," Danforth drew on Du Bartas and cited events like the death of Julius Caesar that according to tradition were prefigured by a comet. Mather cited Josephus, Cicero, Du Bartas, Mede, and Scripture as authorities when preaching on the comet of 1680. His account of a comet that appeared in 1527 was entirely derivative:

> On the eleventh day of August, a most terrifying Comet was seen, of an immense longitude, and bloody colour. The form of it, was like a mans arm holding an huge Sword in his hand with which he was ready to strike. Such terrour and horrour surprized the Spectators of this Prodigy, as that some died away with dread & amazement.[42]

So too the references in diaries and histories to lightning and comets reiterated an old code of reference. The venerable associations between lightning, judgment, and prophecy infused Samuel Arnold's description of a storm that struck the town of Marshfield, when "the most dismal black cloud . . . that ever" anyone had seen passed overhead, shooting forth its "arrows." They colored John Hull's account of a stroke of lightning that "stunned" an Ipswich man: "His Bible being under his arm, the whole book of Revelation was carried away, and the other parts of the Bible left untouched." Simon Bradstreet knew of the "effects" of the star of 1664 on England: "a great and dreadfull plague that followed the next summer; in a dreadfull warre by sea with the dutch; and the burning of London the 2d year following."[43]

From medieval handbooks the colonists also borrowed the language of astrology and used it in their almanacs.[44] Even more appealing was the apocalyptic tradition. Visions, dreams, apparitions, unseen voices—all of these were almost everyday encounters, talked about in private and a matter of experience. John Brock, a minister, noted in a book of memoranda that he "saw a Resemblance of a Trooper in the Air." A young woman suffering from the cruelties of witches had a vision that a minister reported to the public:

> [she] saw in her fitt a White man and was with him in a Glorious Place, which had no Candles nor Sun, yet was full of Light and

Brightness; where there was a great Multitude in White glittering Robes, and they Sung the Song in the fifth of Revelation. . . .

This vision came to Mercy Lewis "several times." Each episode the "White Man" told her "how long it would be before" she fell into another fit, her narrator adding, "it hath fallen out accordingly."[45] The Reverend Noadiah Russell had

heard of a man in Connecticut who was taken with a sudden shivering after which he heard a voice saying that four dreadful judgments should come speedily upon the whole world viz: sword, famine, fire and sickness which should, without speedy reformation prevented, begin at New England.

Nathaniel Morton, the lay historian of Plymouth, reported an unseen "voice" that had alerted the beleaguered colonists to arson in their storehouse.[46]

Dreams, though needing cautious treatment, were nonetheless significant. The mother of John Dane, a farmer, had dreamed that a certain minister would preach at such a time using a specific text, and as Dane remembered in his memoirs, "so it was; the same man, the same day, the same text." John Winthrop and John Wilson, the minister in Boston, shared dream stories. Winthrop in his dream had come into his bedchamber and

found his wife . . . in bed, and three or four of their children lying by her, with most sweet and smiling countenances, with crowns upon their heads, and blue ribbons about their leaves. When he awaked, he told his wife his dream, and made this interpretation of it, that God would take of her children to make them fellow heirs with Christ in his kingdom.

Two years previously, Wilson had told Winthrop "that, before he was resolved to come into this country, he dreamed he was here, and that he saw a church arise out of the earth, which grew up and became a marvellous goodly church."[47] One of Cotton Mather's neighbors, a shipmaster, told him of a dream he had while captive of the Turks, a dream that seemed to promise "speedy redemption," which indeed occurred. John Hull recorded in his diary that a Long Island man had "dreamed he fought with devils, and they took his hat from him." The sequel— "he was soon after found dead . . . killed, as supposed, by lightning, and his hat some few rods from him"—seemed to confirm dreaming as prophetic.[48]

Here we sense ourselves approaching folk belief. As in England, the lore of wonders in America was openly folkloric in certain of its motifs. Much of this folklore becomes evident whenever someone was accused of practicing witchcraft. Stephen Batman had incorporated the folk tradition of spectral, shape-shifting black dogs into *The Doome warning to the Iudgemente*.[49] A century later, people in New England testified at Salem that they had seen this very dog. Sarah Carrier, enticed into witchcraft by members of her family, was promised "a black dog." William Barker came upon "the Shape of a black dog w'ch looked Verry fercly Upon him" as he went into the woods to fetch a cow.[50] Many of the witnesses at Salem had been visited at night by persons crying out for vengeance on their murderers. Such stories were a staple of folk legend and also of the ballad literature.[51] Another folk belief expressed at Salem was the power of white magic (reversed in this case to black) to keep persons dry in rainstorms. A witness testified that she suspected someone of witchcraft when that person passed through a storm on muddy roads with no evident sign of having done so. One source of this story was the legend of St. Cainnicus, who remained dry in spite of rain. Witchcraft cases also contain evidence of fortune-telling and of folk remedies for guarding against occult power.[52]

Because it built upon the wonder tales that people told as stories, Increase Mather's *Essay for the Recording of Illustrious Providences* has something of the quality of a folk narrative. Chapter 1 tells of "sea-deliverances," some of them native, others taken from an English book. In chapter 2, a potpourri of stories, Mather reaches back to King Philip's War of 1675–76 for a captivity narrative and two related episodes; after telling of another "sea-deliverance," he opened up his Clarke's *Examples* and began to copy from it. In chapter 3, "Thunder and Lightning," he quotes from John Bishop's letter and adds several other stories of lightning in New England. But the chapter ends with two German stories, some references to Scripture, and several bits of pedantry. Chapters 4, 6, 7, and 8 are meditations and general arguments on providence, Mather speaking here as a "learned" man. Chapter 9, in which he tells of persons who were deaf and dumb but learned to speak, demonstrates how thin the line was between the wonder and the curiosity.[53] Chapter 10, "Of remarkable tempests," covers hurricanes, whirlwinds, earthquakes, and floods; in chapter 11, "concerning remarkable judgements," he relates how the enemies of God—Quakers, drunkards, and others hostile to New England—have been punished. Mather adds a letter from Connecticut as chapter 12, and in chapter 5 draws together several stories of "things preternatural"—demons, apparitions, and evil spirits.

The many layers of the *Essay* included the esoteric. Like Beard and Clarke before him, Mather had an eye for the unusual event. From a manuscript, presumably of English origin, that descended to him from another minister, he drew a Faust-type story of a young student who contracted with the Devil for money. The black magic of the Devil yielded to the higher powers of a group of faithful ministers, whose prayers forced Satan

> to give up that contract; after some hours continuance in prayer, a cloud was seen to spread itself over them, and out of it the very contract signed with the poor creatures blood was dropped down amongst them.

From this manuscript Mather quoted the tale of a minister named Juxon who drank too much and went to a cockfight on the Lord's Day. As "curses . . . were between his lips, God smote him dead in the twinkle of an eye. And though Juxon were but young . . . his carcase was immediately so corrupted as that the stench of it was insufferable."

From the same collection, finally, Mather copied out a "strange passage" concerning a man suspected of stealing sheep who swore his innocence and

> wished, that if he had stollen it, God would cause the horns of the sheep to grow upon him. This man was seen within these few days by a minister of great repute for piety, who saith, that the man has a horn growing out of one corner of his mouth, just like that of a sheep; from which he hath cut seventeen inches, and is forced to keep it tyed by a string to his ear, to prevent its growing up to his eye.

Here again we sense ourselves confronting folk belief. This story of the sheep's horn had its parallel or antecedent in a medieval legend of a man who stole and ate a sheep, and afterwards discovered a sheep's ear growing out of his mouth. Likewise, the story of a student who compacted with the Devil had roots in legends of the saints and, more remotely, in lore of eastern cultures.[54]

How like it was for wonder tales to build on folk or pagan legends! With its mixture of motifs and sources, *An Essay for the Recording of Illustrious Providences* reaffirmed the traditional tolerance of the genre. What Mather's writings also demonstrate is an enduring fascination with the wonder, a fascination he shared with his correspondents and a host of others in New England. It was almost automatic to take note of wonders and evoke this lore.[55] The repertory in general use among the colonists was closely akin to the repertory amassed in Beard and Clarke, from which, indeed, these people gained instruction. Prophecy, prodigy, providence—these were the stuff of everyday experience. When William

Hibbins stood up in Boston church in 1642 and asked his fellow members to take note of "sea-deliverances"—"what desperate dangers they were delivered from upon the seas, such as the eldest seamen were amazed"—he was expressing a popular awareness of wonders that Increase Mather would reiterate.[56]

This attentiveness to prodigies and portents bespoke deep feelings about communal danger and security. The men who interlaced the Dorchester and Roxbury church records with providential events were consciously performing a public function. So were Winthrop and Bradford in their journal histories, and Edward Johnson in *The Wonder-Working Providence of Sions Saviour*. To chronicle the wonder was to chart the zones of danger through which a community must pass. In early modern Europe, every community had its good times and its bad. The good times were when rain came at the right moment and the harvest was abundant, when neighbors lived in peace and landlords were not greedy, when servants obeyed their masters. The hard times were when food ran low and famine threatened, when disease was epidemic, or when peace gave way to conflict. In many European villages, a craving for protection was satisfied by "miracles" or extraordinary events that promised the return of peace, health, and prosperity. Thus, when epidemics threatened, villagers in late-medieval Spain—young girls, shepherds, old men— had visions of the Virgin Mary in which she demanded that the village build a chapel or renew its vows of faith. In thirteenth-century Burgundy, women washed newborn or ailing infants in water from a well associated with a miracle.[57]

Women were still bringing infants to the well of St. Guinefort in Burgundy when the colonists departed for New England. In the towns from which these people came, many of the customs that once addressed the dangers of everyday life had lapsed into disuse. Once past their own "starving time," these people found themselves becoming prosperous— owners of their land, blessed with healthy children, reaping ample harvests. Yet all of the first generation had risked the dangers of the sea in coming to New England. Then as well as later, the wilderness that lay around them contained hostile Indians and their Catholic allies from French Canada. Back in England, the government (except when Puritans had reigned) regarded them with disfavor. And, as they discovered, there were enemies within—those who lied, cursed, or profaned the Sabbath, old women who allied themselves with Satan, children who grew up rebellious, neighbors who disputed each stray pig and cow, and, increasingly, merchants who lived ostentatiously. Danger pressed as much upon the godly in their new home as in England.

Responding to these dangers, the colonists employed an old language of interpretation in which the key words were "sin" and "judgment." That language reached them via Beard and the ballad writers, and also via poems like *Pestilence* (1625), a narrative of epidemic illness that painted it as God's response to man's indifference. What enriched and made this language relevant was the colonists' assumption that they lived in covenant with God. For them the covenant transformed the body social into a moral order, a "Theocratie" erected on the basis of the laws of God. It was the wonder that made visible this fusion of the social and the moral, at once manifesting God's protection and—more frequently—warning of God's anger at their carelessness.

John Winthrop kept his journal not out of private curiosity but in order to record the flow of "providences" betokening the situation of a covenanted people. "It is useful to observe, as we go along," Winthrop wrote in 1635, "such especial providences of God as were manifested for the good of these plantations." What he meant by "good" was the safety of the whole, and the general welfare. Anyone who put self-interest ahead of the welfare of the whole was likely to become an example of God's judgments—to drown in a shipwreck, die in an explosion ("wherein the judgment of God appeared, for the master and company were many of them profane scoffers at us"), lose some of his property. Perhaps because he sacrificed so much of his own estate, Winthrop was especially attracted to cases of the rich and covetous becoming poor. "Divers homes were burnt this year," he noted in 1642, "by drying flax. Among others, one Briscoe, of Watertown, a rich man, a tanner, who had refused to let his neighbor have leather for corn, saying he had corn enough. . . ." Servants and sea captains who were suddenly enriched at the expense of others often suffered bad dreams or psychological distress, or simply lost their money as rapidly as it had been acquired. Winthrop's conception of the general good extended to those standbys of the Puritan program, Sabbatarianism and temperance. He told of drunkards who drowned and of people who died after having worked on the Sabbath—in one case, after carting dung. He was much relieved when murderers and thieves were detected by special acts of providence; reporting two examples, he summed up their meaning as "show[ing] the presence and power of God in his ordinances, and his blessing upon his people, while they endeavor to walk before him with uprightness."[58] Always portents reaffirmed the rightness of a moral order.

Meanwhile there were constant "plots" spawned by the Devil to "disturb our peace, and to raise up instruments one after another." The "old serpent" tried his hand at "sowing jealousies and differences between us and our friends at Connecticut." But God sent tokens to reveal that he stood by the colonists. Perhaps the most impressive of these tokens for the men and women who came in the 1630s was their safe passage of the ocean. A folklore emerged from the fact that every ship but one (the *Angel Gabriel*) had reached New England safely: "wherein" (as William Hibbins told the Boston congregation in 1642) "it was very observable what care the Lord had of them." Citing Hibbins in the journal, Winthrop added that "indeed such preservations and deliverances have been so frequent, to such ships as have carried those of the Lord's family between the two Englands, as would fill a perfect volume to report them all."[59] A more confusing token was the snake that crawled into Cambridge meetinghouse while a synod of the ministers was listening to a sermon. There was panic before "Mr. Thomson, one of the elders of Braintree, (a man of much faith) trode upon the head of it." Interpretation followed, the ministers agreeing that the snake was Satan attempting "their disturbance and dissolution": "This being so remarkable, and nothing falling out but by divine providence, it is out of doubt, the Lord discovered somewhat of his mind in it." Mixed in with events Winthrop knew how to interpret were others that remained mysterious. It was not clear why "one James Everell . . . saw a great light in the night at Muddy River," or why "a voice was heard upon the water between Boston and Dorchester, calling out in a most dreadful manner, boy, boy, come away, come away," or why at Ipswich in 1646 "there was a calf brought forth with one head, and three mouths, three noses, and six eyes": "What these prodigies portended the Lord only knows, which in his due time he will manifest."[60]

As chronicle of prodigies and portents demonstrating God's protection of the colonists, Winthrop's journal history had its parallel in Nathaniel Morton's *New-Englands Memoriall*. Basing much of what he wrote on William Bradford's then unpublished journal history, Morton celebrated the "simplicity" of life in those early decades when no one had been covetous or proud. Another of his themes was the success of the "weak" and "lowly" Pilgrims in overcoming stronger enemies. Thus the menace of the Indians, who far outnumbered the few people who survived their first winter in New England, was removed by a sickness God had sent among them. "Ancient Indians" told him that not long before the English first arrived, "they saw a Blazing Star or Comet, which was a fore-runner of this sad Mortality. . . ." Reversal struck the proud merchant Thomas Weston. The men he sent to Plymouth mocked the Pilgrims, but then fell short of food and turned to begging. "A strange alteration there was" in Weston himself, after he arrived and was betrayed by the Indians. Likewise the defeat of the Pequots—so "Proud and Blasphemous an Enemy"—was the doing of the Lord. But if God struck some with judgments, he gave godly people strength to persevere against their enemies. The overriding theme of Morton's narrative was deliverance: how the weak, because they rested on God's mercy, came to triumph over every adverse circumstance.[61]

These public texts taught the importance of the Protestant community. So did the record-keeping in such churches as Dorchester and Roxbury. John Eliot, the minister in Roxbury, noted the drowning of two "ungodly" servants who went out at night to gather oysters: "a dreadful example of God's displeasure against obstinate servants." But God protected those in covenant, as in the providential healing of the deacon's daughter from a head wound that exposed her brains, and another of a man so badly hurt blood gushed from his ear; yet "thro' Gods mercy he recovered his senses . . . to the wonder of all men."[62] Similarly, private diaries detailed portents that signified protection of a family or a household. People told the story of their lives in this same fashion, as when John Dane of Ipswich composed "A Declaration of Remarkabell Proudenses in the Corse of My Lyfe," to which he added a long poem that celebrated his prosperity as one of the godly. Always in such texts the private and the public—self, household, church, community—were not differentiated, but conjoined. And always they provided reassurance. Even after learning of a new defeat in King Philip's War, a layman voiced the wisdom that "It is a day of the wicked's tryumph, but the sure word of God tells us his tryumphing is *brief*." The lore of wonders held the lesson that the godly, should they live up to their values, would pass safely through all trial and tribulation.[63]

At a still deeper level, the wonder story embodied confusing lessons about danger and security. The people of New England viewed the world about them as demonstrating pattern. This was the order of God's providence, the order of a theocentric universe. It was also teleological, its structure the grand scheme laid out in the Apocalypse, the war of Antichrist against the godly. Evil was a force of great strength and cunning, so much so, indeed, that the providential order could seem to be "overthrowne and turned upside downe, men speak[ing] evill of good, and good of evill, accounting darknesse light, and light darknesse."[64] Disorder was profound in other ways, as Winthrop half perceived in struggling to make sense of the array of portents. The world was rife with violence—of neighbors angered by stray animals or slander, of death that came to children without apparent cause, of Indians on the rampage, of great storms and terrifying earthquakes.

The people of New England acted out their fear of what such wonders revealed at moments like the earthquake of 1638, which "shook the earth . . . in a very violent manner to our great amazement and wonder" (as the residents of Newbury recorded in the town records) and caused divers men (that had never knowne an Earthquake before) being at worke in the Fields, to cast downe their working tooles, and run with gastly terrified lookes, to the next company they could meet withall.

On Cape Ann in 1692, phantoms roused men into frenzied firing of their guns. A servant girl in Boston, awakened by a fire near the water, saw its "Light . . . reflecting from a Black Cloud, and came crying to [her master] under Consternation; supposing the last Conflagration had begun." People felt uneasy when the sun passed into the darkness of an eclipse, and the officers of Harvard College postponed commencement in 1684 because it fell too close to one of these events.[65] Witches too were terrifying in their power to disrupt community.

Each kind of violence was attuned to every other, as were the forms of order. Certainly the order of the universe often seemed to be hidden or difficult to decipher. If there was purpose and plan, there was also mystery at the heart of things.

One providence seems to look this way, another providence seems to look that way, quite contrary one to another. Hence these works are marveilous. Yea, and that which adds to the wonderment, is, in that the works of God sometimes seem to run counter with his word: so that there is dark and amazing intricacie in the ways of providence.

Death could strike at any moment, the Devil could mislead, the earth begin to tremble. In dramatizing all these possibilities, the wonder tale evoked the radical contingency of a world so thoroughly infused with invisible forces. It came down to this, that nothing was secure, that no appearance of security could hide the mystery beneath.[66]

II

I HAVE spoken of the wonder stories as embodying a mentality that united the learned and the unlearned. Being so pervasive, and so widely credited as real, these stories readily became, as well, weapons in a complex game of politics. When consensus lapsed, competing groups used purported wonders to discredit their opponents. One axis of this conflict in New England placed Baptists and Quakers in opposition to the Orthodoxy. Another set the ministers against the "cunning folk" who offered to help people know the future. A third revolved around "declension," or the perceived decline of community, and whom or what to blame for it. One major result of this politicization was to make the interpretation of wonders generally uncertain. Moreover, embedded in the very books and broadsides that conveyed this lore was a definite skepticism about portents. Was astrology a science? Were dreams and voices mere delusions? Learned culture, Scripture, even popular tradition, warned against false prophets and misleading signals. The many-layered meanings of a portent thus included the possibility of its having no significance at all or of its being overly politicized.

In using portents to discredit others and, at the same time, to legitimize their own position, the colonists were playing an old game. The oracle at Delphi, the Sibyllines in Rome, the texts attributed to Merlin in the thirteenth century, all were preludes to the uses of wonders in the Reformation. Martin Luther helped revive the story of a deformed monster fished out of the Tiber, which he construed as condemnation of the Catholic clergy. John Foxe retold a "prophetical vision or dream" of John Hus and the kindred testimony of the martyr Jerome: "And I cite you all [he declared to his judges in 1416] to answer before the most high and just Judge, after a hundred years."[67] Thus did Foxe propose that someone had foretold the Reformation! His many other tales of portents and prophetic sayings encouraged English Puritans to employ these events in their campaign for reform. Much of the lore amassed in *The Theatre of Gods Judgements* was meant to further this campaign, and an angry man named Phillip Stubbes used it in denouncing Sunday sports and other English pastimes. When fire devastated Tiverton, Puritans read it as a warning to observe the Sabbath. The same people liked to tell of blows inflicted on the Catholics. A much-favored story described the collapse of a gallery in Blackfriars Hall, London, where a clandestine Catholic service was being conducted. A similar tragedy nearly occurred at the funeral of a prominent Puritan when too many people crowded into the gallery of the church and the beams began to crack. Writing to John Winthrop of the incident, Emmanuel Downing thought it was a "miracle" that the "gallery stood . . . for had it faln as blackfryars did under the popish assembly, yt would have ben a great wound to our religion."[68] The politics of portent-watching intensified as Royalists and Parliamentarians maneuvered for support. On the eve of civil war, each side hired astrologers to issue respectively sympathetic readings of the stars and planets. Even when the game was up and Charles II restored to the throne, opponents issued propaganda in the form of portent lore. A frenzy of such portent-mongering occurred as opposition parties worked to exclude James II from the throne.[69]

Well versed in these campaigns before leaving for New England, the colonists discovered in the 1630s that a prophetess was in their midst, a charismatic woman who claimed God had given her the gift of prophecy. Anne Hutchinson arrived in Boston in 1634. She brought with her a reputation as a prophetess. Two specific prophecies or "revelations" survive in the records of her life, one forecasting that her ship would need three more weeks to reach New England, the other a prediction that "a young man in the ship should be saved, but he must walk in the ways" she specified. We may infer that her voyage did last three more weeks, for this prophecy (and doubtless others we know nothing of) was cited by admirers who went on to speak "of rare Revelations of things to come from the spirit." Edward Johnson, a hostile witness, remembered someone saying to a newcomer, "Come along with me . . . i'le bring you to a Woman . . . who hath had many Revelations of things to come, and for my part, saith hee, I had rather hear such a one . . . then any of your learned Scollers. . . ." Questioned by the General Court in 1637 as it acted to suppress the movement known as Antinomianism, Mrs. Hutchinson described herself as bearing "immediate" revelations and cited a key text of Scripture: "And it shall come to pass afterward, / That I will pour out my Spirit upon all flesh; / And your sons and your daughters shall prophesy, / Your old men shall dream dreams, / Your young men shall see visions" (Joel 28–29; the passage goes on to speak of wonders and deliverance). At this session of the court, one of the deputies reported that in London she had told him she "was very inquisitive after revelations and said that she never had any great thing done about her but it was revealed to her beforehand." He remembered too that "when she came within sight of Boston" for the first time, "and looking upon the meanness of the place . . . she uttered these words, if she had not a sure word that England should be destroyed her heart would shake."[70]

Without claiming the same status, her two allies in the ministry, John Cotton and John Wheelwright, both voiced apocalyptic views. At Wheelwright's fast-day sermon in Boston meetinghouse in January 1637, he linked the growing dispute over doctrine to the "combate" between Christ and Antichrist. "The day shall come," the "terrible day" foreseen in Scripture, when all the enemies of Christ would be "consumed" by fire. An audience well versed in apocalyptic speculation understood his meaning when Wheelwright asked rhetorically, "Why should we not further this fire, who knoweth not how soone those Jewes may be converted?"[71]

Statements such as these had an altogether different meaning from the dreams and visions of a Mercy Lewis or a Winthrop. Here, the role of prophetess was turned against the men in power, the ministers Anne Hutchinson denounced for preaching "works." She may have known of Eleanor Davis, an Englishwoman who, in 1625, declared she "heard early in the morning a Voice from Heaven, speaking as through a trumpet

these words: 'There is nineteen years and a half to the Judgment Day.'"
Davis was able to have some of her sayings printed, but she also was
imprisoned for predicting the downfall of Charles I. Or the story may
have reached Anne Hutchinson of Jane Hawkins, a visionary who in
1629 foretold "the downfall of the bishops and the Anglican Church."
In the years when Anne was learning to respect the voices that she heard
as sent from God, still other men and women arose to proclaim the
downfall of the state and church and their own mission as inspired
prophets. One died at the stake for heresy, and others were imprisoned.[72] When she found herself in danger from the magistrates and
ministers, she warned them that, like Daniel in the lion's den, she would
be "delivered" by a miracle from the grasp of persecutors: "and if you
go on in this course you begin you will bring a curse upon you and your
posterity, and the mouth of the Lord hath spoken it." A fuller report
has her telling the court that in England "the Lord did reveale himselfe
to me, sitting upon a Throne of Justice, and all the world appearing
before him, and though I must come to New England, yet I must not
feare nor be dismaied," and insisting to the ministers that "I feare none
but the great Jehovah, which hath foretold me of these things, and I doe
verily believe that he will deliver me out of [y]our hands."[73]

In her footsteps followed other prophetlike outsiders who denounced
the doctrines of the ministers and rejected their authority. A standard
theme among the Quakers, who picked up where she left off, was to
declare that all persecutors of the saints would suffer from God's anger.
Like Anne Hutchinson, moreover, the Quakers used the fearful weapon
of the curse against the magistrates and ministers. From prison Hum-
phrey Norton accused Thomas Prence, the governor of Plymouth, of
transgressing "the laws and waies of God," and warned him that he must
expect "the vengeance of God."

> The day of thy wailing will bee like unto that of a woman that
> murthers the fruite of her wombe; the anguish and peine that will
> enter upon thy reignes will be like knawing worms lodging betwixt
> thy hart and liver: When these things come upon thee, and thy backe
> bowed down with pain, in that day and houre thou shalt know to
> thy griefe, that prophetts of the Lord God wee are, and the God of
> vengeance is our God.

John Hull recorded in his diary in 1661 that "The Quakers have given
out such speeches as gave cause to think they intended mischief unto
our magistrates and ministers, and threatened fire and sword to be our
speedy portion. . . ."[74] When King Philip's War broke out in 1675, Samuel
Groom declared that God was making an example of the colonists for

their extreme cruelty: ". . . and therefore thou must drink of the Cup of terrible Amazement and Astonishment, poured out by a Just Hand, as from God upon thy Inhabitants Oh New-England!" It was also in these troubled years that a Quaker "marcht" through Boston, "crying, 'Repent, &c.,'" and that Quaker women stripped themselves of all their clothes, rubbed their faces "black," and rushed into meetinghouses to proclaim the coming judgment. The entry of such a woman (partly dressed) into Boston Third Church "occasioned the greatest and most amazing uproar that" one eyewitness "ever saw."[75]

This "amazing uproar" lasted through the 1690s. George Keith, who came to Massachusetts to debate the ministers in 1690, defended Quakers for believing that the saints received new revelations and illuminations from the Holy Spirit. "I say it with Sorrow," Keith declared in taking up the classic pose of prophet, "if ye were not blind, ye might see some of the Judgments of the Lord begun to be executed upon you. . . ." Thomas Maule, a Salem Quaker, invoked the Salem witchcraft executions as evidence of "Gods Judgments upon . . . the chief persecuting Priests and Rulers." Citing Foxe, he argued that the ministers belonged in the tradition of false teachers that included Rome, and placed victims like himself in the context of the *Book of Martyrs*. In these years a small group of men and women gathered around a merchant of New London, John Rogers, who claimed to be inspired. Imprisoned, whipped, and fined, the Rogerenes persisted by appropriating the myth of "God's Children" suffering at the hands of their worldly "Persecutors."[76]

From Hutchinson to Keith and Rogers, these radicals relied on Scripture in defending their right to interpret God's commands. More, they drew on motifs which the orthodox themselves articulated—the expectation of the coming kingdom, the role of certain men as prophets. The social memory of the radicals was little different from the memory of the men who punished them; both groups cited Foxe, both were fascinated with the Book of Revelation. Crossing and recrossing a line that was difficult to fix, the radicals played on ambiguities intrinsic to the role of prophet.

A different group of men and women, those who served as fortune-tellers, healers, and magicians, exploited other ambiguities. We learn of fortune-telling from court records, and especially those involving accusations of witchcraft. A servant girl accused of stealing responded with the threat to "burn" one of the girls who had testified against her; according to a witness, "She said shee had a book in which she could read and call the divill to kill Sarah." John Broadstreet of Rowley, "presented" to the Essex County Court in 1652 "for having familiarity with the devil," told someone "he read in a book of magic, and that he heard a voice asking him what work he had for him." He was not persuasive, for the court dismissed him with a fine for lying. Yet others had substantial credibility as healers and fortune-tellers. Margaret Jones of Charlestown, convicted of being a witch and executed in 1648, practiced healing and prophecy. She was critical of the doctors with whom she competed, warning "such as would not make use of her physic, that they would never be healed, and accordingly their diseases and hurts continued, with relapse against the ordinary course, and beyond the apprehension of all physicians and surgeons." John Brown of New Haven, a young man already known for drinking and disorderly behavior, boasted to his friends in 1665 that he could make the Devil appear at his bidding; before their eyes he drew circles and "strange figures which he called the lords of the second, third, tenth and twelfth house," and adduced "the aid of the seven stars and the planets"—though all in vain, apparently. A New Haven woman, Elizabeth Goodman, was accused of witchcraft because she seemed to know beforehand of events or see what was hidden. Mercy Goodwin was empowered by the demon spirit that possessed her to detect where stolen goods were hidden. At the witchcraft trial of Katherine Harrison of Wethersfield, a former servant testified that Katherine "told fortunes." According to this witness, she also boasted "of her great familiarity with Mr. Lilley, one that told fortunes and foretold many matters that in future times were to be accomplished." "Mr. Lilley" was a practicing astrologer who took the side of Parliament in the portent propaganda of the 1640s. His books or others like them may have reached Caleb Powell, who told William Morse, the man whose house was beset by spirits in 1679, that "he had understanding in Astrology and Astronomy and knew the working of spirits." Though Powell escaped charges of witchcraft, Dorcas Hoar of Beverly did not. The owner of a "book of fortune telling," she read palms and told fortunes. Alice Parker was sought out by persons who wanted to know if their sons or husbands were safe at sea. Samuel Wardwell was consulted for advice on lovers and children; he informed one woman that she would have five girls before a son, "which thing is come to pase." Among some of her neighbors, Elizabeth Morse was perceived as a "cunning woman" who had healing powers.[77]

Fortune-telling veered over into remedies and sayings that had roots in folklore. Rebecca Johnson told the Salem court in 1692 that, wanting to know if her son "was alive or dead," she had her daughter perform "the turneing of the sieve . . . and that if the sieve turned he was dead, and so the sieve did turn." To make this device work she used word magic, repeating the phrase "By Saint Peter & Saint Paul, if [the person] be dead let this sieve turn round." Sarah Cole of Lynn "owned" to the same court "that she & some others toyed w'th a Venus glase & an Egg what trade their sweet harts should be of." (John Hale, the minister of Beverly, heard that "there came up a Coffin, that is, a Spectre in likeness of a Coffin.") Drawing on an old folklore, people nailed up horseshoes to protect themselves or struck back by tricks that broke the power of witchcraft—baking a cake made out of a suspected person's urine mixed with flour or else boiling or baking bits of hair.[78]

Prophecy and magic were alike in helping people to become empowered, prophecy because it overturned the authority of mediating clergy and magic because it gave access to the realm of occult force. It may be that some of those who practiced magic and/or witchcraft were explicitly rebellious. One or two at times articulated a worldview that was clearly blasphemous—William Barker at Salem in 1692, and a woman in Connecticut in 1663 who a witness testified had come to her and said that "god was naught, god was naught, it was very good to be a witch," while adding that "she should not ned far going to hell, for she shold not burne in the fire." Perhaps this taint of blasphemy is why many of the colonists confused prophecy and fortune-telling with witchcraft, as though prophets could cause death or sickness. When William Graves of Stamford came to his daughter's house not long before she went into labor, he "suddenly began to counsail" her, "sayeing Abigall fitt thyselfe to meet the Lord." Were his words a curse that caused her death? Was he acting out of love or malice, as witch or caring father? Dozens of such questions arose in the flow of everyday experience, questions springing from the doubleness of prophecy and healing.[79]

Such acts were open to interpretation as white magic—or as black. It was in the interests of the clergy to resolve this situation by declaring *all* magic unlawful. Yet the hostility of elite magistrates and ministers was shared by many of the colonists, who came to see the cunning folk as threatening. In denouncing them at Salem or in other trials for witchcraft, lay men and women resolved their suspicion that the witch who healed was not far removed from the witch who harmed their children. Nor was it clear that prophets and fortune-tellers were depending on the Holy Spirit rather than the Devil.

Hence the fascination in 1637 and 1638 with two medical disasters that were open to interpretation as judgmental portents. In October 1637, Anne Hutchinson's close friend and supporter, Mary Dyer, gave birth to a stillborn and premature fetus, "so monstrous and misshapen, as the like hath scarce been heard of." Winthrop, who promptly ordered the fetus exhumed once he learned of its existence, worked telling clues into his description of the object—a midwife who was "notorious for familiarity with the devill," a sudden illness that struck most of the women who were helping with the birth, a violent rocking of the mother's bed at the moment when the fetus died, the coincidence of hearing of the monster "that very day Mistris Hutchinson was cast out of the Church for her monstrous errours, and notorious falsehood." Not long thereafter, Anne Hutchinson herself gave birth to a deformed fetus that, gruesomely described in Winthrop's journal, was summed up in Thomas Weld's report of the whole controversy as "30. monstrous births" corresponding to the "about 30 [misshapen] opinions" she had expressed. Weld, who was then in England, estimated that these were "such monstrous births as no Chronicle (I thinke) hardly ever recorded the like."[80]

Here was one form of response to the "fearful uproar" of prophesying: describe would-be prophets as deluded liars, and link them with Satan. So the ministers in 1638 informed Anne Hutchinson herself that her revelations were from "Satan."[81] Anyone in later years who prophesied against the orthodox ran the greater risk of being accused of witchcraft. So did those who practiced fortune-telling. Included in the nineteen persons executed in 1692 were Parker, Hoar, and Wardwell. Mary Hawkins, the midwife who assisted Mary Dyer in 1637, had previously been executed as a witch. Though not executed on this charge, Quaker women were stripped and their bodies searched for certain growths that, according to the lore of witchcraft, were unique to witches.[82]

Hundreds of the colonists participated in witch-hunting—and did so with such a vengeance as, from time to time, dismayed the magistrates and ministers. The special contribution of the ministers was twofold. First, it was they who made much of the Devil, portraying him as the grand conspirator ever plotting to subvert the godly and install the "Kingdom of Darkness."[83] Their second contribution was to proscribe certain beliefs as *too* magical, and not suited to a godly people. In *An Essay for the Recording of Illustrious Providences,* Increase Mather denounced several practices and artifacts—"herbs and plants to preserve from witchcrafts," "characters, words, or spells, to charm away witches, devils, or diseases," drawing "blood from those whom they suspect for witches," putting "urine into a bottle," nailing horseshoes "at their door, or the like, in the hope of recovering health thereby"—as "unlawful" customs that drew their force (and Mather said they sometimes worked) from the Devil. He went on to criticize the water trial for witches, "divination by sieves," and the "foolish sorcery of those women that put the white of an egg into a glass of water, that so they may be able to divine of what occupation their future husbands shall be." He labeled all such matters "superstitious," and denounced the people involved in them as "implicitly" in compact with the Devil. John Hale resumed this critique in *A Modest Enquiry,* his effort to make sense of Salem witchcraft. As though to illustrate his own confusion, he told tales of fortune-telling that had been exposed as falsehoods while also citing episodes in which it seemed to work. One basic point, like Mather's, was that visions, charms, astrology, conjuring, and prophecy depended on the Devil. Yet Hale was less rhetorical than Mather, perhaps because he seemed to think that no one in New England really practiced the "foreseeing art" or because he "excuse[d] . . . those that ignorantly" used such means of answering their "vain curiosity."[84]

Hale and Mather each drew on the reasoning of learned men in Europe in decrying certain beliefs as mere superstitions. There was much else in the learned tradition to deploy against practices like prophecy. For one, the ministers insisted on the point that revelations ceased with Christ and the apostles. For another, they evoked the natural world of medicine with its descriptions of the diseases of melancholy and lunacy.[85] For a third, they drew on a critique of dreams that originated with the Greeks. These lines of criticism converged in a book that Marmaduke Johnson, the Cambridge printer, published in 1668, an English translation of a sixteenth-century attack on the Anabaptists. Its main theme was the unreliability of visions, dreams, prophecy, and portents as manifested in the troubled history of Thomas Muntzer and his fellow Anabaptists. Equating dreams with "Satanical illusions," the French author described Muntzer as an opportunist who "preached dreams" in order to "cheat and deceive the poor ignorant people." Deception, not truth, "madness," not sanity, "rage," not peace—such were the qualities or consequences of this way of acting. Nor had Muntzer told the truth in citing portents like a rainbow to encourage his troops. As narrated by this critic, in another city Anabaptists went out into public "quite naked . . . crying after a horrible manner, Wo, wo, wo, Divine vengeance, Divine vengeance." Madmen all in their behavior, the Anabaptists were an object lesson in the danger of uncontrolled interpretation. The New England clergy pointed out this danger time and time again in justifying their repression of "enthusiasm" like Anne Hutchinson's.[86]

But the best defense of all was to take the offense and match prophecy for prophecy, portent for portent. The politicizing of Mary Dyer's "monster" was part of such a campaign, one in which a London printer happily cooperated by issuing *Newes from New England of A most strange and prodigious Birth* in 1642. Down through the years the story lived on—cited in the almanac of 1648, remembered by Nathaniel Mather, remarked on by English writers, retold by Nathaniel Morton in *New-Englands Memoriall*, disputed by Quakers anxious to defend a woman who became an early convert.[87]

Another spate of portent-mongering occurred around the Robert Child affair of 1646, occasioned by a visitor from England, Dr. Robert Child, who protested certain policies of the Massachusetts government. What made his protest dangerous was Child's threat to inform authorities in England that the colonists did not concede the authority of Parliament. Child and his associates made matters worse by revising the official version of God's providence. Instead of falling in with the idea that God "meanes to carry his Gospel westward, in these latter times of the world," they enumerated numerous "afflictions"—not the acts of special providence!—"which God hath pleased to exercise" the colonists "with, and that to the worst appearance." Child made much of events like the death of Edward Winslow's horse "as he came riding to Boston," and an accidental killing in Winslow's brother's family. According to his reading of these events, they signaled God's disfavor toward an "evil" Massachusetts government.

The magistrates and ministers responded in kind. Believing as they did in portents, and aware of their effect on public thinking, the defenders of the government hastened to adduce contrary evidence—an ally of Child's who became lame and others who lost property, including a stray horse. Help came from John Cotton, who told his Boston congregation that God had surely "manifested his gratious presence" to the colonists. Cotton prophesied God's vengeance on the group of malcontents: "speak[ing] as a poore prophet of the Lord according to the word of Grace in my text," he declared that the God who had brought the immigrants safely to New England would make sure that their "enemies shall not prosper . . . but shall bee taken every one of them in the snares they lay for it." He warned, too, that if any of Child's group remained hostile to New England, the Lord would treat them when they left by ship as he did Jonah: "That if any shall carry any Writings, Complaints against the people of GOD in that Country, it would be as Jonas in the ship."[88]

What happened thereafter was an extraordinary demonstration of God's providence. According to the chief propagandist for the colonists, the ship would experience "the terriblest passage that ever I heard on for extremitie of weather." The storm led certain passengers, remembering Cotton's sermon, to demand if anyone on board was carrying Child's petition to the English government. When a paper was produced, they threw it into the sea, whereupon the storm abated. Later in the voyage, the ship struck a sandbar, but by a "miracle" and a "deliverance" worked its way to safety.[89] Edward Winslow published this interpretation of the voyage to counter a quite different version of events offered by Robert Child's brother. What the frightened passengers threw overboard was only a "copy" of the petition; the original and other copies remained on board. No cause-and-effect relationship existed between the "great and wonderful deliverance from shipwreck" and "the throwing of that Writing over-board; for that was thrown over long before, at least 14 dayes."[90]

The humor of this exchange was completely lost on Winslow. Nor did any of the magistrates and ministers regard lightly the task of determining New England's providential situation. Early on, many English (and some of the colonists) were shocked by the harshness of the weather and hard times economically into speculating that it had been a mistake to leave England. In the 1640s, the triumph of the Puritans in England produced similar misgivings.[91] In later years, the effort to elaborate a "myth" of "errand" ran into difficulties as the colonists divided over issues like the halfway covenant and whether to allow Baptists and Quakers some degree of toleration. The struggle between friends and foes of the halfway covenant achieved focus in the much-disputed founding of Boston Third Church (pro-covenant) in 1669. The next spring, the Massachusetts General Court received a petition from many of the townspeople of Hadley in which they affirmed that portents like a recent comet were signs of God's disfavor with Third Church.[92] The ministers fought back with the aid of allies like Nathaniel Morton. But it was the outbreak of King Philip's War in the spring of 1675 that intensified this politics. What kind of judgment was the war? For Quakers, now achieving some small measure of accommodation, the war was punishment on those who made them suffer.[93] For ministers like Increase Mather, the war served as a warning to overcome "declension" and resume a pure way of life. So it went for episodes like Salem witchcraft, the dissolution of the charter government, and further wars against the Indians: always there were clergy quick to read the meaning of these events, yet always someone proposed an alternative interpretation.

No other writer plunged into this politics more intensively than Increase Mather. In book after book, as in scores of letters and unpublished sermons, he addressed the meaning of the wonder for his times. What he wrote and said illuminates the politicizing of this lore. Moreover, his efforts at interpretation make manifest new tensions between learned uses of the wonder and the popular tradition.

Mather used portents to enhance the message of reform. When two young boys fell through the ice on Fresh Pond in Cambridge and drowned while skating on a Sunday, he was quick to note the moral: God punished Sabbath-breakers. Thomas Beard had filled a long section of *The Theatre of Gods Judgements* with similar stories, some of which turned up anew on a broadside (originally English, but reprinted in Boston) that vividly portrayed four "divine judgments" on people who in one way or another broke the moral law. Such warnings of "declension" were endemic in the sermons Mather preached and wrote. Thus he represented King Philip's War as a warning sign from God, and in *Wo to Drunkards* told story after story of the consequences of this "sin," citing in addition to the judgments exercised by (or on) Turks, Indians, rain, and fires, "a Drunkard, that when he was drinking there hapned to be a Spider in the Pot, which he not observing, was poisoned, and died immediately." Always, portents served him as a means of promoting "Reformation," though Mather defined reformation to encompass problems Thomas Beard had never known, like the presence of the Quakers.[94]

Similarly, Mather used the lore of portents to sustain the special meaning of New England. After 1660, with Royalists again controlling England, it was harder to affirm the role that some in his father's generation had imagined for New England and the "Congregational Way." History, ever rich in clues as to God's intentions, seemed to signify the triumph of a wholly different party, the despised Anglicans, who even managed to set up a church in Boston! Yet, like his fellow ministers, Mather continued to insist that prodigies and portents revealed God's favoring of New England. When news reached Boston of "a great Persecution . . . against the Protestants in France," the government proclaimed a fast day for which Mather preached a sermon in which, citing Foxe and Clarke repeatedly, he insisted that the very success of the Catholics was a "token" that "destruction . . . [was] hastening upon" them. Another of his themes was the well-worn plea that godly people "are alwayes the subjects of great persecution: being much hated in the world. . . ." His efforts at collecting portents in the early 1680s served, he hoped, to place beyond all doubt the meaning of New England.[95]

Yet the contradictions increased with each passing year. The Baptists and the Quakers rejected his interpretation of events. "Contention" became more intense as churches split on issues like the halfway covenant, as merchants lobbied for acceptance of a royal government, as towns ran short of land. Even as he pleaded for reform, a few fellow ministers were suggesting an alternative interpretation of King Philip's War, one less keyed to special providences.[96] Lay men and women had reasons of their own for discounting Mather's prophecy-cum-moral exhortation, disliking, as some did, his harsh criticism of contemporary morals and resenting what he had to say about the Baptists and the Quakers. In the midst of war he received "reviling" letters; in 1676 two men came up to him after he had read aloud the General Court's new laws requiring moral reformation and told him "that when ministers did lay a solemn charge upon the people, it might take in the ignorant, but no rational men would regard what was said the more for it."[97] This incident, the foot-dragging of the magistrates on moral legislation (the laws they passed went largely unenforced), the criticism he received from Baptists and Quakers, the unchecked process of "declension," the report of an older colleague who, having read aloud the new laws (including all the fines and whippings prescribed as the punishments), found that the experience "seems to expose us to the reproach & contempt of ill minded people, and to give them occasion to say this & that against the ministers"— all these suggest that ordinary people were becoming more selective in their response to a lore of wonders that had become openly political.[98]

As consensus slowly dissolved in these decades, learned men like Mather had reasons of their own for becoming more selective. An avid reader of imported books, he was learning in the 1680s that scientists in Europe were questioning the physics of the Greeks and Romans. Comets were a case in point; a new understanding of their regularity was making it impossible to view them as providential warnings of impending judgment.[99] Another was the monster, which now seemed a freak of nature unrelated to the workings of the supernatural.[100] A wholly different reason for this disenchantment with the supernatural was the response within learned culture to the outbursts of "enthusiasm" that occurred in England in the midst of civil war. The excitement of those years stirred prophets by the score to declaim that God entrusted them with supernatural inspiration. Afterward, in the cool mood of Restoration England, Anglicans and scientists renounced visions, dreams, and other unseen wonders, like the drummer boy of Tidworth, as tricks of the imagination.[101] A medical interpretation of "enthusiasm" came to prevail, an interpretation tracing it to merely natural factors. Some, like Thomas Hobbes, extended this critique to witchcraft, adding to old doubts that it was being practiced by the women swept up in a witch-hunt.[102] Mather did not know of Hobbes directly. But close to home, in nearby Charlestown, lived Charles Morton, a minister-turned-academic who emigrated to Massachusetts in 1686. Harvard students were soon learning science from a textbook Morton had prepared in England, a far more up-to-date survey in which he denied comets and eclipses any role as portents, offered natural causes for thunder, lightning, and rainbows, and in general liberated nature from the lore of wonders.[103]

The pressures Mather faced to be selective show up in *Kometographia*, his treatise on the comet as a wonder. Desiring to present himself as a man of learning, though admitting he lacked access to the latest books, he assumed the stance of a skeptic judiciously weighing the evidence. Having noted, for example, that eclipses occurred somewhere in the world every year, he questioned whether these events were portents despite what other "Learned and Good Men" had said. In the same tone, he scoffed at an "Astrologer in London" and his prophesying what would follow from a comet. But it was a different tone in which he reckoned with the fact that "[t]here are those who think, that inasmuch as Comets may be supposed to proceed from natural causes, there is no speaking voice of Heaven in them. . . ." He resolved such contradictions by choosing to address a local audience; his "chief design," he announced, was "to inform and edifie the ordinary sort of Readers," not to please the learned. Thus he could reiterate the old associations between comets and their terrifying message, only briefly adding "some things of the nature, place, motion of Comets, which only such as have some skill in Astronomy can understand." [104]

Mather's double sense of audience carried over into his analysis of witchcraft, angels, and possession. Here, morever, he was forced to take account of the widespread recognition that some who died at Salem in 1692 were innocent. Meanwhile, reports continued to arrive from Europe of episodes of fraud, as when someone claimed to see an apparition. Mather was inclined to believe what he read about the Huguenots in Savoy, France, who heard voices singing to them. But as he rummaged through the books he had on hand, he began to realize that the sources he once took for granted should be treated with a grain of skepticism. He emerged from a rereading of the sources and rethinking of the issues with two statements: angels did exist, as did witchcraft and the Devil (to believe otherwise was "Atheism"); yet many of the events that, in popular tradition, were interpreted as supernatural interventions in the world were better understood as "delusions" that had natural causes or were signs of "Satanicall Possession." All in all, the witchcraft episode capped a reappraisal that ended with his questioning the testimony of Eusebius, proposing that appearances of angels have "in a great measure ceased," and doubting most reports of apparitions, dreams, and voices. By the middle of the 1690s, when he published *Angelographia,* he had also more or less conceded much of medicine and nature to the naturalists, agreeing with them that the source of certain spiritual phenomena was not the Holy Spirit but "enthusiasm." [105]

In thus voicing his mistrust of the lore of wonders, Mather fell in step with a broader movement that a historian has aptly named the "reform of popular culture." [106] Here, the meaning of this term was that certain clergy redefined the line between religion and mere superstition—redefined it in such a way that some of what had once been shared in common by lay people and the clergy now was being designated as improper or mistaken. There was nothing new about this effort; Protestants had first redefined this line in breaking with the church of Rome, and redefined it once again in response to the Anabaptists. Increase Mather surely knew of what was said against the Anabaptists and their visions. He knew of Anne Hutchinson, and how a synod which included both his father and stepfather had declared that revelation ended with the apostles. He knew all the reasons why astrologers should not attribute binding power to the stars and planets. In the last two decades of the century, he extended the critique of superstition to include bibliomancy and the healing practices of cunning folk. He agreed with William Perkins and Richard Bernard that the methods of detecting witches must be sharply limited to confession and the testimony of two witnesses; scornful of the test of throwing suspects into water to see if they would drown or float, he had allies in the clergy of Connecticut, who ruled in 1692 (when consulted by the magistrates) against the water trial. In all likelihood, the reluctance of the magistrates to enforce jury verdicts—a reluctance manifested as early as the 1660s—paralleled his growing doubts about what was put in evidence by ordinary people.[107]

By the 1690s, therefore, Increase Mather and his fellow clergy[108] were participating in the dissolution of the lore of wonders that Anglicans and rationalists initiated in the middle of the century. Ahead lay publications like Thomas Robie's anonymous *Letter To a Certain Gentleman,* in which Robie, a Harvard graduate, ridiculed the thinking of the common people, who, as he advised his "gentleman," regarded as "amazing" a meteor that Robie knew had "Natural" causes. He went on to dismiss a whole way of thinking:

> As to Prognostications from [meteors] I utterly abhor and detest 'em all, and look upon these to be but the Effect of Ignorance and Fancy; for I have not so learned Philosophy or Divinity, as to be dismayed at the Signs of Heaven. . . .

Via such remarks, Robie manifested a self-consciousness of separation from the culture of the people; he rejected what had once prevailed, a common culture of the lore of wonders.[109] What also emerged in the early decades of the eighteenth century was a more generalized perception of God's providence, an interpretation that emphasized its regularities and not the interruptions that so fascinated Beard and Clarke.[110]

Yet Increase Mather did not fully overthrow the tradition he invoked so often in his sermons before 1692. The reality of witches was an article of faith, as was the presence of a Devil who enticed men and women into covenant. He continued to accept as true some stories of the supernatural, and in speaking of God's providence, he lingered on its mystery.[111] His son Cotton, who shared with him the recognition that the Devil had deceived witch-hunters, filled the *Magnalia Christi Americana* with scores of events he interpreted as wonders. Condemned in the case of Anabaptists, dreams returned to center stage in the pages of the *Mag-*

nalia as authentic promptings from the supernatural. So did prophesy-ing. Thus he dared report that John Cotton and John Wilson learned in dreams who would be selected by the Boston church to succeed them. Prophetic dreams had come to James Noyes, the minister of Newbury; his son recorded, "I have heard him tell . . . that the great changes of his life had been signified to him before-hand by *dreams*." John Eliot, the great preacher to the Indians, "often had strange *forebodings* of things that were to come." And Mather here added his own affirmation that "I have been astonished at some of his predictions, that . . . were followed with exact accomplishments."

But of all these men the most astonishing was John Wilson, the min-ister who had once shared dream lore with John Winthrop. Wilson, so we learn from Mather, used prayer to affect events; as chaplain of the expedition sent out to subdue the Pequots he had saved someone from death by impromptu prayers that deflected an arrow from its target. He had dreams that worked as prophecy, and his "blessings" healed the sick.

Yet Mather could not wholly endorse such proceedings. Though he went on to affirm the truth of witchcraft (including some events that involved magic), he also noted that John Wilson preached a sermon crit-icizing the claims of "opinionists" that God spoke to them in dreams. After writing of John Eliot he reaffirmed the doctrine that true proph-ecy must coincide with what the Scripture declares, a principle that worked (he said) against the Quakers. Like his father in *An Essay*, Cotton criti-cized the "little sorceries" of people who "would . . . cure hurts with spells" and use horseshoes to ward off the Devil. Responsive though he was to arguments against the long tradition of prophetic dreams and portents, Mather nonetheless gave far more weight to that tradition than to its alternative.[112]

If in his retelling of such stories Mather seemed another Clarke or Beard, he had company in English writers who continued to affirm the truth of certain wonders and to report their sensations of the supernat-ural. A writer who had roots in Puritan nonconformity, Daniel Defoe, defended the "reality" of apparitions, publishing in 1706 *A True Relation of the Apparition of One Mrs. Veal*, an apparition for which he vouched himself.[113] Another nonconformist, the minister George Trosse, repeat-edly experienced divine messages, or so he believed. A *Life* of Trosse published in the early eighteenth century reported these experiences as unquestioned fact.[114]

Where Mather differed from these writers was in linking his belief in dreams and apparitions to the situation of the ministers. It is clear that he regarded ministers in general as gifted with extraordinary powers, along with certain individual laymen. But in lavishing attention on a man like Wilson whom the Quakers had denounced (and Anne Hutchinson, before them), Mather was defending the authority of everyone in office in New England. In effect, he invested his position with a strange two-sidedness: the power both to bless and to wreak destruction. Thus he told a classic wonder story of how someone rebuked by a minister for working on a fast day, and who "made him an obstinate and malapert answer . . . came home . . . [and] found one of his children suddenly dead; upon this he could have no rest in his mind, until he came to this 'reprover in the gate,' with humble and many tokens of repentance." Thus too he revealed the doubleness of blessings by John Eliot: "If he said of any affair, 'I cannot bless it!', it was a worse omen to it. . . ." All this was like magic, albeit godly magic.[115]

The many levels of these texts forbid any simple separation of elite belief from popular. True, the lore of wonders was falling out of favor within learned culture. Yet tradition remained strong, and clergy like the Mathers, anxious to enhance their role, continued to invoke the wonder. But in doing so they had to face the fact that ordinary people sometimes disagreed with them. In effect, the clergy and the people were rethinking the relationship between the lore of wonders and the message of God's judgment. Even in the sixteenth century some lay people had resisted this connection, as when England's Queen Elizabeth rejected the advice of certain of her bishops that an earthquake was a portent of her death.[116] Anglicans, in general, shrugged off Puritan manipulations of the wonder to support a cause like reform of the Sabbath, just as, in the 1650s, moderates among the Puritans fought off would-be prophets who denounced a "hireling" ministry. How lay men and women in New England acted to select among competing versions of the wonder is not easy to discern. What is certain is that they held at arm's distance the specifics of the preachers' message about taverns, drinking, and the like.[117] Interpretation, always open-ended, had become less clear thanks to excess special pleading and to growing doubts about the meaning of God's providence.

III

EVEN HAD there been no politicking of the kinds here described, prodigies and portents would have triggered contradictory feelings in most people. The reason, in a word, was that these events were surrounded by ambiguity. The case of William Lilley is indicative. In the 1640s this astrologer was on the side of good when he complied with Parliament's request that he foretell the King's defeat. But it was a different matter when one of his books came into the hands of Katherine Harrison; the neighbors who declared that "she had read Mr. Lilly's book in England" were voicing a suspicion of such lore and the extraordinary powers that it could bestow. Much else was similarly good or bad, sanctioned or forbidden, depending on circumstances and the individuals concerned—dreams certainly, hearing voices from the heavens, prophesying when the Second Coming would occur, and cursing those who wronged you. A curse pronounced by Increase Mather was presumably a righteous act, but not one pronounced by Quakers.[118]

The contradictions that engulfed the wonder were sustained, not resolved, by the printers and booksellers who manufactured newssheets, chapbooks, and broadside ballads that conveyed the lore of wonders to so many people. Their allies were writers who specialized in tales of preternatural events. Well versed in all the themes that made the wonder story so appealing, these writers produced tales of judgment that rivaled any jeremiad. They took on the guise of prophet and offered up a heady mixture of apocalypticism and astrology. The repertory of these writers was limited only by their powers of imagination and the constraints of the literary form at hand. When imagination failed, they plagiarized competitors or borrowed wholesale from the past.

Early in the seventeenth century, one man active in the business of preparing wonder stories was John Trundle, "that busy miracle monger and father of lies," as someone at the time described him. Two of the stories he included in *A Miracle, of Miracles* (1614) were lifted from publications of the 1580s and redated, one of them to 1613, the other as "lately happened at" an English town, even though, in the original, the event occurred in Germany. The same year as *A Miracle, of Miracles*, Trundle also published *True and wonderfull. A discourse relating a strange and monstrous serpent (or dragon)* that lived in "St. Leonard's Forest" in Sussex. His was a fictive dragon, as were other tales of dragons put out by the broadside publishers. Equally fictive was a mixture of astrology and prophecy, all of it inspired by hostility to James, the Duke of York, that Benjamin Harris issued in 1679. Meanwhile, other printer-publishers were falsifying the imprints of almanacs; Harris, once he returned from New England to the London book trade, stole the title of a widely selling almanac for publications of his own.[119]

Writers and booksellers toyed with the principle of "truth" so crucial to the culture of the Word. Their work offended writers who conceived of printed books as vehicles of divine utterance. Some who took offense were also bothered by the taste of readers who enjoyed ballad tales of monster births.

> Let Natures causes (which are too profound)
> For every blockish sottish *Pate* to sound.)
> Produce some monster: some rare spectacle:
> Some seaven yeares Wonder: Ages miracle:
> Bee it a worke of nere so slight a waight,
> It is recorded up in Metre straight. . . .

Cultural snobbery moved another writer to denounce rhymed versions of the Bible, along with readers who liked "new accounts of hangings at Tyburn and descriptions of monstrosities." Pursuing the same vein of criticism, the Englishman John Earle sneered at the "pot-poet" who composes "Gods Iudgements . . . sitting in a Baudy-house." It was common to denounce these writers and their printer-patrons as "mercenarie liers," men who abused words like "miracle" in order to play tricks on simple-minded readers.[120]

All these remarks point to tension between learned culture and the printers' version of the world of wonders. Yet in violating truth, printers and hack writers were not that unusual. Godly writers such as Foxe reiterated stories that most surely were not true, stories they respected nonetheless as fables that conveyed a higher truth. Fables, marvels, tales of "preternatural" events—as in Foxe's *Book of Martyrs,* so in Increase Mather's *Essay* and cheap forms of print, such kinds of writing passed as versions of reality. Fact and fiction intermingled. Nor were printers unique in their fascination with the theme of violence. Nature was for them a matter of destructive storms and "fiery" meteors that verged on being instruments of human death—and often were, as in the lightning storm that Trundle described in *A Miracle, of Miracles.* Violence was a feature of the witchcraft stories, tales of martyrs undergoing torture, and narratives of murders. But godly writers followed suit.

Where the difference lay, and why godly writers did have reason to be troubled, was the way in which hack writers packaged their material. In their hands the moral message shrank to a bare minimum, a formula to recite before turning to the substance of the story. Or else they inserted a degree of playfulness. How this worked is clear from one hack writer's books, including his retelling of the witchcraft stories Increase Mather published in *An Essay.*

Nathaniel Crouch—R. Burton, to call him by his pseudonym—combined the trades of printer and writer in Restoration England. He specialized in inexpensive books, many of them histories of a sort. (Young Benjamin Franklin bought "R. Burton's Historical Collections; they were small Chapmen's Books and cheap, 40 or 50 in all.") From histories he turned easily to wonders, using scissors and paste to put together *Won-*

derful Prodigies of Judgment and Mercy, discovered in above Three Hundred Memorable Histories (1682), *Delights for the Ingenious* (1684), and *The Kingdom of Darkness: or, The History of Daemons, Spectres, Witches, Apparitions, Possessions, Disturbances, and other supernatural Delusions, and malicious Impostures of the Devil* (1688). The second of these books was superficially moralistic, for its form was that of emblems (pictures), each with an interpretative poem attached. In keeping with the genre, Burton left the meaning of his emblems somewhat cryptic. But he turned the process of deciphering them into a game—literally a game, for at the back each book contained a little pinwheel for readers to use in finding the emblem that had meaning for their lives. In his preface Crouch anticipated being censured for this device; knowing as he did that godly people hated games of chance as contravening Providence, he insisted that his "Lotterie" was harmless. His real excuse was that he was in business to sell lots of books: complaining that "solid and serious Treatises" have "many times undone the Bookseller," and wishing to "advance" his "Profits," he "was moved to invent somewhat which might be more likely to please the Populace. . . ."[121]

When Crouch put together *The Kingdom of Darkness,* he faced the same dilemma as the Mathers did in writing about witchcraft: whether to concede to critics, or persist in representing apparition tales as true. Crouch played both sides of the street. In his opening sentence he adopted an equivocal position, labeling (like the Mathers) critics of this lore as "Atheists and Sadducces," but acknowledging the judgment that "all stories . . . are either fabulous or to be ascribed to Natural Causes." So it went throughout his preface. In the text itself he took pains to cite the sources of his stories and to insist on their truthfulness, promising that he himself would "only relate bare matters of Fact." Yet he struck a different note in affirming, "I shall not positively assert nor deny any thing, but having met with a story to this purpose shall here insert it." Thus licensed, he went on to retell fables of enchanted cats, the magic of Ann Bodenham, students raising devils, witch enchantments causing storms, and dead bodies coming back to life. Interspersed with these adventures were narratives he borrowed almost intact from *An Essay*—the enchanted house of William Morse, the possession of Elizabeth Knapp, the story of Mercy Disborough. Crouch had a good eye for detail. In excerpting yet another published text, Alexander Roberts's *Treatise of Witchcraft,* he eliminated all of Roberts's lengthy disquisition on witchcraft, sparing only the "true Narrative" of one woman's witchcraft.

The commercial purpose showed through in such excerpts. It did also (I would argue) in the frankness with which Crouch repeated fables from the past. And though he proposed certain stories as persuasive even to "the Atheist," the tone of voice, the framework of ideas, never implied that the godly must unite against the Devil. No plea for reformation, no moral purpose intruded in the stories. They were entertainment, like the pictures that went with them, pictures he recycled without much regard for how they fit a given tale.[122]

Using pseudonyms and false imprints, writers such as Crouch inhabited a zone of freedom, a space that let them transgress crucial boundaries in the culture of the godly. Hence Cotton Mather's complaint about "Wretched books . . . among which, I wonder that a blacker brand is not set upon that fortune-telling wheel, which that sham-scribler that goes under the letters of *R. B.* has promised in his *Delights for the Ingenious,* as an 'honest and pleasant recreation.' . . ."[123] But did the freedom of the printing office carry over to the readers of cheap books and broadsides? Did lay men and women find a message in a portent story different from the moralizing framework that contained the tale? And why did local printers produce descriptions of earthquakes, comets, and prophetic dreams, some of them complete with illustrations, long after 1700? It seems certain that portent lore persisted in the culture of the people—the same people who continued to buy and memorize *The Day of Doom,* and who did not worry quite as much as Mather about playfulness. What these people found in wonder stories was like melodrama in containing elements of fear, suspense, and violence. Printers knew their audience!

IV

EVEN THOUGH the wonder became fictive in the hands of printers, and though partisans of different causes shamelessly politicized the process of interpretation, people never stopped believing that God signaled his intentions through extraordinary events like a fire or an earthquake. The colonists who kept diaries or wrote letters repeatedly referred to prodigies and portents as having real significance; in these private statements, as in public, they perceived the wonder as betokening God's judgments.

When Michael Wigglesworth, a Harvard tutor, learned of a "great fire" that destroyed part of Boston, he wrote in his diary that

> my heart was much affected and dejected within me upon
> deep thoughts of these things and what I have heard god
> speak to me in his word, (for he met with sundry of my
> sins and gave dreadful examples of gods judgments that
> should have warned me from them). . . .

Writing of the battles they were fighting in King Philip's War, other men consistently referred to victories and defeats as providential. Still others manifested a mentality of fearfulness by the way they behaved when they thought the Day of Judgment had arrived—the maid who fled to her master when she saw reflected in the clouds another Boston fire, Samuel Sewall's children when an earthquake shook their home.[124] The same kinds of people demonstrated time and time again their belief that dreams, strange sounds, and accidents had occult or prophetic meaning. Not always, but often, people traced misfortune to the powers of a witch. Those who became Quakers believed that they could prophesy. So did others who were orthodox; the sense of having special knowledge of the future—or of serving as the voice of God—was endemic in this culture.

A world so full of wonders, of supernatural forces that seeped into daily life, was a world that many different kinds of people essayed to interpret. The process of interpretation remained open-ended. In part this happened because stories circulated in bewildering confusion, and by routes that no one could control—conversations, rumor, letters, and public demonstrations, and in such forms of print as broadsides and cheap pamphlets. Printers played a crucial role in keeping older lore afloat, and in adding to the stock of stories. Surprisingly, the same role suited learned men like Beard and Clarke. Never, in New England, did the learned culture impose systematic order on the meaning of the wonder. Nor could the clergy silence or suppress the prophesying that lay people or outsiders like the Quakers practiced. It was in the very nature of the wonder that it be "surprising," that it run against the grain of routine expectations. In a culture that empowered every layman to interpret Scripture, the wonder was as meaningful to ordinary men and women—and as open to quotation or retelling—as the Book of Psalms. Bewildered though they often were by prodigies and portents, lay people in New England were free to accept or reject the meanings for these events that the clergy might propose.

Yet the clergy also taught them to prefer a certain set of meanings. One of these concerned God's providential guidance of New England and, more generally, of Protestants. Here the clergy more or less reiterated attitudes that lay writers also voiced, and that had their great original in Foxe's *Book of Martyrs*. A more distinctive meaning, though not solely voiced by clergy, had to do with morals and the good society. A long line of clergy, from Thomas Beard to Cotton Mather, insisted that the lesson of the wonder was that people must give up "Sabbathbreaking" and behave in keeping with a moral code. John Winthrop voiced a broader vision of what portents signified for daily life, an ethic of community or fellowship.

Out of all these uses emerged the most common meaning that the clergy offered for the wonder, that it signified impending judgment. In one sense there was nothing new in this interpretation; the motif of judgment (or disaster) was prefigured in the Bible, the lore descended from antiquity, and the message of exempla in the Middle Ages. The story line of judgment was in every sense a cliché of the times, a convention that hack writers used as freely as the preachers. Yet what made this theme distinctive as employed by the clergy was its kinship to their message about sin. For them a world of wonders was a world of fallen sinners who must learn to plead for forgiveness from a sovereign, judging God. The wonder served this end by instructing people in the doctrine of God's providence and its corollary, the message of man's weakness in God's presence.

> But we should consider that the Most High God doth sometimes deal with men in a way of Absolute Soveraignty. . . . If he does destroy the perfect with the wicked, and Laugh at the Trial of the innocent . . . who shall enter into his Counsels! who has given Him a Charge over the Earth! or who had disposed the whole world! Men are not able to give an account of his ordinary Works, much less of his secret Counsels, and the Dark Dispensations of his Providence.[125]

This evocation of a sovereign God and his "Dark Dispensations" may have been designed to impress laymen who ignored the lesson of the wonder. It was in the preachers' interest to emphasize the insecurity of sinners, to paint the course of life as prone to abrupt interruption.

Hence the many references to sudden death. It exemplified the quickness—the terrifying quickness—by which God could render judgment:

> . . . the voice of the Lord in this Providence [is] Calling upon all that hear of it and, saying Prepare for Death! Prepare for Death! Prepare for Death! . . . The best man in this Congregation, yea upon the face of the earth, may for ought that any one can say, be (as Moses was) suddenly taken out of the world.

Writing to console a mourning widow, a New England minister invoked the long-persisting echoes of the wheel of fortune, reminding her (and readers of his sermon) of how "the late and present rouling posture of the wheels of Providence" had overturned great emperors and caused them to tremble when they saw the king of terrors approach.[126] If death loomed as fearful, and if preachers played upon these fears in order to impose a system of repentance on the people, the lore of wonders was in part their means of doing so. But did lay people in New England turn from contemplating wonders to the practice of this kind of piety?

CHAPTER 3

THE
MEETINGHOUSE

ANYWHERE, at any time, wonders could occur. All space was open to the influence of the supernatural. But only in a meetinghouse did people gather to hear sermons. There they took their children to be baptized; there they celebrated the Lord's Supper. There too they assembled on the Sabbath, the one day of the week that was holy, a moment infused with anticipation of the coming kingdom. Bounded by a special sense of time, bounded by the rituals that occurred uniquely in this place, the members of the gathered church affirmed in covenanting with one another that the "church" was wholly different from the "world."

This perception of the church was implanted in popular belief in Elizabethan England as reformers campaigned against the "mixt multitude" of the Church of England. By the time the colonists reached New England, this campaign had ripened into the felt principle that "there should be a difference between [the] precious and the vile," and its corollary, that the church should *exclude* "unbelievers" and the "disobedient." The brave men and women who crossed the Atlantic on the *Mayflower* in 1620 had more reason than most to perceive themselves as "poor servants of God," and to have memories of their being "scoffed and scorned by the profane multitude." But the people who settled Massachusetts and Connecticut also had a social memory of "hatred" and would quickly institutionalize an extreme separation of the profane from the godly.[1] The church was where this separation became manifest—where in ceremonies like baptism and the Lord's Supper some came forward to participate while others were excluded. Each time a group of people organized themselves into a congregation, they acted out a rite of separation, passing from the world into a disciplined community in which they tried to live according to an ideal moral code.

The everyday meaning of religion thus involved the social experience of withdrawing from one kind of community and uniting with another. Back in England this process often provoked conflict between the "godly" members of a parish and their clergyman, or, if he was on their side, between competing factions in the town. There, the ideal of a pure church was not easily turned into practice. Conflict ebbed among the immigrants, however, for most of them agreed on what they wanted, and consensus had the backing of the authorities.

Yet the reigning myth of purity, a myth that entered deeply into popular religion, somehow failed to satisfy large numbers of the colonists, as its consequences for their children and grandchildren slowly became visible. A new kind of conflict thus emerged by 1650 between men and women who preferred a policy of strictness and those who were thereby denied, but still desired, access to the sacrament of baptism. Very often people came to disagree with their ministers, a disagreement that by 1680 also touched the meaning of the Lord's Supper. Despite the different social circumstances in New England, lay men and women increasingly contested with one another and the clergy the terms of access to the church and the nature of the sacraments.

It was not every week, or even every year, that men and women stood up in the meetinghouse and described their experience of piety. The relative rarity of such occasions made them all the more precious, and their impact all the stronger. To hear these testimonies was to feel the presence of the Holy Spirit; these were moments that affirmed the church as spiritual community. So Roger Clap, a layman, suggested in remembering "the many Tears that have been shed in Dorchester Meeting-House at such Times, both by those that have declared God's Work on their Souls, and also by those that heard them."[2] The bonding that went on among church members was furthered by the message of the ministers. This message had two parts. One part concerned "duties," or the obligation to obey the moral law of God. Inheriting a list of negatives and positives from late-Elizabethan Puritans, the New England clergy harped on these as though they were the substance of religion: strict observance of the Sabbath and temperance in drinking, daily prayer and reading from the Bible. Every child and adult in New England was drilled incessantly in "duties" as crucial to the task of overcoming sin. The other message of the preachers concerned spiritual experience. They asked people to undergo the work of grace, which in essence meant experiencing the curse of sin and—via striving for repentance—the promise of the gospel. Men and women in New England took as model the Christ who went into the wilderness and wrestled with temptation. According to the preachers, they would have to struggle (a common metaphor was "war" or "warfare") before there was any hope of overcoming sin. In their presence the minister spelled out the drama of unending warfare between Christ and Satan. Their lives, too, were caught up in this struggle, which sometimes meant that they were deprived of assurance of salvation.

Thanks in part to sermons, lay men and women became fluent in the language of spiritual experience. Farmers, housewives, artisans, merchants, sailors, aspiring scholars—all went away from the meetinghouse with an understanding of themselves that they owed substantially to their ministers. They saw the Christian life as they were taught to see it. Returning to their homes, they learned these lessons anew from catechisms, from notes they took on sermons and repeated afterward, and from books the ministers had written. At home they also opened up their Bibles, perhaps to read again the verses explicated in a sermon. In doing so, however, they sometimes found that Scripture did not coincide with what the minister had said. Empowered by their literacy and by their access to other printed narratives than sermons, lay men and women possessed the confidence to speak for themselves about the ways in which they had experienced the workings of the law and grace. Having once acquired the basic foundations of their world-view from meetinghouse and minister, they were then capable of building upon these foundations, of exercising self-confident, independent judgment on the major issues of their lives.

Nonetheless, for many this self-confidence was tinged with doubt, and the practice of their faith with inconsistency. Popular religion encompassed an ideal of piety that people may have reverenced even when they did not wholly follow its prescriptions. Here, too, was ground for conflict with the ministers, who complained after 1640 of "declension" or of "formalism" in religious practice. Where we must begin in trying to describe the piety of ordinary people is with the words they used themselves, before we try to estimate the difference between ideal and reality.

I

THE PLAIN meetinghouse in Cambridge was the setting in which scores of men and women spoke in public of their struggle to perceive and "take hold of" the "promise" of the gospel. The minister of the congregation, Thomas Shepard, recorded more than sixty such "confessions" in a notebook. The minister of Wenham, John Fiske, copied testimonies into the church records, and the minister of Malden, Michael Wigglesworth, incorporated several more into his diary. Still others, dating from 1700 and 1701, survive in a notebook kept by Timothy Edwards, the minister of Windsor in Connecticut.³ In these towns, as undoubtedly in others,⁴ many different kinds of people—young and middle-aged, men and women, servants, yeomen farmers, artisans, young college students—stood up before the congregation to describe their piety. Ordinary people also voiced what they knew and felt in narratives they wrote or in private conversation with friends or relatives, or, more rarely, under pressure in a courtroom, as in the Salem witchcraft trials.

These texts tell a common story, the "progress" of the soul to Christ. It was a story rich in dramatic possibilities, as in the terrifying moments when the soul seemed on the "brink of hell" or the Devil beckoned with a tempting offer of release from sin. In describing such experiences, lay writers sometimes turned them into allegory. This literary mode came easily to John Bunyan, the English layman who wrote *Pilgrim's Progress*. The motifs and symbolism of *Pilgrim's Progress* were part of a vernacular tradition that reached the colonists quite independently of Bunyan's narrative.⁵ The same elements of drama—the same motifs and symbolism—figured in the stories people told in Cambridge meetinghouse. Lay men and women in New England drew on a vernacular tradition, a shared thaumaturgy of experience.

Like Bunyan and so many of their English contemporaries, these people relied on the Bible for the central metaphors and images of spiritual experience. And like Bunyan, who read chapbooks in his youth as well as books like Dent's *The Plain Mans Pathway,* they acquired their facility with language from many intervening texts and visual materials. As in the case of the wonder stories, we must infer a process of transmission that conveyed a particular vocabulary from pre-Reformation Christianity to seventeenth-century New England.⁶ How was it, for example, that the themes of medieval lyric poetry reappeared in a different culture? Or certain motifs of the *Gesta Romanorum,* a bulky compilation of old stories that were Christianized in the Middle Ages? One medium of transmission was the imagery in emblem books of warfare between Christ and Satan. Another was the vast literature that played upon the theme of *vanitas.* This too was rendered in an imagery familiar to New England painters and printmakers; in Thomas Smith's self-portrait, he rests his right hand on a skull that sits next to a written text, a poem that declares:

> Why why should I the world be minding
> therein a World of Evils finding;
> Then farewell World: Farewell thy Jarres
> thy Joies thy Toiles thy Wiles thy Warres.
> Truth sounds Retreat: I am not Sorye.⁷

The lore of wonders contained similar assertions, while helping sustain the dramatic framework of Satan warring against Christ.

One other source that can be specified is Foxe's *Book of Martyrs*. Important in transmitting the lore of wonders, the documents that Foxe assembled in his great collection include letters of advice from those awaiting execution to friends and family on the nature of the Christian life. The language of these letters was woven out of metaphors that refer back to Scripture. In the "wilderness" that was the world, the Christian must "build" his life on Christ, the only safe "foundation." There was but one pathway to heaven, the "strait gate and narrow way that leadeth unto life, which few do find." The martyr John Bradford, most prolific of the letter-writers, went on to warn against "hypocrisy and carnal security." True faith was rooted in the "heart." Any other kind was sure to be exposed as false in the struggle against Satan. Likening the Christian life to "warfare," the martyrs compared the godly few to "soldiers" who must endure "adversity" before attaining victory:

> And, forasmuch as the life of man is a perpetual warfare upon earth, let us run with you unto the battle that is set before us, and like good warriors of Jesus Christ, please him who hath chosen us to be soldiers. . . .

These metaphors conveyed a message that Christians must manifest their faith in action. There was "work" to do, the work of overcoming sin, of striving for "good conscience," of "bringing forth fruit worthy of repentance." Religion was a matter of incessant striving to defeat the evil in the world as well as in oneself.[8]

The language of these letters became the language of the lay tradition. With that language passed the propositions that but few were saved, and that faith entailed repentance and an active striving against sin. Not from any formal treatise of theology but from testimonies like those found in Foxe did most people in New England gain their understanding of the Christian life. They learned that no matter how routine or humble someone's situation seemed, the real meaning of existence was far grander. They learned, too, specific techniques for discerning the significance of what it was they felt and saw. The first and most essential of these techniques was the practice of consulting Scripture. A second was to pray. As the merchant Laurence Saunders, who went early to the stake in Mary Tudor's reign, said in writing to his wife, "Wherefore . . . let us, in the name of our God, fight lustily to overcome the flesh, the devil, and the world. What our harness and weapons be in this kind of fight, look in Ephesians vi.; and pray, pray, pray."[9] A third technique was learning how to recognize the patterns of God's providence in everyday events; a fourth was knowing how to link the "types" and metaphors of Scripture with events in their lives.[10]

Thus it was that men and women in New England learned to analyze the inward workings of the Holy Spirit and to recognize the larger structure of God's providence. For some, this recognition was confined to a diary. John Hull thus undertook to write down "Some Passages of God's Providence about myself and in relation to myself; penned down that I may be the more mindful of, and thankful for, all God's dispensations Towards men."[11] Michael Metcalfe of Dedham, a weaver back in England but a farmer here, left but a single page of private text in which he commemorated the mercy of God that enabled him to escape the "ceremonies" of the English church. Recalling how he suffered "many times much affliction, for the sake of religion" in old England, Metcalfe remembered vividly the "many dangers, troubles, vexations and sore afflictions" that complicated his first attempt to transport all his family to New England. Succeeding on a second try, he asked that "Glory be given to God, for all his mercies to me."[12] Edward Johnson expanded on these themes in a published book, *The Wonder-Working Providence of Sions Saviour.* Selectman, town clerk, church member, and captain of the citizens' militia in Woburn, Johnson employed several of the metaphors that pervade Foxe's *Book of Martyrs:* the colonists as "Soldiers" in Christ's "Army," the "wilderness" as the place where the colonists would "re-build the most glorious Edifice of Mount Sion." Like the writers of wonder lore, Johnson relished the surprising inversion that Christ performed in bringing "sudden, and unexpected destruction" on opponents of the Puritans. For him the overriding theme, as indicated by his running title, was the providence of God.[13]

Mary Rowlandson, wife of the minister in Lancaster, drew on the providence tradition in describing the weeks she passed as captive of the Indians in 1676. Her tale was rich in pathos, as in her account of the moaning of the "wounded babe" she carried in her arms, and his death some ten days into their captivity. She told of being famished, and of faltering from exhaustion as she struggled through rough country with her captors. There came easily to her a sense that her "doleful" suffering had its parallel in the lives of Jacob and Lot's wife. Thus, too, she compared herself to the Prodigal Son confessing, "Father, I have sinned against heaven, and in thy sight" (Luke 15:21). There came easily to her also a way of writing that conflated her "wilderness" experience with events in Scripture. The smoke that rose above the burning houses of Lancaster was "ascending to heaven," like the smoke that rose above embattled cities in the Old Testament (see Joshua 8:20–21; Judges 20:38) or that which "ascendeth up for ever and ever" from those who suffer in hell (Revelation 14:10–11). When she was restored to the English settlements and had "bread again," the real food she craved was the "honey" that comes "out of the rock," or God's blessing. Like the martyrs she had surely read about, she praised a God who worked the most amazing inversions—turning victory into defeat or defeat into victory, and delivering the weak and helpless from the proud and mighty: "and though they had made a pit, in their own imaginations, as deep as hell for the Christians that summer, yet the Lord hurled themselves into it." "Victory and deliverance"—these were the work of a "wonderful power" that sustained the faithful.[14]

In such narratives, pattern emerged out of the relationship between individual experience and the providential history of God's people over time. When other men and women wrote or talked about their lives, as in testifying of the "work of grace" before a body of church members, the frame of reference was the "strait and narrow way" that few would find—the way that led to Christ, the moment of "election" to salvation. Hence the questions Roger Clap remembered people asking of each other in the 1630s: "How shall we go to Heaven? Have I true Grace wrought in my Heart? Have I Christ or no?"[15] Hundreds gave their answers to these questions as part of the process of becoming a church member. Early on, the procedure was established in most congregations that those who wished to become members must "make ther faith & holynes visible" by something more emphatic than taking part in the rite of baptism. That extra something included evidence of "a civille restrained life and some religious duties performed," as the founders of the church in Dedham put it. But the more significant task was to make visible the "inward worke of faith and grace."[16] Thus it happened that some decades before Bunyan wrote his tale *Pilgrim's Progress*, the colonists were standing up in church to describe how God worked on their hearts.

The starting point for most of those who testified was how they learned to see themselves as sinners worthy of damnation. William Manning told the Cambridge church of feeling "loathe and ashamed to make my condition . . . known" because he realized he was a "gross" sinner. William Andrews and Jane Winship were convinced of their "guilt" as sinners. John Fessenden acknowledged having "lived in sin." The people testifying in John Fiske's congregation spoke similarly of "unworthiness." The wife of Phineas Fiske thought of herself as in a "worse condition than any toad" by reason of the sins she had committed. She named specific failures, as did Mary Goldsmith, who recalled "the discovery of her sin of disobedience to them over her and her unfaithfulness in her particular calling." The first sentence of Francis Moore's confession in Cambridge sums up what all these people said about themselves: "The Lord revealed his estate to him that he was miserable."[17]

Some people generalized about their sinfulness, as Mary Goldsmith did in reporting the "discovery of her accursed condition in the state of nature." Thereby she voiced a fundamental doctrine of Christianity, that everyone participated in the fall of Adam. "In Adam's Fall / We sinn'd all," ran a couplet in the *New England Primer,* and New England catechisms taught the same fundamental principle. Few people in their testimonies referred specifically to Adam or to the doctrine by name, though Brother Jackson's maid "saw my original corruption," Edward Kemp of Wenham was "convinced of his evil condition by nature," Joan White had "heard of original sin," and Sister Batchelor, perhaps responding to a question about "the doctrine of original sin," spoke of being convinced of it "from Isaiah 44:22."[18]

People were more apt to talk about the state of mind and heart that followed on the heels of "conviction of sin." They used powerful words—"fearful," "accursed," "terrified," and "torment"—in speaking of their feelings. The metaphors that emerged in their speech were equally evocative, as when Sister Geere of Wenham likened the "fearful state of unbelievers under God's wrath" to "a continual dropping of scalding lead." John Stansby of Cambridge, who said of himself that he "came into the world a child of hell and if ever any a child of [the] devil," spoke of having realized that his "hellish, devilish nature" was "opposite to God and goodness," and therefore that he lay before "the brink of hell." John Furnell, having learned of general sin, "considered I must to hell if I die in that condition." Elizabeth Olbon thought of sin as something "heavy," and its taste as "bitterness." As in the lore of wonders, the theme of sudden, unexpected death was frightening to people worried whether they had overcome their state of sin. Martha Collins, recalling the threat of sudden death that Jesus held before a certain rich man ("thou fool, this night thy soul shall be required of thee," Luke 12:20), was "affected" in her "heart." A young man, confessing he had "many slavish fears of the devil," worried when he went to bed "lest before morning I should fall to eternal sorrow."[19]

Yet fear was held in check by the bright hope of grace. That hope rested on the "Promise," Christ's promise of forgiveness and free grace to those with faith. Candidates for membership found that promise stated in Isaiah 55:1, "Ho, every one that thirsteth, come ye to the waters," and in Matthew 11:28, "Come unto me, all ye that labor and are heavy laden, and I will give you rest." Many in Shepard's congregation cited this verse, and so did some in Wenham. From Isaiah 55:1 the wife of James Fiske had realized that "Christ is offered to only [any?] one that be in a need of Him, second, Christ is offered freely, . . . and Third, nothing could hinder her from Christ and joy." Though this woman had no crucifix to gaze upon, she gained hope from the promise that he "love[s] them that love me, and they that seek me early shall find [me]." Another woman could affirm that if she was "willing to come to" him, she would find "rest" and "joy." Hers was the rest Christ offered in Matthew 11:28, the rest (as Mary Goldsmith noted) that flowed from knowing he had promised (John 6:37) that "him that cometh I will in no wise cast out." This promise was "free." Remembering a sermon that explicated the parable of the prodigal son, Goodman Foster twice spoke of God as "freely accepting" the repentant man. This was a God of "mercy" and "rich goodness," a God who "pardons." So also Martha Collins knew of God's "free offer," and Mary Parish, that "He would pardon my sins." Learning of the promise, feeling Christ reach out to them—everyone who testified in Cambridge and Wenham knew such moments of experience.[20]

These patterns of expression flowed from the same techniques that Laurence Saunders practiced back in 1555. The living Word of God became an instrument or mirror for achieving self-perception. Richard Cutter used a verse in the Gospel of St. John to understand the nature of a particular "sin whereby some men pursue their perdition 'tis opposing of His members." Meditation prompted the discovery of unworthiness. For John Green of Cambridge, a sermon got him started thinking on Psalm 130:2 and its lesson of "the miserable estate of all unpardoned sinners." Thereafter he was able to reflect in private on this verse in ways that made him think he "was one myself under the power of Satan an enemy to God and so no way out [but] to perish." For others, the spur to reflection was a spell of sickness like that which led William Hamlet to regret his "evil trade of life" and "pride." Transposing physical illness into the spiritual event of affliction, Hamlet recognized "the justice of God by such a stroke." Once at this point, and in response to prayer, "the Lord did mitigate my pain." Always, meditation reaffirmed the lesson of the *vanitas* tradition. Thus young Roger Haynes found that after prayer he had "many sweet meditations of the vanity of the world." Many also employed the technique of "humiliation," retiring into private space to "seek the Lord."[21]

Practicing the art of meditation, the colonists turned easily to metaphorical language. Richard Eccles referred to his soul as "a ship at anchor," a Scriptural metaphor that complemented his experience of being "sick" at "sea." It was common to describe the "heart" as registering a wide range of feelings. John Stansby told the Cambridge congregation that "God shot arrows in my heart," and a woman imagined that a ser-

mon "struck my heart as an arrow." Here as elsewhere, metaphors originating in the Bible enabled ordinary people to find spiritual meaning in
everyday experience. When the house of Brother Crackbone and his
wife caught fire and burned down, she prayed that the "fire" of the Holy
Spirit would burn her as well: "And as my spirit was fiery so to burn
all I had, and hence prayed Lord would send fire of word, baptize me
with fire." [22]

Another woman who watched as her house burned to the ground
turned the experience into poetry. Anne Bradstreet was more gifted as
a writer than Brother Crackbone's wife, but her technique was the same,
as was the moral that it taught. Sorrowing, Bradstreet shifted from complaint to recognizing it "was just" that God deprived her of so much:

> Then streight I gin my heart to chide,
> And did thy wealth on earth abide?
> Didst fix thy hope on mouldring dust,
> The arm of flesh didst make thy trust?
> Raise up thy thoughts above the skye
> That dunghill mists away may flie.

Bradstreet saw her poems as exercises in the disciplining of the self. In
one poem she dramatized the tension between "The Flesh and the Spirit."
In another, she fused her emotions about death with the figure of the
pilgrim:

> A pilgrim I, on earth, perplext
> with sinns with cares and sorrows vext
> By age and paines brought to decay
> and my Clay house mouldring away
> Oh how I long to be at rest
> and soare on high among the blest.

The struggle to subdue the self and remain conscious of God's presence
infused the prose "meditations" she wrote out and willed to her children.
In them she taught how to see God's purpose even in the humble act of
keeping a house clean: "That house which is not often swept, makes the
cleanly inhabitant soone loath it, and that heart which is not continually
purifieing itself, is no fit temple for the spirit of god to dwell in." Meditation was recurrent and unending if the "pilgrim" was to remain steadfast on his journey. [23]

The technique of turning pain into a blessing was at the heart of the
prose masterpiece in which Mary Rowlandson described her captivity
during King Philip's War. One evening, as she sensed herself about to
faint, she found "sweet cordial" in a verse (Jeremiah 31:16) to which she

returned "many and many a time" in the classic manner of devotional practice. This facility enabled Rowlandson to perceive her captivity as a time of spiritual self-searching and renewal. The outward history of "removes"—her name for changes of location—became a tale of deepening humiliation as she realized her dependence on God's mercy.

> I then remembered how careless I had been of God's holy time, how many Sabbaths I had lost and misspent, and how evilly I had walked in God's sight; which lay so close unto my spirit, that it was easy for me to see how righteous it was with God to cut off the thread of my life, and cast me out of his presence forever.

She remembered too that living "in prosperity, having the comforts of the world about me, my relations by me, my heart cheerful," she took "little care for anything." Knowing she had sinned, Mary Rowlandson acknowledged God was justified in causing her to suffer. Quoting Psalms 119:71 on the blessing of affliction—"It is good for me that I have been afflicted"—she affirmed the lesson of the *vanitas* tradition:

> The Lord hath showed me the vanity of these outward things. That they are the vanity of vanities, and vexation of spirit; that they are but a shadow, a blast, a bubble, and our whole dependence must be upon Him.[24]

Another colonist, the tailor and "Chiriengen" John Dane, was enabled by his knowledge of the Bible and the techniques of meditation to set down the meaning of his life in a prose narrative. Using, like so many others, the metaphor of pilgrim to frame his life—as a youth in England he imagined doing "Jurney work thorow all the Conties in ingland, and so walk as a pilgrim up and doune on the earth"—Dane recounted numerous temptations and bad deeds that, in retrospect, made him lament his "Retched heart." Confessing an initial worldliness, Clap remembered how his parents had rebuked him and how their chastising words encouraged him to meditate on "the Joys of heaven and of the vanetys of this world." He followed the prose version of his memoirs with "some poesie in waie of preparation for death" in which he praised God as his "Choisest friend": "If wede have God to be our friend / In all our meserey / then lets hold out unto the end in / trew senserety." The dozens of unpolished stanzas bear out his confidence that God was not a distant figure but immediately present.[25]

Dane and Rowlandson drew on the same lay tradition that empowered the men and women who testified in Cambridge meetinghouse—the same techniques for self-examination, the same literacy with Scripture, the same narrative structures of temptation and deliverance. This tradition of piety was "popular"—which is to say, independent of the ministry—in that people learned it from one another, from reading the Bible, and from reading books and broadsides that originated in the marketplace. Yet the independence of lay piety was only partial, not complete. Part of the process of becoming a church member was making a "confession of faith," which meant reiterating the basic doctrines of the Protestant system. In these statements the people of Wenham and Cambridge stayed within the framework of the catechisms they had received from their ministers, Shepard's which may have circulated only in manuscript, Fiske's a printed text *(The Watering of the Olive Branch)* for which his congregation paid the costs of publication. And in speaking of the work of the spirit on their hearts, they relied directly on the sermons they heard someone preach, adopting as their own the imagery and formulas repeated every Sunday from the pulpit.[26]

It was the ministers, moreover, who exemplified the ideal Christian. Though Foxe included hundreds of lay men and women in his massive history of faith enduring fiery trial, he gave pride of place to a handful of heroic clergy. Chief among them was John Bradford, whose very name would serve the preachers in New England as symbolic of the Christian way of life.[27] By the early seventeenth century, godly ministers in England were issuing biographies of exemplary shepherds. The New England clergy commemorated one another in similar publications,[28] and were joined in this practice by lay writers such as Johnson and William Bradford.[29] Apart from such publicity, the intense tone of clerical religion was manifested in private or unpublished writings. Few, if any, laymen drew up for themselves a long list of "rules to live by." Nor did laymen explore in extensive diaries their relationship to God, as did the elder Shepard, Wigglesworth, two of the Mathers, Jonathan Mitchel, and, in poetry not prose, Edward Taylor.[30] The great lay diaries are providential but not pietistic; most do not refer to spiritual experience.[31]

These differences do not mean that lay colonists were indifferent to the demands of a strenuous, self-searching piety. They showed how much they valued the ideal by treasuring a handful of extraordinary case histories. Of those that survive, two are autobiographical; a third describes a family member. All three seem to have been addressed to the person's family. Handed down, it seems, from one generation to the next, these texts reveal a heightened piety, an intense state of mind that others, though less pious, honored with their praise.

Sarah Tompson grew up in a "godly" family, and married into another. In the "relation" she composed in private, and that members of her family later copied perhaps for a printer, Mrs. Tompson described how certain sermons and Scripture texts caused her to think that "the

Lord might iustly leave mee to myself and strive no more with mee[.]"
Discouraged by a heart that "was so dead and hard," and by her failure
to make use of an affliction, she worried that her time had come and
gone: "I thought now the lord wold strive no longer with mee I thought
the day of grace was past with me." Reassured by what she read in Shepard's *Sincere Convert* and by hearing her father-in-law, the minister of
Braintree, teach "that when the Lord brought home any soul to him self
he usually puts it into great fear," she resolved to continue seeking "and
not faint . . . though I could merit nothing by my seeking, becaus the
Lord had commanded me to look unto him." In the final pages of her
narrative, Sarah Tompson moved beyond mere striving to awareness of
God's mercy: "I thought there was hope in the mercy of God were my
Condition never so low." Likening herself to the Psalmist, she imagined
she "might say with David have mercy upon mee o God according to the
multitude of thy tender mercyes." The last sentence of the text sums up
her measured hopefulness: "I desire still to wait upon God in the use of
means."[32]

Someone in the family of Mary Clarke Bonner, who died in Cambridge in 1697, wrote down her speech to those who gathered by her
deathbed. Her testimony began with Mary praying for "one Glimpse" of
God's love, a prayer he quickly answered:

> then of a Sudden she broke forth with a great Deal of Joy using
> these and such Like Expressions he is Come he is Come he is Come
> and has Spocken powerfully to my Soul telling me my Sins are for-
> given She seemed to be abundantly filled with Comfort Expresing
> her Self in a Sweet manner Saying reioyce with me O ye Righteous.

But Mary was not spared the classic cycle of the pilgrim's voyage. The
next evening her joy vanished, and to those who watched she seemed
"to be in great teror and agony of spirit." "Satan," she declared, "came
upon me Like a Lyon almost a frighted me out of my wits" by tempting
her to doubt the promise. Slowly weakening, she gave voice the next
night to renewed hope:

> having her father By the hand She lookt on him Saying o father
> now God has answered all your Prayers for me O praise praise for
> God has wonderfuly reveled himself to me And filled me with Joy
> unspeackeble and full of glory She . . . Lookt up in his face & Smil-
> ing on him Said father dont It reioyce your heart to See your Child
> going to Glory

Now she gained perspective on the previous night's temptation: "i feared
the Last night that ye Joy i had was but a Delusion but now I know this

is no Delusion now God has Wonderfuly Discouered him Self to me." In this state of mind and heart she died.[33]

Here was an ideal of faith made real; here was all the drama anyone could ever wish to feel or witness! In 1681, a Boston printer published yet another of these personal narratives, Sarah Goodhue's *A Valedictory and Monitory Writing*.[34] Goodhue's model piety was echoed in the broadside verse in which writers honored deceased friends or family members. John Saffin, a Boston merchant, wrote a number of these elegies, as did Sarah Tompson's brother-in-law, Benjamin.[35] The same goal of teaching an exemplary piety moved Anne Bradstreet to write out and will to her children the "Meditations Divine and moral" that survived in her family until rediscovered in the nineteenth century. Stories, some oral and some written down, circulated of young children. Cotton Mather collected some of these and added them to a New England edition of his literary model, James Janeway's *A Token for Children*.[36] In later years, other ministers would publish similar reports, most famously the descriptions of youthful religion that Jonathan Edwards included in *A Narrative of Surprising Conversions* (1738). Edwards also published, anonymously, his wife's description of her spiritual experiences.[37] Indeed, the clergy sponsored most of the statements by lay men and women that achieved publication.

Published or unpublished, these texts sustained an ideal of lay piety that had wide currency among the colonists. Yet to take them as the norm is to ignore the very kind of evidence they represent: the reason they survived or found a publisher is that they dramatized the outer limits of experience, the most that saints could do. In this respect they belong with the martyr stories. We know that people in New England liked to read such stories, just as they also liked to read Janeway's stories of premature piety. But to read about the martyrs was not the same thing as becoming one. Acknowledging the value of an ideal faith, most people in New England remained more hesitant and cautious, more prone to intermittent zeal and frequent carelessness. As in every army, some marched to a different beat than "Onward Christian Soldiers." There were cowards who turned back from conflict, and some who hastened to the front. Others tried to confront life intensely but found that their courage failed them. Four main patterns emerge from the evidence. A small core of people, mainly women, lived up to the ideal. A second pattern was to live routinely as a formal Christian until provoked to self-searching by a sudden crisis. A third was to persist in the moderation of the "horse-shed" Christian, participating yet creating distance. A fourth was to know despair.

The crucial fact behind these patterns is that half or more of all lay people never found the confidence to testify about the work of grace.

The men and women who stood up in Wenham, Cambridge, and Windsor were listened to in silence by most of their neighbors, who went home year after year without ever qualifying for *full* membership. Perhaps these people hesitated because they knew from books they read or stories passed along in conversation of the danger of spiritual despair. Too much striving after grace, too much straining for assurance, could have sad consequences.

Despair sometimes did befall the colonists. An early case, coinciding with discussions in the Boston church about assurance of salvation, involved a young mother who, in 1637, "having been in much trouble of mind about her spiritual estate, at length grew into utter desperation, and could not endure to hear of any comfort, etc., so as one day she took her little infant and threw it into a well, and then came into the house and said, now she was sure she should be damned, for she had drowned her child." Winthrop, who noted this sad event in his journal (and its unexpected sequel, the rescuing of the child before it died), is our principal informant on other cases of extreme despair. From him we learn of a man who, affected by the despair of a neighbor, "would often utter dreadful speeches against himself, and cry out that he was all on fire under the wrath of God," and of a resident of Roxbury, a woman who "died in great despair" after giving birth to a stillborn infant: "She fell withal into great horror and trembling, so as it shook the room, etc., and crying out of her torment . . . saying . . . now she must go to everlasting torments . . . and still crying out O! ten thousand worlds for one drop of Christ, etc."[38] Many people knew the history of Abraham Warner of Hartford, "who being left of god & prevailled with by satan . . . drowned himself . . . leaveing behind him in his brothers pocket a writting to his father wherein he doe advis his father to look to the ways & walkings of his Brother." The Dedham church contained a woman who was diagnosed as sick from melancholy and who, in dying, judged "very hardly of hir sperituall estate. . . ."[39] Less extreme, though symptomatic of the situation, was the spiritual history of Mary Rowlandson's sister, who "in her younger years . . . lay under much trouble upon spiritual accounts. . . ."[40]

That Rowlandson remembered these sad years and that diarists such as Hull and Winthrop collected stories of despair suggest a widespread fascination with the extremes of religion. The circulation of these stories may also mean that despair was not something distant, something no one could imagine as occurring to himself, as some may still suppose today of mental illness. Let us conclude that these stories involve the perception that faith was never safe from doubt. Nor did Satan ever cease attempting to make Christians think that they were beyond saving mercy.

If this mentality owed much to lore of how the Devil worked, it had a further source in a story that enjoyed remarkable currency in seventeenth-century England and New England. In describing this story and in tracing its repetitions, we illuminate again the role of print culture in the making of popular religion.

Francis (or Francesco) Spira was a lawyer and a Catholic in mid-sixteenth-century Venice. Drawn to Luther's doctrine of free grace, he came under pressure from the Church, his clients, and his family to recant in public. As narrated in *A Relation of the Fearful Estate of Francis Spira,* on the eve of recantation Spira thought he heard a voice urging him to renounce the world for Christ. Once he abjured his Lutheran views, the same voice pronounced "the sentence of . . . eternall damnation. . . ." Thereafter, he was convinced "he was utterly undone: that he could neither hope for grace, nor Christs intercession with God the Father in his behalf." Rejecting friends and clergy who advised him of God's mercy, Spira suffered torments of despair. His worst moments came from "fearful dreames and visions" that persuaded him he was possessed: "I have a whole Legion of divels that take up their dwellings within me, and possess me as their own; and justly too, for I have denied Christ." A swarm of flies that gathered in his room he saw as signifying the presence of Beelzebub, "god of Flies." These agonies of mind and conscience ceased only with his death.[41]

The process by which this story became widely known cannot be traced precisely, but in later years the mere mention of "Spira" summed up a tale that frightened John Bunyan, who "hit upon that dreadful story of that miserable mortal, Francis Spira; A book that was to my troubled spirit as salt, when rubbed into a fresh wound." The passage of this "dreadful story" into everyday religion was well underway by 1555, when John Bradford the martyr employed it in giving counsel to someone who sought his advice. Thomas Beard included Spira in *The Theatre of Gods Judgements,* deriving it, perhaps, from Continental collections of wonder tales. An Elizabethan playwright turned the tale into a play, and a ballad version appeared in 1587. Early and late in the seventeenth century, English and New England ministers referred to Spira in their sermons. In the course of describing how the wicked, having refused to fear God, come to ruin, Thomas Shepard cited Francis Spira: "that famous picture, patern and monument of Gods justice by 7 yeares horror, and grievous distresse of conscience." A half-century later, an English evangelical, recalling "the continual torment in his mind" that Spira faced, asserted that "the damned . . . in hell, endures not the like misery . . . I assure you, this is the dreadfullest example that ever I read in my whole life: the Lord grant that none of us all may ever come to this."[42]

Twice, at each end of the century, people in New England referred to Spira. Once was when young Roger Haynes, telling of his struggle to achieve "a true sight of sin," and fearing he had fallen short, recalled having "many slavish fears of the devil and going to bed lest before morning I should fall to eternal sorrow. And I was now fearful of doing, speaking, lest all should aggravate misery which I thought was as sure to be inflicted as I had a being . . . and thought my sins greater than others . . . and that I was another Francis Spira and so afraid to pray." These thoughts came to Haynes in about the year 1640. Several decades later, Samuel Sewall's fifteen-year-old daughter Betty came into her father's bedroom and told him "the disquiet she had when waked; told me was afraid should go to Hell, was like Spira, not Elected."[43]

Though no one else was this specific, the motifs of the Spira story—the presence of the Devil, a fear of dying suddenly in the night, a sense of the immediacy of hell, and despair at being so unworthy—turn up elsewhere in colonists' testimonies. These same motifs pervaded a religious literature that we may aptly characterize as popular in the sense of being produced for a general audience in large quantities by writers who were usually not religious professionals—that is, the penny godlies written by the likes of Andrew Jones.[44] More loosely, this literature may be referred to as "popular" because of a recurrent formula. As in the Spira story, so here the narrative was structured to convey intense effects around the formula of good contending against evil. Always, good prevails. But the tone and substance of the tale played up the horror that sinners must endure. To us these tales may seem fantastic or contrived: did Spira really undergo his torments? Yet what to us may seem exaggeration was an element of "truth" to those who read these stories. For them the "real" was not the everyday world of appearances, but the half-hidden struggle between moral right and wrong. This simple "plot," this endless "war," was dramatized in stories such as Spira's.

The sensationalism of *The Black Book of Conscience*, one of the most widely reprinted of the penny godlies, had to do with death and Satan. Death was described as a terrifying event, its terror all the greater because God could strike so suddenly. And Satan also threatened the unwary.[45] Though penny godlies acknowledged the possibility of God's mercy, they did so only after lavishly exhorting readers to experience the thrill of terror:

O! how could it chuse but strike Terror to the heart to hear an uncontroulable Sentence past against him, when he was (as he thought) tumbling in Gold and Pleasure, when his mind was most at ease, even, even then, the Lord separated his soul from his body

. . . the next time you lay your head upon your Pillow, may be the
last time: then never defer, do not prolong repentance.[46]

Not surprisingly, these books refer to Spira![47]

Sudden death, the gaping jaws of hell, a Christ who comes in judgment, the torments of despair—these themes were milked by printers
and hack writers because of customer demand. Reprinted well into the
nineteenth century, the tale of Francis Spira was like the wonder stories
in combining piety and violence, though here the violence lay within the
mind. That there was common ground between these genres was evidenced by Beard and Clarke, who included stories of extreme despair
in their collections. A further sign of such common ground was the use
ministers made of terror in their preaching and in publications like *The
Day of Doom*. Here again, printers and preachers worked in tandem, thanks
to a receptive marketplace; eager readers in New England bought up
five successive printings of *The Day of Doom*, and local printers also issued
versions of the Spira story.

The preachers who used terror did not wish to cause despair, though
critics charged that books like Shepard's *Sincere Convert* had that unin-
tended consequence.[48] Unlike Andrew Jones, who reveled in sensationalism, the preachers thought of terror as a short-term means of driving
sinners to begin the quest for grace. Yet in passing they were graphic in
evoking death and judgment, in pressing the imperative of "now or never,"
and in painting sleep as dangerous. Sinners, declared Shepard, were like
criminals awaiting execution on the scaffold:

Thou art condemned, and the muffler is before thine eyes, God
knowes how soon the ladder may bee turned, thou hangest but by
one rotten twined thread of thy life over the flames of hell every
houre.

Sleep was treacherous for sinners. "When you lye downe," Scudder warned
in *The Christians Daily Walke*, "you may thinke of lying downe into your
winding sheete, and into your grave. For besides that sleepe and the bed
doe aptly resemble death and the grave, who knoweth when he sleepeth
that ever he shall awake againe to this life?"[49]

As in the chapbook literature, English and American ministers played
on the realities of hell in building up the "terror" of God's judgments.

What a Screech of Horror will be heard, What Woes and Lamenta-
tions will be uttered, when Devils and Reprobates and all the damned
Crew of Hell shall be driven into Hell, never to return again; down
they go howling and screching, and gnashing of their Teeth. . . .[50]

Joseph Alleine, the English nonconformist minister whose *Alarm to Unconverted Sinners* was such a runaway success in the book market, referred to Francis Spira in evoking the torments of the damned *before* they reached the fiery pit:

> They that have been only singed by this fire, and had no more but the Smell thereof passing upon them: O what amazing Spectacles have they been! Whose Heart would not have melted, to have heard Spira's Out cries, to have seen . . . that Monument of Justice, worn to Skin & Bones, Blaspheming the God of Heaven; cursing himself, and continually crying out O Torture, Torture O Torture Torture . . . ?[51]

"Now or never" was the refrain of hundreds of sermons. A person joining the Cambridge church in 1653 remembered Thomas Shepard preaching thus: "I tell you young persons that have passed your 20 years and slept out your opportunities tis a wonder of wonders if ever God show you mercy." Timothy Edwards taught his Windsor congregation that people "were usually converted before they were thirty years of age," a lesson that made several of them fear it may have been "too late" to "seek for mercy." Increase Mather used a real incident, the accidental death of two young men who fell through the ice on Fresh Pond in Cambridge, to emphasize that "man knows not the Time of his Death," and to warn the living (he was speaking to a group of Harvard students) that God may have "more arrows to shoot amongst you, that shall suddenly strike some of you ere long."[52]

So many sources of this popular tradition, so many ways of pressing home the experience of terror! Everyone who listened regularly to sermons, who read *The Day of Doom,* who knew the "fearful" tale of Francis Spira, was apt to feel a chilling sense of vulnerability, or worse, a sense of being lost. Abigail Rockwell, testifying before Windsor congregation in 1702, attributed her "first awakenings" to "hearing such a question as expressed in a sermon to unconverted sinners, namely, can you bear to live half an hour in fire, and . . . how can you bear to live in hell to all eternity[?]" Young Roger Haynes remembered hearing Thomas Hooker preach on "the sin of offending brethren that they should go where the worm never dies out. And most terrible expressions of wrath came from him." Joshua Willis of Windsor told the congregation that

> what I heard from that text the doctrine from which was that the great work of the soul must be done now or never, was very awful to me, and particularly the thoughts of how long I had put it off etc. And that place, he that being often reproved and hardeneth his

neck shall suddenly be destroyed and that without remedy, was very awful and terrifying to me . . . and made me greatly fear that if God did not suddenly destroy me yet He would never hear me so as to show me mercy.

Elsewhere, in the Cambridge church relations, men and women imagined having committed the unpardonable sin. Jane Winship was "afraid to die" lest she "should forever lie under wrath of God"; she wondered too how anyone "could eat, [or] sleep that had no assurance of Christ."[53]

Assurance of Christ! It was the absence of assurance that made men and women fall into despair, and too much assurance that deceived them into thinking they were safe from judgment. In using terror, the ministers were taking aim at the self-confidence that seemed to underlie the failure of so many people in New England to become church members. The measure of their success with this message is not the cases of extreme despair—these seem but few—but the testimonies of church members in which they attribute their conversion to hearing of an unexpected death or in coming close to death themselves. This was how Anne Fitch of Windsor described her awakening. An early sickness moved her to be "more afraid of hell than before." Taken ill again, she "was much struck with a great and trembling fear of death and hell." On she went in her relation to speak of how she

> expected every hour that I should die and go to hell, and then my sins and God's wrath were so amazing to me that I can't express it, so that though my bodily pain was very great, yet such was the anguish of my spirit that I thought it ten times greater, and so great that no affliction that ever I felt in my life was in any measure like it.

This same sequence figured in a score of narratives where people spoke of death and illness.[54] In doing so they imitated Christians they heard of in sermons, like the case of "Waldo," whose conversion, as described by Increase Mather, was occasioned by "the Sudden Death of one of his Companions."[55] For others, the breakthrough event was "affliction" such as Mary Rowlandson experienced. Beforehand, she slept well at night and was careless on the Sabbath. Afterwards, she lived more intensely and with shame-laden memories of her earlier peace of mind:

> I can remember the time, when I used to sleep quietly without workings in my thoughts, whole nights together, but now it is other ways with me. When all are fast about me, and no eye open, but His who ever waketh, my thoughts are upon things past, upon the awful dispensation of the Lord towards us. . . .

For John Trumbull, a "sore storm" at sea was the equivalent, an event that pushed him into thinking "what would become of me if peace [not] made with God." For Jonathan Pierpoint, a young Harvard student, it was a fellow student's death: "It pleased God to awaken me by the Death of that pious youth, Edw. Dudley. I thought it would go ill with me if God should suddenly take me away."[56]

So it went for many persons, so many as to define another closely related pattern of experience. These were people who in many respects conformed to the pattern of the saint, yet who lived untroubled in "prosperity" (as Mary Rowlandson remembered it) until a crisis triggered latent doubts underlying their seeming assurance. This was the structure of the Antinomian controversy, and the wave of church admissions that followed the great earthquake of 1727, when people crowded into churches out of fear that the world, and therefore the time in which to receive grace, was coming to an end. What such moments tell us is that every congregation contained those who may have lived as Christians in most outward ways, who were inwardly in control, until a crisis shattered this control and let fear rise to the surface.[57]

There were still others, however, who simply refused to be moved by the threat of "now or never." In achieving distance from this message, these lay men and women acted out their preference for a mode of religious response less taxing than the extremes of an ideal faith, on the one hand, or Spira-like despair, on the other.

How they achieved distance was in part a matter of acknowledging the fictive nature of the lore of terror. No one openly dismissed this lore, as some dismissed the lore of wonders. But in responding to the one as to the other, lay people learned to be selective, accepting some of what they read as true and treating other tales as fiction. Again it was the book trade that, in blurring the distinction, cast a cloud of doubt on the whole genre. Printers intervened to publish tales of terror and despair for reasons of the marketplace. Hack writers did for penny godlies what Nathaniel Crouch did for the lore of wonders, turning out a dozen thrillers like *The Black Book of Conscience*. An enterprising London printer sold thirty thousand copies of *The Second Spira* before his rivals in the book trade exposed it as a fake, though some of them soon published a fake of their own, *The True Second Spira*.[58] New England printers republished both.

A deeper reason for this distancing was the resource of ritual. Ordinary people responded to moments of high danger—the life crises of birth, sickness, and death—in patterned ways that served to reduce tension. Ritual practice in New England is the subject of a later chapter. Here I merely wish to note that ritual helped turn fear into assurance.

Fear was also offset in the very preaching of the ministers. Their message fell into two parts, the disturbing doctrine of the limited atonement—"here is matter of terror," Thomas Shepard declared, in that "few shal be saved"—and the reassuring doctrine of the "security" of God's promise to his "people."[59] Every minister in New England talked or wrote at length about God's merciful love for the weak and fallen, and his offer of free grace. They offered "cordials" in the form of statements that a faith no greater than a single grain of mustard seed was faith enough to gain admission to the church, and they urged those in despair, or close to feeling hopeless, that these were sentiments the Devil tried to create in the saints. If there was genuine reason for spiritual confusion, there was also the confusion Satan caused. In making this distinction, the ministers urged people to seek assurance of salvation from their practice of the duties of the Christian life. Outward behavior, they insisted, was a reliable sign of inner or invisible realities. Writers of the penny godlies offered similar advice, paralleling their accounts of judgment with "demonstrations of God's mercy and love illustrated from Christ's actions." "God's people," declared one popular writer, "shall never be forsaken of God." This same theme was a staple of the New England pulpit; no one seemed to tire of proclaiming the "peculiar glory" of the godly in New England, a glory in which many seemed to share.[60]

Hearing these sermons, lay people imagined themselves as participating in a security that extended to everyone within the church covenant. Or perhaps they derived comfort from the facts of good behavior: attending services, supporting the minister, engaging in family prayers from time to time. Theirs was a faith less rooted in ongoing anxiety than in an ethics of "weaned affections," and though they may have wondered if this was "hypocrisy," as some ministers suggested in their sermons, they were willing in most cases to accept one another's practice as sincere. It mattered, for example, that neighbors testified to someone's being like a "Christian."[61]

Theirs was thus a faith that settled at a lower pitch, the pitch of "horse-shed" Christians, of those who hung back from the Lord's Table, of those who may have read *The Day of Doom* or the amazing tale of Francis Spira, yet did not prostrate themselves in terror. Content to read about the martyrs without being such themselves, such ordinary Christians went to church and between services talked animatedly of "their Farms, their Crops of Corn, their Horses, their Cows; or what's the Price of this or that Commodity."[62] For them the tension between church and world had eased, or achieved ritual definition. Some space, some time, was still committed to religion, but there was also time for play and work.

Patterns of experience were multiple, not uniform. Lay men and women in New England confronted an idealized faith in the lives of people they may have known or heard of. Another source of this ideal was the preaching of the ministers; a third, certain literary texts. Many of the colonists were able to reiterate the formulas of this literature—the confession of unworthiness, the acknowledgment of sin, the "warfare" against temptation, the fear of death and judgment, the rapture of experiencing Christ's love. Yet many listened silently as others testified about the work of grace, and though they sat through years of hearing sermons would never testify themselves. These stolid farmers and their families interpreted the world in ways that softened the strict separation of the elect from the reprobate. Only when some crisis or life passage broke up the rhythm of their situation—an earthquake, say, or marriage, or sudden death—did the sermons of the ministers and the rhetoric of the chapbooks become forcefully significant.

II

DOWN THROUGH the years this tempered piety disturbed the ministers. Early on, Thomas Shepard discerned a mood of "deadness" he traced to the immigrants' contentment with their situation. "Doth not plenty of means make thy soul slight means?" he asked his Cambridge congregation. "When you went many miles to hear, and had scarce bread at home, O, you thought, if once you had such liberties; but when they are made yours, now what fruit?"[63] In 1679 the ministers who gathered in a special synod issued a report in which they complained of the "great and visible decay of the power of Godliness amongst many Professors in these Churches." According to their report, the colonists were guilty of excessive "Sabbath-breaking," a lapse in family devotion and too much "affection to the world." Moreover, every meetinghouse contained the spectacle of "men . . . [who] sit in prayer time, and some with their heads almost covered, and . . . give way to their own sloth and sleepiness, when they should be serving God with attention and intention." Invoking God's avenging judgments, the ministers demanded immediate reform: Let all those sleeping men awake![64]

No history of popular religion in early New England can ignore the rhetoric of declension and how it colored the relationship between people and clergy. May we suppose that the repetition of this rhetoric caused more, not less, indifference? Nor did it seem to help when ministers like Increase Mather drew on the lore of wonders or when the synod called on congregations to perform the ritual of "renewal of covenant." To judge from outward evidence—the figures on church membership, the restlessness of many young people, the failure of the state to enforce moral legislation—lay people in the late seventeenth century were marking out more distance from the ministers and their ideal of a zealous faith. But the deeper consequence was one that remains largely hidden from us, a psychological resistance that burst into the open in rare moments like the witchcraft trials and cases of demonic possession.

If new tensions followed from the rhetoric of declension, an older and more visible resistance continued to occur in response to the basic message of the preachers. The reasons for this resistance, and the directions that it took, can be found in the spiritual history of one woman and two men: Anne Hutchinson, Obadiah Holmes, and Peter Pratt.

Anne Hutchinson the prophetess was gifted as a teacher of the way to grace. Arriving in New England at a time of spiritual excitement, she quickly passed into church covenant. It was not long before she and her favorite minister, John Cotton, were noting that most people depended on the wrong means of achieving assurance of salvation. A few brief years into his New England ministry, Cotton was alarmed by the self-assurance of the colonists. Accusing them of "rest[ing] in . . . Deutyes or ordinances," he told a fellow minister in early 1636 that he wanted to "provoke" lay men and women into a deeper searching after grace. He found an ally in Mrs. Hutchinson, who urged the women she attended in childbirth to rethink the basis of their faith. "Shee did much good . . . in [women's] Childbirth-Travells," Cotton would remember, "[and] readily fell into good discourse with the women about their spiritual estates." As he recalled her message, she warned these women not to build "thear good Estate upon thear owne duties and performances or upon any Righteousness of the Law," telling them as well that all their "Conscience of Sabbaths, Reverence of Ministers, Frequenting of Sermons, Diligence in calling"—practices that were the very center of the Puritan program—were "duties" unrelated to "saving Union" with Christ, "being no more but Legall work." Cotton remembered too that "many of the women . . . were much shaken and humbled thereby, and brought to enquire more seriously after the Lord Jesus Christ." Her message and his, he reported, served to "awaken" people "to discover their sandy foundations, and to seek for better establishment in Christ."[65]

In declaring that Christians cannot "make sanctification an evidence of justification," Anne Hutchinson attacked the system of the ministers at a weak point. She offered an appealing alternative to guilt and endless striving after godliness; assurance, she declared, came directly to the saint in the form of "the immediate witness of the Holy Spirit." In her speech, as echoed by her followers, she contrasted "Christ" and "Adam," grace and works, the witness of the Spirit and the classic, prolonged techniques of meditation:

> Here is a great stirre about graces and looking to hearts, but give me Christ, I seeke not for graces, but for Christ, I seeke not for promises, but for Christ, I seeke not for sanctification, but for Christ, tell not me of meditation and duties, but tell me of Christ.

Her dichotomies tore apart the careful interweaving of law and gospel in the system of the ministers. Hutchinson and her followers criticized the language of conditions and qualifications, while rejecting any sort of "works" in favor of free grace.[66]

But the several dozen men and women who thronged her home were less concerned with matters of doctrine than with knowing whether they were saved or not. Anne Hutchinson may have promised them assurance so complete that they would never doubt again; so, at least, her enemies alleged in citing as one "errour" of the Antinomians the assertion that "After the revelation of the Spirit, neither Devill nor sinne can make the soule to doubt." She had reached this point herself, but only after undergoing extraordinary turmoil. The daughter of a minister who got in trouble for his "Puritan" activities, she was disillusioned back in England once she saw that godly preachers compromised their principles instead of separating from the church. Puzzling out the reasons for their imperfection, she reached the point of feeling that "none of those Ministers could preach the Lord Jesus aright": all taught "a Covenant of works, and did oppose Jesus Christ." It was a "troubled" state of mind that turned Anne Hutchinson against the ministers and drove her to the clarity of "an immediate witness of the Spirit." In the end, she rested her critique of the ministers on experience—the confusion she had felt, and the release of assurance once she heard God speak to her.[67]

Obadiah Holmes began to search for grace within the system of the ministers, but also found himself dissatisfied. He remembered years of effort and "perplexity of mind" because he never found the "rest" he craved. At first immigration seemed to help; he "tried all things in several churches, and for a time thought I had made a good choice or change." Yet all the while he remained restless, his "spirit . . . like a wave tossed up and down." At last he broke through to the principle "that there is no preparative necessary to obtain Christ, nor any thing to deserve that love, or to merit the same." Holmes did not become a spirit-mystic. But he drew a sharp distinction between works and "free grace"; what "removed" him "from the covenant of works to the covenant of grace, even that new covenant of life," was the "free pardon" he received from Christ.[68]

The system of the ministers failed to satisfy young Peter Pratt of Connecticut, though later he would change his mind. Pratt grew up in an unusual family; his mother divorced her first husband, John Rogers, on the grounds of his religious heterodoxy, before marrying Peter Pratt senior in 1679. John Rogers was a merchant in New England who came under the influence of Quakers and Seventh-Day Baptists from Rhode Island. Fashioning an eccentric collection of beliefs—he believed in free will and the possibility of perfectionism, and rejected the Puritan Sabbath—and maintaining them in spite of legal penalties, Rogers passed these ideas to a small group of "Rogerenes" that included his son John Rogers, Jr. As a young man Peter Pratt came to know the Rogerenes in the person of his half-brother. Narrating his conversion to the Rogerenes and his recantation, Pratt remembered feeling troubled by the doctrine of election and the theme of now or never. Sometimes, Spira-like, he feared "the Door of Mercy was shut against me, and sometimes that I had Sinned Unpardonably." Like Spira, too, he felt himself beset by "Innumerable Swarms of the Infernal Spirits, rushing towards me with utmost Fury." Disenchanted with his fellow Christians and the ministers, he "could scarce bear to hear" the minister of Lyme preach, and turned to his half-brother for enlightenment. Thrown into jail for working on a Sunday, he found in his Bible the message that he needed to resolve his worries:

> . . . I lit upon the Eighth Chapter to the Romans, and read onto the Thirty Fifth Verse, whereupon I was blown up into an Extatick Joy, I thought I had now Assurance of my Union to Christ, and that nothing should Separate me from His Love. . . .

Yet he could not hold on to this assurance—"this Rapture lasted me that Night, but the next Day totally Vanished"—even though his half-brother insisted that this Bible reading was guided by the "Holy Ghost." For a brief while Pratt became a Rogerene. Still in search of truth, he found, surprisingly, that he agreed with most of what he read in Shepard's *Sincere Convert* and the Westminster Catechism. Another providential experience with Scripture restored his self-assurance and led him back to the town minister.[69]

What lessons do these histories hold? All three detail a disenchantment with the ministry. For these laymen the ministers were threatening figures, too powerful (the Antinomians called them "popish factors"), teachers of a burdensome system, promoters of confusion. The chief source of discontent was the message of the ministers; thus Pratt remembered how, instead of getting assurance of salvation from Shepard's *Sincere Convert*, the book "broke me off from every hold, drave me from every resting place, and brought me many a time to my Wits end."[70] The same longing for assurance, yet the same dissatisfaction, caused dark moments for Holmes and Hutchinson. All three arrived at a common remedy: the certainty denied them by the ministers could be found in personal experience—the direct witness of the spirit, a self-tutoring in Scripture, the emotion of free will. The importance of these narratives lies in the glimpse they give of slow-building anger with the message of the ministers, anger transformed into an assertion of independence.

How widely people shared this anger is unclear. Mary Dyer followed Anne Hutchinson into exile. She and others found in Quakerism a doctrine of assurance that promised the children of God an infallible knowledge of personal salvation. Quakerism also sanctioned contempt for the ordained ministry. What some people found in Quakerism others gained from being Rogerenes or Gortonists. The Baptist way was yet another possibility. But though many may have passed through spiritual confusion, most people remained faithful to the system of the ministers. Not until the Great Awakening of the 1740s did thousands find that what they were experiencing as a work of grace was condemned by their ministers as "enthusiasm." And only then did "New Lights" strike out on their own, organizing churches that restored the primacy of direct experience.

For some of the colonists, experience diverged in other ways from the system of the ministers. A man who became a minister in England, Richard Baxter, complained of being unable to discern the "signs" of new birth as these were customarily outlined. One sticking point was time; in contrast to the manuals which he read for guidance, Baxter could not pinpoint the specific moment of conversion.[71] Roger Clap had the same problem. As he listened in Dorchester meetinghouse to candidates for membership describe "their Experiences of the Workings of God's Spirit in their Hearts," Clap realized he could not discern the same explicit workings of the spirit: "If ever there were the Work of Grace wrought savingly in my Heart; the Time when, the Place where, the manner how, was never so apparent unto me, as some in their Relations say it hath been unto them." It may have been significant that Clap became a member of Dorchester congregation *before* his church required the test of a relation. Proud of being in "Church Fellowship," he remained troubled by his inability to "find as others did, the Time when God wrought the Work of Conversion in my Soul." The vain search for this experience "caused" him "much Sadness of Heart, and Doubtings how it was with me, Whether the Work of Grace were ever savingly wrought in my Heart or no?" Relief came from hearing Cotton preach that constancy was sometimes how God worked. Citing several "Reasons" why he could believe his faith was "rightly Grounded," and remembering a precious moment when the spirit filled his heart with "full assurance," Clap relied as well on the wisdom that "God doth work divers Ways upon the Hearts of Men, even as it pleases him; upon some more sensibly, and upon others more insensibly." In his early disappointment lay the makings of a more radical response. But Clap was contemptuous of the Antinomians and defined "truth" as what he found in the Westminster Catechism. His is a case history of confusion, yet also of a confidence that he and all his children were members of Christ's kingdom.[72]

A different kind of testimony from any hitherto considered consists of confessions that were made not to a church congregation but to a court investigating witchcraft. The Salem witch-hunt of 1692 turned up fifty people who acknowledged having covenanted with the Devil. Their statements to the court, together with another text that describes in detail the outcries of a girl who claimed to be possessed, throw an extraordinary light upon the piety of people who were more confused than not, and who found the preachers wanting.

Some confessing witches were "children" of the church—that is, baptized members who had not advanced to full communion. We know from other sources that such halfway members were the subjects of a double message from the pulpit, the reassuring statement that they could rest upon the covenant *and* the lament that they did wrong in holding back from the Lord's Supper. It was the second of these messages Joseph Green delivered in advising those within the covenant that if no progress occurred in their striving after grace, "being baptized will add to your account at the great day and will also add to your torments in hell for ever. . . ." The published sermons of another minister were equally emphatic in describing children of the church as "Infatuated Souls" who falsely thought of the church covenant as securing them "from all fear of evil."[73]

This preaching troubled Mary Toothaker, a confessing witch at Salem. Asked the standard question in her courtroom hearing, did the Devil tell her to renounce her Christian baptism, she

> answered that she had thoughts she was rather the worse for her baptisme and had wished she had not been baptised because she had not improved it as she ought to have done.

This reasoning—that baptism made her worse, not better—represented her response to the preaching of the ministers. Desperate to remove the burden that the preachers placed on her, she fantasized finding relief from the Devil.

Mary Toothaker suffered for another reason, her failure to experience the same flow of pious feelings that some of her neighbors had enjoyed, or that she heard about in sermons. As she told the court at Salem, "she used to get into a corner alone and Desyred to pr[a]y but her mouth would be Stopt but sometymes she had been helped to say Lord be merce full to me a sinner." Here, the reference to "her mouth . . . Stopt" suggests an alienation that others who confessed to witchcraft also voiced. Ann Foster had once attended church, but stopped going when she found "she could not profit there." Elizabeth Johnson was moved to sign the Devil's book and receive baptism from another witch, thinking this was how "she Should be Saved." Her mother welcomed Satan because he promised her "al glory and happines and joy." Mary Marston, "over come with melancholly" when her mother died, found release from grief in joining with the Devil. Mary Barker signed in order to secure "pardon" for "her Sins." Others craved a happiness that they did not find within the meetinghouse: thus Mary Lacey confessed that the Devil told her "we should have happy days and then it would be bett'r times for me." A search for satisfaction, a search for release from the message of the ministers—is this what the confessing witches represent? Dissatisfaction surely manifests itself in William Barker's striking statement that the Devil had informed him there would "be . . . neither punishment nor shame for sin. . . ." One further sign of craving for release was the statement made by someone who did not confess in 1692 (instead he testified against a neighbor); the Devil had approached him, saying, "I understand you are trobled in mind, and if you will be Ruled by mee you shall want for Nothing in this world."[74]

Elizabeth Knapp also fantasized of overcoming unmet obligations. Household servant of the minister in Groton, sixteen-year-old Elizabeth cried out that the Devil was demanding that she enter into compact with him in exchange for saving her from hell. She was swept with feelings of inadequacy, declaring to onlookers that she "led" an "unprofitable life," and reporting that "the devil told her [that] her time was past and there was no hope unless she would serve him." In this same stretch of speech, Elizabeth behaved as though she were another Spira, beyond any hope of grace:

> And that it was observed in the time of her extremity, once when a little moment's respite was granted her of speech, [that] she advised us to make our peace with God and use our time better than she

had done. The party advised her also to bethink herself of making her peace, [and] she replied, "It is too late for me."

What sins had she committed that made her feel so worthless? Neglecting duties, for the most part, like attending church service. Her confession throws light on the legalistic preaching of the ministers and how it led to feelings of inadequacy. Her description of the Devil makes him appear almost ministerial, as in "terrify[ing] her . . . with sin and misery" and in warning that "her time was past and there was no hope unless she should serve him." Confusing minister and Satan, she acted out her hostile feelings via a strange voice that, emerging from within her (bystanders thought it was the Devil speaking), called the Rev. Samuel Willard a "black rogue" and labeled what he preached as "a company of lies." She was also frightened by the Devil, since she "feared [that] if she were a witch she should be discovered and brought to a shameful end. . . ." Torn between these feelings, and thinking also that both minister and Devil offered relief, Knapp endured the torments of possession for two months before somehow moving to a better sense of self.[75]

Possessed girls and confessing witches did not find in witchcraft an alternative theology.[76] What they voiced was rather an unfocused discontent that followed from the preaching of the ministers: their insistence on the law, or duties, and the parallel insistence on sincere repentance. Even as they made these demands, the clergy complicated things by declaring that mere duties without grace were, for all intents and purposes, worthless, and that differentiating sincere actions of the heart from mere hypocritical emotions was difficult. So too, the ministers were quick to blame Satan for causing spiritual confusion; not they, but the Devil was responsible for "filling" men and women

> with perplexing fears and terrours, making them to travel in the dark: and that whereby he doth mainly advance this, is by drawing of them to wound themselves by such sins as tend to darken their evidences, and make their Consciences to accuse them. . . .

Worse, as Samuel Willard pointed out in enumerating all the skills of Satan, "His ways . . . are full of windings & turnings, are so Meandrous, filled with so many intricacies, that it is impossible to trace them." Moreover, sin was like a "traitor" that permitted—nay, encouraged—men and women to heed Satan.[77]

From the preachers' point of view, the lesson of the Quakers, Spira, and Anne Hutchinson was exactly this: they allowed Satan entrance to the self. But we must view this distress in a different light. Granting that some of the colonists learned to blame the Devil when they felt invaded by self-doubt—this was Mary Bonner's way of dealing with her deathbed crisis—we do better if we pursue the connections between spiritual confusion and the process of conversion. As the Cambridge testimonies reveal time and time again, the system of the preachers fostered deep anxiety about whether one were "sincere" or a "hypocrite." The near-impossibility of making this distinction, together with the paradox of waiting, helpless, for Christ's mercy and yet striving to fulfill the "duties" he imposed, lies behind the statements of uncertainty that recur so often in the Cambridge church relations. Joanna Sill was typical in never seeming to get past the conditional "if": "Lord if thou hast elected me." She reached out for the "promises, yet . . . could apply none till at pit's brink nearly to sink." Grace came, but also vanished; even after coming to New England Joanna was "oft troubled" because the Lord "absented Himself from her."[78] The men and women who fantasized of finding relief via Satan were responding not only to these problems but also to the burdens placed upon them by "declension." The statements made in Salem, like the statements made in Cambridge meetinghouse, hint at underlying strains that must have been widespread, though rarely leading to overt revolt. Yet some would come to think that they were worse off listening to the preachers than to Satan.

Describing the effects of a "good Conscience," a minister lingered on the "inward peace" that "makes every thing easie," that frees the soul "from fear of wrath," that "takes away the poyson and venome of sin." This was the ideal. But as this minister acknowledged, the reality was different: "But here some may ask a Question; If Christ gives such peace, how then comes it to pass that many a gracious Soul meet with so much trouble . . . in Spirit, that the Soul hath lost his peace and sense of the favour of God?"[79] The distress voiced at Salem by confessing witches reveals a group of people who found little satisfaction in the church and who often blamed their problem on the clergy. Not so angry they turned Baptist, not so gifted with the Holy Spirit as Anne Hutchinson, these men and women struggled to resolve ambivalence—were they saved or not, free or enslaved by the Devil?—and to find a missing peace.

III

ON JULY 30, 1630, men and women gathered together in newly founded Charlestown to spend the day in fasting. Once this "exercise" concluded, some of them participated in another ritual, the act of entering "into covenant with the Lord to walke in his ways." Thus came into being a newly gathered church. Within a few more weeks, the congregation elected ministers to office.

These events flowed from a deep antagonism to the "mixt multitude" of English parishes. At long last the colonists were able to achieve the "discipline" they had been denied in England. What this meant in practice, though unfolding gradually for several years, was evident in outline that July day in Charlestown. In their eagerness to purify the church the large group which met to fast agreed to limit membership to those among them who were "godly." By the end of the afternoon, the hundreds who participated in the fast had dwindled to no more than thirty or forty who entered into covenant. Reporting to the crowd that more persons would eventually be received into membership, the organizers of the event made it plain they meant to move slowly, adding only "a few, to witte, such as are well known unto them; promising after to receive in such by confession of faith, as shall appear to be fitly qualified for the estate."[80]

As people formed more churches, the same principle prevailed. Eight men in Dedham agreed to weigh one another's merits in a process that took eighteen months; of the eight who started, seven became founders of the congregation. Once under way, the Dedham church acquired members at a fairly rapid rate. But in general, no one entered the gathered congregations of New England without undergoing public scrutiny. As in Thomas Shepard's Cambridge, it was common practice by 1640 to ask candidates to make a "confession of faith" (or assent to one the church had already prepared) and to describe, however briefly, their humiliation and repentance.[81]

The men and women who thus covenanted together were engaging in a rite of passage. The threshold of the church was the boundary between two very different communities, and when people moved across that threshold they took care to purify themselves beforehand. In joining a gathered church and accepting the church covenant, people imagined themselves as separating from "all ungodliness and worldly lusts, and all corruptions and pollutions wherein in any sort we have walked." The founders of the church in Braintree spoke of themselves as having lived "without Christ and without God in the World." But in the "Fellowship" they now enjoyed, they pledged themselves to "renounce the Devil, the wicked World, and the sinful Flesh, with all the Remnants of antichristian Pollution, wherein sometimes we have walked, and all our former evil Ways." The same language recurs in the pledge that Joseph Green, a future minister, associated with becoming a church member, for Green "renounce[d] the Devil and his service and the lusts of my own heart."

At Woburn, having first confessed to being "unable of ourselves to the performance of any thing that is good," the members voiced abhorrence of their "former defilements in the worship of God." The Concord covenant was more explicit than many others in committing the members to "watch over each other" in order to maintain the purity of the church; referring to the power to cast erring members out, that covenant evoked the ritual purging of "any raging pollution or spiritual uncleanness" that might occur "amongst us."[82]

Opposing purity to "uncleanness," the colonists drew on the complex symbolism of the Bible to enlarge the meaning of church membership.[83] Scripture was the source of three powerful metaphors, the church as "body," "household," and "temple" filled with those the Holy Spirit transformed into "living stones." St. Paul elaborated on these metaphors in a letter to the Ephesians:

> Now therefore ye are no more strangers and foreigners, but fellow citizens with the saints, and of the household of God; and are built upon the foundation of the apostles and prophets, Jesus Christ himself being the chief corner stone; in whom all the building fitly framed together groweth unto a holy temple in the Lord: in whom ye also are builded together for a habitation of God through the Spirit.

In another of his letters Paul likened the church to a human body, a metaphor from which followed an ethics of mutual obligation:

> And whether one member suffer, all the members suffer with it; or one member be honored, all the members rejoice with it. Now ye are the body of Christ and members in particular.

This ethics and these metaphors informed the covenants that each congregation in New England fashioned in becoming organized. Those who entered the church covenant promised one another to "walk in brotherly Love, and the Duties thereof . . . to the common Edification of the Body, and of each Member therein." A recurrent expectation was that "love" prevailed within this fellowship:

> . . . as his covenant binds us to love him and his Christ for his own sake, so to love our brethren for his sake.
> . . . God's people . . . [must] walke in subjection to him, and Christian love to all his people.
> . . . [we] bind ourselves in special to all the members of this body, to walk in reverend subjection in the Lord to all our superiours, and in love, humility, wisdom, peaceableness, meekness, inoffensiveness, mercy, charity, spiritual helpfulness, watchfulness, chastity, justice,

truth, self-denial, one to another, and to further the spiritual good one of another, by example, counsel, admonition, comfort, oversight, according to God. . . .[84]

Sometimes a group confessed that human weakness put this ideal out of reach, as when the Concord church declared that "we . . . are liable to be oppressed and devoured one of another." Yet realism yielded to the vision of a better way of life as the members went on to pledge that they would "carefully avoid all oppression, griping, and hard dealing, and walk in peace, love, mercy, and equity, towards each other, doing to others as we would they should do to us."[85]

A visionary social ethics informed every covenant. The essence of that vision was a sense of fellowship, a "love to the brethren" that only those in covenant experienced. Roger Clap remembered having once disliked a "Stranger," a "Young Man [who] came into the Congregation where I was," until the stranger made it known that "he feard God; and upon the very Report thereof my Heart was knit unto him, altho' I never spake with him that I know of."[86] In popular speech the word "Christian" was a shorthand for this fellowship. That word was applied to men and women who, as witnessed by their neighbors, lived in peace with one another.[87] All too often, peace was shattered in the "world" by malicious, sharp-tongued people who preferred "revenge." It was often said of them that Satan was their master, and that they were witches. But Satan and his followers did not dare to cross the threshold of the church. In this household peace prevailed, and charity to one another. Those who became angry or "oppressed" a neighbor in the course of business were summoned to repent or be dismissed from membership. Thus Roxbury congregation removed a woman baker who was cutting "bits" from every loaf she sold. In Boston congregation, the members took to heart St. Paul's instructions to the Corinthians—"Dare any of you, having a matter against another, go to law before the unjust, and not before the saints?" (1 Corinthians 6:1)—and resolved to use arbitration in disputes with one another. The same church proposed that unless the votes on business were unanimous, no action would be taken.[88]

Yet even as this vision was reiterated in new covenants, conflict made its way into the church. Early on, and especially after 1660, church members often could not agree on the choice of a new minister. In vain did candidates appeal for peace and love, or tie their contract to conditions such as Joseph Green imposed on Salem Village in 1696: "once they began to quarrel and contend: I should look upon myself to be free from any obligation to tarry with them."[89] The tensions springing from such politics were compounded by the strictness of the standards for church membership. From the very start, some colonists were embittered when others shut them out from entering church covenant. Elizabeth How, a candidate for membership in Ipswich, was opposed by a family that suspected her of witchcraft, and How was grieved by the decision to exclude her.[90] The men within the church could vote not only on each candidate, but also on each question of church discipline, the salary of the minister, and any other issue that came up. It was rare that debate ended in unanimity. Writing from Connecticut to a famous English minister, a young minister remarked wryly on the contradictions of church covenant: "An honest Englishman That has nothing But Holynesse is in Some Places Amongst us counted scarce pure enough to Looke in at the Church-window, and yet enormous Censurings, groundlesse Derogations, and unchristian Bickerings are seen and Allowed."[91]

The men and women who made up the membership in Wenham were typical in wanting to review with care all candidates who came before them. Eighteen months of hearings were necessary before they accepted Sarah Fiske, the minister's sister-in-law, into the church; these many months church members debated whether Sarah had wronged her husband (they decided she had) and whether she was adequately repentant. When newcomers to the town requested that their membership be transferred from another church, the members responded that *"even* such should make a declaration of the work of grace. . . ." It was the ideal of the church as spiritual household that justified this policy—that, and the plain fear that godly people could not safely coexist with those who were not saints:

> Resolved because we could not else answer our conscience in exercise of the trust Christ hath reposed in us of receiving in such only as be meet. We are to judge by our own light and not others'. Because it may be a means of engaging of our affections, mutually beholding Christ in such &c. Because such a practice seems most safe for the church &c.

When it came to deciding whether the examination of prospective members should occur before a "mixed congregation" or only those in covenant, the same ideal prevailed: "it was conceived more comely and honorable for those matters to be transacted only before the church, none others present." A few months later, the members were debating whether to exclude nonmembers from the prayers and blessing that were part of the service of communion. Even though John Fiske, the minister, insisted that he had "some relation to and charge over, those that are not in church covenant," some members objected to any kind of "communion in that ordinance with unbelievers." Only after three meetings' worth of debate did Fiske prevail.[92]

Indeed, the ministers in many congregations were sadly disappointed by the stubbornness of the lay members. By the 1640s, Thomas Hooker, the first minister of Hartford, was objecting that lay members were engaging in harmful "inquisitions and niceties" in scrutinizing candidates. Resenting this behavior, the ministers were also troubled by what seemed to be the dwindling numbers of church members. In the same decade a disgruntled layman announced that "thousands" were excluded from the churches, and in 1662 a minister forecast that "the bigger half of the people in this Country will in a little Time be unbaptized." Certainly this seemed the case to John Woodbridge, who "found above 60 unbaptized persons, men, women, and children," when he came to Killington, Connecticut, as minister. Writing to his English correspondent, he complained that "the Common opinion is so riveted in the hearts of men, vid. That the infected and Infectious will steale in at the church-doors unlesse every brother be allowed a feeling of his pulse and smelling of his Breath and handling of his necke."[93]

Out of such discoveries came second thoughts among the clergy, and, because they now protested the behavior of church members, a new round of conflict.[94] Where conflict achieved focus was on access to the sacrament of baptism. No New England minister ever argued that baptism was necessary for salvation. What could be said, however, and what many did articulate in defense of the halfway covenant, was that baptism and covenant worked together to ensure the "continuation and propagation of [God's] kingdome . . . from one generation to another." If everyone who joined in covenant received spiritual benefits, so must everyone who received the sacrament of baptism. This rethinking of baptism, covenant, and church membership generated a more telling argument, that the benefits of covenantal membership passed from generation to generation within the same family. Echoing what lay members of the Cambridge church had long ago affirmed, Increase Mather declared in 1675 that God had "cast the line of Election" so that it ran in part "through the loyns of godly parents." Thus proclaiming the importance of the Christian family, the ministers reasserted in the same breath the function of the church as "household" or "garden" where children grew into faith and obedience. In such a church, declared Shepard, Christ "will prune, and cutt, and dresse, and water" the children of the covenant, and by doing so encourage them to "hope, and pray for the communication of . . . grace, and so feel it in time."[95]

This thinking, and the policy it justified, enraged the members of a score of churches. For them it violated the deep symbolism of the covenant, betokening, as one lay writer put it, "Corruption Creepinge in as an harbenger to old england practice . . . (which god prevent in mercye)." Those who felt this way found spokesmen in ministers who shared their point of view—a young Increase Mather (later on he changed his mind), the patriarch John Davenport, his colleague Nicholas Street. In publications issued by the Cambridge press, the three men attacked the halfway covenant for violating a taboo. Mather used the strongest language, declaring the new policy a "sin" as "dreadful . . . as if a man should administer the Lords Supper unto unworthy receivers; which is as sacrilegious impiety, as if a man should take the Blood or Body of Christ, and prostitute it to dogs." He and Street employed popular rhetoric (they were hoping to mobilize church members) in proclaiming that the halfway covenant meant "Farewell to New-England's Peculiar Glory of undefiled Administrations of holy things," "Corruption and Pollution creeping into the Churches," and a "return to our former state" of the mixt multitude.[96]

Yet for all the power of this rhetoric, a different way of reasoning swayed the people who remained outside the church, and some of those within. More lay people favored than opposed the halfway covenant because of how it fit into their thinking about baptism and children. Theirs was an instinctive response, a projection of their concern for the welfare of their families. In a world so full of danger and where death struck suddenly, it was important to enclose each child within the shelter of religion. Protection came in several forms for newborn infants, like giving them a godly name. What the church could offer was baptism, a rite extending safety to those who received it. The halfway covenant helped satisfy the urge to believe that one's offspring were the heirs of Christ and not of Satan. In the absence of a formal liturgy we cannot know exactly what was said in the meetinghouse when parents presented infant sons and daughters to be baptized. It seems certain that the ceremony made no direct reference to the Devil and retained none of the qualities of exorcism that lingered in the Anglican rite. Yet surely the colonists thought of the ordinance as purifying the newborn. The prayer that Richard Brown, the minister of Reading, recorded in his journal in 1706 the day a son was baptized may indicate the nature of the service:

The Lord love him. Thou has[t] given him to me, O Lord, and I have given him up to thee, in the ordinance [of baptism] & I pray that thou wouldst take him into the number of thy Jewels, into covenant with thyselfe, cleanse him with the blood of Jesus from his original uncleanness, and keep him whilst in the world from the evil of it.

Baptism drew children within the protecting shelter of the covenant, the same covenant that linked Abraham and the Children of Israel with their God, and that was symbolized by circumcision.[97]

Likening baptism to that rite, people in New England imagined that the ordinance separated the clean from the unclean, the godly from the heathen. For some of the colonists, the New Testament furnished the essential symbolism of the rite. Anne Fiske of Braintree affirmed in a "confession of faith" that

> Baptism is that washing of the Flesh with water, in the Name of the Father, Son & Holy Ghost, whereby is signified, Christ in the promise, by whom we are washed from Sin, & made Righteous, delivered from Death, & restored to Life.[98]

Apart from this perception of the sacrament, those within the church as well as those without believed that parents owed it to their children to pass on the benefits of godliness. This way of thinking was articulated in the reasons people gave for wanting to become church members. In making her "relation" to the Cambridge church, Mary Angier explained that she became an emigrant (and now a candidate for membership) because she saw both steps as beneficial for her children: "thinking that her children might get good it would be worth my journey." Nicholas Wyeth acted out of similar concern, believing, as he told the Cambridge congregation, that emigration to New England would benefit his wife and one surviving child, another having died in England. The burden felt by parents was revealed more sharply in Anne Ervington's imagining that "children would curse parents for not getting them to means," a thought that led her to become an emigrant. These themes recur in the Wenham testimonies. There one woman wondered "what would become of her children if she died," a thought that spurred her to apply for church membership in order to secure the sacrament of baptism. Even more suggestive of this way of thinking was a request made in 1674 by a man who, "being married and now having a child," was finally willing to renew his covenant because he "desire[d] baptism for his child."[99]

The men and women who spoke thus were voicing an instinctive tribalism.[100] Consistently they assumed that their parents' faith (or lack of it) was consequential for themselves. If they had "godly" parents, they made a point of saying so. If not, they worried, knowing (as one woman put it) that "she was born of carnal parents where there was not the promise to seed." Grace seemed to run in families—yet only if the chain was not interrupted: if Brother Crackbone's wife could wonder if her children were consigned "to hell . . . because I had not prayed for them," what thoughts occurred to parents who were not church members and who could not bring their children to be baptized?[101] Those *in* covenant brought newborn children to the meetinghouse within a week or two of birth.[102] This urgency was not the making of the ministers, who always kept baptism separate from the doctrine of election. Rather was it the outgrowth of the parents' feelings for their children, feelings of intense love, or of devastating grief when infants died or suffered from afflictions, and a craving to protect them. The "heart-cutting" thoughts that came to Mary Rowlandson as she thought of her children's fate were thoughts that came to every parent in such situations. Concluding, on their own, that grace descended within families and that it would help protect their infants, lay men and women favored the decision of the synod on grounds of their devising.[103]

Nor, in general, were the ministers dismayed by this tribalism. For them, it was a card to play in fending off the Baptists. Responding in the 1640s to their challenge, one minister accused them of "unhumanity" in wanting to "deprive parents of that comfort they may take from the baptism of their infants dying in their childhood." Another who debated Baptists fell back on the concept of "preventing grace" to explain why "Parents" could expect "some comfortable hope of their children's salvation" from the sacrament; "I see no reason," Thomas Shepard affirmed, "for any man to doubt of the salvation of his child if he dyes, or that God will not do good to his child in time if he lives." His son, the minister of embattled Charlestown where Baptists were emerging in the 1660s, associated the group with the record of "hatred, and hostility" between the Devil and "the young ones of Christ's little flock," a history, as he told it, that extended back to Pharaoh's massacre of infants and episodes in which the "evil eye" of "that great adversary of our comfort and Salvation" was directed against children. In the same tradition, Cotton Mather assured readers of *Baptismal Piety* that if children who were baptized died as infants, "They shall none of them be lost, as minute as they are."[104]

In blurring the significance of baptism—did it really convey saving grace, or merely add an element of nurture?—the ministers fell in with popular opinion. They did so at a cost, the opposition of those purists who denounced the halfway covenant. Not until the end of the century, or even decades later, would some congregations accede to the rule announced in 1662, and in the turmoil of the Great Awakening a new wave of separatists restored the strictness they resented having lost. The alternative to purity, the tribalism of the laity, caused other problems for the ministry. As the practice grew up among halfway members of delaying to "renew" their covenant until they reached the point of being married, some ministers would realize that the classic meaning of the ceremony had been wholly displaced by the goal of family continuity. Observing this relationship, a leader of the Great Awakening rebuked his congregation in Northampton for not understanding that the sacrament was meant to be a "token of their being visibly regenerated, dead to sin, and alive to God." Jonathan Edwards wrote angrily of his congregation (and of others also) that "owning the covenant has . . . too much degenerated into a matter of mere form and ceremony; it being visibly a prevailing custom for persons to neglect this until they come to be married, and then to do it for their credit's sake, and that their children may be baptized." When his congregation dismissed him from office in part because he took this stand, they acted to defend the lay tribalism they had fashioned in the seventeenth century.[105]

One way or another, lay colonists imposed their own interpretation on the sacrament. They did so with more unanimity, and in more striking fashion, with the sacrament of the Lord's Table. By the middle of the seventeenth century, and increasingly thereafter, lay men and women were deciding not to apply for admission to this sacrament. Every congregation contained hundreds who belonged within the covenant by virtue of baptism. But when communion day occurred, a mere handful lingered in the meetinghouse to celebrate the Lord's Supper. Hence the lament of the Reverend Benjamin Wadsworth in 1724 that "the so general a neglect" of the Lord's Supper "hath been both a wonder, and grief of heart to me, almost ever since I have been in the Ministry." And hence the distress of Cotton Mather in 1690: "It is a Lamentable Thing to see what Multitudes, and Quantities among us do dayly turn their Backs upon the Table of the Lord Jesus."[106] In acting to frustrate the ministers, lay men and women were responding in their own way to the message of the ministers. What that message was and how the people heard it are matters that reveal with special clarity the complex dialectic of lay people and the clergy.

The forming of lay attitudes involved the clergy and their preaching. Only ordained ministers administered the sacrament. No one knew as well as they the reasons why the Reformation had rejected Catholic doctrine. On them fell the burden of articulating what the "signs" of bread and water meant, and why this sacrament was holy. Rejecting out of hand the Catholic doctrine of the real presence, the New England clergy interpreted the Lord's Supper as strengthening and confirming ("sealing") the grace already present in a person. Declaring it a "sign" or "seal" of grace, they linked it with assurance of salvation and the quest for saving grace. All this was commonplace, as was the likening of the sacrament to marriage, a metaphor that underlay instructions that communicants "search and examine your own consciences, as you should come holy and cleane to a . . . heavenly feast." The Book of Common Prayer, in which these words appeared, cited Paul's advice to the Corinthians—"Wherefore whosoever shall eat this bread, and drink this cup of the Lord, unworthily, shall be guilty of the body and blood of the Lord . . . For he that eateth and drinketh unworthily, eateth and drinketh damnation to himself, not discerning the Lord's body" (1 Corinthians 11:27–29)—in warning would-be communicants that "otherwise the receiving of the holy Communion doth nothing else but increase your damnation." The Devil lay in waiting for the unclean: he will "enter into you . . . and bring you to destruction." But safety did not consist in avoiding the Lord's Table; those who "stand by as gazers and lookers" were setting themselves up for "punishment."[107]

Inheriting these themes, preachers in the Puritan movement had reasons of their own for describing the Lord's Table as a zone of danger. It seems fair to suggest that Puritan reformers, seeking some way of differentiating the saints from the "mixt multitude," placed an even greater emphasis upon the duty of self-examination. John Dod and Robert Cleaver spent hundreds of pages in *Ten Sermons tending chiefely to the fitting of men for the worthy receiving of the Lords Supper* (1610) on the task of preparation in all of its aspects, including repentance for many different kinds of sin, each one of them enumerated. In effect, preachers such as Dod and Cleaver attached their demand for conversion to the sacrament. The message was direct: There must be an "examination" beforehand to see "whether we have attained unto a competent measure of repentance, knowledge, faith, and love," an examination directed to discovering "whether wee bee of the number of the faithful, and have in us the life of grace."[108] Exaggerating the task of preparation, evangelical ministers rushed on to emphasize the frightful consequences of coming to communion without being ready for it. Dod and Cleaver told their readers that a curse lay on the elements if they were eaten by ungodly people. Lewis Bayley spent more pages of *The Practice of Piety* on such warnings than on any other topic.

> If Uzze for but touching . . . the Arke of the Covenant was stricken with sudden death, what stroake of Divine Iudgement mayest thou not feare, that so rudely, with uncleane hands, doest presume to handle the Arke?
>
> · · ·
>
> And seeing that as it ministreth to *worthy* partakers the greatest assurance which they have of their Salvation, so it putteth temporall Iudgements on the Bodies, and (without repentance) eternall damnation on the Soules of them who receive it unworthily.

Body and soul, both were doomed if someone dared to violate the taboo of the sacrament.[109]

This symbolism—we might say, this anthropology—entered the lay tradition via books like Bayley's and its sequels that New England book-sellers were importing after 1660.[110] The marketplace in England and, less certainly, the marketplace in New England absorbed at least twenty-three printings between 1665 and the end of the century of the noncon-formist minister Thomas Doolittle's *Treatise Concerning the Lord's Supper.* No less sternly than his predecessors, Doolittle urged the duty of prep-aration on would-be communicants lest they become "guilty of the Blood of the Son of God!" Likening an "unworthy receiver" to a "Christ-mur-derer," he reiterated the familiar warning from 1 Corinthians 11:27–29: eternal damnation was the fate of those who feasted unprepared at the Lord's Table. "Nowhere in the popular literature," remarks a historian of religious literature in seventeenth-century England, "is there a more horrific statement than Doolittle's comment that . . . at judgement" Christ's "blood will 'cry against you, instead of pleading for you.' "[111] New England preachers followed suit in citing 1 Corinthians 11:28 to justify the duty of self-examination. A taste of what their sermons sounded like is the word of warning Cotton Mather offered "Members of our Churches, in . . . Full Communion," that in coming to communion they "stand in an Holy Place," and were therefore exposed to "the Wrath of God" if they came unclean:

> It may be, some will go Reeking Hot, upon the Gratification of their Filthy Lusts, Either To or From, the Dreadful Sacrament of their Confession at the Table of the Lord. An Horrible Thing! Ye Athe-istical Wretches, I am verily perswaded, a Terrible God will Avenge Himself upon many of you, by Leaving you to some Further Sin. . . .

Another taste of pulpit rhetoric survives in a diary entry in which Mi-chael Wigglesworth described Jonathan Mitchel as showing "the danger and the vile sin of a careless spirit that hath little or no appetite unto christ . . . such frustrate the very end of the ordinance. . . ." Did Mitchel cite 1 Corinthians 11:28? That text follows in the diary entry, and pre-cedes Wigglesworth's confession, "o Lord I am afraid of this."[112]

After listening to such statements, well might Wigglesworth have been afraid! That many others shared his fears seems certain. A woman in John Fiske's congregation confessed that "Going to the seals she thought to turn back," undoubtedly because she was not certain of assurance. Jane Colman Turell, daughter of one minister and wife of a second, delayed renewing her baptismal covenant, the step that gained her ac-cess to the sacrament, because her "Fears were great lest 'coming unworthily she should eat and drink Judgement unto her self.'" According to her father, Mrs. Turell "was often in an Agony, that she might draw near to God with a true Heart, and in the full Assurance of Faith."[113]

What these people said they felt was echoed by the clergy in describing lay religion. Soon after citing 1 Corinthians 11:29, Lewis Bayley imagined someone saying, "It were safer to abstaine from comming at all to the Holy Communion." These words have the ring of popular speech. More, they embody the commonsense reasoning that lay Christians often practiced. We may say this confidently because the same reasoning turns up in descriptions of how people spoke to preachers in New England. "I fear, I am not fit for the Supper of the Lord; and it is a dangerous thing to come unworthily thereunto," Cotton Mather recorded as the "most common" reason people gave in 1680s Boston for refusing to advance to the Lord's Table. In Wadsworth's *Dialogue Between a Minister and his Neighbor,* the "neighbor" sounds like Bayley's layman from a hundred years before: "because those who in this Ordinance eat and drink unworthily, do eat and drink Damnation to themselves, I'm so startled and frightened hereby, that I dare not come." When Wadsworth went on to assert that "too many are apt to argue in their own minds" that "it's most safe to stay away and avoid the danger," he was surely voicing objections he heard in his parish.[114]

Wadsworth knew another reason why so many people refused to attend communion. The "neighbor" in his *Dialogue* believes that those who come to the Lord's Table are obliged to be at "peace" with one another. But in his frank way he acknowledges that "I have some Difference & Controversy with some of my Neighbours, and know not how to sit down with them in so holy an Ordinance as the Lord's Supper is." Intervening in his own voice, Wadsworth confirmed that it was "too common" for townspeople to use their "Differences" as the reason for abstaining "from the Lord's Table, pretending they can't Join with [their enemies]."[115] As he knew firsthand, the lines of tension that rippled through so many towns did not stop at the church door—not in Salem Village, where the families of the victims in the witchcraft craze refused to come to the Lord's Table, or in nearby Topsfield, where John Gould refused for different reasons to attend. Gould had spoken out in public against the government imposed by royal fiat on Massachusetts in 1685. Three men in Topsfield reported him for treason, and Gould was forced into apologizing. When the wheel turned with the overthrow of royal government in 1689, Gould exacted his revenge by refusing to attend the Lord's Supper if his church continued to receive one of the men who had denounced him in 1686. Such pressure to prevent someone else from attending was brought to bear in Beverly, where the minister was visited by a woman in full communion who asked him to exclude another woman until she "had given her . . . satisfaction for some offences that were against her." Though Cotton Mather did not name the "quarrelsome woman" who, "having accus'd a man in the church of a fault that she could not prove, . . . remained so irreconcilable, that she would never come to the Lord's Table as long as that man liv'd," his story has the ring of truth. For sure, a Dorchester man refused to attend the Lord's Supper because of "some prejedice he had taken against" Henry Flint, the pastor. More normal, though perhaps but little less inciting, were decisions by a congregation to exclude a member from communion on grounds of pending discipline.[116]

Enemies and anger—these two did not mix with the ritual of communion. In observing this distinction, the colonists were responding to another of Paul's teachings in his first letter to the Corinthians. Church members were united "into one body," he told the Corinthians, the very "body" of Christ that was the spirit: "For as the body is one, and hath many members, and all the members of that one body, being many, are one body: so also is Christ" (1 Corinthians 12:12). United as they were by "covenant" into a fellowship of love, the colonists knew that love should prevail in the celebration of the Lord's Supper. Many still remembered the requirement in the Book of Common Prayer that those who wished to attend must "bee in love and charity with your neighbours," and the blessing that gave closure to the ritual process: "The peace of God which passeth al understanding kepe youre heartes and mynds in the knowledge of God."[117] That this ethic weighed on laymen is apparent from the "Apologia" of Robert Keayne, a Boston merchant censured by his church for overcharging. Expressing, in his will, his anger at the church for an action that had occurred long before, Keayne imagined "some" demanding "how could I with any comfort receive that blessed sacrament of love and keep communion with such either publicly or privately of whose carriages and actions I have such hard thoughts . . .?" The same ethic disturbed a man who joined Windsor church in 1700. Referring to "what I heard from that subject of loving our neighbor as ourselves," he acknowledged that the ideal "made me to see that I had not done it nor could do it, and that I had a spirit of envy and hatred against my neighbors, and especially those that were godly, and that I did not desire the good of my neighbors' soul but was against it." Here the consequence of recognizing anger was to pass beyond it. But for many of the colonists this transcendence was not easy to sustain. In acknowledging the norm, they were led into the very contradiction Wadsworth would describe: unable to accept a neighbor, they preferred to abstain from the sacrament instead of using it to achieve reconciliation.[118]

Lay people abstained by the thousands from communion because it had a troubling significance. Their actions indicate how well they understood the message of the clergy, and how strongly they preferred to compromise. The compromise was to enter the church covenant and gain access to the sacrament of baptism, but to hang back from attempting more. According to one witness, some were almost as reluctant to join in a quasi-sacramental ceremony, the renewal of covenant that many of the ministers pressed on their parishioners after 1675, "Lest it should encrease the guilt of the Churches through neglect of performance."[119] Here as with the sacrament of the Lord's Supper, the bottom line was safety—the safety of not promising too much, of not risking to profess that you had saving faith. If it was safer in the church than out, there was still a zone of danger to avoid. In effect, this response to the sacraments was in keeping with the basic strategy of "horse-shed" Christians, to participate but only in a way that allowed for some distance.

The colonists maintained this compromise despite a change of mind among the ministers. The man who made the boldest change was Solomon Stoddard. He urged his parishioners to come to the Lord's Table whether they were saved or not because he felt the sacrament itself would function as a means of their conversion. Others changed the tone and substance of their sermons. Echoing a famous English minister who downplayed the dangers of 1 Corinthians 11:28, and who urged that people look upon participation as a way of *gaining* confidence, Wadsworth, Willard, and Cotton Mather all denied that candidates for the Lord's Supper must feel assured of salvation. When Willard cited 1 Corinthians 11:28–29, he added a new twist to its interpretation by inverting the significance of doubt. As he paraphrased the text, he imagined someone thinking, "I may be most unworthy in my self, and yet at the same Time be accounted worthy in Christ; that, though I am most unworthy, yet I may partake worthily, and most so, when I labour under the deepest Sense of my own Unworthinesss. . . ." Wadsworth made the same inversion while suggesting that "damnation" in verse 29 meant a mere "external chastisement." Mather emphasized the dangers of neglect, which he painted as far greater than the dangers of participating! Yet little followed from these gestures, perhaps because, in these and other sermons, the ministers continued to complain that the church was filled with lifeless, formal Christians none of whom were saved unless they had a "principle of Grace within," and to hector the baptized to advance to communion.[120]

Despite these tensions between ministry and people, the church retained its aura of a special fellowship. It was in token of that fellowship that people paid the cost of buying silver plates and goblets to add beauty to the service of communion, and in wills gave money to the church to benefit its poor.[121] Tension vanished when the meetinghouse was filled with song, for though the text and tunes were plain, that very plainness symbolized the presence of the Word. It seemed to some that church membership made would-be mothers fertile.[122] For sure, the church was shelter from the Devil. And if outside its walls some people denounced those within as liars—an Essex County man was punished for saying he knew seven or eight liars, "and if one would lye soundly he was fitt for the church," and another whipped for declaring "hee hoped to meete some of the members of the Church in hell err long, and hee did not question but hee should"—inside the colonists continued to experience "the communion of Gods saints, and the sweete and comfortable enjoyment of God in all his holy ordinances."[123]

IV

IN SOME villages of seventeenth-century New England there were men like Benjamin Murries, who "did not care if he were in hell a fortnight, and he did not care if the devil plucked the soul out of him, and a pox take him, he did not care"; or like Philip Read of Concord, who was brought before the court because he "did sometime . . . blaspheme the holy name of christ & also on a motion then & there made to pray to God for his wife when sick blasphemously Cursed bidding the Divill take you & your prayers." In these same villages, young men and women slipped away from Sunday services or lectures to have a different kind of fun in houses emptied of churchgoers. In detailing such behavior, the court records do not suggest that the women who got pregnant out of wedlock or the men who drank too much were consciously rejecting the creed of the ministers.[124] However restless and indifferent, the colonists were rarely able to articulate a real alternative to Christianity. Few were full-fledged atheists, and my cautionary "few" should probably read "none."[125] William Barker offered a conventional confession to the court at Salem after having voiced his picture of a sinless world;[126] young people ceased their "frolicking" on Sundays as they moved into the stage of parenthood.

More important in the long run than misconduct are the glimpses the court records provide of piety infusing daily life. Many were the people who, in dying, voiced a faith in Christ. Many were the moments when someone responded to a crisis by regarding it as Job had learned to understand his plight. When neighbors warned Rebecca Nurse of Topsfield that her name was being mentioned in the witchcraft trials at Salem, she told them that she was as "Innocent as the child unborne but surely shee said what sine hath god found out in me unrepented of that he should Lay such an Affliction upon me. . . ." Indeed the witchcraft records reveal not only latent distress but a well-informed and active piety. Mary Bradbury accompanied her plea of not guilty with a statement that could almost be a "relation" spoken to a church:

> . . . I am the servant of Jesus Christ & Have given my self up to him as my only lord & saviour: and to the dilligent attendance upon him in all his holy ordinances, in utter contempt & defiance of the divell . . . and accordingly have endevo'red to frame my life; & conversation according to the rules of his holy word. . . .

Sarah Good, asked "what god doe you serve," answered briefly, "the god that made heaven and earth." Elizabeth How was described by her neighbors as someone who, "when shee met with eny Afliktion she semid to jostifi god and . . . she yust To bles god that she got good by afliktions for it med her exsamin hur own hart." When someone asked Elizabeth "what hopes she hade of her salveation," she told him "that she did bild her hopes upon suer rock Jesus christ." A neighbor remembered her sadness when a congregation voted down her application for church membership. The same kinds of records make it clear that people talked of religion in settings other than the meetinghouse—farmyards, households, taverns, streets. They asked questions of each other, gave and heard advice on how to read the Bible, and participated in what they referred to as "private meetings."[127]

An enduring aspect of lay piety was the perception of the church as different from the world. That perception figured in the reasons why so many English left their homeland in the 1630s for New England. It figured in the Salem witchcraft controversy when Samuel Parris, the minister of Salem Village, preached a sermon on the theme of how the Devil had infected some church members. His distress—it was as though a taboo had been violated—was shared by one of his parishioners, whose sister was among the suspects. Sarah Cloyse got up and left the meetinghouse as Parris started preaching; according to some witnesses, she slammed the door behind her. Did her leaving mean she was affiliated with the Devil, and was forced to reveal her allegiance by the sermon? Or was it the case (as another woman accused of witchcraft reportedly declared) "that all Church members were Devills & that her husband was going to be a Devill too he was then going to Joine with the Church"? Purity and danger converged on the meetinghouse: both were somehow intermingled in perceptions of the passage from the "world" into the "church."[128]

Lay people sensed this intermingling in the sacraments as well. Again the witchcraft records are revealing. The evidence against George Burroughs, a suspected witch and sometime minister of Salem Village who had moved to Maine, included his neglect of the Lord's Supper and the failure to baptize all but the eldest of his children.[129] That people thought this relevant suggests a sensitivity to the symbolism of the covenant: those within belonged to God, those without to Satan. The surest sign of this mentality is the struggle to prevent the coming of the halfway covenant. But the struggle to *secure* the sacrament by those outside the church, or but partially within, is almost equally significant. In or out, lay men and women valued what baptism did for children and the family line. Where they varied is in how they perceived the relationship between purity and danger; for some, the slightest compromising of a pure church threw protection into jeopardy. Whatever their position, lay people constructed their own meaning for the sacrament. They also disagreed with one another, as they did so visibly with the Lord's Supper, when some advanced to the Lord's Table while others kept their seats or left the meetinghouse.

As these controversies show, lay men and women were not uniform in how they construed the symbolism of water, bread, and wine. But people were more uniformly orthodox on doctrines like the difference between grace and works. And they were able to articulate the story framework that they learned from sermons and the "godly" books they read. The essence of this story was the struggle to work free of sin. That so many of the colonists, and at every social level, were able to retell this story represents a triumph for the Reformation. It was a triumph for the preachers in particular. They were making high demands on lay men and women—that they know the Bible, that they understand the catechism, that they practice disciplined asceticism, that they strive for the "experience" of faith. People in New England could not satisfy their obligations by coming to communion once a year, as was the case in certain Catholic systems. Hence it was that people cared about such matters as the difference between works and grace. In what other culture would an army marching off to battle have paused to debate matters of doctrine, as did the army sent against the Pequots in 1637?[130]

Yet for many of the people there were moments when the story framework did not coincide with what they actually experienced. For some, the difference lay in the turmoil of despair; for others, in not feeling the guilt of their sins. Out of these discrepancies emerged two different movements—the radicals who received grace directly, and the formalists or "horse-shed" Christians who preferred a calmer sense of self. True, some of the colonists experienced to the full the intense piety that they knew of from sermons and biographies. But in the main this piety was practiced by the clergy and lay people close to them through family ties or having the same education. In noting these relationships, we must also note that other kinds of people wrote or talked about their piety. Sarah Goodhue, Roger Clap, John Stansby, Peter Pratt, Jane Winship—these were men and women of more ordinary education who, like many of their brethren who testified in Cambridge, Wenham, and Windsor, were fluent in the language of the "pilgrim's progress."[131]

The meetinghouse was more than just a place to learn about salvation. It made visible the fellowship of Christians; it symbolized a set of rules or ethics that defined the meaning of community. The church was like an ideal order, a place where peace prevailed, and love among the brethren. As in every social system the ideal was not reality, for what went on in the churches was sometimes more like war than peace: "Sinful Heats and Hatreds, and that amongst Church Members themselves, who abound with evil Surmisings, uncharitable and unrighteous Censures, Back-bitings, hearing and telling Tales. . . ."[132] But the values of the people did not change. A yearning to restore the true communion of the faithful found expression in the rituals of the fast day and of covenant renewal. In turning next to ritual, we see again a symbolism of community that also figured in the lore of wonders and in people's quest for grace.

CHAPTER 4

THE USES OF
RITUAL

WHEN THE ship *Mayflower* reached Cape Cod in November 1620, it "fell among dangerous shoals and roaring breakers." Turning northward, the ship and its passengers "got out of those dangers before night overtook them," reaching "safety" the next day in Provincetown harbor. Pent-up fear gave way to joy; the passengers "fell upon their knees and blessed the God of heaven who had brought them over the vast and furious ocean, and delivered them from all the perils and miseries thereof. . . . ." Emotions ran less high on the ship that carried John Winthrop to New England. Yet we sense the same anxiety in Winthrop's references to storms and the incidence of fast days and thanksgivings. Twice en route the passengers participated in a fast, and once (two days after sounding ground beneath the *Arbella*) a "thanksgiving." When the sailing season ended with all ships accounted for, "we had a day of thanksgiving in all the plantations."[1]

Danger, yet deliverance: the rhythm of this sequence was played out in collective rites like fast days and thanksgivings. Fast days were a major resource for the colonists, the main ritual in a repertory that included prayer, the practice of confession, and the ceremony of public execution. Theirs was a repertory that did *not* include most of the feasts and festivals that Anglicans and Catholics commonly experienced. In this reformed culture, people had to do without the Christian calendar and its days of high significance: no Christmas, Easter, or Ascension. Nor was the changing of the seasons marked by other customs. It was a principled decision to relinquish all these ceremonies, as it was to transform funerals and marriages into a civil ceremony. These Protestants rejected the assumption—crucial to most ritual practice—that certain zones of time and space were sacred. For them, all of time and space was holy (or equally profane). In keeping with this principle the Huguenots who gained power in Lyon, France, in 1566 abandoned the elaborate differentiation between sacred and profane that affected where someone was buried, and stipulation of where the married could perform the sexual act. Similarly, the colonists perceived their meetinghouses and cemeteries as civil space, not sacred. The very ground was drained of ritual significance.[2]

What the colonists retained, what they drew afresh from the Old Testament and Elizabethan sources, was the moral allegory of repentance and renewal. In their thinking, God held men responsible for sin, and punished them accordingly. A crucial task was therefore to erase the taint of sin, to cleanse the self or the body social and renew covenantal obligations. Ritual structure recapitulated the great cycle of sinning and repentance that men and women passed through as pilgrims on the way to grace—passed through not once but many times in lifelong warfare against sin. Ritual practice had much to do, as well, with these people's sense of corporate identity. Ritual reaffirmed the ideal nature of the body social and protected it from danger. And ritual had to do with certain rites of passage or life crises such as death and sickness. Here again, people turned to ritual in the hope of passing out of danger into safety. What lay people yearned for is what William Bradford evoked in describing how the passengers responded to the feel of "firm and stable earth, their proper element," deliverance "from all the perils and miseries" of life.[3] Hostile to the magic of the Catholic system, nonetheless these people reinstated ritual practice at the heart of their religion.

The world of the colonists threatened them with many dangers. Nature, always unpredictable, could withhold rain from crops and send fierce storms that threatened ships at sea. The woods were full of wolves and Indians. There the Devil lived, displaced but a little from his "Territories" by the "Church" that "Fled into this Wilderness," and always seeking to "Blow up, and pull down," the church and commonealth.[4] As agents he used people who compacted with him to torment the godly. Witches caused dissension. Quarrels in a town or church, or between magistrates and neighbors, threatened all relationships. Lamenting conflict as destructive, people also worried about acts that visibly betrayed the ethics of the community—a murder that left blood upon the land, the sexual act of buggery, the greediness of merchants. When sickness struck someone, its source could well be witchcraft. Sickness frightened because there was little understanding of its natural causes. Many thought of it as caused by sin and worried lest their own sins, unrepented, were the reason a child of theirs fell ill. Death was perceived as the "King of Terrours" who ushered dying men to hell unless they had repented.

All these dangers had their counterpart in ritual: the witch-hunt, the process by which criminals confessed, public executions, renewal of covenant, prayer notes in a church, the seeking out of blessings, the wording of a will, the "way of death," and most of all, the practices of prayer and fasting. Where these rituals occurred was not limited to churches. Here as with the wonder, a mentality that we must think of as religious impinged on a range of settings, from households and courtrooms to the public space where scaffolds were erected. Always the purpose of the ritual was to enact a reversal, as in turning sickness into health, providing passage out of danger, or making visible the hidden. Ritual was a formalized procedure, a patterned means of connecting the natural and the social worlds to supernatural power.

This pattern was widely known among the colonists. Feeding, as it did, on the lore of wonders and the social ethics of community, ritual did not depend on a single source of information or a symbolism peculiar to the learned. Sectarians shared the same traditions as the orthodox; all parties drew on a well-known repertory of roles. In this culture, almost everyone could pray.[5] Sickness came to many, and death to everyone. Witch-naming and witch-hunting originated locally, in quarrels between neighbors. Executions were perhaps the grandest spectacle that any of the colonists experienced. People filled the streets of Boston in 1686 to watch James Morgan carted to the Common, and three thousand gathered for the hanging of an Indian.[6] Afterward, printers had a busy time of it selling broadside "dying testimony" of the criminal.

Yet within this common culture there were differences and tensions. Witch-hunting troubled certain magistrates and ministers. The clergy had a vested interest in the fast day, especially since it intersected with their complaints of "declension." In representing sickness as a judgment of "affliction" and in pleading for confessions, the ministers assimilated certain crises or life passages to their model of the godly life, a model that some people found too stressful. The ideal way of death was not how everyone preferred to die, and doctors had a role in healing sickness. Were public executions spectacles that people could enjoy? Printers played it both ways with their broadsides. If the meaning of an execution remained open-ended, so did the punishment of Baptists and Quakers. Was the victim of such punishment a heretic or a martyr suffering from cruel persecutors? No one in New England celebrated "carnival," when order relaxed and "the world turned upside down."[7] But witchcraft had much of the same structure, as in the scene of a "a Damned Crew of Devils" feasting on "Red Bread and Wine, in derision of our Lords Body and Blood." When people found themselves besieged by witches, it felt as though things had "turned topsy turvy, Heads and Heels have changed places."[8] The pacing of most rituals was fluid, and the symbolism of these rites was open to conflicting interpretations.

Ritual figured in the religion of lay men and women as a means of dealing with the dangers they encountered, and of reaffirming certain social values. But as with other practices, lay people had to choose between alternative interpretations or else leave the meaning of these rites ambiguous.

I

IN *ancien régime* France, peasants set the church bells pealing when a hailstorm threatened crops, and turned to relics of a local saint for aid in bringing back good weather. The Book of Homilies of the Church of England included prayers "For rain, if the time require," "For fair weather," for good crops and for abatement of the plague.[9] Facing the same dangers, people in New England depended on the fast day and thanksgiving to restore proper order. They staged another ritual, the ceremony of confession, in courts of law and churches. Less often, and with fewer gestures than in Europe, they hanged people in a public execution.

A score of times the farm people of New England turned to fasts to save their crops from unkind nature. Early on, in 1639, a two-week drought in May, which caused "great fear" that all the wheat was "lost," was relieved by a fast that produced "such [a] store of rain, and so seasonably, as the corn revived and gave hope of a very plentiful harvest." In late summer 1642, it rained for almost two weeks straight, "scarce one fair day, and much corn and hay spoiled." No sooner had a fast been ordered by the Massachusetts General Court than "the weather changed, and proved fair after." Three years later a July drought that threatened crops was changed to rain once the General Court declared a "day of humiliation." After July, a swarm of caterpillars did "great harm" to crops, but "vanished" when some "churches kept a day of humiliation."[10] Sometimes fasts miscarried, like one in 1638 that was followed the next day by "so great a tempest . . . as had been since" the colonists' arrival. But more often, God responded as the people hoped he would. They called on him to protect ships at sea and support soldiers sent to fight the Indians. When word reached them of victory in the campaign against Pequots, they celebrated with thanksgiving. Attuned as they were to the progress of reform in England, people held thanksgivings to commemorate the victories of Cromwell and the failure of a "diabolicall intendment" to burn London. In war as on the land and sea, fast days helped preserve a godly people.[11]

Another peril was "contention." The health of the body social was measured by the prevalence of peace and the generosity of people. When these gave way to "differences and dissensions," as peace did in the turmoil of the Antinomian controversy, this change was reason to suppose, as Henry Vane warned publicly in 1637, of "the inevitable danger . . . of God's judgments."[12] Fast days kept this danger at a distance, or so these people hoped. A fast in troubled Scituate (where rival ministers competed for authority) "concluded peaceably" with people reconciled to one another and promising "not to speak of each others infirmityes. . . ." Another time, this church concluded a day of humiliation with everyone in covenant renewing the pledge "to walke in Love & Peace." A third time, in 1637, the church participated in the ritual, hoping it would help compose the same disputes that troubled Vane. If conflict was the sickness of the body social, real sickness, like "a bloodye Coffe amonge children" in June of 1641, was something fasts were also called upon to reverse. Thus in Scituate in late 1649, "In regard of our owne particulars, very many amongst us beeing visitted with colds and coughes in a strange manner especially children theire coughing constraineing casting & bleeding att ye nose & mouth," the congregation pleaded, fasting, with God "to shew mercye." Sometimes the results were satisfying, as when, next spring, the congregation celebrated a thanksgiving to thank God for "restoreing & recovering manye of our Little children who hadd been very nigh death with very violent cooughings . . . wee as duely required, rendered praise."[13] More ordinary moments were when would-be churches had to choose a minister, elect someone deacon, or begin to build a meetinghouse. Here the function of a fast was to induce unanimity, though fasting also underscored the separation between church and world. In dealing with a member who was under sentence of church discipline, congregations sometimes fasted as a means of spurring someone to confess, an action that not only purged the sins that caused the church to impose discipline, but restored wholeness to the group in covenant.[14]

In general, fast days and thanksgivings reaffirmed the myth that also sustained wonders and church covenants, that God protected people who obeyed the moral rules of "Christian" community. The time to call a fast day was when people sensed that God was angry at them for not living up to what they promised in the covenant. The structure of the ritual was designed to manifest repentance, a process that ensured the return of God's favor. As John Davenport explained in a fast day sermon,

> When people who have been formerly under the effects of Gods displeasure, do turn unto him with unfeigned Repentance, and Reformation of their former evil wayes, God will certainly turn unto them in mercy, and make all his Creatures serviceable for their good. . . .[15]

People fasted for a day (they feasted on thanksgivings), as though to purge themselves of sin. Work ceased on such days, and most people went to church to pray collectively for mercy. Fast days mirrored the redemptive cycle that people knew as individuals, the movement that began with "humiliation" and "true sight of sin," and ended in "deliverance." As in their conversions, so in the ritual of fasting, people pleaded with their God to "deliver" them from sin, meanwhile promising repentance and renewed obedience to his laws. Fast days carried people out of ordinary time—or out of time's decay—back to that moment when all things were "new," when time was everlasting, when the ideal coincided with reality.[16]

Fast days were affairs of the moment. True, the colonists experimented in the 1640s with the practice of a weekly fast that rotated among churches.[17] And in some localities toward the end of the century, fasts did come to be more or less routinely ordained to mark the change of seasons, and to that degree assumed a fixed character; but in theory, at least, their timing was supposed to be dictated by unpredictable events. No one could foresee the waves of sickness or bad weather that signaled God's impending anger, just as no one could foretell the progress of reform in Europe. More commonly, the call for fast days arose when it seemed that people were not practicing the covenant. How to make that judgment was a matter of debate. The records suggest that the process of deciding on a fast day was usually initiated by the clergy, either in their congregations or in their role as counselors to the state. In local congregations, a minister was obliged to gain the consent of the members. Richard Mather "made a motion" to Dorchester church in December 1660 for a "day of humilliation" to which "the Church & assembly consented by ther silence."[18] Early on, the magistrates in Massachusetts never called a fast day without asking for permission from the clergy. Tension soon developed, in part because some magistrates complained "about the often reiteration" of the ritual "for the same cause." And tensions increased after 1660, as issues like the halfway covenant and treatment of the Baptists led members of the Massachusetts General Court to quarrel with the ministers. A drought the very summer during which the synod advised churches to adopt the halfway covenant was blamed on that decision; in their defense, the clergy pointed to the rains that fell in response to a fast![19]

Like so many of the wonders, fast days and the events they were keyed to were open to alternative interpretations. People could explain the drought of 1662 two different ways, as a judgment on the ministers or on the churches for opposing the reform. Year after year throughout these troubled decades, the clergy argued that "declension" was the problem that fast days must address. A classic statement of their thinking was the "jeremiad" preached in 1645 by Thomas Shepard in which he traced the loss of ships at sea and recent deaths of children to God's anger at the colonists for wavering in the "love of . . . Truth."[20] Others echoed his lament—his son in *Eye-Salve; Or, a Watch-Word From our Lord . . . unto his Churches* (1673), Samuel Willard in *Useful Instructions for a professing People in Times of great Security and Degeneracy* (1673), and Increase Mather in *A Call from Heaven* (1679). Yet back in 1637 the ministers themselves had offered rival meanings for the fast day held officially to bewail "the dissensions in our churches," with John Wheelwright arguing in a sermon that "those that do not know the Lord Jesus, they are usually given most unto fasting," and pleading that the only rightful "end" of fasting "must be our turning to the Lord."[21] So it went thereafter: consensus on the basic myth gave way to arguments among the ministers over toleration and church membership. Meanwhile the deputies and magistrates had reasons of their own for wanting or rejecting fast days. As King Philip's War neared its end, the Massachusetts General Court proclaimed a day of thanksgiving despite Increase Mather's plea for renewed fasting. In retrospect he saw himself the better judge, though others disagreed.[22]

All this politicking did not deter local congregations from assuming that a fast would help them overcome dissension. Fasting remained deeply meaningful to Samuel Sewall even though he witnessed at close range the struggles within the Massachusetts government over what was said in fast-day proclamations.[23] To others, surely, the rite became formulaic. But at its heart remained the central motif of religion in this culture, the confession "I (or we) have sinned; Lord, pardon me (us) for doing so."

Confession was a ritual in its own right. It occurred in several different settings, but never more dramatically than when John Underhill, a former "Antinomian" who was accused of adultery, returned from exile in 1640 to ask Boston church to lift its sentence of excommunication. He spoke before the church on the weekday of a public lecture.

He came in his worst clothes (being accustomed to take great pride in his bravery and neatness) without a band, in a foul linen cap pulled close to his eyes; and standing upon a form, he did, with many deep sighs and abundance of tears, lay open his wicked course, his adultery, his hypocrisy, his persecution of God's people here, and especially his pride (as the root of all, which caused God to give him over to his other sinful courses) and contempt of the magistrates.

As though he were a candidate for membership, or mindful of the tale of Spira, he went on to describe

how his presumptuous laying hold of mercy and pardon, before God gave it, did then fail him when the terrors of God came upon him, so as he could have no rest, nor could see any issue but utter despair, which had put him divers times upon resolutions of destroying himself, had not the Lord in mercy prevented him, even when his sword was ready to have done the execution . . . all along he discovered a broken and melting heart, and gave good exhortations to take heed of such vanities and beginnings of evil as had occasioned his fall; and in the end he earnestly and humbly besought the church to have compassion of him, and to deliver him out of the hands of Satan.

Once the church had voted to accept him back, Underhill repeated this performance before the General Court, which grudgingly released him from most penalties. The final step in his ordeal, one he took "to make his peace the more sound," was to kneel before the man whose wife he had seduced and beg forgiveness.[24]

This extraordinary scene—so public, so fully staged, so rich in gestures—was archetypal in its structure. The action began with a demonstration of reversal in the clothes he wore, clothes that emblemized the transformation of his pride into humility. Like the kings and tyrannizing bishops described in the lore of wonders, Underhill had fallen from high rank to low. Kneeling and crying (Winthrop noted that his "blubbering" interrupted the flow of the confession) were gestures emphasizing his "fall," and as Winthrop said, his broken heart. Another action was to bring out in the open what was hidden. Underhill had started on this process some months before, when "he made a public confession both of his living in adultery with Faber's wife (upon suspicion whereof the church had before admonished him) and attempting the like with another woman. . . ." Now he added details of these crimes. Built into the structure of confession was another requirement, to "justify . . . the church and the court" for having punished him. Underlying the whole spectacle was the premise that sin left unexposed turned the guilty into slaves of Satan; referring to himself as a "bondslave" of the Devil, Underhill "declared what power Satan had of him since the casting out of the church."[25] Thereby he dramatized anew the fearful dangers awaiting those outside the church and the safety of the covenant.

The ritual structure of confession came into play in many other cases. A year before this scene in Boston church the man who headed Harvard College, Nathaniel Eaton, was charged with "cruelty" to students by the General Court. Overnight, his fellow ministers "convinced" him to confess, and "in the open court, before a great assembly," Eaton "made a very solid, wise, eloquent and serious (seeming) confession, condemning himself in all the particulars." Eaton hoped for pardon. But when the court imposed a fine and banned him from schoolteaching, he broke the rhythm of the ritual by refusing to accept the punishment:

> A pause being made, and expectation that (according to his former confession) he would have given glory to God, and acknowledged the justice and the clemency of the court, the governor giving him occasion, by asking him if he had ought to say, he turned away with a discontented look, saying, "If sentence be passed, then it is to no end to speak."

What happened afterward confirmed the court's doubts, for Eaton "soon discovered [revealed] himself" by fleeing before he could be excommunicated from the Cambridge congregation. Once he disappeared, other crimes of his were revealed, and Winthrop closed his story of the episode by surmising that Eaton had been enduringly corrupted by his youthful training with the Jesuits.[26]

Sometimes people played the role of penitent and fulfilled expectations; sometimes they rebelled against neighbors who attempted to rebuke them. Happy was the day when a woman excommunicated from Boston church for "wicked and blasphemous courses . . . came to see her sin and lay it to heart, and to frequent the means." Repenting, she was received back into the church. The Chelmsford/Wenham church tried time and time again to persuade certain members they had misbehaved. It was satisfying when a woman who cursed others by calling them "rogue, rascal, hellbound, the devil will take them" made "open confession" and was released from church discipline, but not at all so when a "sullen" George Norton told visitors "that the church would force him to confess that he sinned against knowledge which were, he said, to sin the sin against the Holy Ghost." In contrast to Underhill, Norton told church members that "he had not trouble in his soul," and "had not sinned wittingly &c."[27] Human nature being what it is, churches often ran up against stubborn men and women who affirmed their innocence or who simply moved away from towns where they were under sentence of church discipline.[28] But nothing changed the framework of assumptions or the structure of the ritual: confession released people from their punishment and restored them to the body of God's people.

This same process figured in the civil courts. From the standpoint of the magistrates, the purpose of the courts was fundamentally religious in the sense of making people conform to the rules of righteousness. It was "sin" that courts existed to expose, and, by doing so, to cleanse the commonwealth of guilt. The law was like an icon, a monument to pure truth.[29] According to their self-perception, the magistrates were God-fearing men who undertook to "further the execution of justice according to the righteous rules of God's word." They went about this business in a manner that depended on the ritual of confession. With but rare exceptions, the people charged with crimes in New Haven Colony appeared before the magistrates and acknowledged they were guilty. The "truth" was not at issue once these cases reached this point; rather, it was crucial that a person charged with some offense reveal the truth and manifest repentance. Otherwise, the consequences were far worse than any fines or whippings that the court imposed. As one New Haven magistrate explained to someone being questioned,

> [You had] best speak the trueth, for if [you] shall hide or cover it, it will encrease both your sin and punishment and therefore [you are] wished to confess [your] sinne and give glory to God, and to remember what Solomon says, he that hideth his sin shall not prosper.

Another time, a magistrate reminded someone accused of rape of the crucial distinction between justice here on earth and justice in the world to come, "for though the court might, God would not cleare him if guiltie. . . . [And] therefore [the judge] desired him not to leave God and himself" by refusing to confess. Confronted with this expectation, and accepting it themselves, people in New Haven gave in and confessed to the court in most cases. Like Underhill before the Massachusetts General Court, they also affirmed the correctness of the court's decision.[30] Confession functioned both to purge sin from the body social and to reassert the basic rules that governed this community.

Certain crimes called for special treatment because they violated deep taboos. The codes of law enacted by the several governments segregated most of these as crimes for which the penalty was death: blasphemy, murder, bestiality, homosexuality, adultery, false witness, treason. Three times in New Haven Colony someone was suspected of committing bestiality, and in the one case that resulted in an execution, confession played a crucial role. Interpreting a deformed piglet as evidence of crime, the townspeople of New Haven directed their suspicion at a servant, George Spencer, who was not one of the godly. Confessing under pressure, though recanting when he realized that the consequence was execution, Spencer "died despairing and unrepentant," and in the eyes of those convicting him "a terrible example of divine justice and wrath." Someone else who confessed to the crime of bestiality, a church member, pointed out each of the animals he had polluted. They were killed before his eyes as he awaited execution on the scaffold. In the Spencer case, and again in the pursuit of a man named Thomas Hogg, it was supposed that the likeness of the criminal was revealed in the monster birth. A related folk belief (it also had support in learned culture) was acted on when the New Haven magistrates forced Hogg to scratch the sow that gave birth to the monster, and cited its reaction as proof of his guilt.[31]

Always, confession figured as a means of bringing crimes to light. It was not uncommon for someone accused of one offense to acknowledge others. Where confession failed to work, folk measures sometimes helped, as with the crime of buggery. The lore of wonders contained many tales of crimes successfully concealed until a wonder made them visible—the earth opening up, the Devil making an appearance, some sympathetic magic. Another of these folk beliefs or wonders was that blood would flow from corpses touched by persons guilty of the murder. Twice John Winthrop knew of or participated in this test. Once was when a woman of "lewd" reputation and a man who may have been her lover were led to her husband's corpse, which "bled abundantly." The second time came three years later, in 1647, when a woman who acknowledged giving birth to a stillborn illegitimate baby was asked by a jury "to touch the face of it, whereupon the blood came fresh into it." The woman promptly "confessed the whole truth" and was duly executed. The magistrates in Plymouth Colony ordered a suspected murderess "to touch" the body of an infant, "but there was nothing thereby did appear respecting its death." In one other case, the murder of a Christian Indian, the corpse "fell a bleeding a fresh as if it had been newly slain" when a suspect "came near the dead body."[32]

Thus was the folk proverb fulfilled, "Murder will out." Cited in *The Canterbury Tales* and a staple of the lore of wonders,[33] this action mimicked the archetypal structure of confession—the revealing of the hidden, the upwelling of a sin that God alone can see and forgive. That ordinary people imagined God as knowing all their secret crimes, and as obligating them to confess, is clear from the court records. An Essex

County woman who was pursued by a man to perform "the act of un-cleanes" described the "Sinn" as "odious" and warned her would-be lover, "Will you venture to lay under these temptations & concealed wickednes, you may Provoak God to Leave you & then you will come under Great Blame." A witness shared this feeling:

> These things are not to bee kept private, wee may Justly Provoake God, that further mischeife may follow & then wee shall come un-der Great Blame: Besides the trouble that will bee to my conscience as long as I live.

As she explained to the county court, she acted on this principle by "Re-veal[ing] all to a wise man in ye Towne. . . ." In another case it was nighttime when Ruth Shaw, a married woman, found herself alone with a man who told her that his "yarde was so stiffe that it Hindred him." She refused his plea to make love, and refused a second time when he offered her five shillings. Why not, he asked, since "no body seeth us: she replyed god seeth us: Well come saith hee I will give you ten shill-ings. Then she replyed No for how shall I do this wickedness and sin against god." This staunchness was repeated in the response made by Elizabeth Dane, a married woman, when a man asked her to go to bed with him. It was dark inside the house, and her would-be lover reassured her by advising that "Nobody sees." "But God sees," Elizabeth re-sponded, "if nobody [else] sees, for God sees in the dark." The expec-tation that God knew of crimes attempted or committed and would swiftly punish those responsible was also voiced by people like the Springfield man who halted an attempted rape because "God smote him with a trembling that at last he lett her goe."[34]

The homely wisdom of these women amounted to the principle that sin will out: it cannot hide forever. The ministers affirmed the same idea, Samuel Danforth warning in an execution sermon that the "eye" of God sees every "secret" sin.[35] Another piece of wisdom, one that many different people voiced, was that "guiltless blood" cries out for ven-geance. Articulated by the martyrs under Mary Tudor, this belief was reaffirmed by writers such as William Turner, who cited Cain's sad fate as illustrating how God listened to "the voice of the Innocent Blood crying from Earth to Heaven for Vengeance," and by ordinary people in testi-mony to the courts.[36] Thus a woman warned that "there is a wittnesse above all that sees all . . . and my father said the lord will avenge my wrongs one day." In one version of this belief, the victim returned as an apparition to tell others of the crime that had occurred. Stories of this sort combined two motifs, those of vengeance and discovery. A further piece of wisdom shared by people in New England was that murder and related crimes, like bestiality, stained the land with blood that must be cleansed. Increase Mather likened murder to a curse upon the land, and William Turner, in describing "Divine Judgments upon Murder," explained that "there was no other means allowed for the expiating the guilt of Murder, and purging the Land that was defiled therewith, but by the Blood of him that committed the Fact."[37] The principle of necessary "revenge" figured in the deliberations of the Connecticut General Assembly in 1649, when it ruled, in answer to the question "what may bee done according to God in way of revenge of the bloude of John Whitmore," that it was "lawfull and according to God to make warr uppon" the Indians who had killed him. So too Samuel Danforth, justifying the death sentence on a Massachusetts youth convicted of bestiality, declared, "The Land cannot be cleansed, untill it hath spued out this Unclean Beast."[38]

Where all these threads of meaning converged was in the ceremony of public execution. The procedures of this ceremony dramatized the cleansing of the land, the righteousness of law, and the healing powers of the gospel. As described by the ministers, the crucial moment in the ceremony was the scaffold speech in which the prisoner confessed to his crime and begged for mercy. But was this how crowds perceived the ceremony, or why printers publicized the event?

Executions in New England followed a strict pattern. Even more than confessions, they involved certain gestures and a set of roles. The repertory of these roles and gestures was drawn from English precedents as modified to suit the circumstances of New England. No one in New England was beheaded, as happened to an English king and others of high birth. Peculiar to that form of execution were such gestures as the kiss bestowed upon the ax and the gift of money to the executioner.[39] The colonists retained the procession to the scaffold, the scaffold speech, and the parting prayers and sermon that a minister delivered.[40] A prop that sometimes figured in the staging of the ceremony was a coffin for the victim's body.[41] The pace of things was also crucial. It was customary for the magistrates to grant the ministers' request that someone not be executed quickly, but have time to reflect and, if all went well, confess. For some of those who gathered to observe an execution, the drama lay in whether someone would confess or not, and if so, in judging whether the confession was heartfelt. What counted were the gestures that a person made and how he looked.[42]

Esther Rogers, a young servant executed in 1701 for the crime of murdering an illegitimate child, acted out this transformation into penitent. As described by a minister, Rogers chose to walk "the dolorous way" to the scaffold instead of riding in the usual cart, a gesture that helped manifest humility. When she came in sight of the scaffold, she overcame a brief reluctance and "Marched on with an Erected, and Radiant Countenance, as unconcerned with the business of Death." By her side walked two or three ministers, one of whom remarked on the coffin and the "few Minutes" that remained to her, and asked, "How can you bear the sight of all these things?" Again she answered properly: "She turns about, and looking him in the face with a very smiling countenance, sayes, I know I am going to the Lord Jesus Christ." Climbing to the scaffold without hesitating, she listened to a reading of the warrant for her death, and requested prayer. She prayed herself, and the ministers responded. A handkerchief was placed across her face, a minister asked if her faith was firm, she answered yes, and, as the noose enclosed her head, she "Cryes, . . . O Come Lord Jesus by Thy Pardoning Mercy, to Save me Now, or I perish for ever." In the weeks before she died, Esther Rogers had been visited in prison by "gentlewomen" of the town, and ministers who taught her that she must repent. When she did, in a statement to one of the gentlewomen, she lamented having ignored many opportunities for grace, described her crimes (including a second child murder), acknowledged that the court was just in sentencing her to die, and said she now loathed sin. She told too of prayer notes she sent to the church, notes in which she spoke of herself as a sinner. As though he remained unpersuaded, one minister requested "leave to make a more exact scrutiny into the State of" her soul. After talking with her privately, and making "Tryal of the Firmness and manner of her Faith," he was finally convinced.[43]

Two others who were similarly penitent were James Morgan, executed on Boston Common in 1686 for the crime of murder, and Joseph Quasson, an Indian who had killed a fellow Indian. Morgan confessed to his crime. He went on to lament other breaches of the moral code, from drunkenness to Sabbath-breaking. He was present (as was, in her turn, Esther Rogers) for a public lecture in which Increase Mather turned to him directly, told him this was the "Last Sermon" he would ever hear, and asked if he were "willing" to "go into that Dungeon, where is Blackness of darkness for ever." Walking from the church to Boston Common, Morgan had as company young Cotton Mather, who reviewed with him the rules, like hating sin, that were conditions of Christ's mercy. From the scaffold Morgan voiced a "solemn Warning" to the thousands gathered there to "beg of God to keep you from this Sin which hath been my ruine."[44] Joseph was exemplary in using well the extra time the court allowed him. People lent him several steady sellers (as a servant he had learned to read) and a copy of the narrative of Esther Rogers! Ten days before his execution, he was still not sure he had repented, though a visitor observed that he had "scores of Leaves turned down" in his Bible and approved the decision of the court. Only after hearing his last sermon did people observe "a very remarkable Alteration" in him, as in losing "Fear of Death." Like Esther Rogers, he declared that his "first sight of the Gallows" did not terrify him. Those who walked with him the final distance to the scaffold noted that "his Countenance, his Words . . . his whole Behavior . . . shewed plain eno' that he was very much above the Prevalency of . . . slavish Fear." From the scaffold he warned others not to fall into his wicked ways; questioned once again about assurance, he responded in a way that moved the audience "almost beyond Example."[45]

Joseph, James, and Esther Rogers were models of repentance. Others also confessed—the Hartford woman whose dead baby's face changed color when she touched it; Hugh Stone, who killed his wife; another woman who killed her bastard child; a group of pirates Cotton Mather described in an execution sermon.[46] But from the outset some refused to play the role marked out for them. Winthrop noted two such cases, the first when Dorothy Talby was executed in 1638 for killing her three-year-old daughter. It seems certain she was mentally deranged, which may be why she confessed only after being threatened with the punishment of being "pressed to earth." Yet remorse did not follow. Instead,

> When she was to receive judgment, she would not uncover her face, nor stand up but as she was forced, nor give any testimony of her repentance, either then or at her execution. The cloth, which should have covered her face, she plucked off and put between the rope and her neck. . . . Mr. [Hugh] Peter, her late pastor, and Mr. Wilson, went with her to the place of execution, but could do no good with her.

Another troubling execution occurred in 1644, when "one Franklin" was condemned for having so mistreated a young servant that he died. The sentence stirred qualms in certain members of the General Court. Nor did Franklin admit he was guilty. Instead he died "professing assurance of salvation, and that God would never lay the boy his death to his charge, but the guilt of his blood would lie upon the country."[47] Cotton Mather tells us briefly of a man who, thinking he would be reprieved, did not confess, and of a Springfield woman who slept through the sermon preached to benefit her soul.[48]

Still others broke the rhythm of the ceremony in some way—repudiating a confession, acting inconsistently, making the wrong gestures. The pirate William Fly, who died on Boston Common in 1726, mocked the deepest meanings of the ritual in his passage to the scaffold.

Fly briskly and in a way of bravery jumpt up into the Cart, with a nose-gay in his hand, bowing with much unconcern to the Spectators as he pass'd along, and at the Gallows he behaved still obstinately and boldly till his face was covered for death. . . .[49]

Another pirate leader, Captain John Quelch, who died on Boston Common in 1704 with four others of his crew, began well by piously declaring to a minister, "I am afraid of a Great God, and a Judgment to Come." But he acted very differently for the crowd that gathered at the scaffold:

> . . . when on the Stage first he pulled off his Hat, and bowed to the Spectators . . . now being called upon to speak what he had to say, it was but thus much; Gentlemen, 'Tis but little I have to speak: What I have to say is this, I desire to be informed for what I am here, I am Condemned only upon Circumstances.

When one of his crew members appealed to the crowd to "beware of Fal[se]-Company," Quelch rejoined, "They should also take care how they brought Money into New-England, to be Hanged for it!" A servant who committed infanticide confused people by denouncing well-intentioned visitors after she had made a statement of repentance: "I wish, Oh! I wish, the Testimonies of a thorough Repentance in her, were more Conspicuous" was how Cotton Mather put her case.[50]

Though some refused to confess or gave mixed performances, the meaning of the ceremony remained what the ministers prescribed. They were almost always present, and their testimony about someone's struggle for repentance was the sole source of such information. Who could have overheard the conversation between Cotton Mather and James Morgan, a problem Mather overcame by publishing a unique version of the dialogue? It seems likely, too, that they were mediators of the scaffold speech or written statement made by those about to die. Not that someone wrote these statements for the victims (though this cannot be ruled out); the process was one of approval, as when Increase Mather read James Morgan's confession to five thousand people crowding into Third Church. In making themselves central to the ceremony, the clergy used it to enhance the message they preached weekly in their sermons: repent or suffer terrifying judgment. Apart from all the other meanings of an execution, its focus was conversion. In their final sermons to the victims, the clergy described the right way to grace while sounding once again the theme of "now or never." How fresh that jaded theme, and how frightening, when, as preachers often said, there was but a short interval of time—so "little little time before I go," as James Morgan complained from the scaffold—for someone to repent. Preaching the mercy

of a Christ who listened to repentant sinners, and reminding people of
the moral rules that had been broken, the clergy dramatized the godly
program of reform and the cleansing process of confession.[51]

In so regulating the performance of the ritual, the ministers had allies
in the magistrates and printers—magistrates who believed that law coincided with the will of God, printers who saw opportunities to sell lots
of books and broadsides. How it happened that printers and the clergy
joined forces is not possible to reconstruct, though English precedents
existed, and collaboration on the lore of wonders was another model
they could follow.[52] Gallows speeches were a well-known genre, as were
tales of "divine vengeance against" criminals, which figured in the lore
of wonders. But not until the 1670s did New England printers think to
publish an execution sermon. The first to include a full text of someone's "true confession" was Increase Mather's *Sermon Occasioned by the
Execution of a Man* (1686), to which Cotton Mather added what he preached
before James Morgan's final moments. Two booksellers, one of them the
visiting John Dunton, who saw an opportunity to make a quick profit,
acted as the publishers. No doubt they shared Cotton Mather's satisfaction with the sales, for he reported in his diary that "the people,
throughout the Country, very greedily desired the Publication of my
poor Sermon," and that it "sold exceedingly." To sweeten the second
edition, issued the next year, Cotton supplied his "Discourse with the
poor Malefactor walking to his Execution."[53] Thereafter, printers issued
gallows sermons almost as frequently as there were executions. Meanwhile they were also turning out a cheaper form of publication, broadsides that described an execution and reported someone's final words of
warning. The earliest of "dying warnings" to be published in New England was James Morgan's, which belatedly appeared in Cotton Mather's
compilation *Pillars of Salt*. Others followed, like *An Account of the Behaviour and last Dying Speeches Of the Six Pirates . . . Executed on Charles River.*[54]

It is surely symptomatic of the printers' world that pirates should be
given such attention. Their appeal to the public was demonstrated again
when thirteen-year-old Benjamin Franklin wrote a ballad, "The Taking
of Teach the Pirate," and yet again in 1717, when a Boston printer published *overnight* the gallows speeches and confessions of a group of pirates executed in Rhode Island. It seems likely that a printer enticed
Cotton Mather into capitalizing on this same event, for Mather, though
absent from the execution, hastily composed *The Valley of Hinnom. The
Terrours of Hell demonstrated,* with a gallows speech appended.[55]

Broadsides relating the "last Dying Speeches" of a criminal became
more frequent in the years to come. By the 1730s they included woodcut
illustrations of the execution or the crime, a sure sign of reaching out to

common readers. In this decade, New England printers also issued rival versions of these narratives with warnings not to trust another's text: "Note, There being a foolish Paper printed, called *Julian's Advice to Children and Servants,* said to be published at his Desire; this may certify, that the said Paper is false and spurious, and disowned by the said Julian in the Presence of three Persons."[56] Tales of pirates, woodcut pictures of the scaffold, fictive (or competing) versions of what happened—in these ways the book trade imposed its priorities upon the ceremony as it had upon the wonder. The deeper way in which the book trade mediated executions was in setting up a formula for dying speeches and confessions. The outlines of this formula were established long before the founding of New England and came into play in 1644, when a Massachusetts man and woman, executed for adultery, "died very penitently, especially the woman, who had some comfortable hope of pardon of her sin, and gave good exhortation to all young maids to be obedient to their parents. . . ."[57] Local printers took their time to use it, as they took their time to resume printing almanacs in keeping with the English format. But the remark of an English minister in 1692, "the people expect a confession always at the time of any man's execution,"[58] suggests that printers and the clergy had to conform to the expectations of their audience for both genres. Whatever the exact dynamics of the situation the book trade in New England was significantly involved in the burst of execution sermons that circulated after 1686.

Yet in mediating the significance of executions, printers and booksellers joined with the ministers in presenting executions as warnings to the living (though especially youth) of what they would suffer if they failed to repent and reform themselves. Together, ministers and printers enforced the theme of terror. As in narratives like that of Francis Spira, execution sermons and the histories of these events lingered on the agonies of conscience that criminals experienced—the suffering of a New Haven man, who when he approached the scaffold "was awaken'd into a most unutterable and intolerable anguish of soul, and made most lamentably desperate out-cries," and of a "W.C.," who "when he came to the gallows, and saw death . . . never was a cry, for 'Time! time! a world for a little time! the inexpressible worth of time' uttered with a most unutterable anguish." Where they could not quote the very words of someone, writers filled the gap with prose that evoked inner feelings; hence Increase Mather imagined of James Morgan that "the Murderers Soul is filled with hellish horror of heart; so that he is as it were Damned above ground, and In Hell whilst he is yet alive." Mather and his fellow ministers deliberately enhanced the element of horror; as Samuel Danforth explained, their tactics were to use such "Fearful Judgements" to "strike

. . . holy fear and dread of God into the hearts of the Hearers and Spectators thereof." Danforth singled out "sinners" as especially needing to be "scared and frighted out of their vile Haunts and lascivious Courses, by the Terrour of Wrath and Judgement."[59] But as every printer knew, texts that played on terror—that dramatized God's vengeance—were read by godly people too!

So too readers were attracted to those texts that painted villainy in all its extreme colors by enumerating the crimes of the victims—their "Riots, Revels, Debauches" and "Horrid Oathes," their sexual behavior, the contempt they had for parents.[60] A broadside of 1737 put in rhyme a brash description of the villains:

> Each Son of Vice, a dreadful Crew!
> the Days in laugh and Merriment,
> and ev'ry Joy of Sense they spent.
> In Drink, and Songs, and noisy Play,
> Quick flow'd their jovial Hours away.
> Now Cards, now Dice would intervene,
> And fill the Day—a hellish Scene! . . .
> The sensual Joys and low Delights
> That Women give, clos'd all their Nights.

Here, the literature of crime moved closer to a genre that was secular, the rogue's tales that common readers had enjoyed since the days of Shakespeare.[61]

Such texts reflect an intertwining of the market with the worldview of the clergy. The phenomenon of vast crowds appearing for these ceremonies is another token of this doubleness; lay people were responding to a set of meanings other than the ones they ordinarily encountered in a sermon. Printers knew the reason in a word: murder. We may also sense the appeal of suspense: Would someone repent at the final moment? Would death by hanging occur cleanly, or become grotesque? Sitting in her yard the June day in 1704 when pirates were executed, Hannah Sewall heard from far away the "Screech of the Women" responding "When the Scaffold was let sink."[62] Was this like a cheer, or closer to a mournful groan? Were executions more like festivals than not? Let us suppose that these crowds preferred to hear the criminal confess, and that they went home disappointed when the rhythm of the ritual remained incomplete. But let us also suppose that they went away contented with the spectacle of death no matter how the criminal behaved.

Confession was the central event of the fast day, cases in the civil courts and in the meetinghouse, and public executions. It was *the* New England ritual, the one that ordinary people witnessed, read of, and reiterated countless times. The importance of confession was consistent with the broader culture of the colonists, the vernacular religion that reached them via Foxe, the Bible, and the "godly" of the sixteenth century. The penitential psalms were favorite reading in this culture, as were stories and examples of sinners struggling to achieve repentance.[63] People valued rites that restored moral order to the body social. Confession put Satan at a distance, and reaffirmed the godliness of rulers. It helped satisfy the craving for revenge; it deflected anger into channels that were culturally acceptable. All these different meanings were sustained by printers, and in turn were voiced by ordinary people. Confession, like the lore of wonders, had significance for many men and women in New England.

But this is not to ignore how the rite was used by different groups. Fast days and thanksgivings were invested with political significance as ministers and magistrates advanced rival reasons for their purpose. Always, the clergy tried to make the ritual conform to their outcry of "declension." Printers had their own agenda, together with a formula that lingered well into the eighteenth century. As for those confessing, whether criminals or people in a fast-day observance, there was always the question of sincerity. Were people merely going through a form, or genuinely moved to confess their sins? The formula for executions played it both ways in allowing doubts to intrude in the voice of the minister, though also seeming to affirm that someone who confessed was saved. Fast-day sermons posed this question for the people as a whole. In private statements many asked it of themselves. Indeed, some of the resistance to fast days and the ceremony of renewal of covenant sprang from popular concern that rituals performed in a "formal" manner made things worse instead of better.

The most forceful critique of confession came from Robert Keayne, the Boston merchant who donated books and money to the town in 1653. Back in 1639, Boston First Church, accusing him of charging too much for his goods, voted to admonish Keayne for unchristian behavior. Keayne, confessing, was restored to covenant. But in his lengthy will, a document he intended to be circulated, he insisted on his innocence and accused the church members of self-interest. Never did his "conscience . . . convince [him] that the censure was either equal or deserved by me." In effect, Keayne repudiated his confession by making a distinction between conscience and the ritual. He went on to invoke the authority of death: "I now speak the words of a man as if ready to die and leave the world, when there is no cause to daub with my own conscience to justify evil nor to extenuate my own faults, which will again be called to account, if not before washed away in the precious blood of Jesus Christ."[64]

Keayne was almost unique in renouncing a confession, and he limited his protest by acknowledging the duty of the magistrates to punish sin.[65] But suppose that people really acted on this principle and put conscience first? Or that the magistrates depended on confessions to order people hanged for crimes they had not committed? The first of these situations occurred when governments attempted to suppress the Baptists and the Quakers; the second, in a witch-hunt.

II

MURDERERS AND pirates were joined at the scaffold by people condemned for their beliefs. Between 1659 and 1661 the Massachusetts government hanged four Quakers. One was Mary Dyer, she whose monster birth in 1637 was represented as a portent. All four died because of their insistence on returning to Massachusetts after being banished. Baptists were not executed; but the Massachusetts government sentenced members of both groups to "be openly and severely whipt, by the executioner . . . not exceeding forty strokes, unless he shall publickly recant before his sentence. . . ." In 1661, with the death penalty suspended, the court described more carefully the punishment for Quakers: "[to] be stripped naked from the Middle upwards, and tyed to a Carts tayle, and Whipped through the Town. . . ." Returnees would suffer branding on a shoulder, and a second severe whipping. The reason for these punishments was clear to those prescribing them: false doctrine and "Rebellion" threatened church and commonwealth.[66] So other governments declared, in justifying extreme treatment of outsiders—slaughter of the Huguenots, exclusion of the Jews, burning of Catholic priests in Elizabethan England and of Protestants in Mary Tudor's reign.

Yet, as Foxe informed his sympathetic readers, the heretics who died in Mary Tudor's reign were godly Protestants who transformed their ordeal into proof that they were really martyrs. In describing how to die a martyr's death, Foxe provided the vernacular tradition with a means of overturning the official meaning of an execution. To the priest who stood by hoping for a final change of heart and who urged the crowd to hearken to God's will, execution at the stake manifested the defense of truth by ordained institutions. But as Foxe presented these events they manifested something else, the triumph of the saints as they turned weakness into strength, dying into rebirth in the arms of Christ. As in other ceremonies, the key symbolism lay in gestures and the victim's final words. Did the person at the stake embrace the flames? Did he remain uncomplaining despite agonizing pain? Did he deny that he suffered?

Did he call on Christ, proclaiming his assurance of salvation? This was how lay men and women in the *Book of Martyrs* died, and in doing so transposed themselves from heretics to martyrs. Quoting sources from the times, Foxe asserted (in the words of Thomas Bilney) that "in the flame they felt no heat. . . ." He described others, like the young man William Hunter, who greeted his "weeping" father at the place of execution with the words ". . . be of good comfort; for I hope we shall meet again when we shall be merry," and whose final cry was "Lord, Lord, Lord, receive my spirit." More pointedly, the martyr-minister John Rogers, affirming his assurance that in "conscience" he was not a heretic but a member of Christ's church, declared that the men who judged him belonged to the church of "Satan." To complete the rite, Rogers "washed his hands in the flame, as though it had been in cold water."[67] Two other groups, the printers and the crowd on hand to watch, participated in this process of reversal. Working with the book trade, Foxe and writers like him publicized these events to the Protestant community. Printers helped subvert the church's message. So did those who came to watch the spectacle. Not always, but quite often, the crowd sided with the victims, praying for quick death, reaching out in sympathy, and afterward collecting bones as relics.[68]

All the pieces of the ritual of martyrdom were familiar to the colonists. Thus it happened that lay people acted out the role of martyr in protesting the official system.

Obadiah Holmes, a Baptist from Rhode Island, came to Massachusetts in 1651 in search of sympathetic brethren. Sentenced by the court to pay a fine or suffer whipping, Holmes prepared himself to be a martyr. He spent the night before his punishment in prayer and meditation, begging God for "strength . . . not to shrink or yield to the strokes, or shed tears, lest the adversaries of the truth should thereupon blaspheme and be hardened, and the weak and feeble-hearted discouraged. . . ." The next day he told the crowd that gathered to observe the whipping that he was "to suffer for . . . the Word of God, and testimony of Jesus Christ." A magistrate corrected him: "No, saith Mr. Nowel, it is for your error, and going about to seduce the people." Responding, Holmes compared the whipping he was about to endure to the sacrament of baptism: "I am now come to be baptized in afflictions by your hands, that so I may have further fellowship with my Lord." As the whip began to fall he prayed aloud, the while experiencing "such a spiritual manifestation of God's presence as the like thereof I never had nor felt. . . ." The crucial testimony (rendered in a narrative a fellow Baptist quickly published back in London) was that Holmes "could well bear . . . the outward pain . . . yea, and in a manner felt it not although it was grievous

as the spectators said, the man striking him with all his strength. . . ."
When the whipping ended, Holmes retorted to the magistrates, "You
have struck me as with roses," a statement borne out by the "cheerfulness" of his manner. These words and gestures stirred some in the crowd
to voice their sympathy; two men came up and "took him by the hand,"
an action that the magistrates angrily interpreted as "discountenanc[ing]
him in his sin."[69]

The role that Holmes performed so well was soon resumed by Quaker
missionaries. They had the martyrs Foxe described in mind as they were
whipped or led up to the scaffold.[70] From prison they wrote letters to
the magistrates declaring they knew "true Peace and Rest . . . in all our
Sufferings." Like Holmes, they bore their whippings with an outward
cheerfulness, as though they knew no pain. When the moment came for
Mary Dyer and two others to approach the scaffold (she was reprieved,
only to return again to Massachusetts and be executed), they walked
"Hand in Hand, all three of them, as to a Weding day, with great cheerfulness of Heart. . . ." This language had been used by martyrs under
Mary Tudor. As all three Quakers knew, the key was not to reveal any
change of countenance that might suggest a fear of death. (If Quakers
were false prophets, as the magistrates alleged, their courage would de-
sert them in the end.) Attempting to address the crowd, the three men
and women found their voices drowned out by the rattle of drums. What
they said in court and from the scaffold was publicized from London.
These Quakers uttered holy curses:

> Give Ear ye Magistrates, and all who are guilty, for
> this the Lord hath said concerning you, who will perform
> his Word upon you, That the same Day ye put his Servants to Death,
> shall the Day of your Visitation press over your
> Heads, and you shall be Curst for evermore. . . .

The central message of this curse was vengeance, the vengeance God
would wreak on persecutors of the saints. So Mary Dyer declared from
the scaffold, and so declared the writers who narrated her martyrdom:

> Whose Innocent Blood cries aloud for Vengeance against you,—
> who have shed Innocent Blood; God's Judgments draw near; all you
> who had a Hand in shedding Innocent Blood, the Blood of the In-
> nocent is upon you; Wo will be to you for evermore, except you
> Repent.[71]

Here, the rite of martyrdom achieved its ultimate inversion of the meaning of such punishment: appropriating the motif of vengeance by a
wrathful God, Quakers turned it against magistrates and clergy, whom

they painted as "mad-drunk with blood."[72] It was in keeping with this strategy that, like Foxe before them, Quaker publicists enumerated judgments that befell their judges—the strange death of Endecott ("he stunk alive"), the death of John Norton's grandchildren, the hangman dying "in great Horror of Mind, and Torment of Body."[73]

Echoes of Anne Hutchinson! She too had prophesied the downfall of her persecutors, and, from exile in Rhode Island, continued to cite wonders that betokened (so she thought) God's providential blessing on her cause. Quakers liked to think her blood still called for vengeance. In keeping with the ritual of martyrdom, the writers who described these events also told of people in the crowd who protested they were witnessing "the Sufferings of the People of the Lord," or who became Quaker converts.[74] But what if people in the crowd were hostile? The Rogerenes, the sect that borrowed some ideas from Quakers and others from the Baptists, suffered *their* persistent beatings and imprisonments in front of crowds that rarely expressed sympathy; accordingly, their publicists described the "great Revilings, Mocks, [and] Scoffs" as symbolizing the great "Enmity that is between the seed of the Woman and the Seed of the Serpent." Otherwise, the Rogerenes employed the same rhetoric that the Quakers used before them.[75]

New England's martyrs were but few in number, and their sufferings, though well publicized in London, did not succeed in discrediting the ministers and magistrates. A more consequential event was the collapse of witch-hunting in the aftermath of the witch craze of 1692. Witch-hunting, or the process of identifying witches and imposing proper punishment, involved fasting, execution, and confession. One of its motifs was heresy, for like Baptists and the Quakers, witches were accused of joining with the Devil to subvert Christ's kingdom. Another was the theme of murder, for people often blamed a "witch" for unexpected deaths of children. Men and women testified of seeing apparitions of dead people who demanded that their murder be revenged. There was even more to witchcraft and witch-hunting. As a "hidden Work of Darkness," witchcraft was something that godly men must struggle to make visible. Witchcraft was a mighty "Judgment," a sign from God of sins that must be purged.[76] These sins included the longstanding, much-lamented problem of anger between people; witches seemed especially discontented and disruptive of the Christian ethic. In using witch-hunts to purge witches, the colonists were resorting to familiar instruments, the fast day and the public execution, to cleanse their land of sin. But what if those who died as witches were innocent, not guilty?

In telling whether someone was a witch, the colonists counted on confession as the surest of the several kinds of evidence. Confession had a singular importance for two reasons: it made visible the hidden (no one actually saw the occult lines of force that witches were supposed to use), and it confirmed that the root of witchcraft was a compact with the Devil. Hence it happened that, interrogating men and women charged by neighbors with the crime of witchcraft, magistrates and ministers inquired of them if they had entered into such a compact. Some said yes. Mary Johnson, a servant girl in Wethersfield, Connecticut, admitted to "Familiarity with the Devil"; furthermore, she confessed that "she was guilty of the Murder of a Child, and that she had been guilty of Uncleanness with Men and Devils." A Springfield woman told a Massachusetts court in 1651 that she had "entred into covenant with Satan and became a witch." As though she could not resist the unfolding of the ritual, she went on (apparently) to confess the crime of infanticide. A Hartford woman, Rebecca Greensmith, confessed in 1662 that "she . . . had had familiarity with the devil. Being asked whether she had made an express covenant with him, she answered, she had not, only as she promised to go with him when he called. . . ."[77]

Where confession blossomed was in hearings and court trials arising out of presumed witchcraft in a farming village attached to the town of Salem. Tituba, a servant in the household of the Salem Village minister, confessed to entering into compact with the Devil; as one eyewitness reported afterward, she added a description of "the times when & places where they met, with many other circumstances to be seen at large." William Barker confessed that he signed a "design" to "destroy the Church of God, and to set up Satans Kingdom, and then all will be well." In all, some fifty persons, most of them from Andover, confessed in 1692 to covenanting with the Devil, and to taking part in counter-rituals deep within the woods.[78] Almost simultaneously, a man in Fairfield, Connecticut, acknowledged having "made a Contract with the devell five years senc with his heart and signed . . . the devells book and then seald it with his bloud. . . ."[79]

The crime to which these people confessed was making Satan master of their souls in place of God. But in several of these cases, and especially in the testimony neighbors offered of their suffering from suspected witches, it was said that witches used occult powers to cause death or sickness. The minister of Springfield blamed Mary Parsons for the sickness of his children, she in turn accused her husband of bewitching a young child to death, and neighbors testified of other children's deaths that seemed connected to her threats. When a Newbury woman "was ill, she would often cry out and complaine" that Elizabeth Morse "had bewitched her." A daughter testified that once when Goodwife Morse came to the house, "my Mother Cryed out, that wicked Woman would kill her,

be the Death of her, she could not beare it, and fell into a grievous Fitt.
. . ." Another neighbor declared that after Morse had "stroakt Goodwife
Ordway['s] Child over the Head, when it was sick . . . the Child dyed."[80]

The evidence assembled in the Salem trials included apparitions of the
dead returning to seek vengeance; thus, Ann Putnam saw "a man in a
Winding Sheet; who told her that Giles Corey had Murdered him, by
pressing him to Death with his Feet." Her tale had credibility because it
prompted people to remember that a man who lived with Corey many
years before had died inexplicably. The same Ann Putnam had seen
apparitions of two former wives of George Burroughs, who came to her
and declared "that their blood did crie for vengeance against him." The
murderer himself had told her he had killed several persons! Susannah
Sheldon testified that she had seen the apparition of Bridget Bishop,
another accused witch, and "immediately" thereafter "t[w]o little children" who "said that they ware Thomas Greens two twins and tould
Bridget Bishop to hir face that she had murthered them in setting them
into fits wher of they dyed."[81] On the stories flowed, stories mainly rooted
in the suffering of bewildered people who watched children or their
spouses die or suffer agonizing fits—thus William Brown of Salisbury,
who blamed the "miserabl[e]" condition of his wife (her "strang kind of
distemper & frensy uncapible of any rasional action") on Susannah Martin,
and the man who traced the "grevious fitts" of his child ("who promised
as much health & understanding both by Countenance and actions as
any other Children of his years") to Bridget Bishop. It was the illness of
his wife that moved Joseph Ballard to ride from Andover to Salem Village, a step that rapidly engulfed his town in witchcraft accusations and
confessions.[82]

How else did witches violate the order of God's people? Neighbors
described those accused of witchcraft as contentious, angry people,
or else (as Martha Corey said) as "idle sloathfull persons [who] minded
nothing that was good." Many were the stories of a quarrel over animals
that strayed into another person's garden or over work and how it was
not fully performed, of requests for help that went unanswered, of bar-
gains gone astray. Apparently because the Morses complained of an un-
completed task, their next-door neighbor described Elizabeth Morse as
having "Malice and Envy [in her] Heart." Several persons described the
"threatninge" manner of Hugh Parsons when they protested about the
quality of his brickmaking or some business matters. A man linked the
death of a calf to "a bargaine about" cattle he was engaged in with Thomas
Disbrough; "they not agreeing . . . sd Disbroughs wife was very angry
and many hard words pased . . ." A New Haven woman, not accused
of witchcraft though "suspitious" on that "poynt," was described in court

as someone who made "discord among neighbors," and who uttered "filthy
& uncleane speeches."[83] Someone's speech was often used against him:
curses, in particular, betokened antisocial anger that was felt as threatening by townspeople. Rebecca Eames, accused in 1692 of witchcraft and
of promising her son Daniel to Satan, acknowledged that she feared Daniel
was a witch "becaus he used dredfull bad words when he was angry: and
bad wishes. . . ."[84] Often, accused witches had been refused loans or
gifts by neighbors who subsequently suffered illness or an accident.[85]
Summing up these kinds of social interaction, John Hale noted in his
retrospective history of New England witchcraft that "in many of these
cases there had been antecedent personal quarrels, and so occasions of
revenge. . . ."[86]

Revenge! Associated with the wonder, a motif of the ritual of martyrdom, a favored curse of apparitions representing murdered souls, revenge was central to witchcraft and witch-hunting as these people
understood them. What were witches but malicious people bent on
harming Christians, in imitation of their wicked master? Rebecca Eames,
confessing she had covenanted with the Devil, explained that he had
"promised her . . . [the] powr to avenge her selfe on them that offended her." What was witch-hunting but a process of returning blow
for blow, of defeating Satan's "plot" against New England? Hugh Parsons,
soon to die because of his wife's testimony, came home one day and told
her that he hoped "that God will find out all such wicked Persons and
purge New England of all Witches. . . ."[87] Such cleansing of the land
from witches was acted out in public executions.

But the process often started with a fast day. Associating witches with
social strife and sickness, people looked to prayer and fasting as a means
of vanquishing the Devil and the evils he inflicted on the godly. Thus
when Samuel Parris, the minister at Salem Village, learned of odd events
among a few of his parishioners, he summoned neighboring ministers
to hold a day-long fast. A fast was called in hopes of healing Ann Cole
of Hartford, another in Salisbury to heal a woman rendered ill by witchcraft, and several were attempted in the town of Groton to relieve Elizabeth
Knapp from her possession. The possessed Goodwin children were subjects of a fast.[88]

A third ritual intruded in witch-hunting, the practice of confession.
Not only were confessions the best evidence of witchcraft; they also were
a means of reconciling with the covenanted community, of reenacting
(or restoring) someone's passage out of bondage into grace. The men
and women who confessed to being witches were acknowledging the power
of a rite that promised them redemption if they brought all hidden sins
to light. Mary Parsons had not really killed anyone, but she fell into

confession because other sins (or guilt) weighed upon her. Elizabeth Knapp, a possessed girl who nearly was accused of witchcraft, had likewise to confess her "many sins, disobedience to parents, neglect of attendance upon ordinances, attempts to murder herself and others."[89] At Salem, people had what seem like modest sins to admit; for most, it was a matter of acknowledging indifference to the ordinances or their wish to have more property. Yet upon listening to a minister insist that only by confessing could they save their souls, some fantasized of covenanting with the Devil. Poor Martha Tyler did so after being told by her minister, "Well I see you will not confess! Well, I will now leave you, and then you are undone, body and soul, for ever."[90]

Most striking, in the records, is the exchange between Ann Foster, her daughter Mary Lacey, and her granddaughter, Mary Lacey (Jr.), and four of the magistrates:

Q. [By the magistrates] Are you willing your daughter should make a full and free confession? A. Yes. Q. Are you willing to do so too? A. Yes. Q. You cannot expect peace of conscience without a free confession. A. If I knew any thing more, I would speak it to the utmost.—

The next voice is that of Mary Lacey, Sr.:

Oh! mother! how do you do? We have left Christ, and the devil hath gat hold of us. How shall I get rid of this evil one? I desire God to break my rocky heart that I may get the victory this time.

Further questions followed, most of them addressed to acts that witches were thought to perform with the Devil. The granddaughter, Mary Lacey, Jr., came into the courtroom and was sharply queried by the magistrates.

Q. Do you acknowledge now you are a witch? A. Yes. . . . Q. Do not you desire to be saved by Christ? A. Yes.—Then you must confess freely what you know in this matter.

Mary went on to describe her motives for accepting Satan (he helped her disobey her parents) and meetings she attended with Andover neighbors.[91]

Not only witches confessed guilt. In a culture saturated with descriptions of declension, it was easy to suppose that *everyone* was guilty of allowing Satan to invade the land. Hence the kindred rituals of fasting and confession worked two ways: as in the Faustlike stories, prayer and fasting were means of overcoming Satan, though the deeper overcoming lay within, in a thorough purging of the self and body social of "unrepented" sin.[92] Fast days thus required that the very people who were suffering face up to their guilt. When Mercy Goodwin and her siblings were afflicted with possession, their father, a church member, asked the congregation (it was Cotton Mather's) to hold a day of prayer. When it seemed to work, he interpreted the suffering of his children as a rebuke to himself for living in "a prosperous Condition." Afterward, like Mary Rowlandson, he vowed that, "awake" from affliction, he would remain steadfast in his love of Christ.[93] In late-seventeenth-century New England, witch-hunting thus became a means of moral "reformation," as Cotton Mather said in trying to explain why witchcraft had occurred in Salem. If witchcraft was a great affliction on New England, a matter of divine revenge, then godly people must restore their land to cleanliness by executing witches while confessing their own sins.[94]

Yet the rhythm of this cleansing process was disrupted by the failure of some would-be witches to confess, and the force with which others declared their innocence. Mary Parsons renounced her confession. A Charlestown woman refused to confess to witchcraft, though admitting another crime.[95] Passing by the many others—among them Rachel Clinton, Katherine Harrison, and Elizabeth Morse—who defied suspicion and maintained their innocence, we come to Salem, where the pressure to confess increased as more and more did so. Rebecca Nurse, cried out against by several of the women who claimed the gift of "spectral" sight, denied that she was guilty: "I can say before my Eternal father I am innocent, & God will clear my innocency." What she said in court she also said in private, as friendly neighbors testified: ". . . I am Innocent as the child unborn." Mary Bradbury told the court that she "was wholly inocent of any such wickedness . . . I am the servant of Jesus Christ & Have given my self up to him as my only lord & saviour. . . ." Martha Corey remained firm despite the court's reminding her that "If you expect mercy of God, you must look for it in Gods way by confession." A church member, she reminded people that "she had made a profession of christ and rejoyced to go and hear the word of god and the like." Abigail Faulkner, spared from execution because she was pregnant, insisted to the magistrates that she was "altogether Innocent . . . as will appear at the great day of Judgment." Sarah Cloyse and Mary Easty, sisters of Rebecca Nurse, declared they were not "conscious . . . of any guilt in the least degree of that crime . . . in the presence of the Living God we speake it, before whose awfull Tribunall we Know we shall ere Long appeare. . . ."[96]

A few days before she died, Mary Easty introduced a theme familiar to the Quakers and the Baptists and to any reader of the *Book of Martyrs:* let "no more Innocent blood be shed." In steadfastly refusing to confess, she appealed again to the "Lord above who is the Searcher of all hearts."

The implication of her statement was in keeping with the ritual of martyrdom, though she was more subdued in asking if the judges were thus willing to appear before their Maker; were they certain, she asserted, of "not be[ing] gu[i]lty of Innocent blood"? The horrors of this crime came home to young Margaret Jacobs, a confessing witch whose testimony sent two members of her family to the scaffold:

> The very first night after I had made confesion, I was in such horror of conscience that I could not sleep for fear the devil should carry me away for telling such horrid lies. . . . What I said was altogether false against my grandfather . . . which I did to save my life . . . ; but the Lord, charging it to my conscience, made me in so much horror, that I could not contain myself before I had denied my confession . . . chusing rather death with a quiet conscience, than to live in such horror, which I could not suffer.[97]

But the guilt that Mary Easty warned of was the guilt affecting magistrates and jurors and, more generally, the people who had testified against the witches. Would God not seek revenge on them, as he did on other murderers? Sarah Good resorted to the holy curse as she awaited execution; urged at the last moment to confess, in keeping with the demands of the rite of execution, she replied to the minister, "You are a lyer; I am no more a Witch than you are a Wizard, and if you take away my Life, God will give you Blood to drink." George Burroughs was more subtle. Drawing on a long-established repertory, he responded to the crowd awaiting his last words and watching his appearance with a "Speech for the clearing of his Innocency, with such Solemn and Serious Expressions . . . ; his Prayer (which he concluded by repeating the Lord's Prayer) was . . . well worded and uttered with . . . composedness, and . . . fervency of Spirit. . . ." If Robert Calef can be trusted, the crowd was so affected by George Burroughs (as some people were by watching Baptists suffer) that they almost stopped the execution.[98]

Six more people were to die at Salem, including Mary Easty. But when the court was adjourned by the governor, one reason was the growing recognition that godly magistrates were doing Satan's work by killing their own kind, not witches. That recognition came home cruelly to the minister of Salem Village. Many in his parish thought him stained with blood, which was why they refused to accept communion from his hands. According to the Quakers, it came home cruelly to some of the magistrates and ministers in the form of judgments on them and their children.[99] Hence it was that, four years later, the Massachusetts government commanded everyone to fast, in part to "pardon all the Errors of his Servants" in the "Tragedie" of the great witch-hunt.[100]

When witch-hunting ceased in 1692, with it ceased the confidence to differentiate the true witch from her specter. Fast days would continue, as would public executions. But in the aftermath of Salem there was deep confusion about these events. Cleansing, reconciliation, affirmations of authority—these were what the fast day, executions, and witch-hunting had as goals. Yet at Salem they had functioned to increase, not decrease, conflict between neighbors and between the people and the clergy. Thinking through his own confusion about witchcraft and witch-hunting, John Hale, the minister at Beverly, decided to reject "most of [the] principles" that constituted learned thinking.[101] Ordinary people did not theorize about judgments and authority. What they sensed, however, was that rites designed to heal could also harm. Confessing made things worse, not better; curses, though forbidden, dramatized injustice; victims of an execution became martyrs, and their judges suffered from the wrath of God. Ambivalently good and bad, these practices were perceived by people as too charged with hidden danger. Like the sacrament of the Lord's Suppper, they were better left alone.

As witch-hunting declined, so did persecution of outsiders and the practice of confession. In their heyday these rites of renewal rested on beliefs that lay men and women easily articulated. Some of these beliefs were very old, and owed little to the Reformation. Others (or the same ones) were the common stock of Europeans, whether Protestants or not. Like the lore of wonders, this shared culture was enriched with themes distinctive to the godly. What gave it force was the intensity with which these people valued the coherence of the body social. All these currents converged on the meaning of the martyr, murder, and witch-hunting. But as neighbors fell to quarreling, as outsiders like the Baptists settled down, as towns became distended, the symbolism of community came to lose some of its significance. With it waned the power of the rites that restored fellow feeling.

III

FASTING AND confession were means of healing sickness in the body social—the "heats" and "fever" of "contention," the polluting crimes of murder and infanticide, the conspiracies of witches. This same ritual structure served people who were stricken with disease, or who knew that death approached. But lay men and women did not always turn to ritual to ward off disease and terrifying death. Two alternatives were doctors, with their merely "natural" explanation of the problem, and the "cunning folk" who healed by occult means. Contesting these alternatives, the ministers insisted on repentance as good medicine. It was they who framed a model "way of death" in opposition to folk attitudes. When lay people worried about death and sickness, they often used the language of the preachers. Yet rarely did they approach death despairing of assurance, and from time to time they relied on occult or merely natural modes of healing.

The men and women who testified in Cambridge meetinghouse imagined sin as something almost physical. In the thinking of these people, the health of their bodies depended on their overcoming sin. So they were instructed to believe by Lewis Bayley and James Allin. Bayley, writing early in the century, laid down the principle that "Sicknesse comes not by hap or chance . . . but from mans wickednesse." From this followed the instruction to confess one's sins and beg for mercy. James Allin reviewed the connection between sin and sickness in sermons he preached as the town of Boston suffered from a smallpox epidemic. He reiterated Bayley's point; "our sins," he told his congregation, were the "provocation" for "chastisements and afflictions" such as sickness. Allin urged his readers to repent, while warning that "continuance in sin" was dangerous. Telling how he urged repentance on a woman, Allin painted her refusal as sufficient cause for God to "throw her on a bed of sickness."[102] Sin was dangerous to the body.

Knowing this, and deeply worried about illness because ordinary healing methods had so little chance of success, people turned to ritual to safeguard their passage either back to health or to everlasting life in heaven. The facts were that many children died in infancy, and many mothers as a consequence of childbirth. Illness usually signified a time of suffering, for the means of easing pain were few. When epidemics struck, as in waves of smallpox or diphtheria, they made death and illness that much more mysterious.[103]

But sickbeds were a zone of tension for still other reasons. Friends and kinfolk gathered to provide encouragement, but also to observe if the sufferer viewed his illness appropriately, as God-sent "affliction." Privacy was lacking for the sick and dying. Watching someone die, people often wondered who lay in waiting, Satan or the risen Christ. Death was like a special version of the "theatre of Gods judgments." Many were the stories of "remarkable" behavior as the end approached, stories Beard and Clarke enjoyed telling, and that figured in the conversation of lay people. Some concerned despair. Others told of how the Devil sent "temptations" at the final moment. Here was yet another reason for concern, since the Devil liked to disrupt souls at peace. As if this were not enough to make a sickbed fearful, another person present was the "King of Terrours," Death himself. According to a European folktale, Death stood by the bedside watching as a candle sputtered to its end. Emblem books depicted Death and Father Time cooperating to put out a candle, an image that a gravestone carver in New England borrowed as the design for a stone. Folk tradition and the lore of wonders thus enhanced the drama of the situation.[104]

In fashioning their response to death and sickness, the colonists abandoned many of the practices that other Europeans used—graveside liturgy, funeral sermons,[105] burial on sacred ground, anointing of the sick, ringing of consecrated bells, a final service of communion for the dying. They went on to reject other healing practices. One of these was the king's touch, a ceremony directed at particular diseases. English men and women by the many thousands relied on successive Stuart kings to bring them relief from scrofula and kindred ailments. But people in New England had to do without the practice. In general, they also had to do without a systematic medicine that relied on astrology, while any preference for the remedies of cunning folk was strongly opposed by the clergy. Like other gestures of reform, these changes were in keeping with a deeper bias against ritual. What mattered more was the free movement of the Holy Spirit, together with an inward piety focused on one's conscience.[106]

The place of older rites and folk traditions was taken by a different set of practices and attitudes. The English minister-cum-theologian William Perkins, addressing the significance of dying, asked lay people to imagine death not as "the day of greatest woe and miserie," but as a "passage or mid-way between this life and eternall life." Criticizing two assumptions he attributed to lay people—that someone dying in despair was unredeemed, and that sudden death was the worst kind of all—Perkins argued for a routinizing of the art of dying well: "preparation" must begin beforehand, and continue all through life. Lifetime preparation was far better than delaying till the final moment; repentance on a deathbed could be counterfeit, but not the prolonged practice of asceticism. Hence his commmonsense downplaying of sudden death and the violent outcries sometimes made by dying men and women, outcries he interpreted as having natural causes. Perkins turned death into a message for the living: live well as Christians, and you will die in peace of conscience. But he also emphasized the fearsome consequences of sin, and how it caused a judging God to inflict men with sickness unto death. Lewis Bayley, the more evangelical, insisted on the "fearfull" possibility of "sudden death." He urged people to prepare for death and not postpone repentance, lest they perish in their sins for want of "time or space to have called on [God] for grace and mercy." Either way, the colonists inherited the strategy of lifelong meditation as the best remedy for sickness. It would never do to stop, or feel at ease. James Allin told his congregation, "I remember I have heard of one in England . . . that had such expressions upon a great afliction; that God had now done his worst, but God made her a living monument of his sorer Judgements, & that for many years." Self-examination and self-discipline must be constant, Allin warned, or worse was sure to follow.[107]

Thus it happened that as sickness came upon them people thought about the pattern of their lives and meditated on affliction. Friends who visited a man in Cambridge on his sickbed ("afflicted with the stone") took notes on what he said: first, the pious lament "that he could not in the extremity of the paine submitt with cheerfulnesse to the will of God," and then the satisfaction of finding "that God spake many things to him under this exercise." Anne Fitch (the wife of Joseph) told Windsor congregation that she perceived "sickness . . . as a warning to me to prepare for death"; her train of thought continued with her feeling that "if I did not improve it, another severe sickness of which I should not recover would come and that in a little time." More spells of illness led to an "amazing" sense of how she sinned and of "God's wrath." Stephen Sewall, sick for a whole month of fever, privately renewed his covenant as a means of gaining back his health; according to his brother he was "very desirous to live, and makes vows to serve God better, if his life be spared. . . ." A person testifying in Cambridge recalled that "the Lord has visited me by some illness and then I have resolved to seek and follow the Lord." In John Green's "relation" to the Cambridge church, he reported that "God visited me with the small pox yet I thought it nothing in comparison of the sickness of my soul. . . ."[108] For some, like Sarah Goodhue and Anne Bradstreet, it was childbirth that occasioned these reflections, for childbirth was a threat to every pregnant woman's life. Goodhue, anticipating she would die from her ninth pregnancy, declared that "sudden death" would not disrupt the calmness she enjoyed as a person who was steady in her faith and practice. Using her experience as the basis of a moral lesson, she urged her children to "improve your youthful days unto God's service, your health and strength whilst it lasteth, for you know not how soon your health may be turned into sickness, your strength into weakness, and your lives into death. . . ."[109]

This way of thinking moved the sick or dying to engage in prayer and fasting. As understood by men and women in New England, prayer was penitential, a means by which (as Joseph Green informed his congregation) a "sinner flys to God and confesses . . . sins . . . with shame & sorrow & resolves never to sin more." It was also, Green reported, "a means whereby Christ communicates gracious blessings to returning sinners." Both of these assumptions lay behind the use of prayer at times of illness. Stricken with a fever "which brought him near death," John Winthrop "was restored" to health because of "many prayers" that people "put up to the Lord for him." Such was his perspective on a case involving a church member's child who fell from the gallery of a meetinghouse. He mentions only the "prayers of the church . . . that the place where [God's] people assembled to his worship might not be defiled with blood," and the outcome, "this child was soon perfectly recovered."

Prayer was Increase Mather's response to the sickness of his children—that, and fasting mixed with personal confession. Like so many others he interpreted family illnessess as judgments on himself: "I have not bin thankfull and humble as I should have bin, and therefore God is righteous in afflicting me." He prayed sometimes in the presence of the family, and sometimes privately: "This day I Fasted and prayed in my study, begging for the Lives of my two sick children Nath. and Sam." His duties as a minister included going to the bedsides of the sick and dying, who wanted him to pray. Thus he went to pray with several men wounded when a gun exploded. People came to him at night to ask that he attend the dying: "Called out of my bed before day to pray with mrs Hodges."[110]

The lay men and women who called him to their homes would probably have prayed themselves. But it was also common practice to request a special prayer (or mention in a prayer) in Sunday services. These requests, handwritten on small slips of paper known as prayer notes, were posted in a church or given to a minister. Lacking kings to heal by touch, people in New England viewed these bits of paper as possessing special efficacy. When Samuel Sewall "asked [a sick man] whether I should put up a Note for him," his response suggests the folk perception of these texts: "He seem'd very desirous of it; and said he counted it the best Medicine." Sewall put up notes himself, as did his son. A failure to put up notes could arouse suspicion; in 1692 at Salem, Mary Warren testified that John Proctor, soon to die for witchcraft, was "always very averse to the putting up Bills for publick prayer." Sewall was aghast when a man on his deathbed asked a group of ministers to desist praying for him. On the spot, they spoke "pretty roundly" to him, and the dying man relented. As Sewall summed up the reaction, "his former carriage was very startling and amazing to us."[111]

Ordinary people surely assumed that prayer had real power. Sharing this assumption, ministers prayed for hours in their Sunday services; prayers could last as long as sermons.[112] John Dod and Robert Cleaver affirmed the significance of prayer in language that, to modern ears, is astonishingly anthropomorphic:

> For seeing that it is Gods good hand over us, that doth defend us and all our familie in the night from outward dangers, and giveth us freedom from feares and terrours, and from Sathans rage, and also giveth us rest & comfortable sleepe, or the refreshing of our fraile bodies, is it not meete we should begge it at his hand by prayer. . . .

Protection flowed from prayer, and even revenge. It was an English minister (a brother of the Boston Mathers) who affirmed the latter function. Warning English churchmen who were persecuting nonconformists that "when Saints pray, God will hear," Samuel Mather declared he would "rather be environed with Armies of armed men, & compassed round about with drawn Swords . . . then that the least praying Saint should bend the edge of his Prayers against me, for there is no standing before the Prayers of the Saints."[113]

Stories in support of this hyperbole circulated in New England—of prayers that gained the release of a captive from the Indians, exorcised apparent ghosts and purified a haunted house, saved a ship from storms, rescued prisoners in faraway Turkey, and enabled the Mohegan Indians to defeat the Narragansetts. So too, stories circulated of its power to heal illness. John Collins, wounded by a fall "which had like to have cost him his life," was preserved by prayer: ". . . whilst he lay gasping, the renowned Mr. Thomas Shepard came to him with this consolation: I have just now been wrestling with the Lord for thy life, and God hath granted me my desire; young man, thou shalt not dye but live; but remember, that now the Lord says, Surely, thou wilt fear him, and receive instruction." A minister's son was "taken up for dead" after falling "from a loft four stories high," but recovered thanks to the prayers of his father. When a daughter of this minister "fell sick of a malignant fever," he summoned others to perform with him the rites of prayer and fasting, which saved her (as the story went) from dying.[114] Jonathan Pierpont, the minister of Reading, credited a "public" day of prayer he called in 1690, at a time when soldiers were invading Canada, for the fact that "not a man that went from this town was slain" in a battle coinciding with the ceremony. Late that year, as soldiers returned sick from Canada, Pierpont noted in his diary that "we spent time in prayer" for them. The result was encouraging: "though many of them were likely to die, yet they all soon recovered." Similarly, Pierpont and some others "kept a day of Prayer" for a young woman who "was deprived of the use of her reason." Once again the results were "remarkable": "before the day was ended, the use of her understanding was wonderfully restored to her."[115]

Yet prayer was not infallible or without competition as a remedy. In explaining the significance of prayer, sixteenth-century Protestants warned against the "error" of supposing that mere reiteration of a written or "set" prayer was useful. It was customary for the English primer to include such prayers, and in folk tradition certain mumbled phrases, some of them in Latin, were conceded healing power. The Protestant position was that prayer must emerge from the heart; its power, like the power of the sacraments and the reading of good books, depended on the faith of those participating in the act. Nor were theologians in England and New England sympathetic to the "magic" of a phrase or muttered prayer.[116] Their animosity extended to the "cunning folk" who competed with them to heal illness; less surely, it extended also to the "learned" practice of alchemical and astrological medicine, which fascinated certain colonists.[117] But in New England as in old, lay people searched for ways of overcoming illness, whether these were orthodox or not. For sure, the cunning folk had customers and midwives plied their craft without regard to pious ritual. John Rogers, founder of the Rogerenes, declared himself a healer who worked with the Holy Spirit; Quakers back in England touted "miracles" that George Fox had performed.[118]

Other rivals were the men who practiced medicine professionally, the apothecaries, surgeons, and physicians who relied on bleedings, drugs, and instruments to induce healing. The reputation of professionals rested on undoubted cures as well as on their aura of learning. It was to them that Boston townsfolk looked for help in 1646 when sixteen persons were infected with the "lues venerea." Winthrop's report of the incident reveals the urgency with which people turned to doctors rather than to prayer; noting that none of the doctors then in Boston "had been practised in that cure," he told of the "good providence" that at this "very season there came by accident a young surgeon out of the West Indies, who . . . took them in hand, and through the Lord's blessing recovered them all in a short time." Similarly, magistrates and juries depended on postmortems performed by trained professionals in deciding whether someone's death was accidental.[119]

We may surmise that these different modes of healing were not perceived by most people as in conflict; lay men and women were content to tolerate confusion and remain eclectic in their search for remedies. It was different for the ministers. They were wary of the cunning folk, and also of midwives. A rival like John Rogers, who based his standing as a prophet on his prowess as a healer, was disposed of by an unexpected providence: certain he was immune from disease, Rogers came to Boston while the smallpox raged in 1721 to give witness to his faith, only to be fatally infected.[120] But what of doctors? In a telling passage, William Perkins had insisted that the sick man ask first for a minister: "Where the Divine ends, there the Physitian must begin; and it is a very preposterous course that the divine should there begin where the physitian makes an ende."[121] The tone of this advice/complaint suggests that many people preferred otherwise.

What was true of England in his day was probably the practice of lay people in seventeenth-century New England. The colonists at Plymouth depended mainly on the ministrations of Samuel Fuller to pull them through their suffering that first winter, and when Edward Winslow went to visit a sick Massasoit, he applied the remedy of chicken soup! Winthrop cited the success of surgeons. When the Reverend Thomas Thacher issued *A Brief Rule to Guide the Common People . . . in the Small-Pox and Measles,* he borrowed most of his advice from Thomas Sydenham, an English doctor. Thacher was a learned man, a minister who also practiced medicine. He regarded sickness as "natural" within the framework of the learning he and other ministers accepted.[122] Yet somehow the preachers were obliged to teach another message, that its source was sin. Was this second message only metaphorical?[123]

The thinking of lay men and women is not easily described. Doubtless they shared with the ministry the sense that certain kinds of illness lent themselves to diagnosis from both points of view. One such illness was possession; another was despair, or as doctors called it, melancholy. In healing either of these problems people often used the ritual of prayer and fasting. But they also called on doctors. When young girls in Salem Village behaved strangely, Samuel Parris invited other ministers to join him in prayer and fasting. Yet doctors also came to observe and advise. A few days into the "possession" of Elizabeth Knapp, "she sent to Lancaster for Mr. Rowlandson, who came and prayed with her, and gave her serious counsels; but she was still followed . . . with these fits." Six days into her affliction, a doctor came to see her and, diagnosing "her distemper to be natural," prescribed a "physic" that eased some of the "violence" of her fits. More prayer and fasting followed, though with little result; summoned back, the doctor "consented that the distemper was diabolical . . . [and] advised to extraordinary fasting." Three ministers turned up to help. Another time, the "company" observing her were asked by Samuel Willard, the town minister, "to join in prayer." Elizabeth herself proposed that she "be carried down to the Bay in all haste; she should never be well till an assembly of ministers was met together to pray with and for her, and in particular Mr. Cobbett." (Thomas Cobbett, soon to receive credit for the success of his prayers in rescuing the captives of King Philip's War, was the author of a treatise on the art of prayer.) Looking back upon her months of illness, Samuel Willard was not absolutely certain that the Devil was the cause of her "distemper." Yet he preferred this interpretation to one that ascribed her illness to "natural" causes. His strategy for healing was to induce full confession, as though she suffered from a "case of conscience." Thus he assumed that her fits occurred because of sins that remained hidden; as her fits continued, he remarked that "there was something yet behind [them] not discovered by her," and begged that she "make use of" him to "relate any weighty and serious case of conscience."[124]

The struggle that occurred between his judgment and the doctor's was latent in cases of the kind that Pierpont described. In other cases doctors and the ministry agreed that nature was to blame; in still others, no one could decide.[125] Uncertainty (and, despite the intervention of the ministers, the failure of their prayers) marked the situation of two Boston women whom John Hull described as prone to "raving and madness." His report of alternative interpretations put more weight on sin and Satan than on nature:

> Men know not the human cause. Some think, and not unlike, they were left to some notorious sin, but could not confess it; others think Satan took advantage of a spirit of discontent with their own condition, as being poor and conflicting with sundry wants.[126]

Here as elsewhere in the witchcraft cases, physicians and the preachers jointly ruled out exorcisms. Anyone who imitated Christ in casting out the Devil was suspect.[127] But in cases of despair, the rivalry became more open. Though Perkins in *A Salve for a sicke man* explained despair as having natural causes, the clergy in New England were determined in the main to mark it off from melancholy, and to insist on a privileged role in dealing with its effects. Young Thomas Hooker achieved fame because he saved a woman from despair. Printers issued tales of other healings performed by the clergy. Even so, and despite many sermons on the theme of sickness caused by sin, lay people may have preferred the humoral explanation, which Chaucer cited in the fifteenth century, and which had new support by 1660.[128]

Prayer was thus an instrument to use selectively, and less often, perhaps, than the ministers advised. But what of death? The rivalry between the preachers and physicians ended at the bedside of a dying man or woman. Here religion came into its own in determining the meaning of the moment and in offering rites of passage. As we know already, the ministers made much of death in preaching to their congregations. It was they who took the lead in saying what death meant. Yet others also took part in this process. Gravestone carvers acted on their own in choosing designs for their stones. Printers reached into their stock of ornaments to decorate a broadside elegy. Both groups relied on an iconography of death that owed little to the ministers.[129] The wisdom of this iconography was reiterated in books, like the *New England Primer,* which printers put together on their own. Lay people, initiating the procedures of a funeral, expressed their thoughts in elegies for friends and kinfolk. Facing death themselves, they wrote out wills in which they often spoke of death and what it signified. Much of what they said in wills and elegies was formulaic. This very fact suggests that people counted on an older wisdom as well as on the teachings of the ministers.[130]

The message of the ministers was double-edged. The New England clergy told the living to behave as though at any moment they might die. "Behold and think of death": this motto was inscribed on gravestones and reiterated in a thousand sermons. Death was thus a warning, a reinforcement for the rules of disciplined asceticism and repentance. In keeping with the Protestant tradition, the clergy also informed people that they need not fear the King of Terrors. Living well meant dying well; a peaceful conscience ensured a smooth passage from this world to heaven. It was standard to declare that God and God alone knew whether someone on his deathbed was assured of mercy. Such advice was meant to ease the tensions of the moment. So was the advice that people should not worry overmuch.[131] Yet these "cordials" for the grieving and those slipping into death were matched by statements in a different tone. Leonard Hoar, reminding readers that "Death is . . . consequent of sin," told awful stories of the dying process—of people trembling when they saw the King of Terrors, of despair as Satan flung his final arrows at the dying. Hoar could not resist a reference to Spira:

> O the Ravings and restless tossings of some poor wretches when they come to dye, that cry out as if their breath were already made up of Fire and Brimstone, as Francis Spira and Hadrian the Emperour. . . .

What is more, he played on popular fears of darkness in a passage that evoked the terrors of the night, the presence of the Devil, and death itself as darkness. But Hoar concluded with the message of assurance and likened death to crossing into paradise.[132] Chapbooks tended to prefer the motif of terror, as did poems like Wigglesworth's *The Day of Doom.* Here the emphasis fell on the pangs of conscience that so many persons facing death and judgment would be likely to experience. Chapbooks, broadsides, and the great collections of the wonders added to the stock of stories of despair.

What reached lay people in New England was a medley of motifs. From their reading and from popular tradition they knew of people who, in dying well, could serve them as examples. One model was the final moments of the wife of Thomas Shepard, the first minister of Cambridge. A narrative of her experience was known to members of the church, though not published until early in the eighteenth century. To her bedside (she was dying of consumption) came her husband and a group of persons from the church to welcome her into its fellowship. Thereupon (in Shepard's words), "the Lord . . . fill'd her Heart, with such unspeakable Joy and Assurance of Gods Love, that She said to us, She had now Enough; and we were afraid, her Feeble Body, would have at that time fallen, under the weight of her Joy." Yet Mrs. Shepard was not spared the scrupulous self-questioning that her husband in his sermons required as the norm. On the heels of joy she felt terrifying doubt; as she told those gathered at her bedside, she "fear'd, that there might be some flaw in my Heart, Some Sin in my Soul, which might Separate between me & my God, at the Last, which I neither Saw, nor Others could discern." Even though she credited the act of entering into covenant with having "Satisfied & driven away my Fears," she concluded with a statement implying a persistent doubleness of self-perception: "And tho' I know, that Hypocrites are, & may be received into the Bosom of the Church, yet I am willing the Lord should try me, & mend me, that I am not One of them."[133]

Until the moment of her death, Mrs. Shepard continued to articulate the message of the ministers. Death meant her reunion with a loving Christ in heaven. Yet she bracketed that joyful feeling with uncertainty: death was when true saints were separated from mere hypocrites and formalists, and no one knew beforehand how a dying person would be judged. In citing her example, the ministers were clearly saying they preferred that people understand the passage as a test. Death was judgment. Therefore Christians must labor to ensure that Christ accepted them as saints. Even so, the message went, the passage was uncertain and the strain severe. This was how death came to children and young people Janeway offered as examples in *A Token for Children,* and those that Cotton Mather described in the histories he appended to the book. They show people gathered at the bedside of the dying who exhort them to pursue repentance and a godly life. These histories take account of fears while emphasizing the assurance that came to the pious. At first, Priscilla Thornton was "afraid of dying." Later, "asked whether she were afraid of death, with a sweet smile she replied, 'No, not I: Christ is better than life!' "[134] John Clap, who died when he was thirteen, answered the same question with the words " 'No; death has no terrour to me. . . .' " But to deny fear was also to admit its possibility; fear lay just beyond the reach of confidence.[135] Hence the models set before lay people retained both parts of the preachers' message. In publishing these narratives, the clergy demonstrated that religion, rightly lived, provided Christians with safe passage out of darkness. But only if they lived as piously beforehand as the children Cotton Mather described.

That some people died in rapture seems quite certain. Others felt the ravages of terror, or what they thought of as the Devil's efforts to upset them. More common, perhaps, was to pass away while quietly affirming to those at the bedside that death held no fear. Someone witnessing the death of Ebenezer Tucker in 1724 described him thus: "He never seem'd for to fear Death, / But willing to resign his Breath; / And seem'd to look Death in the face, / With Godly Courage, Undaunted Grace." More than once a diary or a letter admits us to a deathbed. George Allin wrote from Sandwich to a friend in 1661 that his nephew "was sensable untill about two houres before hee died and did say, Oh Lord, when shall my change come; hee was not affraid of death. . . ." As James Blake of Dorchester lay dying in 1700, "some of His Last Words were these: 'Amen. Even so come Lord Jesus.' " John Hull reported in his diary that his father Robert "bore all with sweet patience and thankfulness." Almost as revealing is Hull's own reaction: "and though I am very loath to part, yet do desire willingly and thankfully to resign him up to his and my good Father's will, and to the bosom of his and my dear Lord Jesus, where I have, through grace, good hope to be again with him (in God's time) for ever." Joseph Tompson of Billerica noted in his journal that his wife went to her grave "acknowledging her one [own] vilenes & worthlesness . . . but good hope through grace to stand before the father, haveing the righteousnes of Christ imputed to her & sometimes telling of them Christian friends about her that she was going to iesus Christ." The grieving husband consoled himself by musing that the souls of both his wife and his newborn child were "garded into abrahams Bosome," and that "her prayers were answered, "& is this Sabbath triumphing. . . ."[136]

This hopefulness prevailed in elegies and epitaphs that people wrote in such abundance in New England. In them too we hear the voice of someone speaking, as in the dying speech of Joseph Tompson's sister: "Let not your sighs nor groans mine ears molest; Sweet mother, close mine eys & turn aside, My Jesus sends for me." She was not the only person to envisage death as a homecoming. Anne Bradstreet ended her great poem "A pilgrim I, on earth, perplext" with the lines: "Lord make me ready for that day; / then, Come deare bridgrome. Come away." A few stanzas previously, she imagined herself "soar[ing] on high" to heaven.

Jane Turell, who lost two children in their infancy, wrote a poem about their deaths in which she also used this motif:

> But then the King of Terrours does advance
> To pierce it's Bosom with his Iron Lance.
> It's Soul releas'd, upward it takes it's Flight,
> Oh never more below to bless my Sight!
> Farewell sweet Babes I hope to meet above,
> And there with you Sing the Redeemer's Love.

The winged skulls on gravestones (and later, winged soul effigies) rendered visually the statement "Faith hath Wings, and mounts the Soul on high," and its variation, "Ere Mortal Angels bear it to the Tomb, / While the Soul mounts on Wings of Seraph's Home."[137]

One other source of lay people's thinking about death is the language that they used in wills. What people said in wills was overwhelmingly to voice a trust in the "rich mercy of god." Rarely did these statements refer to uncertainty, and never was the tone one of despair. The most common motif was commitment:

> My poare Imortall Soule I do desire, (with some measure of hope) to leave with, and committ unto the everlasting mercies of God the father in Christ Jesus.

Thus a Cambridge farmer of modest means. A widow was confessional and affirmative at once:

> . . . thus humbly comitting my selfe soul and body into the hands of Gods mercy . . . I humbly desir to wayte his pleasure when He will come and give me perfect Deliverance from, and victory over, all those evills both of sin and the just demerits thereof that I either feel or have just cause to fearr acknowledging that hitherto God hath given me cause to say that God hath bin a very good, a very mercifull and faithfull God unto me and doth yet uphold my heart that for the future he will not faile me nor forsake me. . . .

Many people were explicit in referring to the doctrine that the "God who Loveth me . . . hath given his Deare and Beloved son Jesus Christ to Dye for me." Many also expressed their "hope of a joyfull resurection at the last day," a hope that was surely heartfelt in spite of being formulaic. Now and then a different voice breaks through, a more personal vision of a merciful Christ: "I desier to Cast my self only upon him & rest myself only in the armes of his mercy in Christ Jesus intreatinge of him to stay my soule there in the worst howers even of death itself."[138]

The feel of all these statements—the epitaphs and elegies, the reports of someone's dying words, the responses of the grieving—is significantly different from the model that the ministers endorsed.[139] No one ever said that any friend or family member was condemned to hell. No gravestone carver ever differentiated between members of the church (in full or halfway covenant) and those outside its shelter. Strait was the way, and narrow was the gate, yet when these people spoke about a person they had loved they reaffirmed the message of the gospel. No eyewitness refers to the kind of agitation that affected Mrs. Shepard. None make reference to despair. Oddly, even Cotton Mather, in the many lives he wrote of ministers, rarely noted how they died.

True, it seems that people sometimes asked the dying if they feared the King of Terrors. The testimonies people gave in Cambridge, Wenham, and Windsor contain many references to death as judgment. Somewhere in their consciousness people may have feared they might die unworthy. Jane Winship, Roger Haynes, Joshua Willis, Anne Fitch—all attested to being "afraid to die" lest they "should forever lie under wrath of God." Someone else's death often seemed to flush such feelings to the surface. Or the catalyzing event may have been a crisis, as when pirates facing shipwreck hastily recited prayers.[140] The stories of extraordinary death that printers and hack writers kept in circulation encouraged this response. Thanks to printers, ordinary people knew the torments that had befallen a Francis Spira and a Hadrian.

Yet these stories, like much of the lore of wonders to which they were kin, dealt in extremes, This was their appeal to readers, the same readers who enjoyed every form of story that dramatized the "theatre" of good and evil. Death had always the potential of turning into drama! But ordinary people wavered on this point. They wanted not more terror but more certainty. It seems likely, therefore, that most people put aside the model that imposed on them a final bout of self-examination. Death was never distant from their thinking. But as they died themselves, or as they watched dear friends or family members die, they tended to affirm the message of the resurrection. That very word was inscribed by a minister in 1705 on the gravestone of a daughter who was born and died within a span of hours. In declaring that his daughter was "espoused to Christ," Samuel Moody voiced the thinking of lay people and most of his colleagues.[141] Death, both for "horse-shed" Christians and for those who imposed on religion the responsibility for protection of their family, was not overwhelming either for the dying or for those left bereaved.

In part, its dangers were averted through the ritual of prayer and the kindred practice of preparing elegies. Here the ministers were crucial, though lay people also prayed and wrote such verse. Samuel Sewall's diary is unique in demonstrating how prayer was conceived and practiced by lay people and the clergy; leaving to another chapter a full rendering of his experience, we may merely say that prayer was like the wings that carried dying souls to heaven. In doing so, it comforted the grieving. So did verses that Sewall and so many others wrote. Their function was the classic one of consolation. As someone said of verses written by John Wilson, they "passed like to the handkerchief carried from Paul to help and uphold disconsolate ones, and to heal their wracked Souls, by the effectual prisence of Gods holy Spirit." Out of ritual emerged peace, or at least the strength to face the King of Terrors.[142]

IV

PREPARING FOR his daughter's wedding, a New England father chose a turkey that was "fatted" in advance for the feast that lay ahead. No doubt his guests would also feast on cakes baked specially for a wedding. Perhaps they moved on to a tavern where they danced; some ten years before this wedding, the Massachusetts General Court had complained of "dancing in ordinaries . . . upon marriage of some persons," and prohibited the practice, though apparently to no avail. Feasting, dancing, drinking—these were how the people of New England celebrated weddings as a rite of passage. Food had ritual significance. Though feasts were not the largest of the rich and no longer served to symbolize their stewardship, food in great abundance remained an important means of marking certain moments. Thus at Plymouth, after having survived devastating sickness and securing enough food to last them through the winter, the "pilgrims" commemorated the return of health and "plenty" with a feast. Funerals involved food and drink, as did every ordination of a minister; at the funeral of Thomas Cobbett in 1685, the mourners consumed one barrel of wine and two of cider, the whole sweetened with almost a hundred pounds of sugar. Training days, when the town (or county) militia gathered to rehearse a few maneuvers, usually ended with adjournment to a nearby tavern, where it was the custom to get drunk.[143]

In giving food and drink a central place in certain rites, the colonists were acting as Elizabethans. From time to time, and especially later in the century, some people feasted on the day of Christmas, put up maypoles, and played tricks on April Fool's. More rarely, young men mocked a domineering wife in the folk ceremony of a "chivarari." On the evening of Guy Fawkes Day (November 5), bands of young persons roamed the streets of Boston late at night firing guns and destroying fences to get wood for bonfires.[144] If such "Pope's Day" celebrations bothered the authorities, feasts were culturally legitimate. So was drinking, as the quantities consumed at funerals and ordinations indicate. Yet both could take on the significance of play, and play turned upside down the penitential structure of confession. This was why the ministers complained (and, less often, the magistrates reacted) whenever someone feasted on the day of Christmas, put up maypoles, or played tricks on April Fool's. These rites were like laughter in providing release from self-discipline; they advertised the natural (not the reformed) body, or they counterposed an "idle" sense of time to the "now or never" rhythm of incessant preparation for salvation. This was the danger posed by a jestbook. But it was witchcraft that inverted almost every form of order: witches lied, used "filthy, unclean" speech, sang "wicked, and witty" songs, and feasted on red wine in their meetings in the woods.[145]

That people fantasized about turning godly order upside down—and sometimes actually did so, either furtively or openly—is testimony to the fact that "play" is part of every culture. Some cultures devise ritual forms of play that alternate with rituals of penitence and sacrifice: hence the sequence Carnival and Lent, or gluttony and fasting. But this was not the rhythm that took hold among the colonists. Traces of the older pattern may have lingered in the sequencing of fast days and thanksgiving and in stray episodes of Christmas reveling. But the triumph of reform was amazingly complete.

One measure of that triumph is Harriet Beecher Stowe's description of a late-eighteenth-century New England town where no one ever celebrated Christmas. Her story turns on the appearance of Episcopalians who illuminate their new church on Christmas eve. As its windows radiate warm light across the snow, the young heroine, daughter of the minister whose church is *not* illuminated, is strangely drawn to this alternative religion.[146] It may be that many of the colonists hungered for more richness or more play in ritual practice. Yet regardless, play was scanted in this culture. In its place the ministers and godly colonists installed the moral allegory of repentance and confession. The key ritual in the repertory of the colonists was the cleansing moment of confession, which brought hidden sins to light and purged them.

This structure lent itself to many different situations, from sickness to witch-hunting. It even lent itself to marriage; the morning of his wedding, young Joseph Green spent "some time . . . in confesing my sins, and in imploreing pardon that so I may not enter into the Marriage covenant with any old guilt upon my soul,—but may be washed pardoned and sanctifyed. . . ."[147] It is only when we note how other cultures frame this moment that we see what made New England special.

Another case in point concerns sea voyages. No preacher blessed a ship, no sailor painted an ex-voto, no saints befriended mariners.[148] The one alternative was prayer. All demarcations of the sacred, all ways of linking nature, man, and God, rested on moral allegory.

Ritual was a means of checking the disorder of the natural world, of limiting the danger of God's judgment. Ritual also affirmed social order. In most of western Europe, coronations, feasts, and other civic holidays made manifest the hierarchy of high and low. Processions were important means of demonstrating rank: who came first, who wore what insignia or dress.[149] Here again the colonists were different. The main civic ritual was to call a fast day. Though everyone believed in social rank, the mere fact of worldly status had less weight than godliness. Social rituals reaffirmed the order of collective godliness. This was the significance of public readings of the law code, of prose elegies like Bradford's celebrating William Brewster's kindness, and of funerals (the one time when people did process) of great magistrates. Thomas Willoughby, a Massachusetts magistrate and colonel, "was solemnly interred" in 1670 with gunfire, drums, and trumpets, all in honor not only of his rank but (as one bystander noted) of his being a "real friend to piety and learning."[150] Godly order worked only if everyone participated by assenting to the covenant, and rulers retained their legitimacy only if they used their office to advance the will of God. At the center of the "civil" fast days—those the government commanded—was the myth of New England as a "land" that God had specially favored. This was a myth that anyone could use; it lent itself to revolutionary ends, as in the eighteenth century, though its structure was a plea to return to an ideal past, a "primitive" first times. Above all, it was a people's myth, a set of roles and symbols that included them and their initiative.

CHAPTER 5

THE MENTAL WORLD OF SAMUEL SEWALL

S AMUEL SEWALL, merchant, magistrate, Bostonian, and diarist, was born in England in 1652. Sewall's father and grandfather had participated in the founding of New England; returning to their mother country for a decade, the Sewalls settled once again in Massachusetts in 1661. Samuel inherited from his family a dislike of the Church of England and its "Hierarchy." For the rest of his long life (he died in 1730), he believed in and defended the peculiar culture of New England. Early on, a graduate of Harvard College, he intended like most of his class-mates to become a minister. It may have been his marriage that decided him to "follow Merchandize."[1] Hannah Hull, who became Sewall's wife in 1676, was the only child of a rich merchant who sided with the Puritan regime. Sewall added public service to his career as a merchant. A judge for many years (and finally, chief justice of Massachusetts' highest court), he participated in the witchcraft trials at Salem and served on the Council, the upper house of government. Sewall stood near the center of Massachusetts politics, and the diary that he kept through-out his adult life describes in rich detail the inner workings of affairs of state.

But the diary is much more. Week after week, year after year, Sewall noted down the times at which hundreds of events occurred, and the names of those who brought him news. He kept track of rainbows, bolts of lightning, illnesses and deaths, and bearers at a funeral. His reading figured in the diary, as did sermons preached at services he faithfully attended. For several months he worried about whether he was qualified to become a full church member. Sometimes he remembered dreams. He was fascinated with the clues in Scripture and contemporary events about the Second Coming. Each spring he rejoiced to hear the "chippering" of the swallows in the thin sunshine of April (2:683).

Altogether, the notations in the diary represent a mental world very different from our own. Sewall shared with others, like John Hull, an alertness to prodigies and portents. The pages of his diary reopen, once again, that world of wonders. Through its pages we return as well to books and reading. Sewall also published, writing mainly verses that commemorated some particular event. Often it was death that served him as occasion. His response to crises such as death and sickness leads us back to ritual, which meant much to Sewall. So did his relationship to God, for which he sought guidance from the clergy and from godly books. His expressions of anxiety, his moments of assurance, provide an extraordinary portrait of lay piety.

Certain layers of his thinking may not seem especially religious, such as the significance he ascribed to sound or to the passage of time. But in seeking patterned meaning in his entries, we soon come to realize that for him religion was far broader than what happened in the meetinghouse. Versed in matters of theology, Sewall almost never used the language he was trained in as a Harvard student. He thought in terms of wonders and life crises; he yearned to protect his family and New England even as he struggled to accept the lesson of affliction. It is this yearning for protection that, from start to finish, unifies the diary and emerges as the substance of religion.

I

SEWALL'S BOSTON was a dark place at night. Confused by the darkness, someone standing outside Sewall's door swung a club at a small boy, thinking he was a dog (1:29). People coped with the dark by going to bed early and arising at daybreak. The town became so quiet once the streets were empty that any abrupt sound awakened all who slept. "At night a great Uproar and Lewd rout in the Main Street [as a drunken man wandered about]. Many were startled, thinking there had been fire, and went to their windows out of Bed between 9. and 10. to see what was the matter" (1:144). Time and again, thunderstorms roused Sewall from his bed (1:400). At night he could not distinguish thunder from "Great Guns" (1:330), like those the soldiers out on Castle Island fired late one evening after news arrived of a son being born to James II. The guns, bells, and drums that heralded the birth of Prince Charles caused "Alarm" for "fear of fire . . . the thing was so sudden, People knew not the occasion" (1:175).

At any hour of the day or night, the cry of "fire" sent Sewall and his fellow townspeople to their windows or into the streets. No minister could hope to hold his audience if the alarm—someone shouting or a bell ringing furiously—reached the ears of the congregation. "Uproar in N[orth] M[eeting] House by Cry of Fire" (1:301). "When Mr. Willard was in his first Prayer, there was a Cry of Fire, which made the People rush out" (1:262). ". . . About the middle of Sermon fire was cry'd, which made a great disturbance, by many rushing out" (1:131). Panic followed from the peril people faced in a town of closely packed wooden houses and without effective means of putting fires out.

The dangers of this urban life were many. A robber crept into Sewall's house one night and made off with a load of silver (1:568). Fires were not always accidental; disgruntled people "threatened" to burn down some houses, and a fire two months later may have been their doing (1:34, 37, 531). Waves of disease swept through the town, taking scores of lives. Twice within a month in 1693 the town was "much startled" with news of "Fever of the Fleet" (1:311). Sewall came close to dying from a case of smallpox in 1678 (1:xxxiii). Thereafter he had a fear of the disease that was much akin to his distress over fire. When the news of a fresh case reached him, it caused a "great startling, lest it should spread as in 1678" (1:126). With the safety of his children in mind, he noted the location of the sick, since distance was some indication of peril or safety (1:100; 311). Nonetheless, his children caught the smallpox, though none died from the disease (1:258–60). Nor did any die from falling in a well (1:306), as happened to a friend's child. None became so hungry as to riot for food, as poor people did in the winters of 1710 and 1712 (2:638, 715). No Sewall offspring were victims of a massacre like that the French and Indians inflicted on Schenectady—"Women with Child rip'd up, Children had their Brains dash'd out" (1:251). More fortunate in some ways, the Sewalls were not spared in others. Samuel buried eight of his own children (LB 1:236). Asleep at night, he "dream'd that all my Children were dead except Sarah" (1:328) and that death had taken his wife, Hannah (1:239).

The street life of provincial Boston occasioned other nightmares. Carts rumbled by, conveying pirates, Indians, and young women guilty of infanticide to the Common to be executed (1:21, 22, 310). Beforehand, people jammed into a meetinghouse to view the condemned as they listened to their final sermon (1:99). Going to the Common once when pirates he had helped to apprehend were being executed, Sewall was astonished by the crowd; "the River was cover'd with People" packed aboard at least a hundred boats. The sound effects were equally remarkable: "When the Scaffold was let sink, there was such a Screech of the

Women that my wife heard it sitting in our Entry next the Orchard" on the other side of town (1:509). Some months later came a different level of response. "Last night I had a very sad Dream that held me a great while. As I remember, I was condemn'd and to be executed" (1:518).

Sewall's dream life came closer to reality in his recurring nightmare that the French were attacking Boston (1:544; 2:829), even though on-going war between France and Britain never led to such a battle. Yet in times of peace Sewall and his fellow townsmen were kept on edge by "Rumors and Fears" (1:76) of Indian conspiracies. He was absent when the town rebelled in April 1689 against the royal governor. Thereafter, as others sometimes declared in his presence, "Convulsion" and "Mutiny" (2:918) always remained possible. Sewall's uneasiness about the future was rooted in a broader, more general fear of change. As he walked about the town or listened to the sounds that reached him from the street, the rhythms of unwelcome change became apparent in the noise of a dueling ceremony (1:137) or intrusions on the Sabbath (1:502). Anglicans and Royalists were resuming customs (1:140, 117) Sewall thought of as corruptions of the moral system.

The changes overtaking Boston were changes sure to anger the God who had singled out and guarded the founders of New England. Inheriting the vision of a reformed commonwealth, Sewall did all he could to maintain the old ways. He broke up street games and encouraged shopkeepers to stay open on December 25 (2:795); it was cause for satisfaction when most did (1:90). In court he urged passage of a law against incest, believing it would signal the determination of the people to remain in covenant (1:333–34). It pleased him when "true New England" men (1:385), those leaders who still cherished the traditions of the founders, reassembled at an ordination or a funeral (1:180). Leaders, he believed, should act as one: "Agreement makes Kingdoms flourish" (LB 1:278). The quarreling he overheard among the ministers (1:270) or encountered in meetings of the Council (1:363) was disturbing evidence that unity had given way to conflict. The Quakers were a case in point. He was present in Third Church when "in Sermon time there came in a female Quaker, in a Canvas Frock, her hair disshevelled and loose like a Periwigg, her face as black as ink. . . . It occasioned the greatest and most amazing uproar that I ever saw" (1:44). Back home, he followed anxiously the signs of the times. Good news was any victory over the French in North America or Europe (1:306), or defeats of the Turks (1:340). All too often, the news was discouraging: Expeditions against the French have ended in disaster (1:574); the king of France, the dreaded Louis XIV, still lives, contrary to rumors he has died (1:492); the Huguenots are being persecuted (1:102). Such "evil tidings" seemed to portend a far greater "Darkness" than that of the streets at night, the vaster gloom that was the "Night" of God's disfavor (LB 2:31–32). Were the Quakers right in prophesying that "great Calamities of Fire and Sword . . . would suddenly come on New-England" (1:67)? Would the darkness of the final days foretold in Revelation ever be succeeded by the sunrise?

Coming home at night, Sewall moved from darkness into light as he entered the house that he shared with Hannah's mother. Here he was on safe ground; here peace and quiet reigned: "Laus Deo" (1:470). The same feeling of transition from a zone of danger to one of safety came over him as he reentered Boston from a trip: "by this means I had the pleasure to view the Wall of our City, and pass in, and out at the Gate. . . . The LORD keep the City!" (2:860). Safety also sprang from friendships of the kind he formed with Harvard classmates and some kin. "Glad to hear that you intend to visit us again," he wrote a cousin, "because real friends are the principal comfort and relief against the evils of our own Life" (LB 1:86).

II

CRAVING SAFETY for himself, Sewall sought it earnestly for others as well. As he went about this task, he could not separate the welfare of his wife and children from the welfare of New England. Family, church, town, and country, all shared a collective destiny. He linked them together at a private fast: "Pray'd for Sister Dorothy, my family, New England, that God would fit me for his good pleasure in doing and suffering" (1:277). At another fast, he begged for blessings upon his children and their kin, the governor and the General Court, Third Church and missionaries to the Indians, Connecticut and New York, "all the European Plantations in America," the Queen and "Europe" (1:589). The close at hand and the distant were both deserving of his care. Yet the family always had priority. There were steps he took to safeguard his children that they alone enjoyed.

A new addition to his house was under way. Before construction began, Sewall consulted with a minister as to whether the times were propitious (1:287). While the floor was being laid he drove a pin into the frame (1:317), an act he repeated for the houses of close friends and kin, and for ships and meetinghouses (1:11, 178, 300, 500, 529; 2:639, 822). Soon after he and his family moved into their new rooms, they held a private fast asking God to bless the place where they now lived (1:377). Some years later, Sewall set up stone carvings on gateposts in front of the house, two "cherubims heads" that symbolized the presence of protecting forces (1:400; see Exodus 25:18–22).

The children born to him and Hannah were carried to the meeting-house their first week of life to be baptized. In later life Sewall looked back fondly on those moments when he held a newborn child in his arms "upon the Sabbath Day in the Solemn Assembly of God's saints" (1:313, n. 14). Giving names to newborn children was no casual task, since the right choice could add protection. "I named Joseph, in hopes of the accomplishment of the Prophecy, Ezek. 37th and such like: and not out of respect to any Relation, or any other person, except the first Joseph" (1:175). "I named my little daughter Sarah . . . I was strugling whether to call her Sarah or Mehetabel; but when I saw Sarah's standing in the Scripture . . . I resolv'd on that side. Also Mother Sewall had a sister Sarah. . . ." (1:324).[2] For his children he also sought the benefit of "Blessing" from old men; on one occasion he transported the whole family to the bedside of a man whose word (or touch?) he deemed of special worth (1:282), and on another he presented "all my stock" to the Reverend Nehemiah Walter of Roxbury and "desired his Blessing of them; which he did" (1:407).

Back within their home, father, mother, and children gathered daily for a service of devotion. The routine they practiced was that prescribed by the clergy, who envisaged every household as a "little commonwealth" exemplifying moral order. Year in and year out the Sewalls sang psalms and read Scripture at these family meetings. The prayers they offered were explicit in their reference to family problems like a son's quest for a suitable apprenticeship (1:327). Scripture-reading proceeded by a schedule that took them "in Course" from Genesis to Revelation (1:115), a sequence they resumed once the cycle was completed. Everyone within the family took his turn at reading, Joseph starting at age ten (1:384), one sister at age eight (1:249, 404).

The psalms they sang together had particular significance. Sewall listed them by number in the diary. Here he also listed psalms he sang in Third Church, in the "closet" of his bedchamber, and in private meetings he shared with a group of laymen. This attention to the psalms was in keeping with their place in popular tradition—not the popular tradition of maypoles and Christmas, but the new vernacular tradition that emerged in post-Reformation England. For Sewall, the music that his friends and family made together was a means of imitating life as saints in heaven. "I give you this Psalm-Book," he told a relative, "in order to your perpetuating this Song; and I would have you pray that it may be an Introduction to our Singing with the Choir above" (2:731). Noting the death of a Harvard classmate, he recalled that they had "sung many

a Tune in Consort; hope shall sing Hallelujah together in Heaven" (2:878).
Together with his family he anticipated heaven as they sang the stanzas
of their favorite psalms.

III

SEWALL CAME to know the Bible practically by heart. After all those
hours of reading Scripture he could very nearly think in terms of Bible
texts. When a woman died from choking on a piece of meat, Sewall's
mind ran to 1 Corinthians 10:31: "Whether therefore ye eat, or drink,
or whatsoever ye do, do all to the glory of God." Visiting with a woman
who was ill, they talked of the fatal accident, whereupon she cited the
same verse (1:287). The coincidence was significant to Sewall. He was
ever alert to relations between daily events and the Scripture. A stormy
scene in Council was preceded by his reading accidentally "Mr. Strong's
Notes on Rev. 12. . . . The last words were, prepare for it" (1:363).
Could this really have occurred by accident? One way of finding out was
by keeping track of texts. Hence the hundreds of entries in the diary,
for the process of recording references to Scripture was essential were
he to perceive and profit from coincidences that in hindsight might become important.

The hundreds of references to time were complementary, in that
keeping track of the rhythms of the universe was another way of comprehending interventions of the supernatural. Sewall actually lived amid
several modes of time. As a merchant he had slow, uncertain communications with his business partners overseas. Months went by before he
knew whether ships were lost or safe in port (LB 1:86). But while the
rhythm of the world of work was irregular and slow-paced, the rhythm
of historical time was fixed in a certain pattern. The bits and pieces of
news that reached Sewall from abroad fell in order as evidence that the
sequence described in Revelation was rapidly unfolding. Historical time,
like the phases of a war and events in Massachusetts politics, was really
prophetic time, and Sewall struggled to decipher the relationship between the two.[3] Time for him was also a complex structure of coincidences. And time was finally "GOD's time" (2:660) in that he alone determined what would happen. As Sewall lay in bed at night listening to the
clock tick away the minutes, this sound was cause for reflection on the
profound contingency of life. To know this, to know time, was to feel
that life could end abruptly, without warning.

Sewall followed the passing of time in several ways. For him as for
everyone who lived in preindustrial society, the rising and setting of the

sun were key reference points in the cycle of the hours. When meetings of the Council or Superior Court ran late, it was "Candle-Light" when they ended, not this or that hour of the evening (2:773; 1:360). Traveling once to Springfield without a watch, Sewall was entirely dependent on light and dark as his temporal frame of reference: "a little after sunset," "by duskish," "when night came" (2:829–30). But in Boston he usually knew the time in hours, either by consulting his watch or (if at home) the clock he owned (1:177; 2:675) or by listening to the town bells. His notations of the time in hours were invariably in the form of a "between," as in "between 3 and 4. p.m." (1:383), which suggests that his watch told time only by the hour. To tell the time in minutes, he had to use his clock (2:742).

Spared the modern urgency to be punctual, Sewall worried nonetheless about right and wrong ways of observing time. The days of the week were God's creation, the seven days of Genesis carried over into human history. Arguing unsuccessfully for legislation to replace "Tuesday, Thursday, and Satterday" with "Third, fifth and seventh," Sewall reminded his fellow councillors that "the Week only, of all parcells of time, was of Divine Institution, erected by God as a monumental pillar for a memorial of the Creation perfected in so many distinct days" (1:351). This being understood, it followed that the calendar should be cleansed of corruptions like the pagan names for days of the week. In his diary he kept up the practice of using numbers in place of names long after the New England almanacs had reverted to the usual English practice. And though the government would not reform the calendar, he used his powers as a magistrate to impede the celebration of New Year's Day and April Fool's. Hearing that some Boston schoolchildren were playing tricks on April 1, Sewall exploded in a letter to their schoolmasters. "What an abuse is it of precious Time; what a Profanation! What an Affront to the Divine Bestower of it!" (LB 1:365). Sewall's sense of what was sacred had been rubbed the wrong way; for him the units of the calendar were a mark or measure of God's presence here on earth.

Meanwhile Sewall used the diary to make note of events that would help him understand their temporal relationships. To find that the "very day" a child had died he himself "accidentally lit upon, and nail'd up the verses" commemorating one of his own children was cause for reflection (1:429). As the diary lengthened, it enabled him to search out connections between past and present. Turning back its pages, Sewall discovered in 1691 that a fast he kept "to pray that God would not take away but uphold me by his free Spirit" occurred "the very day of the week and year as much as could be that I set out for New York, which made me hope that twas a token for good that God would pardon that Sin and

Sins since committed" (1:277). The coincidences were many, and some of them distressing, like the deaths of prominent persons "one after another" (1:16). Others reassured him, like the "News of the 18. Indians kill'd, and one Taken last Tuesday; which heard of just after the Appointment" of a day of prayer for the military expedition against Port Royal (1:562). All such relationships bespoke the moral condition of the people of New England and whether God was angry with them. The sequence of things, indeed the very flow of time, fluctuated in accordance with individual and collective faithfulness.

Day in and day out, Sewall was constantly aware of portents that betokened either God's anger or his protection of the colonists. Early on, with King Philip's War underway, he responded strongly to an eclipse: "Morning proper fair, the wether exceedingly benign, but (to me) metaphoric, dismal, dark and portentous, some prodigie appearing in every corner of the skies" (1:12). In his brief role as bookseller, Sewall published Increase Mather's *Heavens Alarm to the World.* Twenty years thereafter he heard Mather preach on "Revelations 22:16—bright and morning Star." The next evening Sewall "saw a large Cometical Blaze, something fine and dim. . . ." A friend informed him "that a Line drawn to the Comet strikes just upon Mexico, spake of a Revolution there, how great a Thing it would be." Sewall thought this all prophetic (1:462), as he did another comet that he viewed in 1702 (LB 1:268). Nature was for him the source of other portents, like a "bloody-colour'd Eclipse of the Moon" (1:52), the birth of deformed children (1:52), the "rare and awful Sight" of Siamese twins (2:730), and most commonly, lightning and rainbows. Dozens of entries indicated his concern. Nor was he unique in this regard: "Much Lightening . . . toward the Castle, which many observ'd and talk'd of" (1:280). Likewise a rainbow that appeared in 1687 attracted wide attention: "People were gazing at it from one end of the Town to tother" (1:131).[4] And he shared with others his reaction to an earthquake. "I congratulat with you [he wrote a friend] our having survived the late terrible Earthquake. . . . Yet the crashing Noise was very amazing to me. . . . The young people were quickly frighted out of the Shaking clattering Kitchen, and fled with weeping Cryes into our Chamber, where they made a fire, and abode there till morning" (LB 2:229). The hysteria is evident, as is Sewall's artless attempt to reproduce in words the jumble of sounds he had heard that morning. But there was more to report and ponder on. The rumbling continued, and someone living in Portsmouth had "heard a fine musical sound, like the sound of a Trumpet at a distance. He could not distinguish any Tune that he knew; but perceiv'd a considerable Variety of Notes" (LB 2:232).

In some part of Sewall's mind lay a reasoned understanding of thunder, lightning, comets, and earthquakes.[5] But in his immediate behavior, and again in the diary, he responded to these events as "portentous" (2:730). He knew much of the old lore of portents, repeating, at one point, the story of the collapse of the building at Blackfriars (LB 2:139–41) that one of Winthrop's correspondents had referred to in 1637. From his partisan position, he viewed certain events as fit punishment for deserters of the cause, like a minister who switched to Anglicanism: "Mr. Dudley Bradstreet quickly after he had received Orders, dy'd of the small Pocks" (2:765). In keeping with tradition, most of what he saw or heard became associated in his mind with anxiety and fear— fear for the welfare of his family and New England, anxiety about his own relationship to God, fear of being caught up by God's judgment before he was ready. "There was great Lightening with sharp Thunder . . . I humbly and Thankfully bless GOD that we saw the quick and powerfull Fire; heard the Terrible Voice, and yet we live!" (2:919; LB 2:80).

Yet portents also brought him reassurance. Rainbows were especially cause for celebration. Sewall felt much better when a rainbow appeared in 1707, at a time of worries for the government: "A Rainbow is seen just before night, which comforts us against our Distresses as to the affairs of the Expedition" (1:568; 2:665). In his letter book he expanded on his feelings about rainbows:

At Boston upon the Lord's Day . . . about 6. p.m. a Noble *Rainbow* was seen in the Cloud, after great Thundering, and Darkness, and Rain: One foot thereof stood upon Dorchester Neck, the Eastern end of it and the other foot stood upon the Town. . . . For the entire Compleatness of it, throughout the whole Arch, and for its duration, the like has been rarely seen. . . . I hope this is a sure Token that CHRIST Remembers his Covenant for his beloved *Jews* under their Captivity and Dispersion; and that He will make haste to prepare for them a City that has foundations, whose Builder and Maker is GOD. [LB 2:248]

Here as in the case of other portents his mind flowed easily from rainbows to prophecy, and from prophecy to assurance or, more frequently, unease.

The deeper, more far-reaching rhythm that Sewall sought to capture in the diary was the rhythm foretold in Revelation. When would the symbolic actions described in that part of Scripture—the pouring of the vials, the unfolding of the seals—be accomplished? Sewall thought so often about these events that they figured in his dream life, as when he imagined "that our Saviour in the dayes of his Flesh when upon Earth, came to Boston and abode here" (1:91). His thinking about the last judgment was influenced by a minister, the Reverend Samuel Lee, who preached frequently in Boston about the approaching of the end: "Mr. Lee . . . Spake of the inverted Rainbow, God shooting at sombody. And that our Times better than the former, and expected better still, Turks going down, a sign on't: Jews call'd, and to inhabit Judea and old Jerusalem" (1:131; 177–78). An eager reader of each "news letter" reaching Boston from abroad, Sewall tried to discern in contemporary history any further signs that prophecy was being realized. "Out of the State of Europe for April, I read the project of the Marquis de Langalerie, formerly a great General, Of planting a Colony of Protestants in the Morea, supposing that he is the person God will improve for pulling down the Throne of Antichrist, is so designed in the Revelation" (2:826). News of the Company of Scotland and its scheme to colonize the Isthmus of Panama excited him to write the ministers of the Darien expedition about the meaning of their venture. "So soon as I was informed of it, and of their Expedition to Darien, I said within my self Surely the Company of Scotland is the Sixth Angel; And within this week, I am confirmed in my Opinion, having seen the Golden Girdle wherewith the Officers and privat Souldiers are girded" (LB 1:228). Closer to home, there were other coincidences in which he rejoiced. Discussing the prophecies with a houseguest, he was told "of a converted Turk, and of strange Visions at Meccha, in the year 1620, to be seen in Clark's Examples. It being the same year with Plimouth it affected me" (1:393). Here the emotion sprang from the possibility of associating the downfall of Antichrist with the founding of America. Sometimes he resisted this connection, as when Joseph Dudley—part Royalist, part Puritan—received 666 votes in an election (1:61). His endless puzzling over witnesses and seals could aggravate his fear of what might lie ahead (LB 2:53–54). But on the whole, prophetic time assured him of the promise of America and the coming triumph of the saints.

Yet Sewall sensed that time was never to be understood as permanent or regular. Though prophecy unfolded, though the clock ticked away the hours by an unvarying beat, though the seven days of Genesis were stamped immutably upon the calendar, the will of God stood over and above any structures, even structures God created. All existence was contingent, all forms of time suspended, on his will. The unexpected crash of a glass to the floor (1:378) was like the crash of God's anger breaking in upon the flow of time: "How suddenly and with surprise can God destroy!" (1:418). The diary entries pile up as Sewall notes the happening of the unexpected—the roaring of a cow in the street (1:288), the cry of fire, the "amazing News" (1:564) of someone's sickness, and most frightening of all, the deaths that happen without warning. Sewall was fascinated by such cases:

> all the town is filled with the discourse of Major Richards's Death, which was very extraordinarily suddain; was abroad on the Sabbath, din'd very well on Monday. [1:318]

> Captain John Wincoll mounting his Horse to ride . . . to the Point, falls off his Horse; in falling cries, Lord have mercy upon me, and dies immediately. [1:322]

> We have had many very sudden deaths of late; but none more amazingly sudden, than that of the Learned President of Harvard . . . who when he was calld to pray in the Hall . . . was found dead in his Bed! [LB 2:166]

> Our Neighbor Gemaliel Wait . . . dyed extream suddenly about Noon . . .: To the Children startled about him he said, here is a sudden Change, or there will be a great Change, to that purpose. [1:87]

Other entries reveal that Sewall had a special interest in those deaths where, a "day Sennight," he himself encountered someone in good health who now lay in his grave (1:326).

The words that recur in entries of this kind are "sudden," "surprising," "unexpected," "startled," and "amazing." When Sewall adds the words "doleful" or "awfull," as he sometimes does (1:58; 2:796), the language is suggestive of his inner feelings. For himself a time had been appointed (1:81), yet he knew it not, and he therefore lived in fear that he would fall before he was prepared.

IV

SEWALL'S SENSE of hearing was like his sense of time, a faculty attuned to meanings. The slightest sound could carry meaning. The beat of a drum and the rumble of guns, the "Hew and Cry" of the sheriff and the voice of the "cryer of fish" (1:10, 97, 78)—these made up a system of sounds that were commonplace events in a culture that depended upon such sounds for communication. Yet when an eccentric old woman wandered into Sewall's house one day and "much scare[d]" his children, the cries they made were "amazing" (1:369) to him, something unexpected and therefore frightening. The natural world provided many such experiences. However pleasant the "chippering" of the swallows every spring, the thunderstorms that awakened him at night were something else (2:851). Abrupt and unexpected sounds derived their meaning from prophecies of judgment. Describing Christ's return to earth in *The Day of Doom*, Michael Wigglesworth made much of its sound effects—the crash of thunder, the blare of trumpets, the shrieks of the distressed. Any encounter with thunder, trumpets, or shrill cries in everyday life stirred associations in Sewall's mind with their meaning in Revelation. Abrupt sounds were the sensate medium of God's anger. Hence Sewall's automatic response to the cries of his children when the old woman frightened them: "The Lord save me and his people from astonishing, suddain, desolating Judgments" (1:369).

Like Scripture texts and time, moreover, sound derived its meaning from the structure of coincidences. It was rare for Sewall not to feel that thunder was related to some other signal of God's presence. His mind ranged widely in seeking out these associations. The "day of the Coronation of K. Charles the 2d," dimly remembered from his childhood in England, was also a day of remarkable sounds: "the Thunder and Lightening of it" (1:xxx). At home one evening, Sewall listened to Cotton Mather "mentioning that more Ministers Houses than others proportionably had been smitten with Lightening; enquiring what the meaning of God should be in it." All at once a storm of hailstones smashed the windows of the room. Amid several efforts at interpretation, Sewall reminded Mather that "Monmouth made his discent into England about the time of the Hail in '85, Summer, that much cracked our South-west windows" (1:330, 331). Here the pattern of sound was fused with a Protestant uprising against Catholics and, more broadly, with prophecy. Indeed the person who listened closely to the sounds of the universe could hear the spirit speak, as in music that echoed through the woods (LB 2:232), or perhaps in the mysterious "Noise of a Drumme in the air, Vollies of Shot, Report of Cannons" described in letters from Connecticut (1:49), or in the words emerging from a child too young to know their meaning. "About Monday night last as Joseph was going into the Cradle, He said, News from Heaven, the French were come, and mention'd Canada" (1:281). To a father who dreamed of the French fleet descending on Boston, and who perceived Louis XIV as an agent of the Antichrist, these words had to seem of supernatural origin.

It was from heaven, after all, that the Holy Spirit would descend in the final days, bringing peace to some and judgment to others. Sewall knew of one moment in recent times when the spirit had thus appeared, a miraculous occasion at a college in Edinburgh when "the Lord came down with the Shout of a King among them," creating in that instant a "Heaven on Earth" (1:352). He would not himself experience such a moment, though it happened to the New Lights in the 1740s. But in his eagerness to hasten on the Second Coming, he arranged for sound effects anticipating those of Revelation. On New Year's Day of 1701, Sewall's townsfolk awoke in the morning to the sound of trumpets heralding the new year and century, and by implication the kingdom that lay just ahead (1:440). This was the hope of the man who arranged for the salute.

V

SEWALL WAS certain he had sinned. Sin was the reason why his children became sick and died, and why he might not get to heaven. The sins of all the colonists, collectively, were why he suffered from the fires that swept Boston. Sin was why the world in which he lived was less agreeable than heaven. "Sir, [he wrote to a friend]—The world we live in is so very evil by reason of sin and mortality that you will not be offended if I begin my letter with the mention of it" (LB 1:214). To another friend he extolled heaven: "Canaan is infinitely the best Country, wherein all are Friends and no Enemies; all Conveniences and no Inconveniences, for perpetuity." His conclusion was to make this other world his goal: "whatever we doe, and wherever we goe we should always be travailing towards Canaan . . ." (LB 2:88). How then cleanse himself of sin? How navigate the passageway of death?

Sewall listened carefully to scores of sermons that instructed him in answers to these questions. He filled pages of the diary with brief summaries of important lessons:

> Doct[rine]. Men ought with the utmost diligence to prepare for the Eternal Estate while this life lasts, because this is the only time to prepare in. [2:752]

> Mr. Solomon Stoddard preaches . . . shewing that there is a principle of Godliness in every true Believer; and how it differs from Moral Vertue, &c. [1:67–68]

> D[octrine]. They who would always be in a readiness for Christs uncertain coming; must see that they have Grace in their hearts, and that they always keep it in exercise. [1:375]

In addition to such entries, he filled several notebooks with outlines of sermons he heard preached. An incessant reader, he immersed himself in printed sermons of the Puritan tradition. Always he sought guidance from the clergy, and especially Samuel Willard of Third Church.

In his mid-twenties, Sewall faced the issue of church membership. The decision to advance to full communion took him months to make. He was bothered by "the weakness, or some such undesirableness in many" of the members, and "exceedingly tormented" by another question, whether Third Church had done right in seceding "from the old" (1:35, 39).[6] But he was also troubled by the classic feelings of "unfitness and want of Grace." A few days before he was admitted, he "resolved to confess" in his public testimony "what a great Sinner I had been" (1:39). Doubts persisted to the very end, in part because an older man, a member, said nothing to him on the eve of the event, and in part because the warnings compressed into 1 Corinthians 11:28–30 roused him to new heights of fear, so much so that on the day itself he "could hardly sit down to the Lord's Table."[7] Never had he "experienced more unbelief. I feared at least that I did not believe there was such an one as Jesus Xt., and yet was afraid that because I came to the ordinance without belief, that for the abuse of Xt. I should be stricken dead. . . ." Yearning for a "glimpse of" Christ, but finding "none," he nonetheless gained the courage to look forward to his next appearance at communion (1:40).

Once within the bonds of full communion, Sewall ceased to feel the same anxiety. He welcomed sacramental Sundays in a different spirit, urging, later on in life, that his church administer the service once a month (1:528). In times of trouble, like the imposition of royal government on Massachusetts in the 1680s, the church gave him shelter. There he heard his minister declare that "God would not forget the Faith of those who came first to New England, but would remember their Posterity with kindness" (1:127). There he heard the message—so in keeping with the Puritan tradition!—that "there was a radicated Antipathy between the Wicked and Godly" (1:142). Thinking of himself as godly, Sewall left behind the profane world and all the changes that perplexed him when he entered church to worship. Noting the admission of his daughter Hannah to Third Church, "Lord grant it may be in order to her being taken into Heaven!" (2:843).

But as he learned repeatedly from sermons and his reading, the way to heaven lay in constant preparation: "The Lord help me to redeem the time" (1:349). To this end Sewall practiced the technique of meditation, turning, as did Mary Rowlandson and Anne Bradstreet, everyday events into lessons for the spirit. On a "winterly" day in March after a great snowstorm, "yet the Robbins cheerfully utter their Notes this morn. So should we patiently and cheerfully sing the Praises of God, and hope in his Mercys, though Storm'd by the last efforts of Antichrist" (1:483). At a family picnic a wineglass "fell down and broke all to shivers: I said twas a lively Emblem of our Fragility and Mortality" (1:378). A meal of fresh fish, the first since his ship left England for New England, prompted him to pray, "Lord, give me to taste more of thyself everywhere, always adequately good" (1:244). More often he was prompted to these meditations by misfortune or by circumstances like a funeral: "Lord grant that I may be ready [he wrote after going to a funeral] when the Cry shall be, Behold, the Bridegroom cometh" (1:286). Misfortune happened all too often in his life—the illnesses he watched his children struggle with, the deaths of friends and family, conflicts in the government, the woes of urban life that threatened his security. Contemplating these events, he prayed that they put him "in a preparedness for my own dissolution. And help me to live upon Him alone" (1:417).

For Sewall it was necessary to perceive such events as "affliction" (1:xxxiii). Death and illness were not accidental but events that God ordained to instruct the living to depend on him. God "appointed . . . pain," Sewall told his aunt, though he added that the reasons for his doing so were sometimes hidden from the people who were suffering (LB 1:80). Yet in general sin was the root cause of death and sickness: "Sin is the Sting of death" (LB 1:391). Hence the proper response to affliction was to pray for release from this curse, and to perform the act of repentance. Sewall's brother shared the same mentality. "Went to Salem and visited my sick brother, who has had a fever all this month; Is very desirous to live, and makes vows to serve God better, if his life be spared" (1:299). Sewall took such vows himself.

Meditations, most of them on his "mortality" (2:894), punctuated Sewall's daily life. They became intense at moments like a birthday (2:655) or a voyage. Returning from a voyage to New York, he wrote a much longer entry in the diary than was usual, remarking on a "heaviness" of "Spirit" and resolving

> that if it pleas'd God to bring me to my family again, I would endeavour to serve Him better in Self-denial, Fruitfulness, Not pleasing Men . . . Labouring more constantly and throwly to Examin my self before sitting down to the Lord's Table. [1:258]

A year later, reviewing this vow to do better, he was "pressed with the sense of my doing much harm and little good, and breach of Vows at my return from New York." Worried lest "God . . . take away" the blessings of the spirit, Sewall held a special fast and "Prayed . . . that God would fit me for his good pleasure in doing and suffering" (1:277).

The death of his wife's mother caused him to reflect anew on whether he was "fit" for heaven. At her deathbed Sewall "thank[ed] her for all of her Labours of Love to me and mine, and ask'd her pardon of our undutifullness; She, after a while, said GOD PITY 'EM." In the broadside "Epitaph" he composed in her honor, Sewall described Mrs. Hull as

"Diligent" and "Constant." He went on to liken her to Sarah, Hannah, and Elizabeth in Scripture: "Performing what her Name did signifie" (1:335–36). Afterward, recalling how he felt "at prayer" the evening she fell ill (but before he knew of the impending crisis), Sewall noted he "was wofully drowsy and stupid" (1:334). Judith Hull was a true saint. Compared to hers, the rhythm of his inner life was marked by spells of drowsiness and "sins" he had "committed" (1:277, 328). Had he ever really cleansed himself of sin? Early in his life, he visited a dying man who "feared all [that] he had done for God was out of hypocrisy." The self-doubt that figured in his prompt reflection—"If so gracious and sober a man say so, what condition may it be expected many will be in on a Death-bed" (1:33)—never left him, though he only verbalized it in response to situations such as these.

Certain events made him feel peculiarly wanting. The worst of these was when one of his children died. Hearing, while away in Salem on court business, the "amazing" news that his wife had been delivered of a stillborn son, Sewall meditated: "The Lord pardon all my Sin, and Wandering and Neglect, and sanctify to me this singular Affliction" (1:350). His *own* sins were the cause of his children's suffering. Dreaming all but one were dead, he then had "Reflexions on my Omission of Duty towards them" (1:328). It was this reasoning, together with the special circumstances of the event, that led Sewall to ask "pardon" for his actions as a judge in the Salem witchcraft cases. Not long after the deaths of two children, and on a fast day proclaimed to repent the witch-hunt, he wrote out a statement that Samuel Willard read aloud in Third Church, Sewall "standing up at the reading of it":

> Samuel Sewall, sensible of the reiterated strokes of God upon himself and family . . . Desires to take the Blame and Shame of it [the mistakes of the court], Asking pardon of Men, And especially desiring prayers that God, who has an Unlimited Authority, would pardon that Sin and all other his Sins. . . . [1:366–67]

Well aware of what the Quakers had declared would happen to their "persecutors" and of the curse that Sarah Good had uttered on the scaffold, Sewall acted to regain God's favor by repenting.[8] When he learned, to his astonishment, that Increase Mather blamed him for the loss of Harvard's presidency and was prophesying that "some great Judgment will fall on Capt. Sewall, or his family" (1:455), Sewall felt the same distress, though here his recourse was to inform Mather of the truth.

The intertwining of the practice of religion and the situation of his family went much further. Like so many others in New England, Sewall became a full church member at the time he was forming his own family. He made his reasoning explicit in a passage that throws light on thousands of decisions made by others to renew their covenant or become "full" members of the church: "because of my child (then hoped for) its being baptised, I offered myself . . ." (1:39). If church membership was tied to having children, having children was in turn a function of God's blessing on a would-be mother's womb. Some months after burying his stillborn son, Sewall prayed that God "would make up our Loss . . . and . . . give us a Child to Serve Him" (1:366). Writing to express his pleasure that another's daughter had "become a fruitful vine," Sewall proposed that "The fruit of the womb is a reward, the reward of the LORD. And therefore when parents lay up for, and lay out upon their children, it is a most convenient expression of their gratitude to God the giver of them" (LB 2:94). When one of his daughters was "delivered of a Living lively Daughter" after having had a stillborn birth, Sewall thought of the event as "an Answer of Peace to our many Prayers. *Laus Deo*" (1:496). Fertility, longevity, a life marked by peace—these were "blessings" (1:337) God disposed of to the faithful Christian and his family.

But only if that family remained faithful. Blessings were conditional on practice and belief. Hence Sewall "pray'd in the Family, that might have an Interest in God, Signed, Sealed and Delivered, and that all that tended to make it sure, might be perfected" (1:252). He impressed on his children the message of incessant preparation. In tandem with the catechism he taught them the doctrine that, by nature, all were sinners. His children learned to regard death as fearful and to worry about judgment. Telling his son Samuel of another young child's death, he warned him

> to prepare for Death, and therefore to endeavour really to pray when he said over the Lord's Prayer: He seem'd not much to mind, eating an Apple; but when he came to say, Our father, he burst out into a bitter Cry, and when I askt what was the matter and he could speak, he burst out into a bitter Cry and said he was afraid he should die. [1:249]

Some years later, daughter Betty "burst out" after dinner

> into an amazing cry, which caus'd all the family to cry too: Her Mother ask'd the reason; she gave none; at last said she was afraid she should goe to Hell, her Sins were not pardon'd. [1:346]

Like so many others in this culture, Betty (then fifteen) felt as though the duties of religion she so carefully performed had not been "heard . . . because her Sins not pardon'd" (1:346).

Here was doctrine gone awry. Sewall sent for Samuel Willard, who "pray'd excellently" (1:346). Sewall prayed himself, and, as with his son, "read Scriptures comforting against death" (1:249). What else was there to do? He had bestowed godly names on them, and gained the blessings of old men. All his children had been baptized; all participated in the family service of devotion. Yet still his children were oppressed with feelings of unworthiness, of being vulnerable to judgment. Death was constantly on Sewall's mind as well, whether manifested in his dream life or a topic of explicit reflection (1:183–84). Death was when God separated true from false believers, the humble from the proud. Was there no assurance of salvation?

VI

THE TENSIONS between judgment and assurance were lessened or resolved in ritual practice. Confronting sickness and death, Sewall turned to prayer and prayerlike gestures as a means of aiding himself and his family through their crises. The remedy for sin was clear—to seek pardon and relief from the "Great Physician" (LB 2:12). Prayer was how Sewall turned doubt into hope, fear into assurance, sickness into health, death into eternal life.

Hannah awakens him at night and says she is going into labor. Sewall rises, *prays*, then sends for the midwife. Once the dawn appears, he walks to the house of Samuel Willard "and desire[s] him to call God." When he returns, "The Women call me into chamber and I pray there." He sends for Cotton and Increase Mather to pray, and, when problems persist, for yet another minister (1:459). A friend of his, a figure in the government, has a badly infected foot. A group of ministers and councillors gather at his bed to pray. "Major Walley was easy all the time of the exercise, had not one Twinging pain" (2:674). Soon after giving birth, Sewall's daughter Mary experiences "extream illness." It is after midnight, yet at once the family "try'd to call up Mr. Wadsworth; but could not make the family hear." Finally "Mr. Mayhew . . . came and pray'd very well with her." Alas, "my dear child expired," though Sewall has the comfort of remembering how, the last evening of her life and before the crisis occurred, she "ask'd me to pray with her, which I did; pray'd that GOD would give her the Spirit of Adoption to call Him Father" (2:644–45).

With death the ritual was more rigorously pursued and its meaning became more explicit. "My little Judith languishes and moans, ready to die. . . . About 2 *mane* [in the morning] I rise, read some Psalms and pray with my dear Daughter. Between 7. and 8. . . . I call Mr. Willard, and he prays. Told [the Reverend Nehemiah] Walter of her condition at [a funeral the day before], desiring him to give her a Lift towards heaven" (1:266). The grief, though real, was greatly eased by these routines. Toward his daughter Elizabeth, dying as an adult, he stretched out every possible "Lift towards heaven." There was prayer in a private meeting, there were prayers at her bedside by some five different ministers, there were prayers requested of the minister who preached Thursday lecture and of Willard. Sewall and his wife were continually at her side in prayer (2:823–24; see also 1:89).

Sewall often left his household to pray by the bedside of a friend or neighbor. The father of a schoolmate of his son's "sent for me, and I pray'd with him in the morning. . . . In the morn, I ask'd him what I should pray for, He answer'd, that God would pardon all his Sin" (1:434; 437). Often he arranged for special prayers in a church service. "Dame Walker desires me to pray with her Husband, which I do and write two notes, one for our House [church] and one for the Old" (1:141). Sewall wrote out such a note to celebrate his own recovery: "I am restored from sickness to the publick Celebration of the Lords day; for which I put up a Note, that GOD may have the Praise, and that He would teach me to profit by my Afflictions" (2:699). His son Joseph acted similarly (2:695). Every now and then he encountered a dissenting voice, the man who on his deathbed asked the ministers on hand *not* to pray. Someone Sewall labeled as "one of the vilest Men that has ever set in Boston" concluded his "Debauchery and Irreligion" by refusing "to have any Minister call'd to pray with him during his Sickness" (1:479).

Those who welcomed Sewall to their bedsides voiced a patience with affliction and assurance of salvation (2:641) far more often than anxiety. To be sure, the pain was difficult to bear when no medicines could ease it (2:866). Many prayed for death to come quickly and spare them distress; the sooner it arrived, the sooner they would be with Christ. Sewall's friend John Bayley had to wait for many months. Visiting him in January 1706, Sewall found Bayley "in a very pious humble frame in submitting to the afflicting hand of God" (1:539). That October, Bayley "said he had been a long time in a storm at the Harbours Mouth, hop'd he should not be swallow'd on Quicksands, or split on Rocks. God had not yet forsaken him. . . . Said, Here I Wait!" (1:553). The next month, responding to a comment Sewall made that "Heaven" was "the Christian's Home," he said that "I long to be at home; why tarry thy chariot wheels?" (1:555). Death came at last in January 1707. If few had to wait this long, others shared with Bayley the hope of seeing Christ. A Quincy relative of Sewall's, feeling death approach, spoke "pretty freely to me.

Saith he must run with open arms to a dying Saviour" (1:384). As reported by a minister, a Roxbury man "had great Assurance of the Love of God to him before he died; though he had much darkness before" (1:587). Others whom he visited affirmed "patience" or craved more of it (1:389, 425). A dying woman who at first complained that dying was hard went on to pray "that God would take her to Himself"; a grandchild told Sewall "she heard her Grandmother say, How long Lord, how long? Come Lord Jesus!" (1:342–43).

These were the closing words of Anne Bradstreet's poem "As weary pilgrim now. . . ." What they signified to women such as Bradstreet and Dame Walker was the mercy of a risen Christ. The God who appointed pain also pardoned the repentant and welcomed them to heaven. "Our HULDAH's gone to Gods Jerusalem," Sewall affirmed in his epitaph for Judith Hull; this faithful wife and mother had "Triumph'd over . . . DEATH. Perfect in *Thoughts, Words, Deeds,* She soars on high" (1:335). For her and, hoped Sewall, for himself and all his family, the trumpet blast that ushered in the day of judgment was also herald of the gospel, the joyful news of God's promise to the faithful. All this was made possible by prayer. Penitential prayer had real consequences. Believing wholly in this ritual, Sewall saw it as an instrument of grace; and when he asked Samuel Willard to give an old woman "one Lift more heaven-ward" (1:343), he meant those marvelous words exactly. The soul rose to heaven on the wings of prayer.

Second only to prayer in importance was the fast day. Sewall took part in close to one hundred fasts in the years the diary covers, and the care he took to describe many of these services is revealing of his hopes for them as means of reconciliation. Fasts were linked to a variety of troubles—drought and military defeat, sickness and death, politics at home and abroad, family troubles. He and his family observed private fasts, as did the religious "meeting" he attended. Third Church, the General Court, the Council—each of these communities practiced the ritual with Sewall in attendance. No governor could declare a fast without having Sewall scrutinize the fast-day bill to see if it was adequate (1:361, 475).

Ever anxious to increase his family's share of blessings, Sewall arranged for private fasts at key moments of transition. The change to new quarters in his house was a step completed by a fast that included three ministers and several members of the Council. "I appointed this day to . . . bless us in our new house. The Lord pardon and doe for us beyond our hopes, contrary to our Deserts" (1:337). Some twenty-odd years later, shortly after Hannah Sewall died, a large group gathered at the house for a "Family Sacrifice" that Sewall spent a week arranging.

The Scripture text central to the exercise was Psalm 79:8: "O remember not against us former iniquities: Let thy tender mercies speedily prevent us; For we are brought very low" (2:878–80).

God was merciful. He answered many prayers and fasts with favoring providences: the rains came (2:857), the sick were restored to health, the dying soared on wings to heaven. Whatever the specific situation, fasting and prayer functioned to transmute anxiety into assurance. They were acts that Sewall performed "incessantly" (1:xxxiii) to give himself security.

VII

"INCESSANT" is indeed the word for much of Sewall's behavior. One other pattern deserves close attention, the reading he did throughout his life. Books were "cordials" (1:559), just like prayer and fasting. Scores of entries tell us what he read, and the uses that he made of books.

Sewall was a learned reader. He owned books in Greek and Latin, and his cousin Samuel Moody, lacking such resources, sought him out to look up words in Greek (1:461; see also 518). Pursuing the significance of Scripture prophecies, Sewall compared texts and, probably, translations (1:442). Yet he only went so far, advising a young minister that "Mere Conjectures lessen the authority of the Scriptures, and betray us to uncertainty and unbelief" (LB 2:48). Sewall ordered books from London, mainly commentaries on the Bible of the kind that educated readers used (LB 1:411). Every year, with rare exceptions, he went out to Cambridge to participate in commencement at the college from which he had graduated, and where he had tutored for a year. One son, Joseph, followed in his footsteps. On a June day in 1703, Sewall listened as young Joseph "was examined" on his competence in Latin ". . . in presence of the President [Samuel Willard] and Mr. Flynt" (1:488), Joseph being asked to explicate a text from Vergil. Four years later, Joseph "held the first Question" at his graduation exercises (1:568–69).

To many of the people crowding Cambridge meetinghouse these exercises must have seemed arcane. But to Sewall they were instruments of learnedness, and learnedness itself an instrument to benefit religion. While in London he bought Matthew Poole's five-volume folio *Synopsis Criticorum*, a compilation of major commentaries on the Bible (1:204); thirty-one years later, he sent the set to Joseph, noting in the diary that "I have enjoy'd them . . . and now have the pleasure to bestow them on a worthy Minister, my Son" (2:741).

But Sewall was as well a common reader, someone who read accounts of the execution of pirates (1:510), bought almanacs each year, and relished steady sellers. Many of his almanacs survive. Most contain brief scribbled annotations: some he interleaved with blank pages on which he wrote more extensive entries.[9] Sewall thought enough of almanacs to give them away to ministers (2:995), and to have his copies bound. Otherwise, the books he liked to peruse were staples in the culture of the godly. He read such older writers as Henry Scudder (2:877), Richard Sibbes (1:139), and John Preston (2:961), and enjoyed works by Jeremiah Burroughs (2:877, 740). The nonconformist writers of the decades after 1660 were important to him: Joseph Flavel, Matthew Henry, Thomas Doolittle, Joseph Alleine, and, by 1711, the rising literary star Isaac Watts with his translation of the Psalms (1:271; 2:681, 840, 712, 828, 668).

Nor did Sewall neglect the New England ministers. He was reading Thomas Shepard's *Parable of the Ten Virgins* seven decades after its initial publication (2:653). Sermons preached by Samuel Willard were to be expected, as were sermons of the Mathers. It seems certain that he read Wigglesworth's *The Day of Doom,* since he gave a copy of it as a present (1:174). More surprising is the pleasure he received from reading and rereading a broadside, *Old Mr. Dod's Sayings,* that originated early in the seventeenth century (1:446; 454). He liked to quote these sayings (1:33).

What gave purpose to this reading was the settings in which it occurred. Sewall actively participated in two groups of readers. As a member of Third Church he took part in "private meetings" at which men and women read aloud from sermons and the Bible and discussed the text at hand. These sessions among "brothers" (2:653, 712, 812) served from time to time to clarify a moral lesson, though in general the intention was to share the "comfort" (1:518) books could offer. Reading in this context defined Christian fellowship. It also helped sustain the duties of the Christian life. The second group of readers was the Sewall family circle. Here, the act of reading focused mainly on the Bible, which the family read "in course," as it also did selected sermons (1:181). For the father of this family, the routine of household reading functioned to protect his children from the world's many dangers. True, the sermons that his children read could make them feel inadequate, as when Sewall's oldest son, still without a trade, found "Mr. Wadsworth's Sermon against Idleness . . . an Affliction" (1:347). But in general, reading sheltered them within God's providence; it eased the turbulence of life and offered steps to heaven. In both reading circles books served yet another function, that of reaffirming the concept of New England as a place where godliness prevailed instead of "superstition" (1:374).

Time and time again, Sewall voiced these meanings for the act of reading and the kindred act of writing. It pleased him (as he wrote to a friend) that his sister Betty "reads through one volume [of] the book of Martyrs, in three months space; improving only leisure times [at] night" (LB 1:19). Pleasing too was that his children—boys and girls alike—became literate. Sewall does not tell us how much they learned in the household and how much at school, though he mentions one son leaving in the morning with his hornbook at the age of three (1:277). The door by which his children entered the great world of books surely involved primers, catechisms, psalm books, and the Bible. Sewall also made these books available to others, buying them in quantities from London and perhaps the local market (LB 1:238, 248; 1:588).

All his life he relished giving books away—books of his composing or commissioning, sets of learned commentaries, psalters specially bound in "Turkey-Leather" (2:731), New England classics like John Cotton's *Gods Promise to His Plantation* (1:120), which he gave to soldiers in his militia company as the old charter government was coming to an end. Active as a writer, he wrote broadside verse accessible to any reader. His one longer book, an essay on prophetic history, had a Latin title and a preface in that language. He was also active as a patron who paid the cost of printing sermons he thought others would find useful. Sewall's eagerness to make such gifts was not that of an author or a patron seeking recognition. He saw the gift relationship as a mode of blessing. Seeking blessings for himself, and especially for his children, he used books to create networks of exchange. Giving and receiving the symbolic goods of "comfort" were reciprocal.

He brought certain needs to books. They were like the prayers he offered at someone's bedside, a means of warding off the evils of the world, of overcoming troubles, of reaching out to God. Often it was death or sickness that initiated comments on his reading or gift-giving. Referring to a broadside elegy by a prolific local writer, Benjamin Tompson, Sewall wrote the man to whom he sent a copy, "It begins with a rich cordial against the revolutions we are many times exercised with, and are constantly exposed to" (LB 1:399). Friends sent Sewall verses to relieve his grief when children died (1:250 n), and he wrote elegies himself commemorating Judith Hull and two of his grandchildren (2:641–42). The circle of consoling friends who supplied him with books included Cotton Mather. Sewall paid the costs of publishing a sermon, *Nehemiah. A Brief Essay on Divine Consolations,* that Mather dedicated to his patron: "THE ESSAY now before you, was made, because you have been Exercised with some funerals in your Family" (2:648 n). Soon Sewall was relaying Mather's *Consolations* to a wider circle, giving half a dozen to the governor (whose daughter had married a Sewall son) and distributing many more at a court session (1:652).

Books thus acquired ritual significance in a complex web of mutual caring and protection. Some were symbols of the Protestant community he labored to defend against its many enemies. Others, like the broadside poem he wrote "Upon the drying up that Ancient River, the River Merrymak" (1:973), signified the coming kingdom. Broadside elegies transformed death into a rite of passage. And *Mourners Cordials* such as Willard's, together with the many sermons that he read and gave away (1:287), were recompense for grief and fear—grief over all the tribulations of the world, fear that he would not be pardoned for his sins.

Reading was inseparable from Sewall's sense of family and community, and how he cared for them. Yet he also came on books that violated that sense of community. Serving briefly as a regulator of the marketplace and witnessing the censorship of Boston's first newspaper, in his role as judge he punished certain men who issued libels harassing the Mathers (2:646), and investigated a "Mock Sermon" (2:680). Someone satirized a poem of his (1:448), and, though it goes unmentioned in the diary, the young son of a man he met with in private meetings used the pseudonym Silence Dogood to mock Harvard College and the culture of the godly.[10] Printed libels were subversive of good order (1:81). The newssheets that arrived from Europe told confusing stories (1:492). Rumor swirled about the streets of Boston. News was carried from one person to another; Sewall had to depend on this system, with its delays and mistakes, for word of public events and even events in his own family (1:78, 80). There was nothing he could do about the process except sift through conflicting stories and hope for the best.

The world of print was like the world at large, more turbulent and conflict-ridden than the space he bounded with the gift relationship. Sewall used books to keep that larger world at arm's length. The curiosity of a Cotton Mather was not his, and he noted with displeasure Mather's preaching on "the Sun being in the centre of our System. I think it inconvenient to assert such Problems" (2:779). What he wanted from the books he read and gave away, what he used his learning for, was something very simple: the security of knowing truth and the obtaining of blessings for himself, his children, and New England.

VIII

SEWALL USED his diary as he used the books he read, to give order to experience. It enabled him to link the small in scale to the large, the microcosm of the Sewall family and events in Boston to the macrocosm of the history of redemption. Turning back to older entries, he could see how all things fit together. Some loose ends remained. But it was reassuring to believe that someday he would see the wholeness of his data.

To any modern reader of the diary, the mental world of Samuel Sewall must seem very distant. We no longer perceive the same interweaving of the natural and the supernatural. His understanding of the world was magical in presuming that the forces flowing through it were not bound by ordinary rules of cause and effect. He thought these forces were responsive to manipulation, as through prayer and fasting: healing remained an elusive fusion of the natural and the spiritual. Sewall's sense of time was ahistorical. Time was reallly time*less* in a world where the coincidences mattered, and not the passing moment. Like the artisans who fashioned New England gravestones, he overrode the rhythm of the clock with the time-scheme of the coming kingdom and the resurrection of the saints.[11]

To us he may seem a deeply anxious man, someone driven by his fear of judgment. It is easy to assume this from the diary's many references to death, and from Sewall's heightened sense of prodigies and portents. And yet, Sewall did not worry constantly about these matters. He passed many moments without thinking about sin and judgment. When a crisis jarred him out of being "drowsy," he responded with expressions of concern. But the structure of his statements became formulaic: "Lord make me ready for thy coming!" (2:869). More crucially, he found sustenance in ritual practice. Fasting, singing, praying, reading, giving—all were means of turning rites of passage into celebrations, of transforming fear into assurance of God's presence. His repertory of such practices was far broader than we might suppose. When Sewall gave away the coin he referred to as an "Angel," he implicitly invoked the ceremony of the king's touch, when such coins were dispersed to those who asked the king to heal them (2:736, 776).[12] When he drove a pin into a building and thereby made it safer to inhabit, he performed an act with roots in pagan folklore.[13] The cherubim that guarded his front gate, the care he took with names, the timing of his decision to become a church member, the fixation with his children's safety, these suggest a faith infused with tribalism. To take Sewall whole, to see all these patterns converge in the diary, is to perceive the complexity of popular religion.[14]

AFTERWORD

EXPLAINING FOR the benefit of future generations why the "pilgrims" came to Plymouth, William Bradford cited the decision of a small group of English men and women that "the lordly and tyrannous power of the prelates ought not to be submitted unto." Accordingly, these plain folk acted to shake "off this yoke of antichristian bondage, and as the Lord's free people joined themselves (by a covenant of the Lord) into a church estate . . . to walk in all His ways." Here in essence was one theme of the lay tradition, an identity summed up in the resonating phrase, "the Lord's free people."[1]

Early in the eighteenth century, Joseph Backus journeyed from his home in Norwich, Connecticut, to Ipswich, Massachusetts. There he conferred with John Wise, a minister well known for denouncing an attempt to increase ministerial authority in church government. Backus did not like the Saybrook Platform (1708), which the clergy in Connecticut had initiated to gain greater independence of their local congregations. Angered when his own church voted its approval of the Platform, Backus withdrew in dissent. A few decades later, Joseph's grandson Isaac, converted in the Great Awakening, withdrew from the Norwich church when it refused to reinstate the test of a "relation" for prospective members. Isaac Backus and his fellow "Separates" formed congregations of their own, despite the opposition of the government. Backus soon evolved into a Baptist. Afterward, he found in the history of New England ample support for a pure church, lay prophesying, and his self-perception as someone persecuted by a power-hungry priestcraft. The version of the past he constructed for himself embraced the Separatists who had founded Plymouth.[2] Together, the mid-eighteenth-century "Separates" and the

Separatists of Bradford's generation affirmed the Word as the sole source of truth. They perceived the Roman clergy (and by implication, others) as usurpers of the Word, always conspiring (as they had in ancient times) to "keepe the Scriptures shut up in an unknowne tongue."[3]

This way of representing Christian history was crucial to the lay tradition. Nowhere was that tradition stronger than in Plymouth, where the people did without a minister for a decade. The "pilgrims" looked back to the martyrs under Mary Tudor as exemplifying the imperative that lay people reject false teachers and read Scripture for themselves. Using Scripture as their standard, they insisted on the liberty of "prophesying."[4] When the members of the church in Wenham were confronted with the Cambridge Platform, they affirmed a parallel idea, that the truth was not yet fully known to anyone. Here and elsewhere in New England, lay people felt empowered to compare their understanding of the Word with that of their minister; when young Robert Breck began to preach in Windham, Connecticut, in 1732, his ideas so disturbed the congregation that they challenged his legitimacy.[5]

Such independence was sustained by oral lore. Describing his "obscure family," Benjamin Franklin told how, in the reign of Mary Tudor, his ancestors "got an English Bible, and to conceal and secure it, it was fastened open with tapes under and within the frame of a joint-stool."[6] More stories of this kind, and others of resistance to a tyrannizing priesthood, found their way into Backus's *History of New England,* just as, a century and a half earlier, they had made their way into Bradford's *Of Plymouth Plantation.*

Declaring themselves "free," the people at Plymouth coupled this assertion with a covenant in which they pledged to live according to the law of God. Theirs was liberation to fulfill the law, to obey it as completely as they could. They demanded of themselves, and of others, obedience to a program of reform. When Bradford intervened on Christmas Day in Plymouth in 1621 to stop certain men from playing in the "street," telling them it was a day of work and not of rest, he enforced a purging of the calendar that figured in a broader movement of reform.[7] Originating in Elizabethan England, this "reformation of manners" (for so we now rename the Puritan movement) found expression in New England in a hundred covenants embodying the ethics of a loving brotherhood, the separation of the "saints" from those deemed "worldly" or "profane," and practices like Sabbatarianism.

Learned men, the clergy trained at Cambridge, Oxford, or their new-world offspring Harvard, were leaders in this campaign for reform and shared in the making of the myth of freedom. Many men and women came to revere clergy who embodied the ideal of disciplined asceticism.

More, these people tried to practice this ideal themselves. The closeness between people and clergy was manifested in the process by which certain towns in Massachusetts and Connecticut were settled, and again in places such as Cambridge meetinghouse when people testified about spiritual experience. The great themes of this religious culture—the moral allegory of repentance and confession, the meaning of the wonder, the role of the Devil—were substantially the doing of the ministers. "God sees in the dark": these words of a woman trying to deter seduction evoke a mentality that people in New England owed in part to sermons, the perception of a judging God who imposed the obligation of confession.[8]

Lay people and the clergy shared much common ground. That common ground included the rejection of traditional popular culture. It embraced a moral vision of community. What lay people added or enhanced was the interweaving of the family and religion. The very human feelings of anger and revenge were absorbed into religion via wonder stories, holy curses, and witch-hunting. So were other feelings, like charity for neighbors and the felt need for peace. But family was the most important bridge between religion and society. Lay men and women used religion to protect their families. Hence the naming patterns in New England (though these also signified the purging of all "pagan" culture) and the pressure on the churches to extend the sacrament of baptism. Life crises (rites of passage) and especially childbirth may explain why people moved from merely "formal" Christianity to critical self-searching, and why women were more likely to become church members. It is surely not coincidental that Anne Hutchinson put her questions about assurance of salvation to women undergoing childbirth.[9]

Much of popular religion involved marking off the zones of danger and securing some means of protection. The movement we call Puritanism was but a reassertion of the dangers that awaited those who sinned, who broke the moral law. This was how reformers used the lore of the wonders. But in the same breath these reformers held out new forms of protection: using the right names for children, separating from ungodly people, entering into covenant, purging sin by prayer and fasting, or conducting executions and witch-hunting. Samuel Sewall's diary shows how deeply he was moved by the yearning for security. What he expressed, others felt as well.

It was the clergy who took the lead in defining what was safe or dangerous. People looked on them as healers who could relieve sickness in their souls and distemper in the body social. Yet this respect for the clergy coexisted with a current of resistance. Often they were perceived as being able to cause harm as well as good. Healers though they were, they could also inflict curses and cause misfortune.[10] Their sermons aroused mixed emotions—fear as well as hope, self-doubt as well as confidence. Lay people took advantage of ambiguity and arranged to their own liking the boundary between purity and danger. Thus, they sought baptism for their children but rejected the Lord's Supper because it added to the risk of judgment. At any moment they could use the wonder lore against the ministers, as Baptists and the Quakers did. Rarely did they wish to punish such outsiders as severely as the ministers insisted.

Ambiguity, or the possibility of seeing things two different ways, was endemic in this system. It engulfed the sacraments and ministry, the heretic and witch, and even printed books. Reflecting this confusion, one of Elizabeth Morse's neighbors puzzled over how to regard her: "What? Is shee a Witch, or a cunning Wooman?"[11] Similarly, people were uncertain whether to see Quakers as agents of the Devil or as saintly martyrs. And how were unseen voices to be understood, or dreams and apparitions? Always in this system the role of the clergy was to regulate ambiguity, or at least to ensure that it worked to their own advantage. But lay people were in general more tolerant, more apt to accept this mix of messages as the way things were. In this manner, popular religion subtly contested the role of the clergy.

The empowering of lay people flowed from all these practices and situations. Yet no form of power was more crucial than what I have referred to as literacy. Lay people were fluent in a language based on Scripture, and that dramatized a sense of self. Implicitly this language communicated the importance of each person's quest for grace. Someone who has studied nineteenth-century English working-class autobiographies has concluded that these more recent

> narratives were based upon the assertion of the right of every individual to determine his spiritual identity. All that stood between him and his maker was the Bible. This conviction was important both for the commitment to free speech which it embodied, and for the encouragement it gave to the most humble and non-literate of individuals to analyse and set down their own experiences.[12]

This statement applies fully as well to lay people in seventeenth-century New England. The ways in which they wrote and spoke about themselves may show how well they hearkened to the ministry. But from another point of view, the speech of these people signified self-confidence.

The making of the lay tradition included books and therefore printers. Long before the founding of New England, English printers were producing plain-style books that taught the story of "warfare" against sin. Such books, together with the Bible and editions of the Psalms, circulated widely among ordinary people. The marketplace thus worked to perpetuate a reformed, godly culture. Yet printers and booksellers had interests of their own that did not fully coincide with the wishes of the clergy. Profit-minded and inventive, printers devised "merriments" as readily as penny godlies. Moreover, printers took control of certain genres—the almanac, descriptions of executions, the narratives of wonders—that clergy in New England tried to adapt to their own ends. The book trade stood astride the line dividing purity from danger, the truthful from the fictive: mediating between learned culture and the lay tradition, printers communicated a mélange of messages.

One may ask, did people "really" believe in wonders, sin, and witches? The commonsense response is yes. It is also common sense to realize that religion was not all these people thought about. Farmers, artisans, and housewives made many practical decisions without reference to God. Much of social life was secular—that is, differentiated from the holy or religious.[13] Always there were elements of choice. Living amid different sets of meanings, people did not by any means always prefer a narrowly "religious" or fully orthodox interpretation. "Horse-shed" Christians may have acted one way, men like Thomas Goold another. But "horse-shed" Christians did not make the choice of whether to believe in God. Nor, in my opinion, did some people opt for occult knowledge in defiance of religion. We must rather understand the two as intermingled.[14]

It is more an art than a science to detect flows of meaning and how people acted on them. Complicated in itself, our process of interpretation must also take account of contradictions in the thinking of these people—of seeing death as terrifying but affirming their salvation, of demanding pure churches but insisting that their children be included in the covenant. Yet people also made consistent choices. Certain story lines prevailed; thinking and behavior occurred mainly within boundaries that lend themselves to charting.

By the 1690s this vernacular religion, this culture of the Word, was beginning to fragment. The first and most important difference concerned literacy. Increasingly the clergy turned away from the vernacular tradition and took up modes of expression that excluded typological symbolism. Rejecting the plain style, they came to think of books and writing not as icons of the truth but as "literary."[15] A "singing controversy" erupted in the 1720s as ministers attempted to replace the psalmody tradition with a different kind of music.[16]

Some lay people also professed a new literary sensibility. Jane Turell wrote poetry and letters to her father (the most cosmopolitan of Boston ministers) in a style completely different from that of Anne Bradstreet's poetry; Turell's model was an eighteenth-century versifier, Richard

Blackmore, not the plain-style writers Bradstreet honored. Young Benjamin Franklin was enchanted with the prose he found in English coffee-house literature. *The New England Courant,* which epitomized the shift away from godly speech, published his "Receipt for a New-England elegy," in which he parodied the kind of poem that ordinary people liked to read and write. "There is scarce a plough jogger or country cobler that has read our Psalms and can make two lines jingle," another writer for the *Courant* declared in 1722, "who has not once in his life at least exercised his talent this way. Nor is there one country house in fifty which has not its walls garnished with half a Score of these Sort of Poems . . . which praise the Dead to the Life."[17]

For Samuel Sewall, the withdrawal of the clergy from a shared tradition was epitomized in the wigs that a few Boston clergy now wore in the pulpit.[18] Less visible, though in the long run of more consequence, was a growing unease with "enthusiasm." Religion, certain ministers were declaring in the 1720s, was a matter more of "reason" than of inward spiritual experience. This trend compromised the lore of wonders and helped end the practice of witch-hunting.[19]

The road thus taken by some clergy generated tensions that eventually erupted in the Great Awakening. Once again, lay men and women testified about spiritual experience; again, they reaffirmed the liberating impact of the Holy Spirit, the true "carnival" for godly people. The Awakening gave new force to the mentality of wonder, the story line of deliverance and confession, and the moral allegory of a land swept clean of sin. All these old assumptions flourished once more among ordinary people. For them printers continued to publish tales of marvels and books like Alleine's *Alarm to Unconverted Sinners.* For that matter, printers continued to reissue *The Day of Doom,* Thomas Vincent's terrifying sermons on the "judgment" of the London plague and fire, the *New England Primer,* and Mary Rowlandson's account of her captivity. And, in contrast to this world of print, other readers were withdrawing into fiction or the kinds of history in which providence was generalized and distant.

Renewed in the Great Awakening, the religion of the people gave color to the Revolution and to further outbreaks of revivalism. In nineteenth-century America, popular religion merged with the tide of democratic nationalism to become a celebration of "free people" in ways that would have seemed quite strange to William Bradford.

Here our story ends. But let us conclude briefly with four assertions about culture and religion. Culture and religion (or religion as a culture) must be understood as partly independent of the social system in which they occur. That so much old debris was transmitted to New England—in a word, so much that was Elizabethan—argues for a process of survival and transmission that was curiously separate from the modernizing social forces which were elsewhere manifested in the colonies. The play of meaning, or ambiguity, that I have emphasized was also partly independent; no social group was immune from this play of meaning or could shut it off.

These comments bear upon the exercise of power. We may want to describe power as unequally distributed in seventeenth-century New England: clergy had more than lay people, men than women, merchants than mere farmers. All this is true. Yet the hegemonic system that prevailed in New England was, if understood as culture, rich in countervailing practices and motifs.[20] The vernacular tradition accepted clerical authority, but also contained techniques for reversing every premise on which this authority depended. From this perspective, then, power was more fluidly arranged than it seems when viewed in terms of the social structure.

This fluidity limits the significance of "high" and "low," "elite" and "popular," as descriptive of how culture was related to society.[21] I have here argued for the notion of a shared culture, and against division; at the same time I have looked for tensions that grew up between the clergy and the people.

Throughout, I have described literary formulas that people found in books and used in daily speech. When lay men and women testified in churches about spiritual experience or when Quakers played the role of martyr, they drew on well-charted scripts. What else is culture but a set of scripts? These stories worked for people in New England—worked despite their formulaic nature and their derivation from sources other than the world of work, or local circumstances.

These four statements deserve fuller testing and more criticism of the kind that Roger Chartier is contributing via his studies of popular literature in early modern France. Whatever the eventual significance of these propositions, I offer them to demonstrate that a history of popular religion in seventeenth-century New England is inevitably a history, not of certain parts or fragments, but of culture as a whole—that is, of how structures of meaning emerge, circulate, and are put to use.

A NOTE ON BOOK OWNERSHIP
IN SEVENTEENTH-CENTURY
NEW ENGLAND

How many people in New England owned books, and at that, how many books? A minister in 1673 lamented that "in multitudes of Families there is (it may be) . . . no Bible, or onely a torn Bible to be found[.] I mean, but a part of the Bible . . ." (Thomas Shepard, *Eye-Salve* [Cambridge, Mass., 1673], 50). Indirectly, however, some of his contemporaries sketched a different picture—Increase Mather, to take one example, remarked in 1677 that "many" in his congregation possessed James Janeway's *A Token for Children.* (See note 74, chap. 1.) Like every Bible in New England (though not editions of the Psalms), these copies of *A Token for Children* had to be imported from England.

Probate inventories are the one consistent source of evidence about who owned books, and how many of them. Their limitations as a source are twofold. More often than not, books are listed not by title but as an inclusive category: "books" or "old books," or other language of this sort, although the valuation may nonetheless enable us to estimate the total number or to make comparisons. The other limitation is that wills and inventories represent an unknown fraction of the population of colonial New England. Even when we study all surviving inventories, the data is selective.

In *The Puritan Pronaos,* Samuel Eliot Morison reported the results of a survey made by Clifford K. Shipton of probate inventories from two Massachusetts counties, Essex and Middlesex. For the period 1635–1681 in Essex County, 39 percent contained books. One-fifth of this group listed only Bibles. The Middlesex records covered a slightly later period (1654–1699), and the percentage was distinctly higher: 60 percent included books, of which only 8 percent were limited to Bibles. Shipton's sample (the data base is not specified) showed little change over time; about as many colonists owned books in 1650 as would own them in 1690. (Morison, *The Puritan Pronaos* [New York, 1936], 137–38.)

More recently, Gloria Main has sampled probate inventories in Boston (Suffolk County) and several counties west of Boston (not including Middlesex) from 1640 to 1764. She counted consumer goods, including books, in attempting to evaluate the standard of living. She divided her data into three "wealth classes," an arrangement that enabled her to correlate the rate of bookholding (but not the quantity of books themselves) with wealth distribution. According to her figures, in the quarter-century between 1640 and 1674, 59 percent of estates in the lowest class (£1–49) owned "religious books." The percentage rose to 74 for persons in the middle group (£50–249) and 100 for the top (£225 and up). There was little change in the quarter-century 1675–1699, though the highest wealth class slipped back to 71 percent ownership. Her figures indicate that "secular books" (far less often cited) were owned almost exclusively by the richest cohort. (Main, "The Standard of Living in Southern New England, 1640–1773," *WMQ* 3d Ser., 45 [1988], 133–34.)

Anne Brown and I have analyzed all the Middlesex County wills and probate inventories that survive in the county Probate Registry for the period 1648–64, using transcripts at the New England Historic Genealogical Society. These total 118, not counting a few documents without inventories. Forty-seven of these inventories, or 40 percent, do not mention books. Our survey therefore coincides with Shipton's; three-fifths of the people for whom wills and inventories survive were book owners, and two-fifths were not. Unlike Main and Morison, we were also interested in how many books these people owned. Nine inventories (just under 13 percent) list a single Bible and no other book. Including these nine, forty-eight persons (68 percent of book owners) owned books valued at £1 or less, a figure we can translate into a maximum of 5 books. Another twelve persons, or 17 percent, owned books valued in the inventories at £1–3. Eleven, or 15 percent, owned more sizable collections, worth from £3 up into the hundreds; the three ministers in the group owned books on a scale out of all proportion to the holdings of lay people.

These figures underscore the difference between "active readers" (as I termed them in Chapter 1) and persons who satisfied their needs by owning two or three books, one of them invariably a Bible. When we take into account the total value of estates, these figures modestly confirm what we would expect: the persons who owned many books were in general better off or had occupations—the ministry, medicine, the magistracy—for which books were crucial. But a few were men of modest means, with estates (as indicated in the inventories) of less than £300.

The men and women whose inventories did not list a single book were a diverse group—some well-to-do, some with scant resources (like the six widows in the group), and others of a middling status. Almost 25 percent (11 of 46) had estates of more than £200, the highest being £822; and since many of the inventories fail to include real estate, this figure must be taken as a minimum. The persons owning a few books also varied in affluence, the range being from a low of approximately £5 to a high of £176. Half of this group had estates of less than £100. Imprecision in the inventories deters us from attempting stricter correlations.

In general, this evidence—Shipton's, Main's, and ours—supports the hypothesis of a literate society. Book ownership is never universal. Certain occupations depend on books; others, not at all or very little. Many books, moreover, get used up or discarded. This happened in seventeenth-century England (as Margaret Spufford proves in *Small Books and Pleasant Histories*) with chapbooks. London printer-publishers issued them in astonishing quantities. Yet almost never were they mentioned in a probate inventory unless concealed in the phrase "small books." Primers, almanacs, and catechisms go unmentioned in New England inventories; psalm books do get cited, though not as frequently as the supply would indicate they should be. We may surmise from the records of the book trade (as Spufford does for seventeenth-century England) that listings in probate inventories understate the extent to which people owned or used books in the course of their lifetimes.

The situation in New England may be compared with book ownership in France. In sixteenth-century Amiens, 20 percent of all inventories included books. Among artisans and merchants, a mere 11 percent owned books at death, and half of this group owned no more than one or two. In seventeenth-century Paris, as in Amiens, wealth and occupation sharply influenced who owned books; again, artisans were usually not book owners, or bought very few. (Roger Chartier, *The Cultural Uses of Print in Early Modern France* [Princeton, 1987], 146–48.) Book ownership in Kent, England, more closely resembled the New England situation. By 1640, after rising from a low of approximately 15 percent in 1560, nearly half of the estates that Peter Clark has surveyed included books. Again, wealth (or occupation) was significant. (Peter Clark, "The Ownership of Books in England, 1560–1640: The Example of Some Kentish Townsfolk" in Lawrence Stone, ed., *Schooling and Society* [Baltimore, 1976], 95–111.) The higher percentage for New England is arresting in light of the fact that, before 1660, little was produced by the local printing press.

Rarely do we glean specific titles from the probate inventories. Nor can we determine whether someone ever read the "old books" to which those who did the inventory assigned a few shillings' worth of value. *Pace* Thomas Shepard, Jr., Bibles do seem relatively abundant, some households owning two or even three. But perhaps he had his eye on the 40 percent of households where, it seems, no Bible was available.

ACKNOWLEDGMENTS

THIS BOOK is a child of circumstances as well as the outcome of my ongoing education as a historian. That education involves teachers, most of whom are my contemporaries. At the outset I want to acknowledge my indebtedness to Richard Bushman and Roland Delattre. My first efforts at describing ritual occurred in a seminar that Bushman and I co-taught at Boston University; that this topic was important I learned from Delattre. Norman Fiering and James McLachlan nurtured my initial curiosity about books and reading; each provided me with references I knew nothing of. Much later, after setting aside a book-in-progress on nineteenth-century Victorianism, I met Keith Thomas, Margaret Spufford, Roger Chartier (through the kind services of François Furet), and Peter Burke; the histories they have written and the advice they have offered me in person have been crucial. From Roger Thompson I received much encouragement, and the stimulation of his own work on court records. My debt is also large to work by John Bossy, Patrick Collinson, and the late Victor Turner.

The circumstances out of which this book emerges originated with an invitation to participate in a conference on intellectual history. The essay I wrote for that conference was revised and published as "The World of Print and Collective Mentality in Seventeenth-Century New England." Some time later, moved by the examples of Alan Macfarlane's *The Family Life of Ralph Josselin* and Robert Mandrou's *Introduction to Modern France,* I opened Samuel Sewall's diary and began to read it closely. The essay that resulted, "The Mental World of Samuel Sewall," was presented to a conference in New Haven, and, rewritten and expanded, published in the *Proceedings* of the Massachusetts Historical Society; it reappears, revised and expanded for a second time, as Chapter 5. I am grateful to Malcolm Freiberg, then editor of publications, for advising me to change the way the essay initially ended.

A conference at the American Antiquarian Society on "the history of the book" led to "The Uses of Literacy in New England, 1600–1850," in which I attempted to define a mode of reading and describe "steady sellers." At still another conference on "popular culture in Europe and

America" at Cornell University the other speakers present (Chartier among them) introduced me to a range of problems and interpretations that inform the introduction to this book; my introduction to the conference papers (for which I received much aid from Steven Kaplan) offered me the chance to reflect on the general proposition of "popular culture." In April 1983, I attempted (prematurely) to summarize my thinking about popular religion in a paper for the Organization of American Historians; I am grateful to Joyce Appleby and the commentators (Harry S. Stout and Richard Trexler) for making this a useful session.

Another circumstance, long in the making, was the exhibition "New England Begins: The Seventeenth Century," at the Boston Museum of Fine Arts. A conference attached to the exhibition, and sponsored by the Colonial Society of Massachusetts, was the forum for an early version of chapter 2 of this book, "A World of Wonders," subsequently published in *Seventeenth-Century New England.*[1] More recently, I have benefited from presenting parts of chapters in two seminars (Chartier's and Jacques Revel's) at the Ecole des Hautes Etudes en Sciences Sociales; in a series sponsored by the Department of History, Brandeis University; in J. R. Pole's Seminar in American History at St. Catherine's College, Oxford University; at the Anglo-American Conference, University of London; at a History Workshop Conference on Radical Religion; and in my own department. Early on, the Columbia University seminars in Early American History and American Studies provided sympathetic audiences.

My research and writing were accomplished thanks to generous support from several agencies: the John Simon Guggenheim Memorial Foundation; the National Endowment for the Humanities through its Centers for Research Program; the American Antiquarian Society; the School of Historical Studies, Institute for Advanced Study, Princeton; the American Council of Learned Societies; and last but not least, Boston University. I am deeply grateful to them for this support. I want also to thank Daniel W. Howe and John M. Murrin for letters on my behalf. I am grateful to Jane Garrett for her encouragement.

Without help from many others I would not have been as well informed about the topics I take up. Ross Beales handed me a sheaf of notes on literacy and reading that was crucial to Chapter 1, "The Uses of Literacy." Roger Thompson shared the results of his work in the Middlesex court records, and Nina Dayton passed on information from the New Haven court. My colleague Robert St. George contributed the widow's inventory I cite in Chapter 1; aside from giving me other items from his research, he has also listened critically to some of my arguments. Barbara Dailey, then a graduate student at Boston University, shared her notes on religious dissent. Mary Rhinelander gave me access to her transcripts of unpublished "confessions" from the Cambridge church. Carolyn Travers reproduced a listing of books owned by Plymouth colonists. William Schoeffler of the New England Historic Genealogical Society let me consult transcripts of Middlesex County wills and inventories. Others who have passed on their research with great generosity include Jennifer Monaghan, Robert Trent, Michel Alexander, Electa Tritsch, Carol Karlsen, and Margaret Spufford. The late D. P. Walker directed my attention to certain secondary sources. Jean-Claude Schmitt has influenced my thinking by his acute response to "A World of Wonders." Chapter 3 owes much to Charles Hambrick-Stowe's *The Practice of Piety;* chapter 4, to the thoughtful comments of Michael MacDonald. Anne Brown, Kathryn Grover, and Eric Hahr ably accomplished specific research tasks.

The remarkable resources of the American Antiquarian Society, together with the skills of its staff (especially Nancy Burkett), were crucial to this book. I want to thank the curators and librarians of the Houghton Library, Harvard University; the Pepys Library, Magdalen College, Cambridge; the Massachusetts Historical Society; the Connecticut Historical Society; the Bodleian Library, Oxford; and the British Library in London, for services on my behalf.

My late friend and former teacher Sydney Ahlstrom introduced me to the history of American religion; his great curiosity, and that of Allan Ludwig, who introduced me to New England gravestones, are part of the background of this book. And I thank Joan Brigham for her generous enthusiasm.

At some moment in my childhood I was handed the Shorter Version of the Westminster Catechism, though, if I remember rightly, I was never really asked to memorize it. In my family, true piety was embodied in the person of my grandmother; as in families of the seventeenth century, ours respected her example in spite of falling short of it in certain ways. There cannot have been many households in the 1940s in which someone liked to recall the novels of Harriet Beecher Stowe—not *Uncle Tom's Cabin,* but *Oldtown Folks* and *The Minister's Wooing.* They were rich in incidents and characters that my grandmother regarded as more fact than fiction. Remembering, myself, the strict family rule of attending church on Sundays, there comes back to me the heat of Virginia summers, the boredom of the sermon, the solemnity of communion Sundays, the wonderful release of singing hymns; and afterwards, around the family dining table, the arguments about the minister's ideas and those of Jesus: Was it right, for example, that Martha did the work while Mary sat and listened to him? It was then I learned the lesson that the respect that my family had for our good minister did not deter freedom of opinion. It was then, in these church services and Sunday schools, that I absorbed certain ways of feeling that, for me, defined religion. Those ways of feeling have undoubtedly affected my perception of the seventeenth century, and of what I describe as religion for the people of those times. Sadly, my description of the thinking of those people also draws on a more recent crisis in my family, as those to whom I dedicate this book will recognize.

NOTES

SHORT TITLES USED IN CITATIONS

AC	David D. Hall, *The Antinomian Controversy, 1636–1638: A Documentary History* (Middletown, Conn., 1968)
Acts & Mon.	*The Acts and Monuments of John Foxe*, 8 vols., ed. Stephen Reed Cattley (London, 1837–41)
CSM Pub.	Colonial Society of Massachusetts, *Publications*
Essex Court Recs.	*Records and Files of the Quarterly Courts of Essex County, Massachusetts*, 9 vols. (Salem, Mass., 1912–75)
Fiske Notebook	Robert G. Pope, ed., *The Notebook of The Reverend John Fiske, 1644–1675* (Publications of the Colonial Society of Massachusetts, *Collections* 47 [Boston, 1974])
Johnson, *WWP*	Edward Johnson, *The Wonder-Working Providence of Sions Saviour* (1654), ed. J. Franklin Jameson, Original Narratives of Early American History (1910; repr., New York, 1959)
Magnalia	Cotton Mather, *Magnalia Christi Americana*, 2 vols. (1702; repr., Hartford, 1853)
MHS Coll.; Proc.	Massachusetts Historical Society, *Collections; Proceedings*
NEHGR	*New England Historical and Genealogical Register*
NEHGS Transcript	Transcript of Middlesex County, Massachusetts, probate records (New England Historic Genealogical Society, Boston; forthcoming)
NEQ	*New England Quarterly*
[Rowlandson], *Soveraignty*	[Mary Rowlandson], *The Soveraignty & Goodness of God, Together With the Faithfulness of His Promises Displayed; Being a Narrative of the Captivity and Restauration of Mrs. Mary Rowlandson* (1682), repr. in Richard Slotkin and James K. Folsom, eds., *So Dreadfull a Judgment: Puritan Responses to King Philip's War, 1676–1677* (Middletown, Conn., 1978)
Sewall Diary	M. Halsey Thomas, ed., *The Diary of Samuel Sewall*, 2 vols. (New York, 1973)
Shepard Notebook	George Selement and Bruce C. Woolley, eds., *Thomas Shepard's "Confessions"* (Publications of the Colonial Society of Massachusetts, *Collections* 58 [Boston, 1981])
SWP	Paul Boyer and Stephen Nissenbaum, eds., *The Salem Witchcraft Papers: Verbatim Transcripts of the Legal Documents of the Salem Witchcraft Outbreak of 1692*, 3 vols. (New York, 1977)

Winthrop Journal   *John Winthrop's Journal "History of New England,"* 2 vols., ed. James K. Hosmer, Original Narratives of Early American History (1910; repr., New York, 1953)

WMQ   *William and Mary Quarterly*

INTRODUCTION

1. The term "Puritanism" is so lacking in precision that I have tried to do without it. In general, the term may be understood as referring to a tendency within the Church of England to practice stricter "discipline," as in limiting access to the sacrament of the Lord's Supper.

2. The interpretation that I briefly sketch may be found in several influential studies of popular culture and popular religion, among them Robert Muchembled, *Culture Populaire et Culture des Elites dans La France Moderne* (Paris, 1978); Carlo Ginzburg, *The Cheese and the Worms: The Cosmos of a Sixteenth-Century Miller*, trans. John and Anne Tedeschi (New York, 1980); and Emmanuel Le Roy Ladurie, *The Peasants of Languedoc*, trans. John Day (Urbana, 1974), Pt. 2. See also Stuart Clark, "French Historians and Early Modern Popular Culture," *Past and Present* 100 (1983), 62–99; and Jean Delumeau, *Catholicism Between Luther and Voltaire: A New View of the Counter-Reformation* (London, 1977), chap. 3. Three very different studies of *mentalité* and popular culture also figure in my thinking: Keith Thomas, *Religion and the Decline of Magic* (London, 1971); Robert Mandrou, *Introduction to Modern France, 1500–1640: An Essay in Historical Psychology*, trans. R. E. Hallmark (New York, 1977); and Peter Burke, *Popular Culture in Early Modern Europe* (Harper Torchbook, New York, 1978). I share with certain other historians of early modern Europe the feeling that the contrast has been overdrawn between an isolated or autonomous peasant culture and the culture of the middling classes or elites. Since I wrote this introduction an essay has appeared that adopts substantially the same point of view: John Van Engen, "The Christian Middle Ages as an Historiographical Problem," *American Historical Review* 91 (1986), 519–52. Van Engen makes the point that the late medieval church was reaching out effectively to ordinary people in ways that make the Reformation seem less revolutionary.

3. Henry James, *Hawthorne* (1879), reprinted in Edmund Wilson, ed., *The Shock of Recognition: The Development of Literature in the United States Recorded by the Men Who Made It*, rev. ed. (New York, 1955), 459–60.

4. Marc Bloch, *Feudal Society*, 2 vols., trans. L. A. Manyon (Chicago, 1961), 1:82.

5. Imogene Luxton, "The Reformation and Popular Culture," in Felicity Heal and Rosemary O'Day, eds., *Church and Society in England: Henry VIII to James I* (London, 1977), 65.

6. William Christian, Jr., *Local Religion in Sixteenth-Century Spain* (Princeton, N.J., 1981).

7. Some historians have stressed the "localism" that prevailed in New England towns; see especially Kenneth Lockridge, *A New England Town: The First Hundred Years* (New York, 1970). Yet no one would deny the uninterrupted presence of the "great tradition" in those towns that had a minister and engaged in the wider market economy. Similarly, I assume that the processes of emigration and mobility eliminated most of the elements of regional culture the colonists brought with them. To trace these out as they affect religion is, I agree, an important task, though not one I undertake.

8. Margaret James, "The Political Importance of the Tithes Controversy in the English Revolution, 1640–1660," *History* 26 (1941), 1–18; Christopher Hill, *Economic Problems of the Church* (Oxford, 1956), chaps. 5–6.

9. William H. Whitmore, ed., *A Bibliographical Sketch of the Laws of the Massachusetts Colony* (Boston, 1890), 57, 47; David D. Hall, *The Faithful Shepherd: A History of the New England Ministry in the Seventeenth Century* (Chapel Hill, N.C., 1972), chaps. 6, 10. It is remarkably instructive to compare the social, economic, and cultural functions of the French clergy of the *ancien régime* with the situation of the clergy in New England; the French situation is admirably described in John McManners, *French Ecclesiastical Society Under the Ancien Régime: A Study of Angers in the Eighteenth Century* (Manchester, 1960).

10. Claire Cross, *Church and People, 1450–1660: The Triumph of the Laity in the English Church* (Fontana Paperbacks, London, 1979), 170, 196, 210. Most of the evidence for "radicalism" in New England before 1660 is assembled in Philip Gura, *A Glimpse of Sions Glory: Puritan Radicalism in New England, 1620–1660* (Middletown, Conn., 1984). My argument for the limitations of radical dissent owes much to several essays by Stephen Foster, especially "English Puritanism and the Progress of New England Institutions, 1630–1660," in David D. Hall et al., eds., *Saints and Revolutionaries: Essays on Early American History* (New York, 1984), 3–37.

11. Thomas, *Religion and the Decline of Magic*, passim.

12. Increase Mather, *A Testimony Against several Prophane and Superstitious Customs, Now Practised by Some in New-England* (London, 1687).

13. For a typical argument to this effect, see Keith Wrightson and David Levine, *Poverty and Piety in an English Village: Terling, 1525–1700* (New York, 1979), 144–45.

14. R. C. Scribner, *For the Sake of Simple Folk: Popular Propaganda for the German Reformation* (Cambridge, 1981).

15. Charles C. Butterfield, *The English Primer, 1529–1545* (Philadelphia, 1953), 202; *Acts & Mon.* 6:443–47, a reference I owe to Cross, *Church and People*, 73; Margaret Spufford, *Contrasting Communities: English Villagers in the Sixteenth and Seventeenth Centuries* (Cambridge, 1974), 246–47.

16. Christopher Haigh, "Puritan Evangelism in the Reign of Elizabeth I," *English Historical Review* 42 (1977), 30–58. William Haller, *The Rise of Puritanism* (New York, 1938), describes the emergence of a "spiritual brotherhood" of ministers committed to the evangelical program.

17. Quoted in Arthur Dent, *The Plain Mans Pathway to Heaven* (London, 1610), 25.

18. *A parte of a register* [Middleburg, 1593], 305; Dent, *Plain Mans Pathway*, 123. An important text is William Perkins, "To All Ignorant People that Desire to be Instructed," in *The Workes of that Famous and worthie Minister of Christ M. W. Perkins*, 3 vols. (Cambridge, 1608–9), 1:32–33.

19. Christopher Hill, *Society and Puritanism in Pre-Revolutionary England* (New York, 1964); see also Keith Wrightson, "The Puritan Reformation of Manners with Special Reference to the Counties of Lancaster and Essex, 1640–1660" (Ph. D. thesis, Cambridge University, 1973).

20. Patrick Collinson, "Cranbrook and the Fletchers: Popular and Unpopular Religion in the Kentish Weald," *Godly People: Essays on English Protestantism and Puritanism* (London, 1983), 399–428; Arihu Zakai, "The Gospel of Reformation: The Origins of the Great Puritan Migration," *Journal of Ecclesiastical History* 37 (1986), 584–602.

21. Roland G. Usher, ed., *The Presbyterian Movement in the Reign of Queen Elizabeth as Illustrated in the Minute Book of the Dedham Classis, 1582–1589* (Royal Historical Society, *Publications*, 3d Ser., 8 [London, 1905]), 99–101. Stephen Foster describes the

significance of this text in "The Godly in Transit: English Popular Protestantism and the Creation of a Puritan Establishment in America," in David D. Hall and David Grayson Allen, eds., *Seventeenth-Century New England, CSM Pub.*, 63 (1984), 185–238.

22. This paragraph rests on a reading of books that describe English folk customs. Very few of these customs made it to New England or had any popular support among the colonists. Since the folklorists I cite rarely date their materials or weigh the significance of the one or two examples they may give, it is impossible to judge how many of these customs were widely practiced in early modern England. An older survey, based on an early-eighteenth-century collection, is John Brand, *Observations on the Popular Antiquities of Great Britain: Chiefly illustrating the origin of our vulgar and provincial customs, ceremonies, and superstitions* (1777; repr. with additions, London, 1849). More recent studies include Christina Hole, *A Dictionary of British Folk Customs* (London, 1978); Katherine Briggs, *The Anatomy of Puck: An Examination of Fairy Beliefs Among Shakespeare's Contemporaries and Successors* (London, 1959); and I find useful another older study, T. F. Thiselton Dyer, *Folk Lore of Shakespeare* (London, 1887). An important description of the decay of collective custom in the sixteenth century is Charles Pythian-Adams, "Ceremony and the Citizen: The Communal Year at Coventry 1450–1550," in Peter Clark and Paul Slack, eds., *Crisis and Order in English Towns, 1500–1700* (London, 1972), 57–85. The *locus classicus* for the disenchantment with traditional customs is Philip Stubbes, *The Anatomie of Abuses*, 3rd ed. (London, 1585). See also Wrightson, "Puritan Reformation of Manners," noting that "the puritan attack accelerated an existing trend" (p. 40), and the same, "Alehouses, Order and Reformation in Rural England, 1590–1660," in Eileen and Stephen Yeo, eds., *Popular Culture and Class Conflict, 1590–1914: Explorations in the History of Labour and Leisure* (Atlantic Highlands, N.J., 1981), 9–10; Jeremy Goring, *Godly Exercises or the Devil's Dance? Puritanism and Popular Culture in Pre-Civil War England* (London, 1983); and the evidence assembled in Richard Greaves, *Society and Religion in Elizabethan England* (Minneapolis, 1981). I exaggerate, but only slightly, in saying that no one celebrated Christmas or put up a maypole; see below, Chapter 4, for a few examples of these actions.

23. Burke, *Popular Culture in Early Modern Europe*, chap. 8.

24. The prescriptive argument appears in John Dod and Robert Cleaver, *A godly forme of housholde governement* (London, 1621), sig. Q1 verso; John Warden, *A Practical Essay on the Sacrament of Baptism* (Edinburgh, 1724), 210–11. The practice of the colonists is described in David Fischer, "Forenames and the Family in New England: An Exercise in Historical Onomastics," *Chronos: A Journal of Social History* 1 (1981), 76–111.

25. These statements run against the grain of much that has been written on the social history of New England. I am grateful to two former students, Susan Green and Kathryn Grover, for papers on the New England town that emphasize the absence of tight organization; James T. Lemon argues similarly in "Spatial Order: Households in Local Communities and Regions," in Jack P. Greene and J. R. Pole, eds., *Colonial British America: Essays in the New History of the Early Modern Era* (Baltimore, 1984), and I have also benefited from R. Cole Harris's comparative perspective; see "European Beginnings in the Northwest Atlantic: A Comparative View," in Hall and Allen, eds., *Seventeenth-Century New England*, 119–52.

26. David D. Hall, "The World of Print and Collective Mentality in Seventeenth-Century New England," in John Higham and Paul Conkin, eds., *New Directions in American Intellectual History* (Baltimore, 1979), 169.

27. Two major demonstrations of this argument are Edward Eggleston, *The Transit*

of Civilization from England to America in the Seventeenth Century (New York, 1901); and George Lyman Kittredge, *Witchcraft in Old and New England* (Cambridge, Mass., 1929). Perry Miller, *The New England Mind: The Seventeenth Century* (Cambridge, Mass., 1939).

28. *Magnalia*, 1:437.

29. Hall, *Faithful Shepherd*, chaps. 1–2 and especially pp. 5–13.

30. Chandler Robbins, *A History of the Second Church, or Old North, in Boston* (Boston, 1852), 8–9, 210–11. In the course of the seventeenth century, perhaps as many as twenty different "unlearned" persons preached in New England. Though their numbers were modest compared to those of the learned clergy, a collective study of this group would add to our understanding of popular religion.

31. Samuel Eliot Morison, ed., "The Commonplace Book of Joseph Green (1675–1715)" *CSM Pub.* 34 (1943), 195.

32. Sumner Chilton Powell, *Puritan Village: The Formation of a New England Town* (Middletown, Conn., 1963), chap. 8; Bernard Bailyn, ed., *The Apologia of Robert Keayne: The Self-Portrait of a Puritan Merchant* (Harper Torchbooks, New York, 1965), 25; and for tension between magistrates (including Winthrop) and the ministers, Hall, *Faithful Shepherd*, chaps. 6, 10.

33. Hall, *Faithful Shepherd*, 188–90; *Mather Papers*, MHS Coll., 4th Ser., 8 (1868), 397–401. Many congregations were disturbed by conflict between ministers and people over the issue of clerical authority; I find especially interesting the controversy that occurred in Newbury, Massachusetts, in the 1670s that I describe in *Faithful Shepherd*, 212–14.

34. Burke, *Popular Culture in Early Modern Europe*, chap. 2, describes the problem. Roger Chartier has proposed that popular culture consists not in a fixed set of artifacts, but in how a common set of texts and practices was appropriated by particular groups. Chartier, "Culture as Appropriation: Popular Culture Uses in Early Modern France," in Steven L. Kaplan, ed., *Understanding Popular Culture: Europe from the Middle Ages to the 19th Century* (Berlin, 1984).

35. As, notably, Christopher Hill has argued in *Society and Puritanism*.

36. Daniel Vickers, "Work and Life on the Fishing Periphery of Essex County, Massachusetts, 1630–1675," in Hall and Allen, eds., *Seventeenth-Century New England*, 111–12; Bernard Bailyn, *The New England Merchants in the Seventeenth Century* (Cambridge, Mass., 1956).

37. Laurel Thatcher Ulrich, *Good Wives: Image and Reality in the Lives of Women in Northern New England, 1650–1750* (New York, 1982); Mary Maples Dunn, "Saints and Sinners: Congregational and Quaker Women in the Early Colonial Period," in Janet Wilson James, ed., *Women in American Religion* (Philadelphia, 1978), 27–46; and Carol Karlsen, *The Devil in the Shape of a Woman: Witchcraft in Colonial New England* (New York, 1987).

38. Horace Bushnell, "The Age of Homespun, a discourse delivered at Litchfield Connecticut . . . 1851," in [Mary Bushnell Cheney], *Life and Letters of Horace Bushnell* (New York, 1903), 11–12.

39. G. Stanley Hall, *Life and Confessions of a Psychologist* (New York, 1923), 58.

40. Unlike the clergy in some Catholic countries, no New England minister kept a register of attendance at communion. John Fiske conducted a house-to-house survey of his parish in the 1660s, but we do not know the results (*Fiske Notebook*, 187). Only in a few instances, e.g., book ownership and the language in preambles to wills, does quantitative evidence support my argument.

41. Harriet Beecher Stowe, *Oldtown Folks* (Boston, 1869), 479.

42. Solomon Stoddard, *The Danger of Speedy Degeneracy* (Boston, 1705), 17. These

forms of misbehavior are tellingly described in Roger Thompson, *Sex in Middlesex: Popular Mores in a Massachusetts County, 1649–1699* (Amherst, Mass., 1986). See also Keith Wrightson, "Alehouses and the Alternative Society," in Donald Pennington and Keith Thomas, eds., *Puritans and Revolutionaries: Essays in Seventeenth-Century History Presented to Christopher Hill* (Oxford, 1978).

43. *SWP,* 1:66.

44. *Magnalia,* 1:65–66.

45. John Eliot, *The Harmony of the Gospels* (Boston, 1678), 26; Increase Mather, *A Sermon Occasioned by the Execution of a Man found Guilty of Murder* (Boston, 1686), 33; Darrett B. Rutman, *Winthrop's Boston: Portrait of a Puritan Town, 1630–1649* (Chapel Hill, N.C., 1965), chap. 4. It is important to recognize that complaints from the clergy were endemic; as Margaret Spufford argues in "Puritanism and Social Control," in Anthony Fletcher and John Stevenson, eds., *Order and Disorder in Early Modern England* (Cambridge, 1985), 41–57, what they said cannot be regarded as a transcript of reality. The same point is argued in Martin Ingram, "Ecclesiastical Justice in Wiltshire 1600–1640" (D. Phil. diss., Oxford University, 1976); and in Wrightson, "The Puritan Reformation of Manners."

46. Thompson, *Sex in Middlesex,* is sensible in this regard.

47. *SWP,* 1:68–69.

48. See Gerald Aylmer, "Unbelief in Seventeenth-Century England," in Pennington and Thomas, eds., *Puritans and Revolutionaries,* 22–46. Michael Hunter argues that "atheism" may have been primarily an elite phenomenon: "The Problem of Atheism in Early Modern England," Royal Historical Society, *Transactions,* 5th Ser., 35 (1985), 135–57.

49. *Shepard Notebook,* 54.

50. William Bradford, *Of Plymouth Plantation* (New York, 1981), 8. The close relationship between literature and religion in the program of English Protestant reformers is demonstrated in John N. King, *English Reformation Literature: The Tudor Origins of the Protestant Tradition* (Princeton, N.J., 1982).

51. After reaching this conclusion I found support for it in Jane Tompkins's explication of *Uncle Tom's Cabin* in *Sensational Designs: The Cultural Work of American Fiction, 1790–1860* (New York, 1985).

52. Lucien Febvre and Henri-Jean Martin, *The Coming of the Book: The Impact of Printing, 1450–1800,* trans. David Gerard (1958; London, 1984), 252.

53. Ginzburg, *The Cheese and the Worms,* 68. Ginzburg is among the historians who argue that the world view of, say, witches was different from that of their persecutors. I am more inclined to accept Keith Thomas's argument (he is referring to magical techniques for healing) that "these practices did not reflect a single coherent cosmology or scheme of classification, but were made up out of the debris of many different systems of thought." *Religion and the Decline of Magic,* 185.

54. Christine L. Heyrman, *Commerce and Culture: The Maritime Communities of Colonial Massachusetts, 1690–1750* (New York, 1983), chap. 3.

55. I owe much to several essays by Natalie Z. Davis in which she insists that ordinary people in early modern Europe had a certain measure of autonomy: e.g., Davis, "Some Tasks and Themes in the Study of Popular Religion," in Charles Trinkaus, ed., with Heiko A. Oberman, *The Pursuit of Holiness in Late Medieval and Renaissance Religion* (Leiden, 1974), 307–36.

CHAPTER 1

1. *The Autobiography of Benjamin Franklin* (New Haven, Conn., 1964), 50, 59–60; Roger Thompson, *Sex in Middlesex: Popular Mores in a Massachusetts County, 1649–1699* (Amherst, Mass., 1986), 87; probate inventory of Elizabeth Betts of Cambridge (1664), NEHGS Transcript; John Taylor, *The Witchcraft Delusion in Colonial Connecticut 1647–1697* (New York, 1908), 115–16.

2. *Acts & Mon.*, 7:29. Foxe also printed the orders forbidding anyone to write, sell, or read the Book of Common Prayer, and in a famous passage celebrated the "invention" of printing: 7:117–18; 3:718–22.

3. Leonard J. Trinterud, ed., *Elizabethan Puritanism* (New York, 1971), 35; Cartwright is quoted in Peter Lake, *Moderate Puritans and the Elizabethan Church* (Cambridge, 1982), 288. "Now no protestant doubteth but that all the bookes of the scripture should by Gods ordinance be extant in the mother tongue of each nation. . . ." Zoltan Haraszti, ed., *The Bay Psalm Book: A Facsimile Reprint of the First Edition of 1640* (Chicago, 1956), preface.

4. *Acts & Mon.*, 7:29.

5. Roland H. Bainton, "The Bible in the Reformation," in S. L. Greenslade, ed., *Cambridge History of the Bible: The West from the Reformation to the Present Day*, 3 vols. (Cambridge, 1963), 3:6–23; Trinterud, *Elizabethan Puritanism*, 37; Greenslade, ed., *Cambridge History of the Bible*, 3:176.

6. Robert Lemon, comp., *Catalogue of a Collection of Printed Broadsides in the Possession of the Society of Antiquaries of London* (London, 1866), 67; Charles C. Butterfield, *The English Primer, 1529–1545* (Philadelphia, 1953), 105; and for a general description of such iconography, R. W. Scribner, *For the Sake of Simple Folk: Popular Propaganda for the German Reformation* (Cambridge, 1981), chap. 3.

7. C. John Sommerville, "'The Distribution of Religious and Occult Literature in Seventeenth-Century England," *The Library*, 5th Ser., 39 (1974), 223; Barbara Kiefer Lewalski, *Protestant Poetics and the Seventeenth-Century Religious Lyric* (Princeton, N.J., 1979), 39.

8. Bainton, "The Bible in the Reformation," 20; Larzer Ziff, "Upon What Pretext? The Book and Literary History," American Antiquarian Society, *Proceedings* 95 (1985), 297–302.

9. James Noyes, *A Short Catechism* (1694; Boston, 1797), 3; *Acts & Mon.*, 7:174. As Thomas Shepard (the second) declared to his son, "God's secrets in the holy Scriptures are never made known to common and profane spirits. . . ." *Magnalia*, 2:144.

10. *Acts & Mon.*, 7:314.

11. *The First and Second Prayer Books of Edward VI* (London, 1949), 4; and see John N. King, *English Reformation Literature: The Tudor Origins of the Protestant Tradition* (Princeton, N.J., 1982), 123, 140–42; [Increase Mather], *The Life and Death of that Reverend Man in God, Mr. Richard Mather* (1670), in Perry Miller and Thomas H. Johnson, eds., *The Puritans*, rev. ed., 2 vols. (New York, 1963), 2:494.

12. John Eliot, *The Harmony of the Gospels* (Boston, 1678), 32; Henry Scudder, *The Christians Daily Walke* (London, 1627), 89–90, 27; Leonard Hoar, *Index Biblicus* (London, 1678), sig. A1 verso; *Acts and Mon.*, 6:422.

13. Eliot, *Harmony of the Gospels*, 32, 62, 65; William Turner, *A Compleat History of the Most Remarkable Providences, Both of Judgment and Mercy, which have hapned in this Present Age* (London, 1697), chap. 66, p. 83; "John Dane's Narrative, 1682," *NEHGR* 8 (1854), 154; [Rowlandson], *Soveraignty*, 336. See also *Acts & Mon.*, 4:635; and David

Cressy, "Books as Totems in Seventeenth-Century England and New England," *Journal of Library History* 21 (1986), 92–106. Examples of the Bible being used as a charm are given in George Lyman Kittredge, *Witchcraft in Old and New England* (Cambridge, Mass., 1929), 146–47.

14. Stanley E. Fish, *Self-Consuming Artifacts: The Experience of Seventeenth-Century Literature* (Berkeley and Los Angeles, 1972), differentiates a presentation that is "dialectical" from one that is "rhetorical"; the former, he argues, ends in a "transformation of the visible and segmented world into an emblem of its creator's indwelling presence," 3, and passim. Cf. Brian Vickers, "Analogy Versus Identity: The Rejection of Occult Symbolism, 1580–1680," in Vickers, ed., *Occult and Scientific Mentalities in the Renaissance* (Cambridge, 1984), 95–163.

15. *Bay Psalm Book*, preface.

16. Ibid. Cf. King, *English Reformation Literature*, 128–29, for the format of John Day's English Bible in octavo and folio. Harry S. Stout has argued that some lay people in New England perceived the Geneva edition of the Bible as allowing them more freedom of interpretation. In view of the apparatus of that Bible, I do not agree with his reasoning and find no independent evidence to sustain it. Stout, "Word and Order in Colonial New England," in *The Bible in America: Essays in Cultural History*, ed. Nathan O. Hatch and Mark A. Noll (New York, 1982), 26.

17. William Dyer, *Christs Famous Titles* (London, 1672), 230.

18. Richard Bernard, *The Faithfull Shepherd*, rev. ed. (London, 1621), 53; David D. Hall, *The Faithful Shepherd: A History of the New England Ministry in the Seventeenth Century* (Chapel Hill, N.C., 1972), 52–55; *Magnalia*, 1:342–43.

19. *Magnalia*, 1:284; Lemon, comp., *Catalogue of Broadsides*, 109; John Harvard Ellis, ed., *The Works of Anne Bradstreet in Prose and Verse* (1867; repr., New York, 1932), 3; Thomas White, *A Little Book for Little Children* (Boston, 1702), 19.

20. M. T. Clanchy, *From Memory to Written Record: England, 1066–1207* (Cambridge, Mass., 1979), 216–17.

21. Scudder, *Christians Daily Walke*, 112, 96, 91–92; Richard Rogers, *The Practice of Christianitie* (London, 1618), sig. al verso; Robert Russel, *Seven Sermons* (1699; Boston, 1767), 70; Richard Mather, *A Farewel Exhortation* (Cambridge, Mass., 1657), sig. A2 verso, 26.

22. William Greenhill, "To the Christian Reader," in Thomas Shepard, *The Sincere Convert* (London, 1646).

23. John Davenport, "The Epistle To The Reader," in Scudder, *Christians Daily Walke*.

24. George Parker Winship, *The Cambridge Press, 1638–1692: A Reexamination of the Evidence Concerning the Bay Psalm Book and the Eliot Indian Bible as Well as Other Contemporary Books and People* (1945; repr., Freeport, N.Y., 1968), 252.

25. Richard D. Pierce, ed., *The Records of the First Church in Boston, 1630–1868*, *CSM Pub.*, 39 (1961), 52.

26. Geoffrey Chaucer, *The Canterbury Tales*, trans. Neville Coghill (Baltimore, 1952), 194.

27. Clanchy, *From Memory to Written Record*, 149, 177; *New Englands First Fruits* (1642), repr. in Miller and Johnson, eds., *The Puritans*, 2:701.

28. Kenneth Lockridge, *Literacy in Colonial New England* (New York, 1974), 13, and passim. David Cressy presents data for contemporary England in *Literacy & the Social Order: Reading & Writing in Tudor & Stuart England* (Cambridge, 1980). See also Linda Auwers, "Reading the Marks of the Past: Exploring Female Literacy in Colonial

Windsor, Connecticut," *Historical Methods* 13 (Fall 1980), 204–14. This is not the place to review the strengths and limitations of the signature-count method for measuring literacy; but see Ross W. Beales, Jr., "Studying Literacy at the Community Level: A Research Note," *Journal of Interdisciplinary History* 9 (1978), 93–102.

29. *Essex Court Recs.*, 5:67, 229; 4:374, 7:31; *Fiske Notebook*, 91; *Essex Court Recs.*, 4:342; 6:352; *SWP*, 2:476.

30. *Essex Court Recs.*, 6:101–2; William H. Whitmore, comp., *The Colonial Laws of Massachusetts* (Boston, 1889), 149; J. Hammond Trumbull and Charles J. Hoadly, eds., *The Public Records of the Colony of Connecticut*, 15 vols. (Hartford, Conn., 1850–90), 1:21 (written names for voting), 85 (written pleas), 37 (every town a ledger book), 38 (for written inventories), 39 (copy laws into the town book), 47–48 (publish marriage contracts); *Fiske Notebook*, 16, 17, 19, 22, 224; *SWP*, 1:96, 163; *Essex Court Recs.*, 7:357; John Rogers, *Death the certain Wages of Sin to the Impenitent* (Boston, 1701), includes "The Declaration & Confession of Esther Rodgers," who described herself (121) as apprenticed in Newbury where she "was taught to Read, Learned Mr. Cottons Catechism. . . ."

31. I quote a later statement: *Essex Court Recs.*, 5:427. The return from Topsfield is printed in *Essex Court Recs.*, 4:212–13. Another return (to an earlier inquiry) is summarized in *History of the Town of Dorchester, Massachusetts* (Boston, 1859), 223–24; the town cited five men for idleness but only one of them had sons "who were found very ignorant, not being able to read."

32. Thomas W. Laqueur, "Toward a Cultural Ecology of Literacy in England, 1600–1850," in Daniel P. Resnick, ed., *Literacy in Historical Perspective* (Washington, D.C., 1983). Literacy correlates with wealth, occupation, gender, and region, as Cressy and Lockridge demonstrate. I am after something that is not adequately represented by their figures, a competence or fluency that overflowed these factors. To take an extreme example, the Lollards in late-fifteenth- and early-sixteenth-century England were only partially literate, being able to read but not write; yet copies of the Bible circulated in abundance among them, and knowledge of Scripture was extensive. Similarly, Protestants in eighteenth-century Bohemia preserved a knowledge of the Bible in spite of adverse conditons that included illiteracy. The same was true (I am informed by Jean Hebrard) of French Protestants in the Cevennes. Each of these examples compromises the distinction between "oral" and "print" modes of knowledge that some historians employ. As I observe later in this chapter, some of the men and women who testified in Cambridge meetinghouse refer to specific books; others, a majority, do not. Yet these statements (excepting those too brief to analyze) manifest a fluency in citing Scripture that constitutes a kind of literacy. Moreover, these testimonies have a distinctly literary texture. Unlike Furet and Ozouf, I am reluctant to describe this competence in reading/reciting as "restricted literacy." Cf. Margaret Aston, "The Lollards and Literacy," *History* 62 (1977), 347–71; Marie-Elisabeth Ducreux, "Lire à en mourir. Livres et lecteurs en Bohème au xviii siècle," in Roger Chartier, ed., *Les usages de l'imprimé* (Paris, 1987), 253–303; François Furet and Jacques Ozouf, *Reading and Writing: Literacy in France from Calvin to Jules Ferry* (Cambridge, 1982), 304–08; Stephen Foster, "The Godly in Transit: English Popular Protestantism and the Creation of a Puritan Establishment in America," in David D. Hall and David Grayson Allen, eds., *Seventeenth-Century New England, CSM Pub.*, 63 (1984), 188.

33. Nathaniel B. Shurtleff, ed., *Records of the Governor and Company of the Massachusetts Bay in New England*, 5 vols. (Boston, 1853–54), 2:6–7, 203. Similar laws existed in Connecticut and New Haven colonies; e.g., Trumbull and Hoadly, eds., *Public*

Records of Connecticut, 1:520–21, 554–55; 3:9; for apprenticeship, see above, n. 29, *Essex Court Recs.,* 5:37; and Sarah Loring Bailey, *Historical Sketches of Andover* (Boston, 1880), 53.

34. This point is emphasized by Jennifer Monaghan, who is writing a general study of instruction in reading in early America, and I am grateful to her for allowing me to read her work in progress; *NEHGR* 5 (1851), 171. A court case in *Essex Court Recs.,* 6:156–57, reveals the workings of a dame school. See also the case history, demonstrating the assumption that children learned to read at home, in New Haven County Court Records, Book I, 148 (Connecticut State Library).

35. Margaret Spufford, "First Steps in Literacy: The Reading and Writing Experiences of the Humblest Seventeenth-Century Spiritual Autobiographers," *Social History* 4 (1979), 407–35; the same, *Small Books and Pleasant Histories: Popular Fiction and Its Readership in Seventeenth-Century England* (Athens, Georgia, 1981), chap. 2; Cressy, *Literacy and the Social Order,* chap. 2. Instruction in the Middle Ages made the same distinction; Clanchy, *From Memory to Written Record,* 182–84.

36. Franklin B. Dexter, ed., *Ancient Town Records,* Vol. I, *New Haven Town Records, 1649–1662* (New Haven, Conn., 1917), 48, 97 (I owe these references to Jennifer Monaghan); Peter Thacher diary, Massachusetts Historical Society, 644; "An Account of Indian Churches in New-England, In a Letter Written A.D. 1673 By Rev. John Eliot, of Roxbury," *MHS Coll.,* 1st Ser., 10 (1809), 127.

37. "Deacon John Paine's Journal," *Mayflower Descendants* 8 (1906), 230; Michael G. Hall, ed., "The Autobiography of Increase Mather," American Antiquarian Society, *Proceedings* 71 (1961), 278; Lilley Eaton, *Genealogical History of the Town of Reading, Mass., from 1639 to 1874* (Boston, 1874), 53; Albert Matthews, "Extracts from the Diary of Josiah Cotton," *CSM Pub.* 26 (1927), 278; Herbert and Carol Schneider, eds., *Samuel Johnson, President of King's College, His Career and Writings,* 4 vols. (New York, 1929), 1:3.

38. Mather Papers, *MHS Coll.,* 4th Ser., 8 (1868), 439–40; *Sewall Diary,* 1:277; "Autobiography of the Rev. John Barnard," *MHS Coll.,* 3rd Ser., 5 (1836), 178; White, *Little Book for Little Children,* 74; James Janeway, *A Token for Children* (1671; Boston, 1771), 7. Isaac Watts designed his *Young Child's Catechism* for three- and four-year-olds, Clifton Johnson, *Old-Time Schools and School-Books* (1904; repr., New York, 1963), 13.

39. *Shepard Notebook,* 54.

40. Schneider and Schneider, eds., *Samuel Johnson,* 1:3; Benjamin Colman, *Reliquiae Turellae, et Lachrymae Paternae* (Boston, 1735), 61.

41. Joseph T. Buckingham, *Personal Memoirs and Recollections of Editorial Life,* 2 vols. (Boston, 1852), 1:16, 19, 9. I have cited other late-eighteenth-century testimonies in "The Uses of Literacy in New England, 1600–1850," in William L. Joyce et al., eds., *Printing and Society in Early America* (Worcester, Mass., 1983), 1–47.

42. In 1690, John Locke observed that "the method" in elementary education in England "is to adhere to the ordinary road of the Hornbook, Primer, Psalter, Testament, and Bible; these are the only books used to engage the liking of children and tempt them to read." Quoted in Johnson, *Old-Time Schools and School-Books,* 185. The transformation of the primer from its function as a service book to elementary schoolbook in the vernacular is symbolic of a broader transformation in the functions and parameters of literacy.

43. Richard Baxter, *A Christian Directory or Body of Practical Divinity* (London, 1673), Pt. 2, 90–91.

44. John Wilson, *Song of Deliverance* (1626), repr. in Kenneth B. Murdock, ed.,

Handkerchiefs from Paul being Pious and Consolatory Verses of Puritan Massachusetts (Cambridge, Mass., 1927), 31. Cf. Charles L. Nichols, "The Holy Bible in Verse," American Antiquarian Society, *Proceedings* 36 (1926), 71–82; Geraint H. Jenkins, *Literature, Religion and Society in Wales, 1660–1730* (Cardiff, Wales, 1978), 52. A young New England woman voiced the same convention in addressing a sister captured by the French: "Dear Sister, For your sake now I / these Verses Written have. / Bear them upon your Memory, / As going to the Grave. / Dear Sister, Bear me in your Mind; / Learn these few Lines by heart . . ." [Cotton Mather], *Good fetch'd Out of Evil* (Boston, 1766), 33.

45. Butterfield, *The English Primer;* Paul Leicester Ford, ed., *The New-England Primer: A History of Its Origin and Development with a Reprint of the Unique Copy of the Earliest Known Edition* . . . (1897; repr. New York, 1962).

46. Shurtleff, ed., *Massachusetts Records,* 2:203; Furet and Ozouf, *Reading and Writing,* 167, 174–75.

47. Alonzo Lewis and James Newhall, *History of Lynn* (Lynn, 1890), 122; Ellis, ed., *Works of Anne Bradstreet,* 3. The messages of the primer are explicated in David H. Watters, " 'I spake as a child': Authority, Metaphor, and The New England Primer," *Early American Literature* 20 (1985–1986), 193–213.

48. *Shepard Notebook,* 107–8, 115, 112–13.

49. *Fiske Notebook,* 10, 33, 36–37.

50. Peter Pratt, *The Prey Taken from the Strong* (New London, 1725), 24.

51. Kenneth P. Minkema, "The East Windsor Conversion Relations 1700–1725," *Connecticut Historical Society Bulletin* 51 (Winter 1986), 28.

52. Edmund S. Morgan, ed., *The Diary of Michael Wigglesworth 1653–1657* (1951; repr. New York, 1965), 114.

53. Jenkins, *Literature, Religion and Society in Wales,* 131; Johnson, *WWP,* 24.

54. Colman, *Reliquiae Turellae,* 112; *Diary of Michael Wigglesworth,* 100–101; *The Apologia of Robert Keayne,* ed. Bernard Bailyn (New York, 1965), 28–29.

55. *Shepard Notebook,* 50, 95–98, 104–5.

56. Patrick Collinson (in a personal communication) has stressed the custom among English "godly" Protestants of reading or reviewing sermon notes. Lewis Bayley counseled this practice, as follows: ". . . [after Sunday dinner] call thy family together, examine what they have learned in the Sermon: . . . Turne to the Proofes which the Preacher alleadged, and rubbe those good things over their memories againe." *The Practice of Pietie* (London, 1631), 476. A good number of such notes survive from seventeenth-century New England, though I have not studied them. Specific references to taking such notes or reading groups are harder to come by; but cf. Waters, *Ipswich,* 1:519; *Dedham Historical Register* 10 (1899), 22–23; *Essex Court Recs.,* 7:186. Some church members in New Haven (men and women) formed a group that was "intended for edification, after the repeating of sermons, there was a question propounded. . . ." Connecticut Historical Society, *Collections* 1 (1860), 24. Certainly in some situations the colonists read aloud to one another. But there is also abundant evidence of private reading, as when a young woman sat by candlelight to read (*Essex Court Recs.,* 7:300). See below, Chapter 5, for a description of Sewall's participation in two reading communities where reading aloud was practiced.

57. *Magnalia,* 2:460–62.

58. Thomas Goddard Wright, *Literary Culture in Early New England, 1620–1730* (New Haven, Conn., 1920), 36, 127.

59. "Elder Brewster's Library," *MHS Proc.,* 2nd Ser., 5 (1890), 82; Wright, *Literary Culture,* 33–34, 126–27; *The Library of The Late Reverend and Learned Mr. Samuel Lee*

(Boston, 1693); Worthington C. Ford, ed., *The Diary of Cotton Mather*, 2 vols. (1911; repr., New York, 1957), 1:368.

60. *Apologia of Robert Keayne*, 7, 9; Franklin B. Dexter, "The First Public Library in New Haven," *Papers of the New Haven Colony Historical Society* 6 (1900), 301–13; Michael J. Canavan, "The Old Boston Public Library, 1656–1747," *CSM Pub.* 12 (1911), 116–32; C. H. Walcott, *Concord in the Colonial Period* (Boston, 1884), 128.

61. *Magnalia*, 1:454; Winship, *Cambridge Press*, 180, 54–61; *Sewall Diary*, 1:120; *Mather Papers, MHS Coll.*, 4th Ser. 8 (1868), 247; see also 480, 477, 291–96, and for the significance of this gift-giving, see below, chapter 5; *Fiske Notebook*, 198. George Selement describes ministerially distributed books in *Keepers of the Vineyard: The Puritan Ministry and Collective Culture in Colonial New England* (New York, 1984), chap. 4. See also Natalie Zemon Davis, "Beyond the Market: Books as Gifts in Sixteenth-Century France," Royal Historical Society, *Transactions*, 5th Ser., 33 (1983), 69–88.

62. Winship, *Cambridge Press*, chaps. 6, 8; Whitmore, ed., *Colonial Laws*, 93–96 (quoting *Massachusetts Records*), and the calculation in note 57, p. 95, that 600 copies of the *Laws and Liberties* of 1648 were printed; Joseph Smith, ed., *Colonial Justice in Western Massachusetts, 1639–1702: The Pynchon Court Record* (Cambridge, Mass., 1961), 219.

63. Lewis and Newhall, *History of Lynn*, 122; Wright, *Literary Culture*, 50; *Essex Court Recs.*, 1:121. The possible references to this practice are many.

64. *Autobiography of Benjamin Franklin*, 59; *Essex Court Recs.*, 3:165; for another example, see "Abstracts of the Earliest Wills upon Record in the County of Suffolk, Massachusetts," *NEHGR* 5 (1851), 242.

65. Winship, *Cambridge Press*, passim; Worthington C. Ford, *The Boston Book Market, 1679–1700* (Boston, 1917). Less reliable is George E. Littlefield, *Early Boston Booksellers, 1642–1711* (Boston, 1911).

66. An excellent description of this network of customers for a mid-eighteenth-century Boston bookseller is Elizabeth Carroll Reilly, "The Wages of Piety: The Boston Book Trade of Jeremy Condy," in Joyce et al., eds., *Printing and Society in Early America*, 83–131.

67. Ford, *Boston Book Market*, 163–82; the references that follow to Perry's inventory are based on this list, as corrected recently by Roger Thompson, "Worthington Chauncey Ford's *Boston Book Market, 1679–1700*: Some Corrections and Additions," *MHS Proc.* 76 (1974), 68–78; Littlefield, *Booksellers*, 136.

68. Inventory of Mrs. Eliza Cutler, Middlesex Probate docket 5511; Hazel A. Johnson, comp., *A checklist of New London, Connecticut Imprints, 1709–1800* (Charlottesville, Va., 1978), 444; and on printings of schoolbooks in England, Donald F. McKenzie, "Printers of the Mind: Some Notes on Bibliographical Theories and Printing-House Practices," *Studies in Bibliography* 22 (1969), 58.

69. The invoices are published in Ford, *Boston Book Market*, 81–161.

70. C. John Sommerville, *Popular Religion in Restoration England*, University of Florida Social Science Monographs, No. 59 (Gainesville, Fla., 1977), enumerates these books and their printing histories; he calculates that the print run for any single edition was between two and three thousand copies. The figures on Alleine's *Alarm* were given by Edmund Calamy, an English nonconformist minister, and are quoted in the inside back cover of the 1767 Boston edition.

71. Winship, *Cambridge Press*, 282. I describe some of these books in "The Uses of Literacy." Many of these same books were being translated into Welsh in the late seventeenth and early eighteenth centuries; Jenkins, *Literature, Religion, and Society*, 133. For further information on such books and their rivals in the marketplace, cf.

Charles C. Mish, "Best Sellers in Seventeenth-Century Fiction," *Papers of the Bibliographical Society of America* 47 (1953), 356–73. The best brief descriptions of the contents of this literature are Jenkins, *Literature, Religion, and Society*, chaps. 4–5, and Spufford, *Small Books and Pleasant Histories*, chap. 8.

72. *Magnalia*, 1:389.

73. The man behind the pseudonyms Andrew and William Jones was one John Hart; Sommerville was unable to identify him (*Popular Religion in Restoration England*, 45), and I believe (without much evidence to go on) that he was not a practicing minister, or even an ordained one. I harbor similar suspicions of Robert Russell, who cannot be traced in the usual records, though supposedly he was a minister.

74. Increase Mather, *A Call from Heaven* (Boston, 1679), 106.

75. Waters, *Ipswich* 1:500; John Demos, *Entertaining Satan: Witchcraft and the Culture of Early New England* (New York, 1983), 439, n. 92; *Essex Court Recs.*, 5:73, 161; 3:359–60, 449; 2:412; inventory of Michael Metcalfe, *NEHGR* 6 (1852), 172; *Essex Court Recs.*, 5:161; inventory of Richard Webb, *NEHGR* 9 (1855), 155; Frances M. Caulkins, *History of Norwich, Connecticut* (Hartford, 1866), 185. Even more interesting is a Norwich inventory of 1724 (p. 210) that includes Flavel, Henry, Doolittle, Russell, Burroughs, and Bunyan, among others.

76. *Essex Court Recs.*, 1:413; Sumner C. Powell, *Puritan Village* (Middletown, Conn., 1963), 108–9.

77. *Essex Court Recs.*, 3:174; 2:97, 357; and for the inheritance of family Bibles, cf. Caulkins, *Norwich*, 77.

78. White, *Little Book for Little Children*, 19; *Letter-Book of Samuel Sewall, MHS Coll.*, 6th Ser., 1 (1886), 19; Eaton, *Genealogical History of . . . Reading*, 53; will of William Ripley, *NEHGR* 6 (1852), 355. Other references to Foxe include: inventory of Comfort Starr (1659), *NEHGR* 9 (1855), 154; the New Haven town library (Dexter, "First Public Library in New Haven," 310); the library of the Reverend Edward Taylor, in John H. Lockwood, *Westfield and Its Historic Influences, 1669–1919*, 2 vols. (Springfield, Mass., 1922), 2:500; the inventory of Edward Tinge (1653), Middlesex County probate records (I owe this reference to Ellen Smith).

79. See below, 247–49, "A Note on Book Ownership in Seventeenth-Century New England," for a more technical assessment of this matter.

80. Ford, *Boston Book Market*, 131; Winship, *Cambridge Press*, 232; Samuel Eliot Morison, *Harvard College in the Seventeenth Century*, 2 vols. (Cambridge, Mass., 1936), 1:116. Cf. Roger Thompson, *Unfit for Modest Ears: A Study of Pornographic, Obscene, and Bawdy Works Written or Published in England in the Second Half of the Seventeenth Century* (London, 1979); the same, ed., *Samuel Pepys' Penny Merriments* (London, 1976); Blagdon, "Notes on the Ballad Market in the Second Half of the Seventeenth Century," *Studies in Bibliography* 6 (1954), 161–80; J. L. Gaunt, "Popular Fiction and the Ballad Market in the Second Half of the Seventeenth Century," *Papers of the Bibliographical Society of America* 72 (1978), 1–13; Spufford, *Small Books and Pleasant Histories*, chap. 7.

81. Edwin H. Miller, *The Professional Writer in Elizabethan England* (Cambridge, Mass., 1959), 54–55 and chap. 7.

82. I am indebted to a conversation with Geoffrey Nuttall for the concept of a "middling" readership. Cf. Jenkins, *Literature, Religion, and Society*, 300; Miller, *Professional Writer*, 78–83.

83. John L. Lievsay, "William Barley, Elizabethan Printer and Bookseller," *Studies in Bibliography* 8 (1956), 219.

84. Gerald D. Johnson, "John Trundle and the Book Trade, 1603–1626," *Studies*

in Bibliography 39 (1985), 177–99; Albert B. Cook III, "John Bunyan and John Dunton: A Case of Plagiarism," *Papers of the Bibliographical Society of America* 71 (1977), 11–28; and cf. Spufford, *Small Books,* chap 4.

85. Winship, *Cambridge Press,* 280–82, 286, 294; Massachusetts Archives, Vol. 58 (Literacy, 1645–1774), items 60c, 91.

86. Worthington C. Ford, "Benjamin Harris, Printer and Bookseller," *MHS Proc.* 57 (1924), 34–68; *Sewall Diary,* 1:267.

87. Ford, *Boston Book Market,* 84, 104–06, 131, 134, 137, 139; George Lyman Kittredge, *The Old Farmer and His Almanack: Being Some Observations on Life and Manners in New England a Hundred Years Ago* (Boston, 1904), 137–38; Roger Thompson, "The Puritans and Prurience: Aspects of the Restoration Book Trade," in H. C. Allen and Roger Thompson, eds., *Contrast and Connection* (London, 1976), 36–64. For references to fortune-telling books see below, Chapter 2, p. 99.

88. John Tully, *An Almanack* (Boston, 1687), 15–16.

89. Samuel Eliot Morison, "The Reverend Seaborn Cotton's Commonplace Book," *CSM Pub.,* 32 (Boston, 1937), 320–52; *New Haven Ancient Town Records,* 1:56; [Cotton Mather], *Bethiah. The Glory Which Adorns the Daughters of God* (Boston, 1722), 58; *Magnalia,* 1:205.

90. Arthur Dent, *Plain Mans Pathway to Heaven* (London, 1610), 373. For other critics see Lawrence Sasek, *The Literary Temper of the English Puritans* (Baton Rouge, La., 1961), 59–62; Hyder Rollins, ed., *Cavalier and Puritan Ballads and Broadsides Illustrating the Period of the Great Rebellion, 1640–1660* (New York, 1923), 11–27. It is important to remember that Anglicans also censored these kinds of books.

91. Benjamin Keach, *The Progress of Sin* (1684; Boston, 1744), 10, 19.

92. Michael Wigglesworth, *The Day of Doom* (1662), repr. (abridged) in Miller and Johnson, eds., *The Puritans,* 2:588. Stephen Foster offers a more cautious assessment of this book and its sales in "The Godly in Transit," 228, n. 6.

93. Sommerville, *Popular Religion in Restoration England,* 45. Cf. Spufford, *Small Books and Pleasant Histories,* 203–4.

94. Cf. Michael McKeon, *The Origins of the English Novel, 1600–1740* (Baltimore, 1987).

95. This description is derived from Bernard Capp, *English Almanacs, 1500–1800: Astrology and the Popular Press* (Ithaca, N.Y., 1979), 123 and passim, and from a handful of examples, e.g., Daniel Browne, *1628. A Prognostication for this present yeare of our Redemption* (London, 1628). Cf. Cyprian Blagdon, "The Distribution of Almanacks in the Second Half of the Seventeenth Century," *Studies in Bibliography* 11 (1958), 107–16. Several of the almanacs that Samuel Sewall owned, and jotted notes in, survive in the collections of the Massachusetts Historical Society and the American Antiquarian Society; and we know from a stray reference that the Reverend Joshua Moodey owned some thirty almanacs in which he inserted extra leaves for adding comments: *MHS Coll.,* 4th Ser., 8 (1868), 282–87; [Cotton Mather], *The Boston Ephemeris. An Almanack For the (Dionysian) Year of the Christian Era* (Boston, 1683). For its uses as calendar, see Charles L. Nichols, "Notes on the Almanacs of Massachusetts," American Antiquarian Society, *Proceedings,* n.s. 22 (1912), 21.

96. [Samuel Danforth], *An Almanack for . . . 1646* (Cambridge, Mass., 1646); the same, *An Almanack for . . . 1647* (Cambridge, Mass., 1647).

97. William Perkins, *A Resolution To The Countrey-Man. Proving it utterly unlawfull to buy or use our yearely Prognostications,* in *The Workes of That Famous and Worthie Minister of Christ . . . William Perkins,* 3 vols. (Cambridge, 1608–31), 3:655–59. Cf. [Henry Jessey], *1646. A Scripture Almanacke.*

98. Morison, *Harvard College in the Seventeenth Century*, chap. 10; [Samuel Danforth], *The New-England Almanack for . . . 1686* (Cambridge, Mass., 1686).

99. [Samuel Bradstreet], *An Almanack for . . . 1657* (Cambridge, Mass., 1657) is the earliest of the surviving almanacs to use the compromise formula, "first month called March," etc.; for astrology, see [Samuel Cheever], *An Almanack for . . . 1660* (Cambridge, Mass., 1660); [John Sherman], *An Almanack of Coelestial Motions viz. of the Sun and Planets* (Cambridge, Mass., 1674); [John Foster], *An Almanack . . . for . . . 1678* (Boston, 1678); Noadiah Russell, *Cambridge Ephemeris. An Almanack . . . for . . . 1684* (Cambridge, Mass., 1684); H[enry] Newman, *Non Cessant Anni . . . Harvard's Ephemeris* (Cambridge, Mass., 1690).

100. Facsimile copy at Massachusetts Historical Society; *The Minor Diaries, Stonington, Ct.* (Boxborough, Mass., 1976), 127, and passim.

101. [Danforth], *New-England Almanack for . . . 1686.*

102. [Josiah Flynt], *1666. An Almanack* (Cambridge, Mass., 1666); [John Sherman], *An Almanack . . . for . . . 1677* (Cambridge, Mass., 1677); the same, *An Almanack . . . for . . . 1676* (Cambridge, Mass., 1676); [Cotton Mather], *Boston Ephemeris; Sewall Diary*, 1:599.

103. Lewalski, *Protestant Poetics*, 40; [Mather], *Boston Ephemeris;* see also King, *English Reformation Literature*, 209ff.

104. George Keith, *The Pretended Antidote Proved Poyson: Or, The true Principles of the Christian & Protestant Religion Defended* (Philadelphia, 1690), 15.

105. Peter Folger, *A Looking Glass for the Times. Or, The former Spirit of New-England revived in this Generation* (1676; repr., n.p., 1725), 11.

106. *AC*, 315–16; 326.

107. William G. McLoughlin and Martha Whiting Davidson, eds., "The Baptist Debate of April 14–15, 1668," *MHS Proc.* 76 (1964), 111–12, 123, 126.

108. Isaac Backus, *A History of New England. With Particular Reference to the Denomination of Christians called Baptists*, 2 vols. (1771; repr. Newton, Mass., 1871), 1:292.

109. Francis Howgill, *The Heart of New-England Hardned through Wickedness* (London, 1659), 7–8; Christine L. Heyrman, *Commerce and Culture: The Maritime Communities of Colonial Massachusetts, 1690–1750* (New York, 1983), 131. Quakers also argued that the printed Bible was corrupt; as Joseph Gatchall declared, what the ministers "called the Scriptures was not the words of God, but the sayings of man." *Essex Court Recs.*, 7:407.

110. William G. McLoughlin, *New England Dissent, 1630–1833: The Baptists and the Separation of Church and State*, 2 vols. (Cambridge, Mass., 1971), 1:58.

111. Hall, *Faithful Shepherd*, chap. 6.

112. Bernard, *The Faithfull Shepherd*, 54, 38; William Perkins, *The Art of Prophecying*, in *Workes*, 2:652–56; Samuel Willard, *Brief Directions to a Young Scholar Designing the Ministry, for the Study of Divinity* (Boston, 1735), ii; Bradford, *Of Plymouth Plantation*, ed. S. E. Morison (New York, 1952), xxviii; John Cotton, *The Grounds and Ends of the Baptism of the Children of the Faithful* (London, 1647), 4.

113. Cf. Walter Ong, *Rhetoric, Romance, and Technology: Studies in the Interaction of Expression and Culture* (Ithaca, N.Y., 1971).

114. *AC*, 36–39, 189, 213. Edward Johnson was more optimistic in noting of the Synod of 1646 (*WWP*, 242), "Their disputation was plain and easie to be understood of the meanest capacity, clearing up those points that were most dubious."

115. Cf. *Shepard Notebook*, 157.

116. *Winthrop Papers*, 3:326–332; *Winthrop Journal*, 1:216–17.

117. John Davenport, *Another Essay For Investigation of the Truth* (Cambridge, Mass.,

1663), 1–2; Charles Chauncy, *Gods Mercy, Shewed to his People in Giving Them a Faithful Ministry and Schooles of Learning for the Continual Supplyes Therof* (Cambridge, Mass., 1655); cf. William Ames, *Technometry*, trans. and ed. Lee W. Gibbs (Philadelphia, 1979).

118. Mather, *Farewel Exhortation*, 6, 12.

119. Bernard, *Faithfull Shepherd*, 38, 54; Perkins, *Workes*, 2:665; Ian Green, " 'For Children in Yeeres and Children in Understanding': The Emergence of the English Catechism Under Elizabeth and the Early Stuarts," *Journal of Ecclesiastical History* 37 (1986), 397–425. The relationship between Reformation catechisms, a "negative conscience," and social control is disputed in Gerald Strauss, "Reformation and Pedagogy," in Charles Trinkaus, ed., with Heiko A. Oberman, *The Pursuit of Holiness in Late Medieval and Renaissance Religion* (Leiden, 1974), 272–93; and Lewis W. Spitz, "Further Lines of Inquiry for the Study of 'Reformation and Pedagogy,' " in Trinkaus, ed., with Oberman, *Pursuit of Holiness*, 294–306.

120. Greenslade, ed., *Cambridge History*, 3:180; Johnson, WWP, 127–28, 173–74; *Winthrop Journal*, 2:147–48, SWP, 1:177.

121. *Essex Court Recs.*, 1:70.

122. Cf. Mather, *Call from Heaven*, 47, 50.

123. Increase Mather, *A Discourse Concerning Faith and Fervency* (Boston, 1710), preface, xvii–xviii; the same, "To The Reader," in *Kometographia or A Discourse Concerning Comets* (Boston, 1683). Constraints on the ministers as published authors are suggested by Mather's candor in "To the Reader" (sig.A2r) of *Wo to Drunkards:* "There were sundry other Sermons Preached from this Scripture . . . but they are not herewith published, because lengthy Discourses are not easily Printed, nor do they finde that acceptance with those for whom this is intended, as little Tractates sometimes do."

124. Davenport, "The Reverend Author's Postscript," *Another Essay.*

125. *Fiske Notebook*, 90–91, 96–98; Winship, *Cambridge Press*, 113. I briefly describe the lay critics of the Platform in *Faithful Shepherd*, 116–17. The Newbury church quarrel is another excellent example of confidence among the laity; see, e.g., *Essex Court Recs.*, 4:232.

126. Joshua Coffin, *A Sketch of the History of Newbury* (Boston, 1845), 331–33.

127. Johnson, WWP, 174; *Fiske Notebook*, 83.

CHAPTER 2

1. SWP, 1:246; John Hale, *A Modest Enquiry into the Nature of Witchcraft* (Boston, 1708), 34; Increase Mather, *An Essay for the Recording of Illustrious Providences* (1684); repr., London, 1856), 101 (cited hereafter as *Essay*); "The Diaries of John Hull," American Antiquarian Society, *Transactions and Collections* 3 (1857), 218; *Winthrop Journal*, 2:346; "The Diary of Noadiah Russell," NEHGR 7 (1853), 53–54; Nathaniel Morton, *New-Englands Memoriall* (Cambridge, Mass., 1669), 52; *Sewall Diary*, 1:281.

2. Johnson, WWP; John Sherman, "To the Reader," in Cotton Mather, *Wonders of the Invisible World* (Boston, 1693 [1692]); Kitty Scoular, *Natural Magic: Studies in the Presentation of Nature in English Poetry from Spenser to Marvell* (Oxford, 1965), 5; Increase Mather, *The Latter Sign Discoursed of*, bound with *Kometographia* (Boston, 1683), third pagination, 7–11. Strictly speaking, a "wonder" was distinct from a "miracle," though in everyday discourse, and even among the ministry, the two words became interchangeable. Cf. John Preston, *The Breast-Plate of Faith and Love* (London, 1630), pt 2,

176–77. See also Samuel Willard, *The Fiery Tryal no strange thing* (Boston, 1682), 4–7, for an explication of "strange" events.

3. Hyder Rollins, ed., *The Pack of Autolycus or Strange and Terrible News of Ghosts, Apparitions . . . as told in Broadside Ballads of the Years 1624–1693* (Cambridge, Mass., 1927), 36–43, 117–21, 162–67, and passim; Joseph Frank, *The Beginnings of the English Newspaper, 1620–1660* (Cambridge, Mass., 1961), 17; Bernard Capp, *English Almanacs 1500–1800* (Ithaca, N.Y., 1979), chap. 6; *Strange and wonderful News from Chipingnorton . . . Of certain dreadful Apparitions* ([London, 1679]); Matthias A. Shaaber, *Some Forerunners of the Newspaper in England 1476–1622* (Philadelphia, 1928).

4. Rollins, ed., *Pack of Autolycus*, 62, 139, 82, 23; [John Trundle], *A Miracle, of Miracles* ([London, 1614]), 5; John Gadbury, *Natura Prodigiorum or, A Discourse touching the nature of Prodigies* (London, 1660).

5. Thomas Beard, *The Theatre of Gods Judgements* (London, 1648), 409; Stephen Batman, *The Doome warning all men to the Iudgmente* (London, 1581), 317, 379, 390, 397.

6. Beard, *Theatre of Gods Judgements*, 37, 48, 195; Batman, *Doome warning all men to the Iudgemente*, 403; [R. B.], *Admirable Curiosities, Rarities, & Wonders in England* (London, 1682), passim. Here as elsewhere in this chapter, the possible references run into the hundreds.

7. Samuel Clarke, *A Mirrour or Looking Glasse both for Saints, and Sinners*, 2nd ed. (London, 1654), 92–93 (hereafter cited as Clarke, *Examples*); Beard, *Theatre of Gods Judgements*, Bk. 1, chap. 30; Rollins, ed., *Pack of Autolycus*, 75, 222.

8. Rollins, ed., *Pack of Autolycus*, 62.

9. Miriam Chrisman, *Lay Culture, Learned Culture: Books and Social Change in Strasbourg 1480–1599* (New Haven, Conn., 1982); 257, 369ff; R. W. Scribner, *For the Sake of Simple Folk: Popular Propaganda for the German Reformation* (Cambridge, 1981), 125–27, 131, 184; Jean Céard, *La Nature et les Prodiges: L'insolite au XVI siècle en France* (Geneva, 1977).

10. Simon Goulart, *Admirable and Memorable Histories containing the wonders of our time* (1547; London, 1607); Willen Frijhoff, *Prophétie et société dans les provinces-unis aux xvii et xviii siècles*, in Marie-Sylvie Dupond-Bouchet, ed., *Prophètes et sorciers dans les pays-bas xvi–xviii siècles* (Paris, 1978), 265–362.

11. Rollins, ed., *Pack of Autolycus*, 81. Philip Stubbes incorporated numerous continental stories into *The Anatomie of Abuses*, some of which he learned from Dutch publications: *The Anatomie of Abuses*, 3rd ed. (London, 1585), 121. John R. McNair, in his introduction to Batman's *Doom warning all men* (1581; repr. in facsimile, Delmar, N.Y., 1984), describes sources and precedents.

12. A book of great practical utility, as my citations from it indicate, is S. K. Heninger, Jr., *A Handbook of Renaissance Meteorology* (Durham, N.C., 1960), which opens with an important survey of the encyclopedias that codified and transmitted so much of the wonder lore. No less important is Kester Svendsen, *Milton and Science* (New York, 1969), with its superb discussion (chap. 1) of "The Compendious Method of Natural Philosophy: Milton and the Encyclopedia Tradition." The notes and cross-references in Hyder Rollins's *Pack of Autolycus* remain the best guide to the print culture that I describe briefly. An exhaustive survey is Lynn Thorndike, *A History of Magic and Experimental Science*, 8 vols. (New York, 1923–58), esp. vols. 4–7.

13. Heninger, *Handbook of Renaissance Meteorology*, 12, and chaps. 2–3.

14. Ibid., 30–32; Don Cameron Allen, *The Star-Crossed Renaissance: The Quarrel About Astrology and Its Influence in England* (1941; New York, 1966), chap. 5; Capp, *English Almanacs*, chap. 5.

15. Eusebius, *The Ancient ecclesiastical histories* (London, 1619), 64, 80; *Bede's Ecclesiastical History of the English People*, ed. Bertram Colgrave and R. A. B. Mynors (Oxford, 1960), 141, 361–63; G. R. Owst, *Literature and Pulpit in Medieval England* (Cambridge, 1938), 129–30.

16. Robert E. Lerner, *The Powers of Prophecy: The Cedar of Lebanon Vision from the Mongol Onslaught to the Dawn of the Enlightenment* (Berkeley and Los Angeles, 1983), passim, and 164 (Luther). See also J. S. P. Tatlock, *The Legendary History of Britain* (Berkeley and Los Angeles, 1950); and Rupert Taylor, *The Political Prophecy in England* (New York, 1911).

17. Scribner, *For the Sake of Simple Folk*, 116–17, 140–47, 184; Katharine R. Firth, *The Apocalyptic Tradition in Reformation Britain, 1530–1645* (Oxford, 1979); Joseph Mede, *The Key of the Revelation, searched and demonstrated out of the Naturall and proper Characters of the Visions* (London, 1643), Pt. 1, 84, 88, 94; Keith Thomas, *Religion and the Decline of Magic* (London, 1971), chap. 13.

18. Katharine Park and Lorraine J. Daston, "Unnatural Conceptions: The Study of Monsters in Sixteenth- and Seventeenth-Century France and England," *Past and Present* 92 (1981), 20–54; T. K. Hoppe, "The Nature of the Early Royal Society," *British Journal for the History of Science* 9 (1976), 1–24, 243–47.

19. Geoffrey Chaucer, *The Canterbury Tales*, trans. Neville Coghill (Baltimore, 1952), 70; John Calvin, *Institutes of the Christian Religion*, ed. John T. McNeill, trans. Ford Lewis Battles, 2 vols. (Philadelphia, 1960), Bk. 1, chap. 16; Beard, *Theatre of Gods Judgements*, 88–93; Peter Lake, *Moderate Puritans and the Elizabethan Church* (Cambridge, 1982), 119–20.

20. Cf. Victor Harris, *All Coherence Gone* (Chicago, 1949).

21. Heninger, *Handbook of Renaissance Meteorology*, 87–91; Du Bartas, *La Sepmaine*, quoted on the reverse of title page, Samuel Danforth, *An Astronomical Description of the late Comet or Blazing Star* (Cambridge, Mass., 1665); Pliny, *Natural History*, trans. H. Rackham, 10 vols. (Cambridge, Mass., 1949), 1:235 (Bk II.xxiii); C. Doris Hellman, *The Comet of 1577: Its Place in the History of Astronomy* (New York, 1944), 252–58.

22. Pliny, *Natural History*, 1:275 (Bk. II.liii); Heninger, *Handbook of Renaissance Meteorology*, 72–87.

23. *The Famous and Memorable Workes of Josephus . . . Faithfully Translated . . . by Thomas Lodge* (London, 1620), 738; Heninger, *Handbook of Renaissance Meteorology*, 91–94; Rollins, ed., *Pack of Autolycus*, 38; *Mirabilis Annus Secundus; Or, The Second Year of Prodigies. Being A true and impartial Collection of many strange Signes and Apparitions . . .* ([London], 1662), 2–3.

24. Paul H. Kocher, *Science and Religion in Elizabethan England* (New York, 1969).

25. Capp, *English Almanacs*, 165; Hershel Baker, *The Race of Time* (Toronto, 1967), 57–63; Joseph J. Morgan, Jr., *Chaucer and the Theme of Mutability* (The Hague, 1961); Harris, *All Coherence Gone*, chaps. 4–5.

26. Willard Farnham, *The Medieval Heritage of Elizabethan Tragedy* (Berkeley, 1936), chap. 7; Scribner, *For the Sake of Simple Folk*, 117; Beard, *Theatre of Gods Judgements*, 80.

27. Michael MacDonald, *Mystical Bedlam: Madness, Anxiety, and Healing in Seventeenth-Century England* (Cambridge, 1981), 175, 202.

28. Howard R. Patch, *The Goddess Fortuna in Medieval Literature* (Cambridge, Mass., 1927); J. G. A. Pocock, *The Machiavellian Moment: Florentine Political Thought and the Atlantic Republican Tradition* (Princeton, N.J., 1975), 349–50.

29. Katharine M. Briggs, *The Anatomy of Puck: An Examination of Fairy Beliefs Among Shakespeare's Contemporaries and Successors* (London, 1959); C. Grant Loomis, *White Magic:*

An Introduction to the Folklore of Christian Legend (Cambridge, Mass., 1948); Kittredge, *Old Farmer and His Almanac*, chap. 6; Clarke, *Examples*, Bks. 69–71. As Sydney Anglo observes in "Evident Authority and Authoritative Evidence: The *Malleus Malefica-rum*," in Anglo, ed., *The Damned Art: Essays in the Literature of Witchcraft* (London, 1977), 6: "Throughout the Middle Ages and the Renaissance, arguments in virtually every field of human enquiry proceeded upon the basis of accumulated authority." Hence (p. 10) the Puritan William Perkins cited Homer as an "unimpeachable source" for an understanding of witchcraft!

30. William P. Upham, "Remarks," *MHS Proc.*, 2d Ser., 13 (1900), 126–27; Increase Mather, *Wo to Drunkards* (Cambridge, Mass., 1673), 28; "The Diary of Increase Mather," *MHS Proc.*, 2d Ser., 13 (1900), 345.

31. Worthington C. Ford, *The Boston Book Market, 1679–1700* (Boston, 1917), 149.

32. Kenneth B. Murdoch, ed., *Handkerchiefs from Paul being Pious and Consolatory Verses of Puritan Massachusetts* (Cambridge, Mass., 1927), 109–11; [Samuel Danforth], *An Almanacke for the Year of Our Lord 1648* (Cambridge, Mass., 1648).

33. Samuel Danforth, *An Astronomical Description of the late Comet or Blazing Star* (Cambridge, Mass., 1665); Wiswell, *A judicious observation* (London, 1683); Mather, *Heavens Alarm to the World* (Boston, 1682); the same, *The Latter Sign Discoursed* of (Boston, 1682); and *Kometographia*.

34. *Records of the First Church at Dorchester in New England 1636–1734* (Boston, 1891); *Roxbury Land and Church Records, [Sixth] Report of the Record Commissioners of the City of Boston* (Boston, 1884), 187–212; *Mather Papers, MHS Coll.*, 4th Ser., 8 (1868), 282 (hereafter cited as *Mather Papers*); John Langdon Sibley, *Biographical Sketches of Graduates of Harvard University in Cambridge, Massachusetts*, 3 vols. (Cambridge, Mass., 1873–85), 1:508, for reference to John Cotton of Plymouth's "diary of remarkables."

35. "Diary of Lawrence Hammond," *MHS Proc.*, 2d Ser., 7 (1892), 147–49; "The Diaries of John Hull," 217–18; and see below, Chapter 5, for Sewall's interest in portents.

36. Upham, "Remarks," 127–28; John H. Lockwood, *Westfield and Its Historic Influences, 1669–1919*, 2 vols. (Springfield, Mass., 1922), 1:132. In Arthur Dent's *The Plain Mans Pathway to Heaven* (London, 1610), one of the characters says, "For it is an hard world, and goods are not easie to come by" (p. 91).

37. *Mather Papers*, 282–87.

38. Ibid., 360–62.

39. Ibid., 306–10.

40. Ibid., 466–81. The Marshfield episode, told in a letter from the Reverend Samuel Arnold, was later published by N. B. Shurtleff as *Thunder & Lightning; and Deaths at Marshfield in 1658 & 1666* (Boston, 1850). For a previous effort by Mather to collect stories, cf. Thomas Cobbett, "A Narrative of New England's Deliverance," *NEHGR* 7 (1853), 209–19.

41. *Mather Papers*, 58–59.

42. Danforth, *An Astronomical Description*, 16–21; Mather, *Kometographia*, 96; a probable source was Goulart, *Admirable and Memorable Histories*, 132. Quoting once again the familiar lines from Du Bartas, Mather also spoke approvingly of apparitions in the air. In keeping with tradition, the colonists were sensitive to the shape and direction of comets; cf. Johnson, *WWP*, 40.

43. Shurtleff, *Thunder & Lightning*, 13–15; "Diaries of John Hull," 231; "Bradstreet's Journal, 1664–83," *NEHGR* 8 (1854), 325; Johnson, *WWP*, 143, 39–40.

44. See above, Chapter 1, regarding astrology and the almanac.

45. "Memoranda of John Brock," American Antiquarian Society, *Proceedings* 53 (1943), 104; Deodat Lawson, *A Brief and True Narrative* (Boston, 1692), 8.

46. "Diary of Noadiah Russell," 54; Morton, *New-Englands Memoriall*, 52.

47. "John Dane's Narrative, 1682," *NEHGR* 8 (1854), 149; *Winthrop Journal*, 1:84, 121; see also Sidney H. Miner and George D. Stanton, Jr., comps., *The Diary of Thomas Minor* (1899; repr., Boxborough, Mass., 1976), 192, 65, 67, 163; *Magnalia*, 1:314–16.

48. *Magnalia*, 2:353; "Diaries of John Hull," 220. Michael Wigglesworth dreamed of the last judgment; Edmund S. Morgan, ed., *The Diary of Michael Wigglesworth 1653–1657: The Conscience of a Puritan* (1946; repr., New York, 1965), 51.

49. The folklore of black dogs is summarized in Katharine M. Briggs, *British Folk Tales and Legends: A Sampler* (London, 1977), 115–20. See also George Lyman Kittredge, *Witchcraft in Old and New England* (Cambridge, Mass. 1929), 124, 156–57.

50. *SWP*, 1:74, 202; 2:568; Cotton Mather, *Wonders of the Invisible World* (1693; repr., London, 1862), 144. See also Alan Macfarlane, *Witchcraft in Tudor and Stuart England* (New York, 1970), 83; Hoadly Transcripts, Connecticut Historical Society, testimony concerning Katharine Harrison, Oct. 29, 1669.

51. *SWP*, 1:166, 246.

52. *SWP*, 2:578; cf. Loomis, *White Magic*, 39.

53. The same fascination with curiosities occurs in Beard and Clarke, and has medieval precedents; Tatlock, *Legendary History of Britain*, 276–77.

54. Mather, *Essay*, "Introduction"; H. L. D. Ward, *Catalogue of Romances in the Department of Manuscripts in the British Museum*, 3 vols. (London, 1883–1910), 1:257, 2:595.

55. Further indications of this mentality can be found in *Shepard Notebook*, 162; *Essex Court Recs.*, 7:113, 148; Charles Thornton Libby, ed., *Province and Court Records of Maine*, 9 vols. (Portland, Maine, 1928–1975), 2:31; Wilson Waters, *History of Chelmsford, Massachusetts* (Lowell, Mass., 1917), 527; Lockwood, *Westfield*, 1:179.

56. *Winthrop Journal*, 2:71.

57. William Christian, Jr., *Apparitions in Late Medieval and Renaissance Spain* (Princeton, N.J., 1981); J.-C. Schmitt, *Le Saint Levrier: Guinefort, guérisseur d'enfants depuis le xiii siècle* (Paris, 1979).

58. *Winthrop Journal*, 1:163, 176; 2:9; 1:195; 2:97, 88; 1:115; 2:44; 1:322, 195.

59. Ibid., 1:285, 287, 308; 2:71. Citing the safe voyages of so many of the colonists became common practice. Cf. *Wyllys Papers*, Connecticut Historical Society, *Collections* 21 (1924), 68; Mather, *Essay*, chap. 1 ("Of Remarkable Sea Deliverances"); and Donald P. Wharton, "Providence and the Colonial American Sea-Deliverance Tradition," *Essex Institute Historical Collections* 119 (1983), 42–48.

60. *Winthrop Journal*, 2:347–48; 1:294; 2:156, 264.

61. Morton, *New-Englands Memoriall*, 84, 1, 23, 44, 97.

62. *Roxbury Land and Church Records*, 188, 78.

63. Charles F. Adams, Jr., "Abstract of [John] Marshall's Diary, *MHS Proc.*, 2d Ser., 1 (1884–85), 148–64, and its continuation, Samuel A. Green, "Remarks," ibid., 2d Ser., 14 (1900–1), 13–34; "John Dane's Narrative, 1682," *NEHGR* 8 (1854), 149–156; "Diary of Lawrence Hammond," 147–48; Samuel Deane, *History of Scituate, Massachusetts* (Boston, 1831), 123.

64. Beard, *Theatre of Gods Judgements*, 2.

65. Joshua Coffin, *A Sketch of the History of Newbury* (Boston, 1845), 26; Johnson, *WWP*, 185; Marshall Swan, "The Bedevilment of Cape Ann, 1692," *Essex Institute Historical Collections*, 117 (1981), 153–77; *Sewall Diary*, 1:603; Robert W. Lovett, ed., *Documents From the Harvard University Archives, 1638–1750*, CSM Pub., 49 (Boston, 1975), 150.

66. Increase Mather, *The Doctrine of Divine Providence Opened and Applyed* (Boston, 1684), 43, 30–32, 34, 81, 133; and for the figure of the wheel and the rise and fall of kings, cf. 9, 16–17. The image of the wheel derives from Ezekiel 1:15–16 et seq.

67. L. M. Buell, "Elizabethan Portents: Superstition or Doctrine," in *Essays Critical and Historical Dedicated to Lily B. Campbell* (Berkeley and Los Angeles, 1950), 27–41; *Acts & Mon.*, 4:114, 253, 115.

68. Stubbes, *Anatomie of Abuses*, 160, 225, and passim. The Tiverton fires of 1598 and 1612, cited by Lewis Bayley in *The Practice of Pietie*, 27th ed. (London, 1631), 432–33, were also cited in the broadside *Divine Examples of God's Severe Judgments upon Sabbathbreakers* (London, 1671). Murdock, *Handkerchiefs from Paul*, 54–59; *Winthrop Papers*, 5 vols. (Boston, 1929–   ), 3:370.

69. The best brief treatment of this subject is Thomas, *Religion and the Decline of Magic*, chap. 5 and pp. 342–44.

70. *AC*, 268, 337–39; Johnson, *WWP*, 129, 127.

71. *AC*, 165.

72. Thomas, *Religion and the Decline of Magic*, 137–38, 135. See also Phyllis Mack, "Women as Prophets During the English Civil War," *Feminist Studies* 8, #1 (Spring 1982), 19–45. I hazard the opinion that separatist Puritans (and Anne Hutchinson was like a separatist in questioning the legitimacy of the English church) were prone to prophesying the destruction of England; for one example, see Edward Arber, ed., *The Story of the Pilgrim Fathers* (London, 1897), 246.

73. *AC*, 337–38, 272–73.

74. Isaac Backus, *A History of New-England, with special reference to the Baptists*, 2 vols. (1771; repr., Newton, Mass., 1871), 1:322.

75. "Diaries of John Hull," 202; [Thomas Maule], *New-England Persecutors Mauld With their own Weapons* [New York, 1697], 32; S[amuel] G[room], *A Glasse for the People of New England* ([London], 1676), 15; *Sewall Diary*, 1:44, 18. See below, Chapter 4, for more such demonstrations and statements.

76. George Keith, *The Pretended Antidote Proved Poyson* (Philadelphia, 1690), 204; [Maule], *New-England Persecutors*, sig. A2 recto, 19; John Rogers, *A Brief Account Of some of the late Suffering of several Baptists* ([New York, 1726]), 13.

77. *Essex Court Recs.*, 7:46; 1:265; *Winthrop Journal*, 2:344; R. G. Tomlinson, *Witchcraft Trials of Connecticut* (Hartford, Conn., 1978), 41–43, 14; Cotton Mather, *Memorable Providences, Relating to Witchcrafts and Possessions* (Boston, 1689), 20; Coffin, *History of Newbury*, 123; John Taylor, *The Witchcraft Delusion in Colonial Connecticut, 1647–1697* (New York, 1908), 56; *Essex Court Recs.*, 7:357; *SWP*, 2:397–99, 626; 3:787–88; Samuel G. Drake, *Annals of Witchcraft in New England* (Boston, 1869), 287, 281. For other episodes, cf. Thomas Gage, *The History of Rowley* (Boston, 1840), 72; "Memoir of the Rev. William Adams," *MHS Coll.*, 4th Ser., 1 (1852), 17–18.

78. *SWP*, 2:507; 1:228, 308; Hale, *A Modest Enquiry*, 133; Drake, *Annals*, 275.

79. Ronald Marcus, *"Elizabeth Clawson . . . Thou Deseruest to Dye: An Account* (Stamford, Conn., 1976) [pamphlet at the Connecticut Historical Society]; Hoadly transcripts, Connecticut Historical Society, testimony of Samuel Debell (1667).

80. *Winthrop Journal*, 1:266–68, 277; 280–82, 214.

81. *AC*, 273. John Cotton was interested in exploring whether Mrs. Hutchinson meant by "miracle" a "work above nature or . . . some wonderful providence for that is called a miracle often in the psalms"; Mrs. Hutchinson did indeed revert to the word "providence," but by this time the magistrates were ready to convict her. Ibid., 340–42.

82. [Maule], *New-England Persecutors*, 8.

83. Mather, *Wonders of the Invisible World*, 13–15. This "political" interpretation of the Devil should be compared to the spiritual interpretation I describe in chapter 3.

84. Mather, *Essay*, chap. 8; Hale, *Modest Enquiry*, 143–44, 131–32.

85. But see below, chapter 4, for confusion on this matter.

86. Alice L. Brown, "Religious Dreams and Their Interpretation in Some Thinkers of the Seventeenth Century" (Ph.D. thesis, University of London, 1975), traces dream theory forward from the Greeks (I am grateful to the late D. P. Walker for this reference); Guy de Brez, *The Rise, Spring and Foundation of the Anabaptists, Or Re-Baptized of our Time*, trans. by J.S. (Cambridge, Mass., 1668), 47, 1, 12–13, 20–21, 7; *AC*, 342–43.

87. Clarke, *Examples*, 221–22; Morton, *New-Englands Memoriall*, 108; G[roome], *A Glasse For the People of New-England*, 11.

88. *Winthrop Journal*, 2:317, 321–22; Edward Winslow, *New-Englands Salamander, Discovered by an Irreligious and Scornfull Pamphlet* (1647); repr., *MHS Coll.*, 3d Ser., 2 (1830), 128–29; John Child, *New-Englands Jonas Cast up at London* (1647); repr., *MHS Coll.*, 2nd Ser., 4 (1816), 114–16. The charges made against the Child group included "They lay open the afflictions, which God hath pleased to exercise us with, and that to the worst appearance, and impute it to the evil of our government." *Winthrop Journal*, 2:297.

89. Winslow, *New-Englands Salamander*, 130–33. This story lived on in oral and written tradition, to be cited by John Allin to his son in 1668: ". . . letters written against the country to great ones in England, divers violent storms, to the apparent danger of ship & lives, forced the mesanger to produce them (as Jonas once himself) which being viewed and thrown overboard they had after it an happy and prosperous voyage, which accident is the 6th time that letters against the country hath from time to time miscarried." Sibley, *Biographical Sketches*, 1:297.

90. Child, *New-Englands Jonas*, 115–16.

91. *Winthrop Papers*, 5:126; Sidney Perley, *The History of Boxford* (Boxford, Mass., 1880), 62 n. Cf. Andrew Delbanco, "The Puritan Errand Re-Viewed," *Journal of American Studies* 18 (1984), 343–60.

92. Sylvester Judd, *History of Hadley* (Springfield, Mass., 1905), 77.

93. Samuel Willard, *Ne Sutor Ultra Crepidam* (Boston, 1681), 24, refers to Baptist celebrations of a war hero as one of their own.

94. Increase Mather, *A Discourse Concerning the Uncertainty of the Times of Men* (Boston, 1697); Mather, *Wo to Drunkards*, 12, 20–24. For more in this vein, cf. Increase Mather, *Meditations On the Sanctification of the Lord's Day* (Boston, 1712). It is worth repeating that Mather followed English literary models, e.g, Samuel Ward, *Wo to Drunkards* (London, 1622). Though this way of preaching was disappearing in the early eighteenth century, some ministers continued to employ it; cf. John Barnard, *The Nature and Danger of Sinful Mirth, Exhibited in a Plain Discourse* (Boston, 1728).

95. Increase Mather, *A Sermon Wherein is shewed that the Church of God is sometimes a Subject of Great Persecution* (Boston, 1682), 16, 7, sig. A3 recto.

96. For example, William Hubbard, *A Narrative of the Troubles with the Indians in New-England* (Boston, 1677).

97. "Diary of Increase Mather," *MHS Proc.*, 2d Ser., 13 (1900), 347, 359–60.

98. *Mather Papers*, 279. For a good example of futility, cf. *Essex Court Recs.*, 7:71.

99. Robert Middlekauff, *The Mathers: Three Generations of Puritan Intellectuals* (New York, 1971), 139–43.

100. Park and Daston, "Unnatural Conceptions," 51–54.

101. John Aubrey, *Three Prose Works,* ed. John Buchanan-Brown (Fontwell, 1972), 427–28. Cf. Moody E. Prior, "Joseph Glanvill, Witchcraft, and Seventeenth-Century Science," *Modern Philology* 30 (1932–33), 167–94.

102. Ronald A. Knox, *Enthusiasm: A Chapter in the History of Religion* (1950; repr., New York, 1961), chap. 15; Thomas Hobbes, *Leviathan,* ed. Michael Oakeshott (Oxford, 1957), Pt. IV.

103. Charles Morton, *Compendium Physicae, CSM Pub.,* 33 (Boston, 1940), 35, 93, 87, 111–12.

104. Mather, *Kometographia,* "To the Reader," 20, 129, 8; see also Mather, *Heavens Alarm,* sig. A2 recto, where he cites, as authorities, Cicero and Vergil. The separation of "learned" (or "scientific") belief from any evangelical message was already evident in Samuel Danforth's description of the comet of 1664. The first sixteen pages of *An Astronomical Description* were just that, Danforth's report of his "observations" and his reasoning about the matter and itinerary of a comet, using scientific instruments as best he could. On page 16, he began "A Brief Theological Application," in which he cited Scripture and associated comets with a series of disasters.

105. Increase Mather, *Angelographia, or A Discourse Concerning the Nature and Power of the Holy Angels* (Boston, 1696), sig. B2 recto, verso, 63; the same, *A Disquisition Concerning Angelical Apparitions, In Answer to a Case of Conscience* (Boston, 1696), 5–6, 12, 17–22, 26–28.

106. Peter Burke, *Popular Culture in Early Modern Europe* (New York, 1978), chap. 8, and p. 241.

107. Mather, *Disquisition Concerning Angelical Apparitions,* 31; Mather, *Essay,* 198–203; Middlekauff, *The Mathers,* 155–57; Taylor, *Witchcraft in Connecticut,* 75–76.

108. Notably, John Hale, Samuel Willard, and Thomas Brattle. See, e.g., Samuel Willard, *The Checkered State of the Gospel Church* (Boston, 1701), 36, for the effort to differentiate Scripture predictions from prognostications, which Willard defined as mostly mistakes made by persons who pretend to possess the spirit of prophecy.

109. [Thomas Robie], *A Letter To a Certain Gentleman, &c* (Boston, 1719), 1–2, 8.

110. See, e.g., Nathan Fiske, *Remarkable Providences to be gratefully recollected, religiously improved, and carefully transmitted to Posterity* (Boston, 1776).

111. As Middlekauff points out, Mather did not really listen to the critics. *The Mathers,* 157–59.

112. *Magnalia,* 1:295, 486, 544, 307–14, 312, 544, 205.

113. James T. Boulton, ed., *Selected Writings of Daniel Defoe* (Cambridge, 1975), 132–41.

114. [George Trosse], *The Life Of the Reverend Mr. Geo. Trosse . . . Written by Himself* (Exon, 1714).

115. *Magnalia,* 2:61–62; 1:544.

116. Buell, "Elizabethan Portents," 33.

117. Cf. *Essex Court Recs.,* 7:71. When Richard Brown preached a fast-day sermon in Newbury in 1700 and "concluded . . . to lay open in peticular the sins that most openly abounded and to press them home," his audience was "highly offended, as taking all to themselves. . . . Great was their rage against me, they threatened me to my face, But more Behind my Back"—to the point of open violence. Lilly Eaton, *Genealogical History of the Town of Reading* (Boston, 1874), 54.

118. *Sewall Diary,* 1:455.

119. Gerald D. Johnson, "John Trundle and the Book Trade 1603–1626," *Studies in Bibliography* 39 (1985), 177–99; John Holwell, *Catastrophe mundi* (London, 1682); repr., abridged, *Holwell's Predictions Of many Remarkable things* (Cambridge, Mass., 1690);

Richmond P. Bond, "John Partridge and the Company of Stationers," *Studies in Bibliography* 16 (1963), 61–80.

120. Earle, *Micro-Cosmographia* (1628), quoted in Louis B. Wright, *Middle-Class Culture in Elizabethan England* (Chapel Hill, N.C., 1935), 96, 98, 359; Park and Daston, "Unnatural Conceptions," 30. "The poore Country wench melts like her butter to heare them. And these are the Stories of some men of Tiburne, or a strange Monster out of Germany" (ibid., note 22).

121. [Nathaniel Crouch], *Delights for the Ingenious, In above Fifty Select and Choice Emblems* (London, 1684), "The Epistle to the Reader." The Harvard Library copy is marked with pinpricks, indicating that it has been used.

122. [Nathaniel Crouch], *The Kingdom of Darkness* (London, 1688), sig. A2 recto, 1, 76, 45, and passim; Alexander Roberts, *A Treatise of Witchcraft* (London, 1616).

123. *Magnalia*, 1:205.

124. *Diary of Michael Wigglesworth*, 8–9; Thomas Waters, *Ipswich in the Massachusetts-Bay Colony*, 2 vols. (Ipswich, 1905), 1:172, 178, 183; Deane, *History of Scituate*, 122; "Letter from Benj. Corbyn to Thomas Fuller," *NEHGR* 22 (1868), 296; and for Sewall's children, see below, Chapter 5, p. 221.

125. I. Mather, *Cases of Conscience Concerning evil Spirits Personating Men* (Boston, 1693), 16; Mather, *Doctrine of Divine Providence*, 77–78.

126. Mather, *The Times of Men*, 20; Leonard Hoar, *The Sting of Death and Death Unstung* (Boston, 1680), sig. A2 recto, 6–8.

CHAPTER 3

1. *Shepard Notebook*, 159; William Bradford, *Of Plymouth Plantation* (New York, 1981), 4, 7. The tension between the "godly" and their enemies and the movement to define church membership as voluntary were crucial aspects of the colonists' experience as Englishmen. Cf. Patrick Collinson, "The English Conventicle," in W. J. Sheils and Diana Wood, eds., *Voluntary Religion* (Oxford, 1986), 223–59; Edmund S. Morgan, *Visible Saints: The History of a Puritan Idea* (New York, 1963).

2. [Roger Clap], *Memoirs of Captain Roger Clap. Relating some of God's Remarkable Providences to Him . . .* (1731; Boston, 1766), 8.

3. *Shepard Notebook; Fiske Notebook*; Edmund S. Morgan, ed., *The Diary of Michael Wigglesworth 1653–1657: The Conscience of a Puritan* (Harper Torchbook, New York, 1965), 107–25 (cited hereafter as *Diary of Michael Wigglesworth*); Kenneth P. Minkema, "The East Windsor Conversion Relations 1700–1725," Connecticut Historical Society, *Bulletin* 51 (Winter 1986), 7–63. Mary Rhinelander has discovered and is editing another sixteen Cambridge testimonies; I am grateful to her for sharing with me a preliminary transcript.

4. Such "notes" existed at one time for the Dedham congregation; cf. *The Record of Baptisms, Marriages and Deaths . . . in the Town of Dedham*, ed. Don Gleason Hill ([Dedham Records, 2], Dedham, Mass., 1888), 14 (hereafter cited as *Dedham Records, 2*).

5. The medieval and folk patterns that inform Bunyan's *Pilgrim's Progress* are described in Vincent Newey, ed., *The Pilgrim's Progress—Critical and Historical Views* (Liverpool, 1982), esp. the essays by Brean Hammond and Nick Davis.

6. See, in general, G. W. Owst, *Literature and Pulpit in Medieval England*, second rev. ed. (New York, 1961), 97–109; Samuel C. Chew, *The Pilgrimage of Life* (New

Haven, 1962); U. Milo Kaufmann, *The Pilgrim's Progress and Traditions in Puritan Meditation* (New Haven, 1966).

7. The portrait is reproduced in Jonathan Fairbanks and Robert F. Trent, *New England Begins: The Seventeenth Century*, 3 vols. (Boston, 1982), 3:441; the poem is quoted, 474.

8. *Acts & Mon.*, 6:65, 199–200, 60–61, 58, 56.

9. Ibid., 6:619. A richly informative study of these techniques is Charles Hambrick-Stowe, *The Practice of Piety: Puritan Devotional Disciplines in Seventeenth-Century New England* (Chapel Hill, N.C., 1982); see. e.g., *Diary of Michael Wigglesworth*, 101.

10. J. Paul Hunter, *The Reluctant Pilgrim: Defoe's Emblematic Method and Quest for Form in Robinson Crusoe* (Baltimore, 1966), esp. chap. 4; and Barbara Kiefer Lewalski, "Typological Symbolism and the 'Progress of the Soul' in Seventeenth-Century Literature," in Earl Miner, ed., *Literary Uses of Typology: From the Late Middle Ages to the Present* (Princeton, N.J., 1977), are among the best descriptions of these literary techniques.

11. "The Diaries of John Hull," American Antiquarian Society, *Transactions and Collections* 3 (1857), 141.

12. Ms., Dedham Historical Society, Dedham, Massachusetts.

13. Johnson, *WWP*, 23, 52.

14. [Rowlandson], *Soveraignty*, 326, 334, 365, 323, 365, 360, 323.

15. *Memoirs of Roger Clap*, 8.

16. *Dedham Records*, 2:4.

17. *Shepard Notebook*, 95, 112, 148, 176, 35; *Fiske Notebook*, 43, 61.

18. *Fiske Notebook*, 61, 94, 30, 8; *Shepard Notebook*, 119.

19. *Fiske Notebook*, 9, 33; *Shepard Notebook*, 12, 112, 143, 86, 204, 148, 39–40, 130, 168.

20. *Shepard Notebook*, 48, 71, 87, 131, 137; *Fiske Notebook*, 95, 8, 52, 30, 33, 61, 90.

21. *Shepard Notebook*, 179, 128, 170, 100; *Diary of Michael Wigglesworth*, 114–15.

22. *Shepard Notebook*, 180, 116, 87, 184, 140.

23. Perry Miller and Thomas H. Johnson, eds., *The Puritans*, rev. ed., 2 vols. (New York, 1963), 2:575, 577–79.

24. [Rowlandson], *Soveraignty*, 332, 336, 341, 343, 348, 328, 365–66.

25. "John Dane's Narrative," *NEHGR* 8 (1854), 147–56; I am grateful to Michel Alexander for supplying me with a text of Dane's poem, from the manuscript at the New England Historic Genealogical Society.

26. John Green reported to the Cambridge church, "The Lord began first to awaken me by Mister Shepard's catechize concerning the dread and terror of Christ Jesus coming to judgment[.]" *Diary of Michael Wigglesworth*, 114. Charles Lloyd Cohen has studied the relationship between Shepard's sermons and the statements of his congregation, and I accept his conclusion. Cohen, *God's Caress: The Psychology of Puritan Religious Experience* (New York, 1986), chap. 6.

27. Increase Mather, *Wo to Drunkards* (Cambridge, Mass., 1673), 19.

28. For a brief sampling of this literature, cf. David D. Hall, *The Faithful Shepherd: A History of the New England Ministry in the Seventeenth Century* (Chapel Hill, N.C., 1972), 174, 263–64. An important study of ministerial biographies as the genre developed among English Puritans is William Haller, *The Rise of Puritanism* (New York, 1938).

29. Bradford, *Of Plymouth Plantation*, 359–64.

30. Michael McGiffert, ed., *God's Plot: The Paradoxes of Puritan Piety, Being the Autobiography and Journal of Thomas Shepard* (Amherst, Mass., 1972); Worthington C.

Ford, ed., *The Diary of Cotton Mather*, 2 vols. (1911; repr., New York, 1957). Cotton Mather refers in the *Magnalia* to now lost personal records of Jonathan Mitchel (2:30).

31. See below, Chapter 5, for my account of a lay diary that comes close.

32. Ms., Connecticut Historical Society. The physical appearance of this text, which includes poems by Mrs. Tompson's brother-in-law Benjamin, suggests that it was prepared for a printer.

33. Robert Trent, "'The Deuil Came Upon me like a Lyon': A 1697 Cambridge Deathbed Narrative," Connecticut Historical Society, *Bulletin* 48 (1983), 115–19.

34. Sarah Goodhue, *A Valedictory and Monitory Writing* [Cambridge?, 1681?]; no copy survives, but the text is reprinted in Thomas Waters, *Ipswich in the Massachusetts Bay Colony*, 2 vols. (Ipswich, 1905), 1:519–24. That she appeals to her children to respect the clergy may provide one reason why her narrative was published. A narrative that circulated in manuscript before being published in the eighteenth century was *Mr. [Jonathan] Mitchel's Letter to his Brother* [Boston, 1732?]. Cf. [Samuel Sewall?], *Early Piety exemplified in Elizabeth Butcher* [Boston, 1718], and the spiritual biographies of laymen in the *Magnalia*.

35. Many of these elegies are printed in Harold S. Jantz, *The First Century of New England Verse* (Worcester, Mass., 1944); illustrated broadside elegies are reproduced in Fairbanks and Trent, *New England Begins*, 2:130, 314.

36. [Cotton Mather], *A Token, for the Children of New-England* (Boston, 1700); Mather added these stories to the probable first New England edition of James Janeway's *A Token for Children*.

37. Jonathan Edwards, *Some Thoughts Concerning the present Revival of Religion in New England* (1742); repr., *The Great Awakening*, ed. C. C. Goen, *The Works of Jonathan Edwards*, 4 (New Haven, 1972), 331–41.

38. *Winthrop Journal*, 1:230; 2:29, 93.

39. *Records of the First Church at Dorchester in New England, 1636–1734* (Boston, 1891), 33; *Dedham Records*, 2:38. For others, cf. "Diaries of John Hull," 181, 195–96; "Memoir of the Rev. William Adams," *MHS Coll.*, 4th Ser., 1:17; *SWP*, 1:96, 282; 2:555; "The Diary of Noadiah Russell," *NEHGR* 7 (1853), 56; 1:45, 47, 163; Edward Taylor's brief account of a Cambridge woman "of a troubled Spirit," in John H. Lockwood, *Westfield and Its Historic Influences*, 2 vols. (Springfield, Mass., 1922), 1:133; and for a case of suicide, cf. 179. See also John Winthrop's description of his son Deane, *Winthrop Journal*, 1:120–21. This is by no means an inclusive list.

40. [Rowlandson], *Soveraignty*, 324.

41. Nathaniel Bacon, comp., *A Relation of the Fearful Estate of Francis Spira, In the year 1548* (London, 1649), 15–17, 20–21, 50, 33, 45. The first English printing of this narrative occurred in 1549.

42. Bunyan, *Grace Abounding to the Chief of Sinners*, ed. Roger Sharrock (Oxford, 1962), 49; *Acts & Mon.*, 7: 219; Thomas Beard, *The Theatre of Gods Judgements* (1597; London, 1648), 47; Celeste Wine, "Nathaniel Wood's Conflict of Conscience," *PMLA* 50 (1935), 661–78; Leonard Hoar, *The Sting of Death and Death Unstung* (Boston, 1680), 9; Increase Mather, *A Call from Heaven* (Boston, 1685), 75; Thomas Shepard, *The Sincere Convert* (London, 1646), 54; Robert Russel, *Seven Sermons* (c. 1699; Boston, 1767), 93, where much of the story is retold. For a layman's reference (and a Rogerene's at that), cf. John Rogers, *The Answer To a Book Lately put forth* [New York, 1726], 10. See below, nn. 47, 51. I am indebted to Baird Tipson for other references in English sermons before 1640 that, for reasons of space, I do not cite.

43. *Shepard Notebook*, 168; *Sewall Diary*, 1:348.

44. Margaret Spufford, *Small Books and Pleasant Histories: Popular Fiction and Its*

Readership in Seventeenth-Century England (Athens, Ga., 1982), chap. 8; C. John Sommerville, *Popular Religion in Restoration England* (Gainesville, Fla., 1977). My description is based on the "penny godlies" in the Pepys Library, Magdalen College, Cambridge, England. For examples of these themes in the ballad literature, cf. William Chapel and J. W. Ebsworth, eds., *The Roxburghe Ballads*, 9 vols. (Hertford, England, 1869–97), 1:434.

45. See, e.g., *Morbus Satanicus. The Devil's Disease: Or, The Sin of Pride arraigned and Condemned*, 10th ed. ([London], 1662); Somerville, *Popular Religion*, 45.

46. *A Call to Extravagant Youth* [London, 166?], unpaginated.

47. Andrew Jones, *The Black Book of Conscience* (Hartford, Conn., 1767), 14.

48. As the English minister Giles Firmin did; Hall, *Faithful Shepherd*, 165–66. It was a truism among the ministers that "Bold and presumptuous sinners cannot be saved except they be made afraid of the Wrath and Vengeance of God." Samuel Danforth, *The Cry of Sodom Enquired into* (Cambridge, Mass., 1674), 12. Starting out as a minister, Joseph Green used this theme to the hilt; cf. "Commonplace Book of Joseph Green," 189–90. "Nothing hath a greater tendency to awaken unto Repentance," Increase Mather advised, "than serious Thoughts about the great Day of Judgment and the Infinite Danger which is in mens delaying their Conversion." *The Greatest Sinners* (Boston, 1686), sig. A3 verso.

49. Shepard, *Sincere Convert*, 72; Henry Scudder, *The Christians Daily Walke* (London, 1627), 82. A person joining the Cambridge church testified that he "thought God was become my enemy . . . I thought I was but travelling to the place of execution . . ." *Diary of Michael Wigglesworth*, 108.

50. Isaac Ambrose, *Christ in the Clouds, Coming to Judgment* (Hartford, Conn., 1767), 14; and cf. Richard Baxter, "An Epistle To the Unconverted Reader," in Joseph Alleine, *An Alarm to Unconverted Sinners* (Boston, 1767), xxi.

51. Alleine, *An Alarm to Unconverted Sinners*, 113.

52. *Diary of Michael Wigglesworth*, 118; Minkema, "Windsor Church Relations," 27; Increase Mather, *A Discourse Concerning the Uncertainty of the Times of Men* (Boston, 1697), repr. in Miller and Johnson, eds., *The Puritans*, 1:348. See also Arthur Dent, *The Plain Mans Pathway to Heaven* (London, 1610), 130; Russel, *Seven Sermons*, 89.

53. Minkema, "Windsor Church Relations," 42, 30, 36–37; *Shepard Notebook*, 166, 176, 148; *Diary of Michael Wigglesworth*, 100.

54. Minkema, "Windsor Church Relations," 33; *Shepard Notebook*, 148, 176; *Diary of Michael Wigglesworth*, 116, 118.

55. Mather, *Discourse*, in Miller and Johnson, eds., *The Puritans*, 1:348.

56. [Rowlandson], *Soveraignty*, 365; *Shepard Notebook*, 108; Lilley B. Eaton, *Genealogical History of the Town of Reading, Mass.* (Boston, 1874), 104. As a youth the minister John Brock "was taken sick of the Small Pox"; the illness seems to have prompted him to apply for church membership. "The Autobiographical Memoranda of John Brock, 1636–1659," ed. Clifford K. Shipton, American Antiquarian Society, *Proceedings* 53 (1943), 97. John Winthrop meditated on the significance of a "dangerous . . . feaver" in his "Experiencia, 1628," *Winthrop Papers*, 5 vols. (Boston, 1929–   ), 1:412–13.

57. Edmund S. Morgan has suggested that many of the colonists hesitated to apply for church membership because they were too scrupulous in their self-examination: "New England Puritanism: Another Approach," *WMQ*, 3d Ser., 18 (1961), 241–42. Despite arguments to the contrary by Patricia Caldwell, Gerald Moran, and others (cf. David D. Hall, "On Common Ground: The Coherence of American Puritan Studies," *WMQ*, 3d Ser., 44 [1987], 216–20), the refusal of so many people to participate

in the Lord's Supper (see later in this chapter) would seem to support Morgan's argument.

58. John Dunton, *The Life and Errors of John Dunton*, 2 vols. (1705; London, 1818), 1:154–57.

59. Shepard, *Sincere Convert*, 134.

60. E.g., Samuel Willard, *The Child's Portion* (Boston, 1684); John Allin, *The Spouse of Christ Coming out of affliction, leaning upon Her Beloved* (Cambridge, Mass., 1672), a rare example of a sermon preached at the administration of the Lord's Supper; Spufford, *Small Books and Pleasant Histories*, 208–09.

61. *Shepard Notebook*, 118; *Dedham Records*, 2:6; Minkema, "Windsor Church Relations," 23, 30. My awareness of this "ethical" testimony owes much to Patrick Collinson, " 'A Magazine of Religious Patterns': An Erasmian Topic Transposed in English Puritanism," in *Godly People: Essays on English Protestantism and Puritanism* (London, 1983).

62. Increase Mather, *Meditations on the Lords Day* (Boston, 1712), 45. A Dutchman visiting Boston in the 1670s noted in his journal, on a fast day he attended, "There was no more devotion than in other churches. . . ." One Sunday he reported, "The auditors were very worldly and inattentive." Miller and Johnson, eds., *The Puritans*, 2:407.

63. John Albro, ed., *The Works of Thomas Shepard*, 3 vols. (Boston, 1853), 2:259, 169, 92.

64. Williston Walker, *The Creeds and Platforms of Congregationalism* (New York, 1893), 428–30.

65. *AC*, 32–33, 371, 412.

66. Ibid., 239, 246, 229.

67. Ibid., 227, 271–73, 336–37.

68. Obadiah Holmes ms., quoted in Isaac Backus, *A History of New England with Particular Reference to the Baptists*, 2 vols. (1771; repr., Newton, Mass., 1871), 1:174–76. I have compared Backus's version of this remarkable spiritual history to the text as edited by Edwin S. Gaustad, *Baptist Piety: The Last Will and Testimony of Obadiah Holmes* (Grand Rapids, 1978). For a somewhat parallel English case, cf. *A Legacy for Saints being several Experiences of the dealings of God with Anna Trapnel, In, and after her Conversion* (London 1654), 1–2: "I ran from Minister to Minister, from Sermon to Sermon, but I could find no rest; I could not be contented to hear once or twice in the week, but I must hear from the first day to the last. . . . I followed after that Ministry that was most pressed after by the strictest Professors. . . ."

69. Peter Pratt, *The Prey Taken from the Strong* (New London, 1725), 4, 6, 10, 15, 16, 23, 24.

70. Ibid., 24.

71. *Reliquiae Baxterianae: or, Mr. Richard Baxter's Narrative of The Most Memorable Passages of his Life and Times* (London, 1696), Pt. 1, 3, 22.

72. *Memoir of Roger Clap*, 9, 11, 8–9, 12–13.

73. "Commonplace Book of Joseph Green," 200; Samuel Willard, *The Barren Fig Trees Doom* (Boston, 1691), sig. A3 recto. This set of sermons embodies the double message I have described; for the trusting part, cf. 33, 27, 123, 34, 7.

74. *SWP*, 3:767; 2:343, 503, 500, 546; 522, 1:60, 282, 66, 100.

75. Samuel Willard, "A brief account of a strange and unusual providence of God befallen to Elizabeth Knapp of Groton," in John Demos, ed., *Remarkable Providences, 1600–1760* (New York, 1972), 365, 363, 368, 361.

76. That doctrines like predestination made people anxious was acknowledged by the ministers; cf. Robert Middlekauff, *The Mathers: Three Generations of Puritan Intellectuals, 1596–1729* (New York, 1971), 377, n. 4. For resentment of the ministry, see Minkema, "Windsor Conversion Relations," 35.

77. Samuel Willard, *The Christians Exercise by Satans Temptations* (Boston, 1701), 80, 107, 84.

78. *Shepard Notebook,* 51–52, 59, 80, 88, 94, 109, 113, 206; Minkema, "Windsor Conversion Relations," 35. Cf. *Diary of Michael Wigglesworth,* 77–78, 112.

79. Allin, *The Spouse of Christ Coming out of affliction,* 14, 16, 18. Historians cannot agree on the extent of anxiety among Puritans; for a brief résumé of this debate, see Hall, "On Common Ground," 216–21.

80. Bradford, *Of Plymouth Plantation,* 260–61; Walker, *Creeds and Platforms,* 126 n., 128, 80.

81. *Dedham Records,* 2:13–17. The emergence of these rules is traced in Morgan, *Visible Saints,* chap. 3, and in Patricia Caldwell, *The Puritan Conversion Narrative* (New York, 1983).

82. Milford Church Records (ms., Connecticut State Library); John Hancock, *A Memorial of God's Goodness* (Boston, 1739), 36–37; "Commonplace Book of Joseph Green," 244; Johnson, *WWP,* 179; Lemuel Shattuck, *A History of the Town of Concord* (Boston, 1835), 151.

83. John S. Coolidge, *The Pauline Renaissance in England: Puritanism and the Bible* (Oxford, 1970), 35, and passim.

84. Walker, *Creeds and Platforms,* 155–56.

85. Shattuck, *History of . . . Concord,* 151.

86. *Memoir of Roger Clap,* 10; *Shepard Notebook,* 126.

87. "Commonplace Book of Joseph Green," 217–18; Samuel G. Drake, *Annals of Witchcraft in New England* (Boston, 1869), 265; *Essex Court Recs.,* 4:76–77; and many other places.

88. *[Sixth] Report of the Record Commissioners of the City of Boston* (1884), 83–84; "Boston Town Records," in *[Second] Report of the Record Commissioners of the City of Boston* (1877), 5.

89. "Commonplace Book of Joseph Green," 245. For the larger story, cf. Hall, *Faithful Shepherd,* chap. 8.

90. *SWP,* 2:449.

91. Raymond P. Stearns, ed., "Correspondence of John Woodbridge, Jr., and Richard Baxter," *New England Quarterly* 10 (1937), 564. James Bird of Farmington "departed the house" rather than accept the implications of a closely divided vote on his application for membership. Farmington Church Records (ms., Connecticut State Library).

92. *Fiske Notebook,* 3–5, 11–12.

93. Hall, *Faithful Shepherd,* 99, 201 n. 12; Stearns, ed., "The Correspondence Between John Woodbridge, Jr., and Richard Baxter," 576. A layman's dissatisfaction with excessive purity is vividly expressed in Richard C. Simmons, "Richard Sadler's Account of the Massachusetts Churches," *NEQ* 42 (1969), 411–20.

94. Walker, *Creeds and Platforms,* chap. 11; Robert G. Pope, *The Half-Way Covenant: Church Membership in Puritan New England* (Princeton, N.J., 1969).

95. Increase Mather, *Pray for the Rising Generation* (Boston, 1679), 12, quoted in E. Brooks Holifield, *The Covenant Sealed: The Development of Puritan Sacramental Theology in Old and New England, 1570–1720* (New Haven, Conn., 1974), 189; Walker, *Creeds*

and Platforms, 330–31; Thomas Shepard, The Church-Membership of Children, and their right to Baptism (Cambridge, Mass., 1663), 6, 10; "[Michael] Wigglesworth's Elegy on the Rev. Benjamin Bunker, of Malden," NEHGR 26 (1872), 12.

96. Records of the First Church at Dorchester, 168; John Davenport, Another Essay for Investigation of the Truth (Cambridge, Mass., 1663), sig. A4 recto, verso, 71.

97. Eaton, Genealogical History of Reading, 55.

98. [Ann Fiske], A Confession of Faith: or, A Summary of Divinity (Boston, 1704), 8.

99. Shepard Notebook, 66, 194–95, 185, and see also 140, 148; Fiske Notebook, 7, 234.

100. This term was introduced into Puritan studies by Edmund S. Morgan as part of his effort to explain why church membership declined in the late seventeenth century; Morgan, The Puritan Family: Religion and Domestic Relations in Seventeenth-Century New England, rev. ed. (1944; New York, 1966), chap. 7. But I follow Gerald F. Moran's reinterpretation of the relationship between family structure and church membership in viewing tribalism as positive in its consequences, that is, as producing more church members. Moran, "Religious Renewal, Puritan Tribalism, and the Family in Seventeenth-Century Milford, Connecticut," WMQ, 3d Ser., 36 (1979), 236–54.

101. Shepard Notebook, 167, 140, 211; Fiske Notebook, 9, 95; Diary of Michael Wigglesworth, 118; "Commonplace Book of Joseph Green," 234–35. Conversely, Richard Mather, responding to the news of Abraham Warner's suicide, warned Dorchester young people "not to pleass themselves with this that they weer the Children of godly parents as it seems this yong man was. . . ." Records of the First Church at Dorchester, 33. Thomas Shepard warned young people in Cambridge that "there were many sons of perdition in godly families," a message that a person who grew up in such a family (and cited it in his relation) "thought . . . was spoken to me." Diary of Michael Wigglesworth, 119. As the witchcraft cases indicate, people believed that evil also descended within families.

102. Seaborn Cotton baptized a newborn son one day later, or two; cf. "Record of the Rev. Seaborn Cotton, of Hampton, N.H.," NEHGR 33 (1879), 35. Similar haste is indicated in "Diary of Rev. William Homes of Chilmark, Martha's Vineyard, 1689–1746," NEHGR 48 (1894), 448. Benjamin Franklin was baptized the day he was born. The emotions of parents are suggested in the minister John Bayley's reflections: Magnalia, 1:620–21. There is no specific indication of the folk belief (John Brand, Observations on the Popular Antiquities of Great Britain [London, 1849], 335) that children were highly vulnerable to witches before they were baptized. Yet I surmise that it lingered in the background. A newborn child, gravely ill (she died the next day), was "baptised in her father's House" in 1716: Sewall Diary, 2:837–38.

103. [Rowlandson], Soveraignty, 329; Fiske Notebook, 7. No scholarly cliché is more misleading than statements to the effect that Puritans did not allow themselves to love their children or mourn them when they died. Many of the witchcraft cases involved sick or dying children, and the grief of parents was intense. Mary Johnson's grief was so overwhelming that she fantasized the Devil would enable her to see her child again; John Hale, A Modest Enquiry into the Nature of Witchcraft (Boston, 1702), 19. The distress of John Kelly at the death of his daughter is indicated in his testimony accusing a neighbor of witchcraft; Hoadly transcripts, Connecticut Historical Society, 82. The evidence against another accused witch included his not grieving when a child died; Samuel G. Drake, Annals of Witchcraft in New England (1869; repr., New York, 1967), 239, 245. See also "Commonplace Book of Joseph Green," 250, 253; and below, Chapter 3, p. 155. Recent studies substantiate this argument: Laurel Thatcher Ulrich, Good Wives: Image and Reality in the Lives of Women in Northern New England 1650–1750 (New

York, 1982), 153–63; Michael MacDonald, *Mystical Bedlam: Madness, Anxiety, and Healing in Seventeenth-Century England* (Cambridge, 1981), 80–82; Alan Macfarlane, *The Family Life of Ralph Josselin* (1970; repr., New York, 1977), 116–18, 164–66.

104. William McLoughlin, *New England Dissent, 1630–1833: The Baptists and the Separation of Church and State,* 2 vols. (Cambridge, Mass., 1971), 1:46; Shepard, *The Church-Membership of Children,* 22–23, sig. A2 recto, verso; Cotton Mather quoted in Holifield, *Covenant Sealed,* 190. Cf. John Warden, *A Practical Essay on the Sacrament of Baptism* (Edinburgh, 1724), 105. It suggests the power of popular belief that even a minister as puristically inclined as Charles Chauncy spoke of the "great blessing, and precious priviledges" accruing to children who were "born of such Parents," though Chauncy hastened to add that "spiritual Freedome comes not by discent. . . ." *The Plain Doctrine of the Justification of a Sinner* (London, 1659), 28.

105. Jonathan Edwards, *An Humble Inquiry Into The Rules of the Word of God* (Boston, 1749), 36; and cf. 125. See also an English nonconformist minister's similar complaint: Warden, *Practical Essay,* 61.

106. Benjamin Wadsworth, *A Dialogue Between a Minister and his Neighbour* (Boston, 1724), preface, sig. A2 recto, verso; Cotton Mather, *A Companion for Communicants,* 62. See also Samuel Willard, *The Child's Portion: or the Unseen Glory of the Children of God* (Boston, 1684), 190. For other complaints, cf. Holifield, *Covenant Sealed,* 204–6. James Obelkevitch, remarking the phenomenon in nineteenth-century Lincolnshire of infrequent participation in the sacrament, interprets it as socially determined: "What appears to have made [poor people] fearful was not its intrinsic sacramental power but the 'solemn' and 'awful' consequences in store for unworthy and presumptuous recipients. Considering themselves too sinful and unworthy, they mentally reserved it for the gentry. . . ." *Religion and Society: South Lindsey, 1825–1875* (Oxford, 1976), 271–72. But in New England many persons of high status hesitated to attend, and more women than men qualified for the sacrament. See the citations in n. 113, below.

107. John Cotton, *Spiritual Milke for Boston Babes,* repr. in Everett Emerson, *John Cotton* (New York, 1965), 130; *The First and Second Prayerbooks of Edward VI* (London, 1949), 383; *Shepard Notebook,* 158. The theology of the ministers is sketched in Holifield, *Covenant Sealed,* chaps. 5 and 7; and see Hambrick-Stowe, *Practice of Piety,* 125–26.

108. John Dod and Robert Cleaver, *Ten Sermons tending chiefely to the fitting of men for the worthy receiving of the Lords Supper* (London, 1610), 2.

109. Ibid., 106; Bayley, *Practice of Piety,* 521–22, 586.

110. Boston booksellers ordered Thomas Doolittle's *Treatise* repeatedly, and requested manuals by Joseph Flavel and Jeremiah Burroughs less frequently. Worthington C. Ford, *The Boston Book Market, 1679–1700* (Boston, 1917), 118, 141, 155, 160, 101, 111, 127.

111. Thomas Doolittle, *Treatise Concerning the Lords Supper: with Three Dialogues for the more full Information of the Weak, in the Nature and Use of this Sacrament* (1665; London, 1687), 42–44, 60, sig. A4 verso; Somerville, *Popular Religion in Restoration England,* 41.

112. Mather, *Companion for Communicants,* 81, 84; *Diary of Michael Wigglesworth,* 24; Cotton Mather, *Pillars of Salt* (Boston, 1699), 46–47. See also *MHS Proc.,* 2d Ser., 12 (1871), 97.

113. *Fiske Notebook,* 9; Benjamin Colman, *Reliquiae Turellae, et Lachrymae Paternae* (Boston, 1735), 110–11. Like others in New England, Mrs. Turell consulted Matthew Henry's *Communicants Companion* (p. 112). Not surviving, though known to her father, is her spiritual diary in which she wrote about her doubts. Elizabeth Price, who died

when she was seventeen, perceived the Lord's Supper as "designed only for Christians of more than ordinary attainments in holiness, and satisfaction about their good estate," and reasoned that "she dare not venture to approach to it. . . ." Charles Chauncy, *Early Piety recommended and exemplify'd* (Boston, 1732), 17. Michael Wigglesworth tried to ease his struggle to feel qualified for communion by articulating two meanings for the sacrament, each of which relieved him of the dangers of unworthy participation. *Diary of Michael Wigglesworth,* 44. I pass by several other references to ministers.

114. Bayley, *Practice of Piety,* 529; Mather, *Companion for Communicants,* 76; Wadsworth, *Dialogue,* 2, 38.

115. Wadsworth, *Dialogue,* 74–75. The English Puritan minister Thomas Goodwin viewed the Lord's supper as "a communion, the [highest] outward pledge, ratification, and testimony of love and amity among his members themselves . . . a lovefeast, in that they eat and drink together at one and the same table." J. Sears McGee, *The Godly Man in Stuart England: Anglicans, Puritans, and the Two Tables, 1620–1670* (New Haven, Conn., 1976), 203; for other important statements of this ethic by Puritan ministers whose writings circulated in the colonies, cf. 172–82.

116. "Danvers Church Records," *NEHGR* 11 (1857), 316; Francis A. Pole, "The Treason of Lieut. John Gould," Topsfield Historical Society, *Collections* 3 (1897), 179; *SWP,* 1:95; *Magnalia,* 2:397; *Dorchester Church Records,* 79; *Fiske Notebook,* 67, 197; and cf. *Essex Court Recs.,* 4:281.

117. *First and Second Prayerbooks of Edward VI,* 398.

118. Bailyn, ed., *Apologia of Robert Keayne,* 62; Minkema, "Windsor Church Relations," 30. A minister's plea that neighbors not engage in "revenge" is noted in *Essex Court Recs.,* 6:253.

119. Willard, *Child's Portion,* 190.

120. Matthew Henry, *The Communicant's Companion: or, Instructions and Helps For the Right Receiving of the Lord's Supper,* 10th ed. (Boston, 1731), 40–45; Samuel Willard, *Some Brief Sacramental Meditations Preparatory for Communion at the Great Ordinance of the Supper,* 2nd ed. (1711; Boston, 1743), 34–35, 42; Wadsworth, *Dialogue,* 67, 35; Mather, *Communicants Companion,* 76–78; Willard, *Barren Fig Trees Doom,* quoted in Hall, *Faithful Shepherd,* 255. For all of Thomas Doolittle's fearful language, the real emphasis of his manual was encouragement.

121. Some of this silver is illustrated in Jonathan Fairbanks and Robert Trent, *New England Begins: The Seventeenth Century,* 3 vols. (Boston, 1982), 2:143–44; gifts to churches and ministers are reported in *Dedham Historical Register* 2 (1891), 132, and many other such records.

122. "Diaries of John Hull," 189.

123. *Essex Court Recs.,* 6:423, 274; 7:49–50; Connecticut Historical Society, *Collections* 22 (1928), 54.

124. *Essex Court Recs.,* 5:354; S. E. Morison, ed., *Records of the Suffolk County Court, 1671–1688,* 2 vols., *CSM Pub.* 29–30 (1933), 1:115.

125. A ship captain was described by a witness in 1672 as "an Athest beleving that there was nither god nor Devell hell or heaven" (*Suffolk Court Records,* 1:86), but he was probably not a resident of New England. My interpretation of moral misbehavior owes much to Roger Thompson, *Sex in Middlesex: Popular Mores in a Massachusetts County, 1649 to 1699* (Amherst, Mass., 1986). Interpretations of atheism in seventeenth-century Europe are cited in note 48 of the Introduction. On the basis of ecclesiastical court records in early-seventeenth-century Wiltshire, Martin Ingram concludes that "cases concerning the expression of heretical views were exceedingly rare.

. . . The instances I have quoted at least suggest that atheistic or near-atheistic ideas were not unknown. . . ." "Ecclesiastical Justice in Wiltshire, 1600–1640" (D. Phil. thesis, Oxford, 1976), 81.

126. *SWP*, 1:68–69.

127. *SWP*, 2:594; 1:116–17; 2:357, 441, 448, 452; *Essex Court Recs.*, 6:298; 7:138; *Sewall Diary*, 1:284, 287. Cf. the exchange of texts between Ann Putnam and Rebecca Nurse described by Deodat Lawson, *A Brief and True Narrative Of some Remarkable Passages Relating to . . . Witchcraft* (Boston, 1692), 6–7.

128. Paul Boyer and Stephen Nissenbaum, *Salem Possessed: The Social Origins of Witchcraft* (Cambridge, Mass., 1974), 173. Sarah Cloyse's behavior is described by Robert Calef in *More Wonders of the Invisible World* (London, 1700), 93; *SWP*, 1:231.

129. *SWP*, 1:153.

130. Shattuck, *History of . . . Concord*, 150 note.

131. Cohen, *God's Caress*, chap. 6.

132. Walker, *Creeds and Platforms*, 429–30.

CHAPTER 4

1. William Bradford, *Of Plymouth Plantation* (New York, 1981), 69, 25, 42, 46, 51.

2. James Walsh, "Holy Time and Sacred Space in Puritan New England," *American Quarterly* 32 (1980), 79–95; Natalie Zemon Davis, "The Sacred and the Body Social in Sixteenth-Century Lyon," *Past and Present* 90 (1981), 40–70.

3. Bradford, *Of Plymouth Plantation*, 69. My narrative does not take account of Sabbatarianism and household devotions, two practices that distinguished the lifestyle of the "godly" in England and New England from their neighbors.

4. Cotton Mather, *Wonders of the Invisible World* (1693; repr., London, 1862), 13–14.

5. For an amusing story in this regard, cf. Samuel Goodrich, *Recollections of a Lifetime*, 2 vols. (New York, 1857), 1:158–59.

6. Samuel Moodey, *A Summary Account of the Life and Death of Joseph Quasson* (Boston, 1726), 25.

7. Peter Burke, *Popular Culture in Early Modern Europe* (New York, 1978), chap. 7.

8. [Joshua Scottow], *A Narrative Of the Planting of the Massachusetts Colony Anno 1628* (Boston, 1694), 48, 46.

9. Pierre Goubert, *The Ancien Régime: French Society 1600–1750*, trans. Steve Cox (1969; New York, 1974), 279; Paul H. Kocher, *Science and Religion in Elizabethan England* (New York, 1969), 98; Robert Lemon, comp., *Catalogue of A Collection of Printed Broadsides* (London, 1866), 39.

10. *Winthrop Journal*, 1:306–7; 2:81–82, 223–24; "Scituate and Barnstable Church Records," *NEHGR* 10 (1856), 37; Lilley B. Eaton, *Genealogical History of the Town of Reading, Mass.* (Boston, 1874), 104; Nathaniel Morton, *New-Englands Memoriall* (Cambridge, Mass., 1669), 37. Richard P. Gildrie, "The Ceremonial Puritan: Days of Humiliation and Thanksgiving," *NEHGR* 136 (1982), 3–16, enumerates fast days by cause. See also the description by a visiting Dutchman of a Boston fast day: Perry Miller and Thomas H. Johnson, eds., *The Puritans*, rev. ed., 2 vols. (New York, 1963), 2:406–7.

11. Samuel Deane, *History of Scituate, Massachusetts* (Boston, 1831), 39–40; *Winthrop Journal*, 1:238; "Scituate and Barnstable Church Records," 39. John Hull notes a fast

that failed to work: "The Diaries of John Hull," American Antiquarian Society, *Transactions and Collections* 3 (1857), 184.

12. *Winthrop Journal*, 1:202.

13. "Scituate and Barnstable Church Records," 42, 38, 40.

14. *Fiske Notebook*, 78–79. In general see William DeLoss Love, *The Fast and Thanksgiving Days of New England* (Boston, 1895).

15. John Davenport, *Gods Call to His People to Turn Unto Him* (Cambridge, 1669), 20, quoted in Gail Sussman Marcus, " 'Due Execution of the Generall Rules of Righteousness': Criminal Procedure in New Haven Town and Colony, 1638–1658," in David D. Hall et al., eds., *Saints and Revolutionaries: Essays on Early American History* (New York, 1984), 122. According to Lewis Bayley, the purpose of a fast was that "we may escape the iudgement of the Lord: not for the merit of our fasting (which is none) but for the mercy of God, who hath promised to remoove his Iudgements from us, when wee by fasting doe unfainedly humble our selves before him." *The Practice of Pietie*, 27th ed. (London, 1631), 516.

16. Charles E. Hambrick-Stowe, *The Practice of Piety: Puritan Devotional Disciplines in Seventeenth-Century New England* (Chapel Hill, N.C., 1982), 19–22; "Scituate and Barnstable Church Records," 39; *Records of the First Church at Dorchester in New England 1636–1734* (Boston, 1891), 32.

17. *Records of the First Church at Dorchester*, 42.

18. Ibid., 36–37.

19. *Winthrop Journal*, 2:91; *[Sixth] Report of the Record Commissioners of the City of Boston* (Boston, 1884), 200. For this politics, see David D. Hall, *The Faithful Shepherd: A History of the New England Ministry in the Seventeenth Century* (Chapel Hill, N.C., 1972), 228–37.

20. Thomas Shepard, *Wine for Gospel Wantons* (Boston, 1668), 13.

21. *Winthrop Journal*, 1:208; *AC*, 156–57.

22. Love, *Fast and Thanksgiving Days*, 200.

23. See below, Chapter 5.

24. *Winthrop Journal*, 2:12–14.

25. Ibid., 1:329; 2:12–13.

26. Ibid., 1:310–14.

27. *Winthrop Journal*, 2:132–33; *Fiske Notebook*, 207, 66. Many more examples of "confession" in the context of church discipline can be found in Richard D. Pierce, ed., *The Records of the First Church in Boston 1630–1868*, CSM Pub., 39 (1961), and in other published church and court records.

28. Exiled to Rhode Island, Anne Hutchinson was unresponsive to the pleas of Boston church that she reform her ways under sentence of excommunication; *AC*, 390–95.

29. This point is emphasized by John M. Murrin, "Magistrates, Sinners, and a Precarious Liberty: Trial by Jury in Seventeenth-Century New England," in Hall et al., eds., *Saints and Revolutionaries*, 152–206; Marcus, " 'Due Execution,' " 101. See also the preface to the Massachusetts law code of 1648, in Max Farrand, ed., *The Laws and Liberties of Massachusetts* (1648, repr., Cambridge, Mass., 1929).

30. Marcus, " 'Due Execution,' " 121, 129; see also Murrin, "Magistrates, Sinners, and a Precarious Liberty," esp. 164. The Essex County Court records contain many similar statements; for still others, cf. Lawrence W. Towner, "True Confessions and Dying Warnings in Colonial New England," in *Sibley's Heir: A Volume in Memory of Clifford Kenyon Shipton*, CSM Pub., 59 (Boston, 1982), 523–39.

31. William H. Whitmore, *The Colonial Laws of Massachusetts* (Boston, 1889), 55;

Murrin, "Magistrates, Sinners, and a Precarious Liberty," 178–79; *Magnalia*, 2:406; Marcus, " 'Due Execution,' " 115. For similar procedures in Plymouth see Bradford, *Of Plymouth Plantation*, 355–56.

32. *Winthrop Journal*, 2:219, 317–18; N. B. Shurtleff, ed., *Records of the Colony of New Plymouth*, 12 vols. (Boston, 1855–61), 5:262; Increase Mather, *A Relation of the Troubles* (Boston, 1677), 75; *Magnalia*, 2:560. See also R. G. Tomlinson, *Witchcraft Trials of Connecticut* (Hartford, 1978), 29; *Magnalia*, 2:405.

33. George Lyman Kittredge, *The Old Farmer and His Almanac* (Boston, 1904), 71–77.

34. *Essex Court Recs.*, 3:52–53; Roger Thompson, *Sex in Middlesex: Popular Mores in a Massachusetts County, 1649–1699* (Amherst, Mass., 1986), 135; Joseph Smith, ed., *Colonial Justice in Western Massachusetts, 1639–1702* (Cambridge, Mass., 1961), 390. Rebecca Hale told a servant woman who threatened to kill her, "It would be discovered"; when the servant proposed to conceal the crime by destroying the body, Rebecca drew on the lore of wonders to respond, "I had heard of murthers of children that weere discovered." *Essex Court Recs.*, 7:46. Describing "secret" sinners, Obadiah Holmes imagined them reflecting thus: "In the dark, these sinners are often thinking and saying, None sees." Edwin S. Gaustad, ed., *Baptist Piety: The Last Will and Testimony of Obadiah Holmes* (New York, 1980), 119.

35. Samuel Danforth, *The Cry of Sodom Enquired Into* (Cambridge, Mass., 1674), 17.

36. *Acts & Mon.*, 7:159; William Turner, *A Compleat History of the Most Remarkable Providences* (London, 1697), 3rd pagination, chap. 28, p. 113.

37. *Essex Court Recs.*, 3:33; Increase Mather, *A Sermon Occasioned by the Execution of a Man Found Guilty of Murder* (Boston, 1686), 18; Turner, *Compleat History*, chap. 113, p. 28.

38. J. Hammond Trumbull and Charles J. Hoadly, eds., *The Public Records of the Colony of Connecticut*, 15 vols. (Hartford, Conn., 1850–90), 1:197; Danforth, *Cry of Sodom*, 8–9; cf. John Reynolds, *The Triumph of Gods Revenge against the crying and execrable sinne of . . . murther* (London, 1640).

39. Execution in New England was by hanging, though a few burnings occurred of Negroes and Indians convicted of extraordinary crimes. Dorothy Talby (see below) requested execution by beheading, as "less painful and less shameful." Her request was not granted; *Winthrop Journal*, 1:283. For English procedures, cf. *A true Copy of Sir Henry Hide's Speech on the Scaffold* (London, 1650); my description is based on many such broadsides and pamphlets in the Bodleian Library, Oxford, and the British Library, London.

40. I have benefited from essays written by Daniel Cohen (Brandeis University) as part of his Ph.D. thesis on executions in New England; see also J. A. Sharpe, " 'Last Dying Speeches': Religion, Ideology and Public Execution in Seventeenth-Century England," *Past and Present* 107 (1985), 144–67.

41. John Rogers, *Death The certain Wages of Sin to the Impenitent* (Boston, 1701), 144; *Magnalia*, 2:413. (*Pillars of Salt*, Mather's collection of criminal stories, was included in the *Magnalia;* I cite the separate publication as well as this reprinting.)

42. Joshua Moodey, *An Exhortation to a Condemned Malefactor* (Boston, 1686), bound with I. Mather, *Sermon Occasioned*, 2nd printing (1687), 85; Cotton Mather, *A Sorrowful Spectacle* (Boston, 1715), 88.

43. Rogers, *Death The certain Wages*, 143–52, 122, 143.

44. *Magnalia*, 2:410–13; I. Mather, *Sermon Occasioned* (2nd printing), 22–23, 29–30, 35–36.

45. Moodey, *Summary Account*, 9–27, 2.

46. [Cotton Mather], *Pillars of Salt* (Boston, 1699), 61, 85, 99; Cotton Mather, *Useful Remarks* (New London, 1723), 29–43.

47. *Winthrop Journal*, 1:283; 2:187–89 (notable in this account is the disagreement among the magistrates).

48. [Mather], *Pillars of Salt*, 68, 103. William Adams noted in his journal in 1669 that he "was at Boston, saw a thief and an Indian hanged; the Indian turned off singing." "Memoir of the Rev. William Adams," *MHS Coll.*, 4th Ser., 1 (1852), 10. Samuel Sewall mentions someone laughing; *Sewall Diary*, 1:22.

49. Benjamin Colman, *It is a Fearful Thing to Fall into the Hands of the Living God* (Boston, 1726), 35–38.

50. *An Account of the Behaviour and last Dying Speeches Of the Six Pirates . . . Executed on Charles River* (Boston, 1704); Mather, *Sorrowful Spectacle*, 83.

51. I. Mather, *Sermon Occasioned*, 44. It was at Increase Mather's sermon in the "Old Meetinghouse" that "the Gallery crack'd" from the weight of so many people crowding in to hear him preach and see James Morgan; preacher, prisoner, and people promptly moved to Third Church. *Sewall Diary*, 1:99; the quite possibly exaggerated figure of five thousand was John Dunton's estimate; cf. *John Dunton's Letters from New-England* (1867), excerpted in Miller and Johnson, eds., *The Puritans*, 2:419.

52. Sharpe, " 'Last Dying Speeches,' "; John L. Lievsay, "Newgate Penitents: Further Aspects of Elizabethan Pamphlet Sensationalism," *Huntington Library Quarterly* 7 (1943–44), 47–69. Matthias Shaaber emphasizes the formulaic nature of these scaffold narratives, including the feature of last-minute confessions: *Some Forerunners of the Newspaper in England, 1476–1622* (Philadelphia, 1928), 98–99, 144. See also H. S. Bennett, *English Books and Readers, 1558–1603* (Cambridge, 1965), 232ff.

53. John Dunton, *The Life and Errors of John Dunton*, 2 vols. (1705; London, 1818), 1:96; Worthington C. Ford, ed., *The Diary of Cotton Mather*, 2 vols. (1911; New York, 1957), 1:54. See also Thomas J. Holmes, *Cotton Mather: A Bibliography of His Works*, 3 vols. (Cambridge, Mass., 1940), 1:109–13.

54. Executions occurred in the early years of the colonies. That the local book trade took so long to exploit a familiar genre is a puzzle. The first published execution sermon (not counting Danforth's *Cry of Sodom*) was Increase Mather's *The Wicked mans Portion* (Boston, 1675); the printer John Foster had just begun his business.

55. Fragments of a possible text (no original survives) are printed in Leonard Labaree et al., eds., *The Papers of Benjamin Franklin* (New Haven, 1959), 1:7; Holmes, *Cotton Mather*, 3:1148–49.

56. *A Mournful Poem on the Death of John Ormsby and Matthew Cushing . . . executed . . . 17th of October, 1734* (Boston, 1734), and *Advice from the Dead to the Living . . . Occasioned by the untimely Death of poor Julian* (Boston, ca. 1733), reproduced in Ola Winslow, ed., *American Broadside Verse* (New Haven, Conn., 1930).

57. *Winthrop Journal*, 2:163.

58. Sharpe, " 'Last Dying Speeches,' " 150.

59. *Magnalia*, 2:407, 408–9; I. Mather, *Sermon Occasioned*, 12; Danforth, *Cry of Sodom*, 12, 13–14.

60. I. Mather, *Sermon Occasioned*, 30, 20; *Magnalia*, 2:420–21; C. Mather, *Useful Remarks*, 13.

61. *The Confession and Dying Warning of Hugh Henderson* (Boston, 1737); Roger Thompson, *Unfit for Modest Ears* (London, 1979), passim.

62. *Sewall Diary*, 1:509.

63. See above, Chapter 3, pp. 133–34.

64. Bernard Bailyn, ed., *The Apologia of Robert Keayne* (New York, 1965), 61, 49,

52, 47–48. See also John Wheelwright's letter to the Massachusetts General Court in which he distinguished between "liberty of conscience" and "confession" (*Winthrop Journal*, 2:166–67). Ezekiel Cheever rejected pleas that he confess to charges, saying it would harm his conscience: "The Trial of Ezekiel Cheever before the Church at New Haven . . . 1649," Connecticut Historical Society, *Collections* 1 (Hartford, Conn., 1860), 42, 46. Cf. *Fiske Notebook*, 79–81.

65. *Apologia of Robert Keayne*, 61.

66. Whitmore, ed., *Colonial Laws of Massachusetts*, 156, 154, 219–20; N. B. Shurt-leff, ed., *Records of the Governor and Company of the Massachusetts Bay*, 5 vols. (Boston, 1853–54), 2:85. It is tempting to suggest that local communities resisted vigorous prosecution of dissent. Certainly the deputies in the Massachusetts General Court dragged their feet in the 1640s, and again in the 1660s. Yet it is also true that the magistrates and ministers were increasingly divided among themselves. Cf. Hall, *Faithful Shepherd*, 128–29, 230; Jonathan M. Chu, *Neighbors, Friends, or Madmen: The Puritan Adjustment to Quakerism in Seventeenth-Century Massachusetts Bay* (Westport, Conn., 1985).

67. *Acts & Mon.*, 4:635, 728–29, 608, 611.

68. Ibid., 7:91, 82, and passim.

69. John Clark, *Ill Newes From New-England: or A Narative of New-Englands Persecu-tion* (London, 1652), repr., *MHS Coll.*, 4th Ser., 2 (1854), 49–51; Isaac Backus, *A History of New England with Special Reference to the Baptists*, 2 vols. (1771; repr., Newton, Mass., 1871), 1:190–92, 195–98. John Winthrop (*Journal*, 2:177) reported that a man named "Painter" of Hingham, whipped in 1644 for espousing Baptist ideas, "endured his punishment with much obstinacy, and when he was loosed, he said boastingly, that God had marvellously assisted him." The game played itself out with his neigh-bors offering countertestimony; 177–78.

70. [Thomas Maule], *New-England Persecutors Mauld With their own Weapons* (New York, 1697), 19; George Keith, *The Pretended Antidote Proved Poyson* (Philadelphia, 1690), 12.

71. George Bishop, *New-England Judged. In Two Parts* (1661, 1667; repr., abridged, 1703), Pt. 1, 75, 125, 121; John Whiting, *Truth and Innocency Defended* (London, 1702), 188, 185; Backus, *History of New England*, 1:256–57.

72. S[amuel] G[roome], *A Glasse for the People of New England* ([London], 1676), 21.

73. Bishop, *New England Judged*, Pt. 2, 444, 482, 485; [Maule], *New-England Perse-cutors*, 32. That ordinary people shared this perception of the ministers is evident from *Essex Court Recs.*, 3:95; 7:407.

74. *Winthrop Journal*, 1:297; Bishop, *New England Judged*, Pt. 1, 225, 178; Backus, *History of New England*, 1:254.

75. John Rogers, *A Brief Account Of some of the late Suffering of several Baptists . . . in New-London County* (New York, 1726), 13, 23.

76. John Hale, *A Modest Enquiry into the Nature of Witchcraft* (Boston, 1702), 1–2 (I have changed Hale's plural to the singular).

77. Hale, *Modest Enquiry*, 20, 19; R. G. Tomlinson, *Witchcraft Trials of Connecticut* (Hartford, Conn., 1978), 5; Increase Mather, *An Essay for the Recording of Illustrious Providences* (1684; repr., London, 1856), 98. Still another, of Mrs. Glover, is reported in Cotton Mather, *Memorable Providences, Relating to Witchcrafts and Possessions* (Boston, 1689), 6–11. Linguistic difficulties (Mrs. Glover, a washerwoman, spoke Gaelic as her native language) have led several modern historians to suppose that she did not un-derstand the questions being asked, or the significance of her answers. Historians of witchcraft in England, and elsewhere, have suggested that ministers imposed the idea of the Devil's compact on lay people. From this point of view, the statements I have

quoted may represent the answers people gave to leading questions. But I agree with Christina Larner, the late historian of witchcraft in Scotland, that "popular" and "elite" conceptions of the Devil had become confused by the middle of the seventeenth century. Cf. David D. Hall, "Witchcraft and the Limits of Interpretation," *NEQ* 58 (1985), 253–81.

78. Hale, *Modest Enquiry*, 26, 33; *SWP*, 1:65–72. The confessions made by other "witches" may be found in this collection.

79. Taylor, *Witchcraft Delusion in Connecticut*, 118.

80. Samuel G. Drake, *Annals of Witchcraft in New England* (Boston, 1869), 235, 243, 275–76, 280.

81. *SWP*, 1:246–47, 166, 164, 104; see also 2:482; 3:837.

82. *SWP*, 2:559; 1:97–99, 94; Robert Calef, *More Wonders of the Invisible World* (London, 1700), 109. Cotton Mather attributed the death of a Northampton man to "murder" by a witch, as did, apparently, the victim himself: *Memorable Providences*, 56–59.

83. *SWP*, 1:261; Drake, *Annals of Witchcraft*, 286, 224, 228; Taylor, *Witchcraft Delusion in Connecticut*, 68; Dexter, ed., *Ancient Town Records*, 1:245. Carol Karlsen argues that historians should not regard the behavioral traits ascribed to witches as accurate; I think otherwise. Karlsen, *The Devil in the Shape of a Woman: Witchcraft in Colonial New England* (New York, 1987), chap. 4.

84. Sidney Perley, *The History of Boxford . . . from the Earliest Settlement* (Boxford, Mass., 1880), 122. One of the "Grounds for Examination of a Witch" written out by a magistrate in Connecticut was "3. If after cursing, there follow death or at least mischiefe to the party." Taylor, *Witchcraft Delusion*, 40. Cf. Jeanne Favret-Saada, *Les mots, la mort, les sorts: La sorcellerie dans le Bocage* (Paris, 1977).

85. Drake, *Annals of Witchcraft*, 104; the possible citations are innumerable. It was Keith Thomas (following George Lyman Kittredge and C. L'estrange Ewen) who perceived the role of services requested and refused in witchcraft accusations.

86. Hale, *Modest Enquiry*, 37.

87. *SWP*, 1:279–80; Drake, *Annals of Witchcraft*, 234.

88. Hale, *Modest Enquiry*, 25; John Demos, ed., *Remarkable Providences, 1600–1760* (New York, 1972), 361; Mather, *Memorable Providences*, 31.

89. Demos, ed., *Remarkable Providences*, 360–61. Cf. the case of Mary Jones, who confessed to theft under pressure from her neighbors; Hale, *Modest Enquiry*, 17.

90. *SWP*, 1:59, 66; 3:777.

91. Ibid., 2:531–32.

92. Mather, *Memorable Providences*, 2nd pagination, 2, 20; and cf. the fast-day sermon embedded in Mather, *Wonders of the Invisible World*, 79–107.

93. Mather, *Memorable Providences*, 48–53. Cf. Anne Kibbey, "Mutations of the Supernatural: Witchcraft, Remarkable Providences, and the Power of Puritan Men," *American Quarterly* 34 (1982), 125–48.

94. Mather, *Wonders of the Invisible World*, 92.

95. Hale, *Modest Enquiry*, 17–18.

96. *SWP*, 2:584, 594; 1:116, 250, 261, 334, 303.

97. Ibid., 1:304; 2:491–92. Many of the confessing "witches" from Andover eventually renounced their confessions; some of their statements are printed in Charles Upham, *Salem Witchcraft with an Account of Salem Village*, 2 vols. (1867; repr., New York, 1966), 2:404–7. The pressure on them to confess was a theme of Calef, *More Wonders*.

98. Calef, *More Wonders*, 102–4; see also *Sewall Diary*, 1:294.

99. Calef, *More Wonders*, 56–63; Upham, *Salem Witchcraft*, 2:497–98; [Maule], *New-England Persecutors*, 32.

100. Love, *Fast and Thanksgiving Days*, 266–69; Calef, *More Wonders*, 143–44; *Sewall Diary*, 1:367. Michael Wigglesworth wrote Increase Mather in 1704 that he feared "(amongst our many other provocations) that God hath a Controversy with us about what was done in the time of the Witchcraft. I fear that innocent blood hath been shed. . . ." Wigglesworth proposed "a Publick and Solemn acknowledgement of it, And humiliation for it . . . by all that have been actors . . . to turn away his Judgments from the Land, and to prevent his wrath from falling upon the persons and families of such as have been Most concerned." John L. Sibley, *Biographical Sketches of Graduates of Harvard University*, 3 vols. (Cambridge, Mass., 1873–85), 1:277.

101. John Hale's confusion is manifest on every page of *A Modest Enquiry*, but see esp. pp. 10–12.

102. Bayley, *Practice of Pietie*, 625–26; James Allin, *Serious Advice to delivered Ones from Sickness* (Boston, 1679), 26–27, 24. That lay men and women shared these ideas is abundantly evident from the Cambridge testimonies; "John Dane's Narrative," *NEHGR* 8 (1854), 151; "Deacon John Paine's Journal," *Mayflower Descendants*, 8 (1906), 183.

103. Contrary to what others have suggested in attempting to describe the "way of death" among the colonists, the rate of mortality does not explain the attitudes and practices we find in early New England. Children and adults died much younger in most parts of Europe than in New England, something that is often overlooked in interpretations that stress panic or despair. I also dislike the implied determinism in such arguments. For a graphic account of a society riddled with disease and early death, cf. John McManners, *Death and the Enlightenment: Changing Attitudes to Death Among Christians and Unbelievers in Eighteenth-Century France* (Oxford, 1981).

104. Emmanuel Le Roy Ladurie, *L'argent, l'amour et la mort en pays d'oc* (Paris, 1980), though the folk tale he explicates (Aarne-Thompson 332) may not have circulated in America; Allan I. Ludwig, *Graven Images: New England Stonecarving and Its Symbols, 1650–1815* (Middletown, Conn., 1966), 274. Two studies that have much influenced my interpretation are Philippe Ariès, *The Hour of Our Death*, trans. Helen Weaver (New York, 1981), esp. Book 2; and Keith Thomas, *Religion and the Decline of Magic* (London, 1971), chap. 7. The circulation of stories about death, especially sudden death, is evident in Samuel Sewall's diary; see below, Chapter 5.

105. Funeral sermons gradually reappeared, and the colonists used other means—processions, gifts, printed elegies—to commemorate the dead and mark out the rite of passage.

106. Thomas, *Religion and the Decline of Magic*, 57, 192–98. Yet in a marvelous illustration of transatlantic survivals, a Hingham man in 1688 petitioned the Massachusetts government for the right to issue a "brief" (an appeal for funds) to cover his costs of traveling to England to receive the king's touch. Samuel A. Green, *A Centennial Address* (Groton, Mass., 1881), 41–42. It may be relevant that a royalist was governor of Massachusetts at the time. For another evocation of this rite, see below, p. 238.

107. William Perkins, *A salve for a sicke man* (Cambridge, 1597), 5–8, 23; Bayley, *Practice of Pietie*, 629; Allin, *Serious Advice*, 24, 27–28. Proposition 6 in Perkins's list of muddled popular beliefs was "That howsoever a man live, yet if he call upon God on his death-bed, and say, Lord have mercy upon me: and so go away like a lambe, he is certainly saved." *The Workes of that Famous and Worthie Minister of Christ M. W. Perkins*, 3 vols. (Cambridge, 1608–9), 1:32.

108. Lucius R. Paige, *History of Cambridge, Massachusetts, 1630–1877* (Boston, 1877), 69; Francis Minkema, "The East Windsor Conversion Relations," Connecticut Historical Society, *Bulletin* 51 (1984), 33; *Sewall Diary*, 1:299; Edmund S. Morgan, ed., *The Diary of Michael Wigglesworth 1653–1657: The Conscience of a Puritan* (1946; New York, 1965), 121, 116.

109. Sarah Goodhue, "A Valedictory and Monitory Writing," in Thomas Waters, *Ipswich in the Massachusetts Bay Colony*, 2 vols. (Ipswich, 1905), 1:519–24; *The Works of Anne Bradstreet*, ed. John Howard Ellis (1867; repr., Gloucester, 1962), 393–94.

110. Samuel Eliot Morison, ed., "The Commonplace Book of Joseph Green," *CSM Pub.*, 34 (1943), 221; *Winthrop Journal*, 1:270, 210; "The Diary of Increase Mather," *MHS Proc.*, 2d Ser., 13 (1899–1900), 342, 344, 348, 355, 364, 367.

111. *Sewall Diary*, 2:863, 1:267, and see below, Chapter 5; *SWP*, 3:795; 1:96. Cf. Stephen J. Stein, " 'For their Spiritual Good': The Northampton, Massachusetts, Prayer Bids of the 1730s and 1740s," *WMQ*, 3d Ser., 37 (1980), 261–85. Philip Read, a doctor in Concord, got himself in trouble in the early 1670s by such sentiments as these: "on a motion then & there made to pray to God for his wife then sick blasphemously Cursed bidding the Divill take you & your prayers." S. E. Morison, ed., *Records of the Suffolk County Court, 1671–1680*, 2 vols., *CSM Pub.*, 29–30 (1933), 1:114–15.

112. Hambrick-Stowe, *Practice of Piety*, 104–5.

113. John Dod and Robert Cleaver, *A godly form of houshold government* (London, 1621), no page, but follows C4;, Samuel Mather, *A Testimony from the Scripture Against Idolatry & Superstition* (Cambridge, Mass., 1672), 74.

114.. *Magnalia*, 1:521, 382–84, 544, 344, 317; 2:139; *Winthrop Journal*, 2:353.

115. Eaton, *Genealogical History of Reading*, 105.

116. Charles C. Butterfield, *The English Primer, 1529–1545* (Philadelphia, 1953), 61, 75; Thomas, *Religion and the Decline of Magic*, 61–62; George Lyman Kittredge, *Witchcraft in Old and New England* (Cambridge, Mass., 1929), 147.

117. See above, Chapter 2; Michael MacDonald, *Mystical Bedlam: Madness, Anxiety, and Healing in Seventeenth-Century England* (Cambridge, 1981), 25–32. The most prominent of the colonists who pursued astrological medicine was John Winthrop, Jr. Cf. Sibley, *Biographical Sketches*, 1:132; 94–95.

118. Henry J. Cadbury, ed., *George Foxe's "Book of Miracles"* (Cambridge, 1948); and cf. Thomas, *Religion and the Decline of Magic*, 127.

119. *Winthrop Journal*, 2:268, 209–11. Autopsies figured in some of the witchcraft cases and in other investigation of suspicious deaths. Cf. *Records of the Court of Assistants of the Colony . . . Massachusetts Bay 1630–1692*, 3 vols. (Boston, 1901–1928), 3:62.

120. Backus, *History of New England*, 1:381.

121. Perkins, *Salve for a sicke man*, 25.

122. Edward Winslow, *Good News from New England* (1624), repr. in Edward Arber, ed., *The Story of the Pilgrim Fathers* (London, 1897), 553; Thomas Thacher, *A Brief Rule to Guide the Common People . . . in the Small-Pox and Measles* (Boston, 1677). The best brief interpretation of this mixture of "natural" and "spiritual" medicine is Alan Macfarlane, "A Tudor anthropologist: George Gifford's *Discourse* and *Dialogue*," in Sydney Anglo, ed., *The Damned Art: Essays in the Literature of Witchcraft* (London, 1979), 140–55.

123. The most sophisticated explication of the ministers' mixed message and the transfer of metaphors is Margaret H. Warner, "Vindicating the Minister's Medical Role: Cotton Mather's Concept of the *Nishmath-Chajim* and the Spiritualization of Medicine," *Journal of the History of Medicine and Allied Sciences* 36 (1981), 278–95. Were I able to deal more fully with a complicated figure such as Cotton Mather, his at-

tempts to sustain and revive a scientific basis for spiritual medicine would deserve attention.

124. Hale, *Modest Enquiry*, 24; Demos, ed., *Remarkable Providences*, 361–70.

125. The case of Lydia Gilbert is instructive in this regard. After much delay, she was accused of using witchcraft to cause the death of a man who died from the accidental discharge of a gun carried by another man. Though found guilty by a jury, she was released by the magistrates. Tomlinson, *Witchcraft Trials of Connecticut*, 10–13; *Records of the Particular Court of Connecticut 1639–1663*, Connecticut Historical Society, *Collections* 22 (Hartford, 1928), 131.

126. "Diaries of John Hull," 181–82.

127. Gage, *History of Rowley*, 72; C. Mather, *Memorable Providences*, 1–38. Also relevant are the healings he performed of Mercy Short and Margaret Rule; cf. Calef, *More Wonders*, 1–10. For the broader context, cf. Thomas, *Religion and the Decline of Magic*, 51–55; and D. P. Walker, *Unclean Spirits: Possession and Exorcism in France and England in the Late Sixteenth and Early Seventeenth Centuries* (Philadelphia, 1981). Catholic priests in England, and even the rare Protestant, were tempted to assert their power to work the rite; Thomas, *Religion and the Decline of Magic*, 491–92.

128. *Magnalia*, 1:334; Barbara Ritter Dailey, "The Visitation of Sarah Wight: Holy Carnival and the Revolution of the Saints in Civil War London," *Church History* 55 (1986), 438–55; Geoffrey Chaucer, *The Canterbury Tales*, trans. Neville Coghill (Baltimore, 1952), 241; John Sena, "Melancholic Madness and the Puritans," *Harvard Theological Review* 66 (1973), 293–309.

129. Cf. Ludwig, *Graven Images*, passim; Elizabeth Carroll Reilly, *Colonial American Printers Ornaments and Illustrations* (Worcester, Mass., 1975). A fuller study of attitudes and iconography would have to take account of astonishing continuities, but also of important changes. As Ariès points out, European moralists and painters by the middle of the seventeenth century had simplified the representation of skeletons by eliminating the spectacle of decaying flesh. The continuities are evident from Douglas Gray, *Themes and Images in the Medieval English Religious Lyric* (London, 1972); and Terence Cave, *Devotional Poetry in France, c. 1570–1613* (Cambridge, 1969).

130. As Alan Macfarlane has noted of Ralph Josselin, ". . . there is nothing to suggest that he attempted to please, appease, or worship his ancestors. . . ." *The Family Life of Ralph Josselin: A Seventeenth-Century Clergyman* (Cambridge, 1970), 100. Unlike people in medieval France, the colonists were not visited by the ghosts of their ancestors (I owe this observation to J.-C. Schmitt). Nor, of course, did New England children have godparents.

131. Samuel Willard, *The Mourners Cordial against Excessive Sorrow* (Boston, 1691), 71–72, 42, 21; Edward Tompson, *Heaven the Best Country* (Boston, 1712), 67.

132. Leonard Hoar, *The Sting of Death and Death Unstung* (Boston, 1680), 3, 6–7, 9–10, 11, 21–22.

133. Cotton Mather, *The Temple Opening* (Boston, 1709), 30–31.

134. James Janeway, *A Token for Children* (1671; Boston, 1700); Cotton Mather, *An Appendix A Token for the Children of New-England* (Boston, 1700), repr. in *Magnalia*, 2:480–83. It merits pointing out that Priscilla Thornton was the daughter of a minister.

135. *Magnalia*, 2:470–71.

136. *Some Memorials on the Death of that Pious & Vertuous Man, Mr. Ebenezer Tucker, of Milton* (Boston, 1724?); *NEHGR* 6 (1852), 95; *Records of the First Church at Dorchester*, 8; "Diaries of John Hull," 156; Kenneth Murdock, ed., *Handkerchiefs from Paul Being Pious and Consolatory Verses of Puritan Massachusetts* (Cambridge, Mass., 1927), xxii–xxiii.

137. Murdock, ed., *Handkerchiefs from Paul*, 11; Ellis, ed., *Works of Anne Bradstreet*, 43–44; Benjamin Colman, *Reliquiae Turellae* (Boston, 1735), 103; T. Loe, *A Divine Discourse* . . . (New London, 1717); *An Elegy Upon the Death of several Worthy Pious Persons* (Boston?, 1717).

138. Wills of George Bowers, Elizabeth Cutter, and William Baker, Middlesex Probate Recs. transcript, NEHGS; *Essex Court Recs.* 1:87–88. This assessment of the language in New England wills rests on a survey of Connecticut and Massachusetts probate records done by Erik Hahr. Including eighteenth-century wills, he and I surveyed approximately 1100 such statements. John L. Brooke, who has also studied these texts, has shown that, over time, the language grew more pious. His inventory of motifs coincides with mine in demonstrating that the colonists voiced a confidence in salvation. Brooke, "Society, Revolution, and the Symbolic Uses of the Dead: An Historical Ethnography of the Massachusetts Near Frontier, 1730–1820" (Ph.D. thesis, University of Pennsylvania, 1982).

139. But in private the ministers may not have varied from lay men and women. Macfarlane has observed of the English nonconformist Ralph Josselin: "Josselin believed that all his children would go to heaven, which was a comfort when he was facing their loss; the more he missed them the more he stressed his certainty that God needed their company. . . . There is not a single direct reference [in his diary] to hell or to damnation." *Family Life of Ralph Josselin*, 167–68. The ministers had to take account of competition from sectarians who pointed to examples of peaceful death in their communities. As described by his son, John Rogers the Rogerene "had also a very easy Death, without any strugling or striving, as is common to many People." Rogers, *Brief Account*, 11.

140. *The Trials of Eight Persons, Indicted for Piracy* (Boston, 1718), 10; *Sewall Diary*, 1:345–46; Minkema, "Windsor Conversion Relations," 24; and see before, chap. 3.

141. Laurel Thatcher Ulrich, *Good Wives: Image and Reality in the Lives of Women in Northern New England, 1650–1750* (New York, 1982), 162.

142. Murdock, ed., *Handkerchiefs from Paul*, 25.

143. Sarah Loring Bailey, *Historical Sketches of Andover* (Boston, 1880), 45; *Massachusetts Records*, 3:224; Waters, *Ipswich*, 1:84; Bradford, *Of Plymouth Plantation*, 100; Solomon Stoddard, *The Danger of Speedy Degeneracy* (Boston, 1705), 20; Alonzo Lewis and James Newhall, *History of Lynn* (Lynn, 1890), 236. For episodes of dancing in private homes and taverns, cf. *Essex Court Recs.*, 7:80, 50; 1:37. William Perkins sanctioned "feasting and mirth" at marriages so long as they were "orderly" and "sober." *Workes*, 3:686.

144. *Essex Court Recs.*, 7:331; 4:282; *Sewall Diary*, 1:140–41; 2:920–21; Pulsifer Transcript, Middlesex County Court records (Massachusetts State Archives), 274.

145. Mather, *Memorable Providences*, 70. Historians of "carnival" and similar events in early modern Europe have argued that ritualized play functioned as culturally sanctioned rebellion, though it sometimes became more openly politicized. Cf. E. P. Thompson, " 'Rough Music': le Charivari Anglais," *Annales E.S.C.* 27 (1972), 285–312; Bob Bushaway, *By Rite: Custom, Ceremony and Community in England, 1700–1880* (London, 1982). This interpretation is open to debate as too narrowly functional. As I suggest in the Afterword, the comparable event in New England was revivalism.

146. Harriet Beecher Stowe, *Poganuc People* (Boston, 1878), 43.

147. "Commonplace Book of Joseph Green," 249.

148. This point came home to me in 1981 as a consequence of viewing an exhibition of ex-votos at the Musée de la Marine in Paris; interestingly, no northern European country was represented by this form of folk art.

149. See, in general, Edward Muir, *Civil Ritual in Renaissance Venice* (Princeton, N.J., 1981).

150. "Memoir of the Rev. William Adams," 12.

CHAPTER 5

1. *The Diary of Samuel Sewall, 1674–1729,* ed. M. Halsey Thomas, 2 vols. (New York, 1973), xxii–xxxiii; cited hereafter in my text itself by volume and page. I have also used the *Letter-Book of Samuel Sewall,* 2 vols., *MHS Coll.,* 6th Ser., 1–2 (Boston, 1886–88), to which references in the text appear as LB 1 or LB 2. Halsey Thomas's thorough annotations have been of much assistance to me.

2. In naming other children Sewall preferred family names that lacked Scriptural significance, e.g., Henry (1:265).

3. Sewall's major effort to link Revelation to the history of America is *Phaenomena quaedam Apocalyptica . . . Or, some few Lines towards a description of the New Heaven* (Boston, 1697). His thinking is described in James W. Davidson, *The Logic of Millennial Thought* (New Haven, Conn., 1977), 22–23, 65–70.

4. Cotton Mather expanded on the meaning of rainbows in *Thoughts for the Day of Rain. In Two Essay's. I. The Gospel of the Rainbow . . . II. The Saviour with His Rainbow* (Boston, 1712). The relevant Scripture texts are Genesis 9:13 and Revelation 4:3, 10:1.

5. Samuel Eliot Morison, "The Harvard School of Astronomy in the Seventeenth Century," *NEQ* 7 (1934), 3–24.

6. Boston Third Church, which Sewall refers to as Old South, originated in a schism within First Church. The fight over the legitimacy of Third Church rocked Massachusetts politics for several years. Cf. Hamilton Hill, *History of the Old South Church,* 2 vols. (Boston, 1890), 1, chaps. 1–2.

7. There is no specific reference to 1 Corinthians 11:28–30 in this passage, or elsewhere in the diary. But Sewall surely had this text in mind. Later he read Jabez Earle's *Sacramental Exercises* (London, 1707) and Matthew Henry's *Communicants Companion* (2:790, 840).

8. Robert Calef publicized Sewall's confession in *More Wonders of the Invisible World* (London, 1700), 144; for the context, cf. Love, *Fast and Thanksgiving Days in New England,* 266–69.

9. The Massachusetts Historical Society owns a number of Sewall's almanacs. His copies of Thomas Paine's *Almanack* for 1718 and 1719 are interleaved, with extensive notes on the blank pages (I am grateful to Frank Cogliano for this information).

10. Leonard Labaree et al., eds., *The Papers of Benjamin Franklin* (New Haven, Conn., 1959), 1:14–18.

11. Allan I. Ludwig, *Graven Images: New England Stonecarving and Its Symbols, 1650–1815* (Middletown, Conn., 1966); Ian Watt, *The Rise of the Novel* (Berkeley, 1971), 21–23.

12. *Oxford English Dictionary.* During the London plague of 1665, John Allin, a Harvard graduate who returned to England, advised a correspondent, "Freind get a piece of angell gold, if you can of Eliz. coine (that is the best) which is philosophical gold, and keep it always in your mouth when you walk out or any sick persons come to you." John L. Sibley, *Biographical Sketches of the Graduates of Harvard University,* 3 vols. (Cambridge, Mass., 1873–85), 1:95.

13. Henry W. Haynes, "Driving a Pin or Nail," *MHS Proc.*, 2d Ser., 4 (1887–89), 101–2, 219–21.

14. My interpretation of Sewall may be compared to Paul S. Seaver's portrait of *Wallington's World: A Puritan Artisan in Seventeenth-Century London* (Stanford, 1985), and Alan Macfarlane, *The Family Life of Ralph Josselin: A Seventeenth-Century Clergyman* (Cambridge, 1970).

AFTERWORD

1. Bradford, *Of Plymouth Plantation* (New York, 1981), 7.

2. Alvah Hovey, *A Memoir of the Life and Times of the Rev. Isaac Backus* (Boston, 1858), 25, 37, 42; Isaac Backus, *A History of New England. With Particular Reference to the . . . Baptists*, 2 vols. (1771; repr., Newton, Mass., 1871), 1, chaps. 1–2.

3. Hovey, *Memoir of Backus*, 53, 63; Charles Deane, "Governor Bradford's Dialogue between Old Men and Young Men, concerning 'The Church and the Government thereof,' " *MHS Proc.*, 2d Ser., 11 (1871), 411, 451–52, and passim.

4. Bradford, *Of Plymouth Plantation*, 8; Alexander Young, *Chronicles of the Pilgrims* (Boston, 1841), 419–22.

5. Keith Stavely, *Puritan Legacies: Paradise Lost and the New England Tradition, 1630–1890* (Ithaca, N.Y., 1987), 133–35.

6. Leonard Labaree et al., eds., *The Autobiography of Benjamin Franklin* (New Haven, Conn., 1964), 50; he had the story from his uncle Benjamin. Cf. "Commonplace-Book of Benjamin Franklin (1650–1727)," *CSM Pub.*, 10 (Boston, 1907), 191–205.

7. Bradford, *Of Plymouth Plantation*, 107. "Yee have been caled unto liberty; only use not liberty for an occassion to the flesh, but by love serve one another." "Governor Bradford's Dialogue," 463; and cf. 461 for a statement against Antinomians.

8. Roger Thompson, *Sex in Middlesex: Popular Mores in a Massachusetts County, 1649–1699* (Amherst, Mass., 1986), 68.

9. *AC*, 412.

10. An essay that set me thinking along these lines is Mary R. O'Neil, "Sacerdote ovvero strione. Ecclesiastical and Superstitious Remedies in 16th Century Italy," in Steven L. Kaplan, ed., *Understanding Popular Culture* (Berlin, 1984), 53–83.

11. Samuel G. Drake, *Annals of Witchcraft in New England* (Boston, 1869), 287.

12. David Vincent, *Bread, Knowledge and Freedom: A Study of Nineteenth-Century Working Class Autobiography* (London, 1981), 16.

13. As the late Christina Larner argues (following Max Weber) in *Witchcraft and Religion: The Politics of Popular Belief* (Oxford, 1984), Pt. II.

14. That is, I do not think the argument of Keith Thomas in *Religion and the Decline of Magic* (London, 1971) applies to New England.

15. Larzer Ziff, "Upon What Pretext? The Book and Literary History," American Antiquarian Society, *Proceedings* 95 (1985), 304–15.

16. Laura L. Becker, "Ministers vs. Laymen: The Singing Controversy in Puritan New England, 1720–1740," *NEQ* 55 (1982), 82–96; Ola E. Winslow, *Meetinghouse Hill: 1630–1783* (New York, 1952), chap. 10.

17. Benjamin Colman, *Reliquiae Turellae* (Boston, 1735), 79–80; Labaree et al., eds., *Papers of Benjamin Franklin*, 1:23–26; *New England Courant*, November 12, 1722.

18. *Sewall Diary*, 1:448–49.

19. Ronald A. Knox, *Enthusiasm: A Chapter in the History of Religion* (New York, 1961), chap. 15.

20. This is the thesis of Stavely, *Puritan Legacies.*

21. Cf. Roger Chartier, *The Cultural Uses of Print in Early Modern France,* trans. Lydia G. Cochrane (Princeton, N.J., 1987), "Introduction."

ACKNOWLEDGMENTS

1. "The World of Print and Collective Mentality in Seventeenth-Century New England," in John Higham and Paul Conkin, eds., *New Directions in American Intellectual History* (Baltimore, 1979), 166–80; "The Mental World of Samuel Sewall," *MHS Proc.* 92 (1980), 21–44; "The Uses of Literacy in New England: 1600–1850," in William L. Joyce et al., eds., *Printing and Society in Early America* (Worcester, Mass., 1983), 1–47; "Introduction," in Steven Kaplan, ed., *Understanding Popular Culture* (Berlin, 1984), 5–18; "Religion, Literacy, and the Plain Style," in Jonathan L. Fairbanks and Robert F. Trent, *New England Begins: The Seventeenth Century,* 3 vols. (Boston, 1982), 2:102–12; "A World of Wonders: The Mentality of the Supernatural in Seventeenth-Century New England," in David D. Hall and David Grayson Allen, eds., *Seventeenth-Century New England, CSM Pub.* 63 (1984), 239–74. See also "Toward a History of Popular Religion in Early New England," *WMQ,* 3d. ser. 41 (1984), 49–55.

INDEX

A Note About the Author

David D. Hall was born in Washington, D.C., in 1936 and received his A.B. from Harvard College in 1958 and his Ph.D. from Yale University in 1964. Since 1973 he has been Professor of History at Boston University. He has also been a Fellow of the Guggenheim Memorial Foundation and the National Endowment for the Humanities and a member of the School of Historical Studies, Institute for Advanced Study. He is the author of *The Antinomian Controversy, 1636–1638: A Documentary History* (1968) and *The Faithful Shepherd: A History of the New England Ministry in the 17th Century* (1972). With others he has edited *Printing and Society in Early America* (1983), *Seventeenth-Century New England* (1984), *Saints and Revolutionaries: Essays in Early American History* (1984), and *Needs and Opportunities in the History of the Book: America, 1639–1876* (1987).

A Note on the Type

This book was set in Baskerville, a facsimile of the type cast from the original matrices designed by John Baskerville. The original face was the forerunner of the modern group of type-faces. John Baskerville (1706–1775), of Birmingham, England, was a writing master with a special renown for cutting inscriptions in stone. About 1750 he began experimenting with punch cutting and making typographical material, and in 1757 he published his first work, a Virgil in royal quarto. His types, at first criticized as unnecessarily slender, delicate, and feminine, in time were recognized as both distinct and elegant, and his types as well as his printing were greatly admired. Four years after his death, Baskerville's widow sold all his punches and matrices to the Société Philosophique, Littéraire et Typographique, which used some of the types for the sumptuous Kehl edition of Voltaire's works in seventy volumes. Eventually, the punches and matrices came into the possession of the distinguished Paris type founders Deberny & Peignot, who, in singularly generous fashion, returned them to the Cambridge University Press in 1953.

Composed by Maple-Vail Composition, Binghamton, New York. Printed and bound by R. R. Donnelley & Sons, Harrisonburg, Virginia. Designed by Peter A. Andersen.